The Kennel Club's
ILLUSTRATED
Breed Standards

Fula of the Congo
1959 — 1974

The Kennel Club's
ILLUSTRATED
Breed Standards

The Official Guide to
Registered Breeds

EBURY PRESS
LONDON

Illustrations
page 1: *Fula of the Congo*, pastel drawing by Andie Pasinger, 1975. Fula, a Basenji, was found in the
South Sudan in 1959 and brought to Britain by Veronica Tudor-Williams. Although never shown,
she was bred from and did not pass on any real faults. She is thought to have done more for
the progress of her breed than any other dog, in any breed, has ever done.
page 2: An early dog show: a 'Jemmy Shaw canine meeting', 1855. Oil painting by R. Marshall.

First published in Great Britain in 1998

1 3 5 7 9 10 8 6 4 2

Copyright © The Kennel Club 1998

Ebury Press
Random House, 20 Vauxhall Bridge Road, London SW1V 2SA

Random House Australia Pty Limited
20 Alfred Street, Milsons Point, Sydney, New South Wales 2061, Australia

Random House New Zealand Limited
18 Poland House, Glenfield, Auckland 10, New Zealand

Random House South Africa Pty Limited
Endulini, 5A Jubilee Road, Parktown 2193, South Africa

Random House UK Reg. No. 954009

A CIP catalogue record for this book is available from the British Library

ISBN 0 09 185374 5

Designed by David Fordham
Typeset by M.A.T.S., Southend-on-Sea, Essex
Colour origination by Colourpath
Printed and bound by Tien Wah Press, Singapore

Papers used by Ebury Press are natural, recyclable products made from
wood grown in sustainable forests.

CONTENTS

UTILITY GROUP 182

WORKING GROUP 230

TOY GROUP 343

ACKNOWLEDGEMENTS

M Y THANKS ARE DUE to the following: Mike Stockman and Bernard Hall, both members of the General Committee of The Kennel Club, for the authorship and assembly of the contributions on the various breeds; Brian Leonard, Public Relations Officer of The Kennel Club, for his liaison work with our Publishers, Ebury Press; Barbara Walker, Kennel Club Librarian, and her Library team, Elaine Camroux-McLean, Monica Smith, Philip Robinson, Craig Hughes and Lea Lambell for co-ordinating and typing the editorial script as well as assembling both the photographs and other art work; Prudence Cuming Associates Ltd, David Dalton, John Hartley, Marc Henrie, Huisman and Zonderop, Carol Ann Johnson, Diane Pearce, Russell Fine Arts, Sally Ann Thompson, Alan Walker and R T Willbie for their photographic work; The Kennel Club staff who in a plethora of different ways provided information and back-up; the Members of The Kennel Club Breed Standards and Stud Book Sub-Committee on whose continued work this book is based.

T HANKS ARE ALSO DUE to a great number of Breed Club Secretaries who provided vital material about the individual breeds, more especially about those which have been registered since the first *Illustrated Breed Standards* was published in 1989. Also to those breeders and owners who responded to calls for suitable photographs with the sort of rapidity which publishers always expect, but seldom receive!

PETER JAMES

Chairman of The Kennel Club

FOREWORD

BY HRH PRINCE MICHAEL OF KENT

FROM THE TIME OF THE GREAT EXHIBITION in 1851 the Victorians were fascinated with exhibitions of all kinds. The first dog show was held in 1859 and from this point dog shows sprang up all over the country. In 1873 it became clear that a governing body for all canine matters was necessary. The Kennel Club was founded in London and was the first organisation of its kind in the world. Its first Chairman was the then MP for Ettington, Warwickshire, Mr S E Shirley.

The inaugural meeting of The Kennel Club committee formulated an elementary code of rules relating to shows. At the same time the first Kennel Club Stud Book was compiled, which contained records of shows from 1859. The Stud Book has been published annually ever since. In 1996, 5,477 licences were granted for the various canine activities; Shows, Agility Tests, Working Trials and Field Trials.

In 1880 a system of dog registration was introduced by the Committee to overcome the confusion caused by the existence of numerous dogs with the same names. Bobs, Spots, Jets and Nettles were all common. The Kennel Club now registers approximately 260,000 dogs a year and its database comprises over 4.7 million dog names.

The Kennel Club recognises 183 different breeds of dog. Each of these breeds has a descriptive standard – a word picture or specification – which details its essential features and sets them out in a logical sequence consistent for each breed. Almost without exception overseas authorities accept the United Kingdom breed standard for dogs of British origin or development. The standards are also accepted by many overseas Kennel Authorities as definitive statements on other than British breeds.

This new edition of *The Kennel Club's Illustrated Breed Standards* is an indispensable reference book and I recommend it to owners, breeders, judges and anyone with an interest in pure-bred dogs. It has been created as a result of continued demand world-wide for the first edition, which is now out of print.

Michael

THE BREED STANDARDS

HOW ARE THEY FORMED?

EACH BREED OF PEDIGREE DOG registered by The Kennel Club has a breed standard; this is a description of how an ideal specimen of a particular breed looks, behaves and moves. Each of these breed standards contains a series of clauses with identical headings, as is evident from reading individual standards.

The owners/breeders of an individual breed of dog tend in the first place to come together to form a Breed Club under the auspices of The Kennel Club. The breed standard is the subject of considerable discussion in the first instance between the members of the Breed Club in order to decide what features of the dog are most advantageous to fit the purpose for which the type was selected.

Once a degree of agreement has been achieved within the ranks of the breed enthusiasts, the format and content are discussed between the Club and the Breed Standards Sub-committee of The Kennel Club. Once those discussions are complete the final version goes before the General Committee of The Kennel Club for final ratification and publication.

This has been going on with the long-established breeds since the nineteenth century. Whenever a new breed is accepted either as an import from overseas or occasionally, as in the case of the Otterhound and the Lancashire Heeler, from within the UK, the same process takes place.

Usually a breed entering from overseas attracts a band of enthusiasts which applies to The Kennel Club for recognition of the breed onto the 'Imported Breed Register'. Once accepted and numbering at least ten specimens, an interim breed standard is formulated. This process takes a varying number of months before an acceptable version reaches the General Committee.

There is evidence of this in this new publication of *The Kennel Club's Illustrated Breed Standards*; the Beauceron has been entered into the Imported Breed Register, but its progress towards an acceptable breed standard was not complete at the time of going to press, although the customary thumbnail sketch and picture(s) are to be found in the relevant group, Working.

This will repeat itself as other new breeds enter the jurisdiction and the Registers of The Kennel Club; it is a continuing process – some 90 or more breeds have joined since the middle of the twentieth century!

*The Kennel Club Library, where much of the research for
the* Illustrated Breed Standards *was carried out.*

BELOW: *The Open Door (1916) painted in oil on canvas by Briton Riviere (1840–1920). The featured dog is Sir R Buchanan Jardine's Greyhound, Long Span, winner of the Waterloo Cup in 1907.*

HOUND

HOUND GROUP

HOUND

AFGHAN HOUND

GLAMOUR IN THE DOG WORLD COMES IN many forms, but the Afghan must be in the top ten of anybody's list. The breed standard talks of strength and dignity as well as an Oriental expression with which the dog looks at and through any stranger.

The silky coat is to many the greatest attraction of the breed, but those in the showring only look the way they do because someone has regularly put a great deal of experienced effort into grooming.

One of the typical sighthounds of the world, the Afghan – who, as his name implies, comes from the mountains of Afghanistan – is a hunter and will chase electric hare or the neighbour's cat, so basic training, especially the re-call, is not easily accomplished.

The first Afghans arrived in Britain in the early 1900s and one, called Zardin, won in spectacular style at the 1907 Crystal Palace show. The breed is also known as the Tazi, supporting its resemblance to a Russian breed of that name.

Temperamentally the Afghan has a tendency to be aloof with those he doesn't know, but has great affection and faithfulness for his owner.

GENERAL APPEARANCE Gives the impression of strength and dignity, combining speed and power. Head held proudly.

CHARACTERISTICS Eastern or Oriental expression is typical of breed. The Afghan looks at and through one.

TEMPERAMENT Dignified and aloof, with a certain keen fierceness.

HEAD AND SKULL Skull long, not too narrow, with prominent occiput. Foreface long with punishing jaws and slight stop. Skull well balanced and mounted by a long 'top-knot'. Nose preferably black, liver permissible in light-coloured dogs.

EYES Dark for preference, but golden colour not debarred. Nearly triangular, slanting slightly upwards from inner corner to outer corner.

EARS Set low and well back, carried close to head. Covered with long silky hair.

MOUTH Jaws strong, with a perfect, regular and complete scissor bite, i.e. upper teeth closely overlapping lower teeth and set square to the jaws. Level bite tolerated.

NECK Long, strong, with proud carriage of head.

FOREQUARTERS Shoulders long and sloping, well set back, well muscled and strong without being loaded. Forelegs straight and well boned, straight with shoulder; elbows close to ribcage, turning neither in nor out.

BODY Back level, moderate length, well muscled, back falling slightly away to stern. Loin straight, broad and rather short. Hipbones rather prominent and wide apart. A fair spring of ribs and good depth of chest.

HINDQUARTERS Powerful, well bent and well turned stifles. Great length between hip and hock with comparatively short distance between hock and foot. Dewclaws may be removed.

FEET Forefeet strong and very large both in length and breadth, and covered with long, thick hair; toes arched. Pasterns long and springy, pads well down on ground. Hindfeet long, but not quite as broad as forefeet; covered with long thick hair.

TAIL Not too short. Set-on low with ring at end. Raised when in action. Sparsely feathered.

GAIT/MOVEMENT Smooth and springy with a style of high order.

COAT Long and very fine texture on ribs, fore and hindquarters and flanks. In mature dogs from shoulder backwards and along the saddle, hair short and close. Hair long from forehead backwards, with a distinct silky 'top knot'.

On foreface hair short. Ears and legs well coated. Pasterns can be bare. Coat must develop naturally.

COLOUR All colours acceptable.

SIZE Ideal height: dogs: 68-74 cm (27-29 in); bitches: 63-69 cm (25-27 in).

FAULTS Any departure from the foregoing points should be considered a fault and the seriousness with which the fault should be regarded should be in exact proportion to its degree.

NOTE Male animals should have two apparently normal testicles fully descended into the scrotum.

BASENJI

ISTORY TELLS US THAT THIS fascinating dog was a palace dog of the Pharaohs, and for proof offers paintings of the dogs in ancient tombs, to which the modern version certainly bears a striking resemblance. In the seventeenth century they were sighted in the Congo, now called Zaire, and it is from there that they have been imported to Britain.

A first pair were imported to Britain in 1936 and these produced the first English litter. The next year when the puppies were exhibited at Crufts police were required to keep the crowds on the move, so great was the interest.

The Basenji is clean both in outline and habits – cat-like in the way in which he cleans his feet, and odourless – thus making him a perfect household companion.

He is known as the 'barkless dog' – a unique characteristic of the breed – and expresses his pleasure with a crowing-yodelling noise. The wrinkles on his head give him a quizzical expression. He is curious, self-confident and friendly, and becomes very attached to his human family.

GENERAL APPEARANCE Lightly built, finely boned aristocratic-looking animal, high on leg compared with its length, always poised, alert and intelligent. Wrinkled head, with pricked ears, proudly carried on a well arched neck. Deep brisket runs up into a definite waist, tail tightly curled presenting a picture of a well balanced dog of gazelle-like grace.

CHARACTERISTICS Barkless but not mute, its own special noise a mixture of a chortle and a yodel. Remarkable for its cleanliness in every way.

TEMPERAMENT An intelligent, independent, but affectionate and alert breed. Can be aloof with strangers.

HEAD AND SKULL Flat, well-chiselled and medium width, tapering towards nose, with slight stop. Distance from top of head to stop slightly more than from stop to tip of nose. Side lines of skull taper gradually towards mouth, giving a clean-cheeked appearance. Fine and profuse wrinkles appearing on forehead when ears pricked, side wrinkles desirable but not exaggerated into dewlap. Wrinkles more noticeable in puppies, but because of lack of shadowing, not as noticeable in tricolours; black nose desirable.

EYES Dark, almond-shaped, obliquely set, far-seeing and rather inscrutable in expression.

EARS Small, pointed, erect and slightly hooded, of fine texture, set well forward on top of head, tip of ear nearer centre of skull than outside base.

MOUTH Jaws strong, with a perfect, regular and complete scissor bite, i.e. upper teeth closely overlapping lower teeth and set square to the jaws.

NECK Strong and of good length, without thickness, well crested and slightly full at base of throat with a graceful curve accentuating crest. Well set into shoulders giving head a 'lofty' carriage.

FOREQUARTERS Shoulders well laid back, muscular, not loaded. Elbows tucked in against brisket. When viewed from front, elbows in line with ribs and legs should continue in a straight line to ground giving a medium front. Forelegs straight with fine bones and very long forearms. Pasterns good length, straight and flexible.

BODY Balanced with short, level back. Ribs well sprung, deep and oval. Loin short-coupled, deep brisket running up into definite waist.

HINDQUARTERS Strong and muscular, hocks well let down, turned neither in nor out, with long second thighs and moderately bent stifles.

FEET Small, narrow and compact, with deep pads, well arched toes and short nails.

TAIL High set, with posterior curve of buttock extending beyond root of tail giving a reachy appearance to hindquarters. Curls tightly over spine and lies closely to thigh with a single or double curl.

GAIT/MOVEMENT Legs carried straight forward with a swift, long, tireless, swinging stride.

COAT Short, sleek and close, very fine. Skin very pliant.

COLOUR Pure black and white; red and white; black, tan and white with tan melon pips and mask; black; tan and white. The white should be on feet, chest and tail tips. White legs, blaze and white collar optional.

SIZE Ideal height: dogs: 43 cm (17 in) at withers; bitches: 40 cm (16 in) at withers. Ideal weight: dogs: 11 kg (24 lb); bitches 9.5 kg (21 lb).

FAULTS Any departure from the foregoing points should be considered a fault and the seriousness with which the fault should be regarded should be in exact proportion to its degree.

NOTE Male animals should have two apparently normal testicles fully descended into the scrotum.

BASSET FAUVE DE BRETAGNE

(INTERIM)

THIS NEAT LITTLE HOUND COMES, AS his names implies, from France, and is usually a reddish-fawn in colour. A recent arrival in Britain, he is already gaining in popularity because he is lively and friendly and also a handy size, suitable for the small house and garden.

The breed was probably created from crosses of the Griffon Fauve de Bretagne and Brittany Bassetts. The former was a dog which could track down predators molesting the flocks of French sheep and the latter hunted in small packs, normally four in number.

His coat is wiry in texture and not over-long, so grooming is not a great chore. He is a tough little character, ready for all the exercise he's given, though woe betide any rabbits unwise enough to loiter in the area when he's about, because he really is nimble.

His legs are slightly shorter than the length of his back, but he is not as low to ground as his countryman the Basset Hound.

GENERAL APPEARANCE Short-legged, rough-coated hound of moderate length.

CHARACTERISTICS Courageous, hardy, possessing good nose. Very nimble in movement.

TEMPERAMENT Lively, friendly and amenable.

HEAD AND SKULL Medium in length, well balanced. Skull moderately domed, fair width; occipital point well defined. Foreface of medium length, slightly arched; moderate stop. Underjaw strong and well developed. Nose black or very dark. Nostrils wide open.

EYES Slightly oval, neither too deep-set nor too prominent. Dark, hazel, no haw apparent. Lively expression.

EARS Set-on level with eye, extending to the nose when drawn forward, folding inwards ending in a point. Covered with finer, darker and softer hair than body.

MOUTH Jaws strong with a perfect, regular and complete scissor bite, i.e. upper teeth closely overlapping lower teeth and set square to the jaws.

NECK Rather short, muscular.

FOREQUARTERS Forelegs straight; slight crook acceptable; well boned with strong pasterns. Feet turning neither in nor out. Shoulders slightly sloping.

BODY Chest wide and deep. Sternum prominent. Ribs well rounded, carried well back. Level topline; strong loin.

HINDQUARTERS Strong and muscular. Stifles well bent, hocks well let down with good angulation, turning neither in nor out; just under body when standing naturally.

FEET Tight, pads firm and hard. Short nails.

TAIL Set-on high, thick at base, tapering to a point, reaching slightly beyond the hock when lowered, carried like a sickle when moving.

GAIT/MOVEMENT Quick, striding out well.

COAT Very harsh, dense and flat. Never long or woolly.

COLOUR Fawn, gold-wheaten or red-wheaten. White spot on chest permissible.

SIZE Height at withers 32-38 cm (12½-15 in).

FAULTS Any departure from the foregoing points should be considered a fault and the seriousness with which the fault should be regarded should be in exact proportion to its degree.

NOTE Male animals should have two apparently normal testicles fully descended into the scrotum.

BASSET HOUND

DEPICTED BY CARTOONISTS THE WORLD over as a kindly but worried canine buffoon, the Basset deserves his popularity as a family dog. Happy by the fireside or on the moors, he is a dog capable of hunting his natural prey, the hare, persistently at a relatively slow pace over prodigious distances.

The Basset was reputedly bred by monks in France in the Middle Ages to hunt in heavy cover and is able to hold its nose close to the ground. Though closely related to the entire family of French Bassets the breed was developed to perfection in Britain.

Standing only 38 centimetres (15 inches) at the shoulder, but weighing some 32 kilograms (70 pounds), he can present quite a problem if he has to be picked up to be put into the back of a hatch-back.

His skin, especially on the top of his head, is supposed to be a trifle wrinkled, and his ears, which are set low, should be long, reaching beyond the length of his muzzle. He loves to paddle his way through the wet and mud of a winter field, but he cleans up remarkably easily because of his short, close coat.

He is possessed of a deep, sonorous bark, which might suggest he is unfriendly, but nothing could be further from the truth. He has not gained the army of friends he has without good cause.

GENERAL APPEARANCE Short-legged hound of considerable substance, well balanced, full of quality. A certain amount of loose skin desirable.

CHARACTERISTICS Tenacious hound of ancient lineage which hunts by scent, possessing a pack instinct, a deep melodious voice and capable of great endurance in the field.

TEMPERAMENT Placid, never aggressive or timid. Affectionate.

HEAD AND SKULL Domed with some stop and occipital bone prominent; of medium width at brow and tapering slightly to muzzle; general appearance of foreface lean not snipy. Top of muzzle nearly parallel with line from stop to occiput and not much longer than head from stop to occiput. There may be a moderate amount of wrinkle at brow and beside eyes. In any event skin of head loose enough as to wrinkle noticeably when drawn forward or when head is lowered. Flews of upper lip overlap lower substantially. Nose entirely black except in light-coloured hounds when it may be brown or liver. Large and well opened nostrils may protrude a little beyond lips.

EYES Lozenge-shaped, neither prominent nor too deep-set, dark but may shade to mid-brown in light-coloured hounds. Expression calm and serious. Red of lower lid appears though not excessively. Light or yellow eye highly undesirable.

EARS Set-on low, just below line of eye. Long; reaching well beyond end of muzzle of correct length, but not excessively so. Narrow throughout their length and curling well inwards; very supple, fine and velvety in texture.

MOUTH Jaws strong, with a perfect, regular and complete scissor bite, i.e. upper teeth closely over-lapping lower teeth and set square to the jaws.

NECK Muscular, well arched and fairly long with pronounced but not exaggerated dewlap.

FOREQUARTERS Shoulder blades well laid back; shoulders not heavy. Forelegs short, powerful and with great bone; elbows turning neither in nor out but fitting neatly against side. Upper forearm inclined slightly inwards, but not to such an extent as to prevent free action or to result in legs touching each other when standing or in action; forechest fitting neatly into crook when viewed from front. Knuckling-over highly undesirable. Wrinkles of skin on lower legs.

BODY Long and deep throughout length, breast bone prominent but chest neither narrow nor unduly deep; ribs well rounded and sprung, without flange, carried well back. Back rather broad; level; withers and quarters of approximately same height, though loins may arch slightly. Back from withers to inset of quarters not unduly long.

HINDQUARTERS Full of muscle and standing out well, giving an almost spherical effect when viewed from rear. Stifles well bent.

Hocks well let down and slightly bent under but turn neither in nor out and just under body when standing naturally. Wrinkles of skin may appear between hock and foot, and at rear of joint a slight pouch resulting from looseness of skin.

FEET Massive, well knuckled up and padded. Forefeet may point straight ahead or be turned slightly outwards but in every case hound always stands perfectly true, weight being borne equally by toes with pads together so that feet would leave an imprint of a large hound and no unpadded areas in contact with ground.

TAIL (Stern) Well set-on, rather long, strong at base, tapering, with moderate amount of coarse hair underneath. When moving, stern carried well up and curving gently, sabre-fashion, never curling or gay.

GAIT/MOVEMENT Most important. Smooth free action with forelegs reaching well forward and hindlegs showing powerful thrust, hound moving true both front and rear. Hocks and stifles never stiff in movement, nor must any toes be dragged.

COAT Smooth, short and close without being too fine. Whole outline clean and free from feathering. Long-haired, soft coat with feather highly undesirable.

COLOUR Generally black, white and tan (tricolour); lemon and white (bi-colour); but any recognised hound colour acceptable.

SIZE Height 33–38 cm (13–15 in) at withers.

FAULTS Any departure from the foregoing points should be considered a fault and the seriousness with which the fault should be regarded should be in exact proportion to its degree.

NOTE Male animals should have two apparently normal testicles fully descended into the scrotum.

BEAGLE

ONE OF THE MOST POPULAR OF THE hounds, bred down from the larger Foxhound to hunt with men on foot, preferably after the hare. He is still used in packs, very often organised by institutions, including colleges and schools, but it is as a first-class family pet that he really makes his mark. A bustling, eager little dog, full of enthusiasm and vigour, ever ready for any activity which involves him.

Sturdy, bold and active, he is the very essence of quality, and is blessed with an equable and merry temperament. His head is powerful but his expression benign and there is usually a most definite difference between the dogs and bitches.

Everything about the breed gives the impression of athleticism and there is no

better sight than a Beagle pack in full pursuit, their heads down to the scent, their sterns up in rigid order as they concentrate on the chase. This instinct is mimicked in his everyday behaviour in the park; the man with the lead in his hand and no dog in sight owns a Beagle.

An easy dog to keep, he can get as muddy as he likes but cleans up with a sponge and water, and dries off his short dense coat in a trice.

During the reigns of King Henry VIII and Queen Elizabeth I there were wire-haired Beagles, some of which were small enough to be carried in the pocket of a hunting jacket. Size has increased over the years but smaller versions of the breed, called 'pocket Beagles', can still be born.

GENERAL APPEARANCE A sturdy, compactly built hound, conveying the impression of quality without coarseness.

CHARACTERISTICS A merry hound whose essential function is to hunt, primarily hare, by following a scent. Bold, with great activity, stamina and determination. Alert, intelligent and of even temperament.

TEMPERAMENT Amiable and alert, showing no aggression or timidity.

HEAD AND SKULL Fair length, powerful without being coarse, finer in the bitch, free from frown and wrinkle. Skull slightly domed, moderately wide, with slight peak. Stop well defined and dividing length, between occiput and tip of nose, as equally as possible. Muzzle not snipy, lips reasonably well flewed. Nose broad, preferably black, but less pigmentation permissible in lighter-coloured hounds. Nostrils wide.

EYES Dark brown or hazel, fairly large, not deep-set or prominent, set well apart with mild appealing expression.

EARS Long, with rounded tip, reaching nearly to end of nose when drawn out. Set-on low, fine in texture and hanging gracefully close to cheeks.

MOUTH The jaws should be strong, with a perfect, regular and complete scissor bite, i.e. upper teeth closely overlapping lower teeth and set square to the jaws.

NECK Sufficiently long to enable hound to come down easily to scent, slightly arched and showing little dewlap.

FOREQUARTERS Shoulders well laid back, not loaded. Forelegs straight and upright well under the hound, good substance, and round in bone, not tapering off to feet. Pasterns short. Elbows firm, turning neither in nor out. Height to elbow about half height at withers.

BODY Topline straight and level. Chest let down to below elbow. Ribs well sprung and extending well back. Short in the couplings but well balanced. Loins powerful and supple, without excessive tuck-up.

HINDQUARTERS Muscular thighs. Stifles well bent. Hocks firm, well let down and parallel to each other.

FEET Tight and firm. Well knuckled up and strongly padded. Not harefooted. Nails short.

TAIL Sturdy, moderately long. Set-on high, carried gaily but not curled over back or inclined forward from root. Well covered with hair, especially on underside.

GAIT/MOVEMENT Back level, firm with no indication of roll. Stride free, long-reaching in front and straight without high action; hindlegs showing drive. Should not move close behind nor paddle nor plait in front.

COAT Short, dense and weatherproof.

COLOUR Any recognised hound colour other than liver. Tip of stern white.

SIZE Desirable minimum height at withers: 33 cm (13 in). Desirable maximum height at withers: 40 cm (16 in).

FAULTS Any departure from the foregoing points should be considered a fault and the seriousness with which the fault should be regarded should be in exact proportion to its degree.

NOTE Male animals should have two apparently normal testicles fully descended into the scrotum.

BLOODHOUND

A DOG OF GREAT SIZE AND IMPOSING dignity, the Bloodhound must be recognised by even the least doggy people. His amazing ability to follow a human scent over all types of terrain after many hours has given him an almost super-canine reputation fostered by the writers of detective fiction.

The home country of the breed is Belgium and ancestry can be traced back to the monastery of St. Hubert. In Belgium the Bloodhound is known by his other name of St. Hubert Hound. It is most probable that this hound was one of those brought to England by the Normans in 1066.

The looseness of his skin, especially over the head, and his long pendulous ears are possibly the most characteristic features of the breed, but his powerful limbs and body make him a truly big dog, weighing up to a hundredweight or more.

He is generally good-natured and affectionate, but can be surprisingly sensitive. He has the sort of voice which cannot be ignored. His short coat cleans up easily in spite of his tendency when on the trail to plough his way through ditches.

GENERAL APPEARANCE Noble and dignified expression, characterised by solemnity, wisdom and power.

CHARACTERISTICS Possesses in a most marked degree every point and characteristic of those dogs which hunt together by scent (Sagaces). Very powerful, standing over more ground than is usual with hounds of other breeds. Skin thin and loose, especially noticeable about head and neck and where it hangs in deep folds.

TEMPERAMENT Affectionate, neither quarrelsome with companions nor with other dogs. Somewhat reserved and sensitive.

HEAD AND SKULL Head narrow in proportion to length and long in proportion to body, tapering slightly from temples to muzzle, thus when viewed from above and in front having appearance of being flattened at sides and of being nearly equal in width throughout entire length. In profile upper outline of skull is nearly in same plane as that of foreface. Length from end of nose to stop not less than that from stop to back of occipital protuberance. Entire length of head from posterior part of occipital protuberance to end of muzzle 30 cm (12 in) or more in dogs and 28 cm (11 in) or more in bitches. Skull is long and narrow, with occipital peak very pronounced. Brows not prominent, although owing to set of eyes may appear to give that appearance. Foreface long, deep and of even width throughout, with square outlines when seen in profile. Head furnished with an amount of loose skin, which in nearly every position appears abundant, but more particularly so when head is carried low; skin then falls into loose pendulous ridges and folds, especially over forehead and sides of face. Nostrils large and open. In front, lips fall squarely making a right angle with upper line of foreface; whilst behind they form deep hanging flews and, being continued into pendant folds of loose skin about neck, constitute the dewlap, which is very pronounced.

EYES Medium size, dark brown or hazel, neither sunken nor prominent, the lids being oval in shape and meeting the cornea – front window of the eye – perfectly without any irregularity in their contour. Eyes should be free from any interference from the eyelashes.

EARS Thin and soft to the touch, long, set-on low and falling in graceful folds, lower parts curling inwards and backwards.

MOUTH Jaws strong with a perfect, regular and complete scissor bite, i.e. upper teeth closely overlapping lower teeth and set square to the jaws.

NECK Long.

FOREQUARTERS Shoulders muscular and well sloped. Forelegs straight, large, round in bone with elbows well set in. Pasterns strong.

BODY Ribs well sprung, chest well let down between forelegs forming a deep keel. Back and loins strong, the latter deep and slightly arched.

HINDQUARTERS Thighs and second thighs very muscular. Hocks well let down, bent and squarely set.

FEET Strong and well knuckled up.

TAIL (Stern) Long, thick, tapering to a point, set high with moderate amount of hair underneath. Carried scimitar-fashion, but not curled over back or corkscrew any time. When moving carried high.

GAIT/MOVEMENT Elastic, swinging free.

COAT Smooth, short and weatherproof.

COLOUR Black and tan, liver and tan (red and tan) and red. Darker colours sometimes interspersed with lighter or badger-coloured hair and sometimes flecked with white. Small amount of white permissible on chest, feet and tip of tail.

SIZE Height of adult dogs: 66 cm (26 in); bitches: 61 cm (24 in). Dogs usually vary from 63-69 cm (25-27 in); bitches from 58-63 cm (23-25 in). Mean average weight of adult dogs in fair condition 41 kg (90 lb); bitches: 36 kg (80 lb). Dogs attain the weight of 50 kg (110 lb); bitches: 45 kg (100 lb). Hounds of the maximum height and weight preferred, providing that quality, proportion and balance combine.

FAULTS Any departure from the foregoing points should be considered a fault and the seriousness with which the fault should be regarded should be in exact proportion to its degree.

NOTE Male animals should have two apparently normal testicles fully descended into the scrotum.

BORZOI

AN ARISTOCRAT OF A DOG, WITH HIS bearing, his size and his proudly carried head. The wolf hunter of Russia, his name means 'swift' in his native country, and though he may not perform his original function any more, he is still built on lines of speed and grace. The earliest seen in Britain were presented by the Tsar of all the Russias to Queen Alexandra and soon caught on.

Temperamentally not a breed for the masses as he is sensitive and aloof in his view of mankind; to his owners he is faithful with an undeniable courage.

His long silky coat with its slight wave comes in a mass of different colours, and requires dedicated application from the groomer if it is not to be allowed to deteriorate into a tangled mass.

The slightly domed and narrow skull with the almost straight, but slightly convex, topline to the nose gives the dog a refinement which is unique in appearance. A dog of striking quality.

GENERAL APPEARANCE Well balanced, graceful, aristocratic, dignified and elegant.

CHARACTERISTICS A coursing hound which must be courageous, powerful and of great speed.

TEMPERAMENT Sensitive, alert and aloof.

HEAD AND SKULL Head long, lean and in proportion to dog's size and substance. In bitches head finer than in dogs. Well filled in below eyes. Measurement equal from occiput to inner corner of eye and from inner corner of eye to tip of nose. Skull very slightly domed and narrow, stop imperceptible. Head fine so that bones and principal veins can be clearly seen. Viewed from side, forehead and upper line of muzzle form an almost straight, slightly convex line. Jaws long, deep and powerful; nose large and black, nicely rounded, neither cornered nor sharp. Viewed from above, skull should look narrow, converging very gradually to tip of nose. Occipital process very accentuated.

EYES Dark with intelligent, keen and alert expression. Almond-shaped, set obliquely and placed well back but not too wide apart. Eye rims dark. Eyes not light, round, bulbous or staring.

EARS Small, pointed and delicate. Set high but not too far apart. Nearly touching at occiput; when in repose folded back along neck. Should be active and responsive, may be erect when alert, tips sometimes falling over.

MOUTH Jaws strong with a perfect, regular and complete scissor bite, i.e. upper teeth closely overlapping lower teeth and set square to the jaws. Full, strong dentition desirable.

NECK Slightly arched; reasonably long and well muscled. Free from throatiness, flattened laterally, set at an angle of 50-60 degrees to the longitudinal axis of the body.

FOREQUARTERS Shoulders clean, sloping well back. Muscular but not loaded. Fine at withers but not accentuated. Forelegs clean and straight. Seen from front, narrow like blades; from side, wider at elbows narrowing down to foot. Elbows directed backwards, neither turning in nor out. Pasterns slightly sloping, strong and flexible. Length of forearm nearly equal to half total height at withers.

BODY Chest, ribs of narrow oval cut, great depth of brisket reaching to elbows, giving great heart and lung room, especially in mature dogs. Breast bone slightly pronounced with adequate width between elbows and abdomen very tucked-up. Back rather bony, muscular and free from any cavity, rising in a graceful curve with well balanced fallaway. Highest point of curve is situated over last rib. Curve is more pronounced in dogs than bitches. Loins broad and very powerful with plenty of muscular development. Fallaway long and well muscled. Width between hip bones at least 8 cm (3 in).

HINDQUARTERS Quarters wider than shoulders, ensuring stability of stance. Thighs long, well developed with good second thigh; hindlegs long and muscular; stifles well angulated, hocks broad, clean and well let down. Posterior line of hock vertical. Seen from side, legs slightly set back.

FEET Front feet oval, toes close together, well arched over strong, thick pads, turning neither in nor out. Hindfeet hare-like, i.e. longer and less arched.

TAIL Long, rather low-set, when measured between thighs reaches up to top of nearest hip bone. Well feathered, carried low in a graceful curve. From level of hocks may be sabre- or slightly sickle-shaped but not ringed. In action not rising above level of back.

GAIT/MOVEMENT Front, straight with long reach, pasterns springy. Hind, straight with powerful driving hocks. Moving wider than front. Viewed from side, appearance in action should be that of effortless power.

COAT Silky, flat, wavy or rather curly (but never woolly). Short and smooth on head, ears and front legs; much longer on body with heavy feathering on backs of legs and hindquarters, tail and chest. Neck carries a large curly frill. More profuse in dogs than bitches.

COLOUR Any colour acceptable.

SIZE Minimum height at withers: dogs: 74 cm (29 in); bitches: 68 cm (27 in).

FAULTS Any departure from the foregoing points should be considered a fault and the seriousness with which the fault should be regarded should be in exact proportion to its degree.

NOTE Male animals should have two apparently normal testicles fully descended into the scrotum.

DACHSHUNDS

DACHSUNDS HAVE BEEN USED FOR A variety of jobs over many years and the different demands made on the breed have resulted in six varieties, dependent on size and coat type. The larger version can weigh as much as 12 kilograms (26 pounds) while the miniatures should weigh ideally 4.5 kilograms (10 pounds) and certainly no more than 5 kilograms (11 pounds). Each size splits into Smooth-haired, Long-haired and Wire-haired. There are differences in minor points but basically the six are one and the same breed. Similarly some consider that their temperaments vary, but this is probably no more than can be found in most other breeds between individuals. There is no longer any crossing between the varieties.

Colours vary tremendously; the standard states that all colours are allowed with the exception that white is only permitted in a small patch on the chest, but even this is not desirable. In dapples, white is allowed but it must be even all over. The Smooth varieties have dense, short coats, while the Longs show a soft texture with straight or slightly wavy hairs. The Wires should have short, straight, harsh hair with a dense undercoat, with bearded chin and bushy eyebrows. All in all, a marvellous selection of attractive and sporting dogs.

The Dachshund is a long, low dog as befits his purpose in life, entering a badger set and rooting its rightful occupant out of his home. Such a task requires tremendous courage and extremely powerful jaws, a point that is obvious when one compares the muzzle length with that of many larger breeds. The low-slung nature of the breed is, of course, partly achieved by a relatively excessive angulation of the shoulder and elbow joints in front and the hip and stifle joints behind.

The forearm is permitted to incline slightly outward to enable the dog to dig freely, but this must not be exaggerated to such an extent that the legs become bowed inward. The length of the back and the character of

BELOW: *Miniature Smooth-haired Dachshund*

ABOVE: *Long-haired Dachshund*

the discs between the vertebrae of the spine have a tendency to allow a weakening in the area, and it is therefore important that the loin should be short and strong, and that individuals should not be allowed to become obese. The breed's ability to eat anything placed in front of it should never be pandered to.

Temperamentally all six varieties are very good at giving a good account of themselves as guards of property and their relatively low stature should never give anyone the idea that they will be easy meat for the criminally inclined. With their families and friends they make wonderful companions, but firmness is needed in their early training as they can be notably independent.

Germany is the breed's home country where sizes are separated not by weight but by chest circumference, the divisions being based on what size of hole they could enter when going to ground.

GENERAL APPEARANCE Long and low, but with compact, well muscled body, bold, defiant carriage of head and intelligent expression.

CHARACTERISTICS Intelligent, lively, courageous to the point of rashness, obedient. Especially suited to going to ground because of low build, very strong forequarters and forelegs. Long, strong jaw, and immense power of bite and hold. Excellent nose. Persevering hunter and tracker.

TEMPERAMENT Faithful, versatile and good-tempered.

HEAD AND SKULL Long, appearing conical when seen from above; from side tapering uniformly to tip of nose. Skull only slightly arched. Neither too broad nor too narrow, sloping gradually without prominent stop into slightly arched muzzle. Length from tip of nose to eyes equal to length from eyes to occiput. In Wire-haired, particularly, ridges over eyes strongly prominent, giving appearance of slightly broader skull. Lips well stretched, neatly covering lower jaw. Strong jaw bones not too square or snipy, but opening wide.

EYES Medium size, almond-shaped, set obliquely. Dark except in chocolates, where they can be lighter. In dapples one or both 'wall' eyes permissible.

ABOVE: *Wire-haired Dachshund*

EARS Set high, and not too far forward. Broad, of moderate length, and well rounded (not pointed or folded). Forward edge touching cheek. Mobile, and when at attention back of ear directed forward and outward.

MOUTH Teeth strongly developed, powerful canine teeth fitting closely. Jaws strong, with a perfect regular and complete scissor bite, i.e. upper teeth closely overlapping lower teeth and set square to jaws. Complete dentition important.

NECK Long, muscular, clean with no dewlap, slightly arched, running in graceful lines into shoulders, carried proudly forward.

FOREQUARTERS Shoulder blades long, broad, and placed firmly and obliquely (45 degrees to the horizontal) upon very robust ribcage. Upper arm the same length as shoulder blade, set at 90 degrees to it, very strong, and covered with hard, supple muscles. Upper arm lies close to ribs, but able to move freely. Forearm short and strong in bone, inclining slightly inwards; when seen in profile moderately straight, must not bend forward or knuckle over, which indicates unsoundness. Correctly placed foreleg should cover the lowest point of the keel.

BODY Long and full muscled. Back level, with sloping shoulders, lying in straightest possible line between withers and slightly arched loin. Loin short and strong. Breast bone strong, and so prominent that a depression appears on either side of it in front. When viewed from front, thorax full and oval; when viewed from side or above, full volumed, so allowing by its ample capacity complete development of heart and lungs. Well ribbed up, underline gradually merging into line of abdomen. Body sufficiently clear of ground to allow free movement.

HINDQUARTERS Rump full, broad and strong, pliant muscles. Croup long, full, robustly muscled, only slightly sloping towards tail. Pelvis strong, set obliquely and not too short. Upper thigh set at right angles to pelvis, strong and of good length. Lower thigh short, set at right angles to upper thigh and well muscled. Legs when seen behind set well apart, straight, and parallel. Hind dewclaws undesirable.

FEET Front feet full, broad, deep, close knit, straight or very slightly turned out. Hindfeet smaller and narrower. Toes close together, with a decided arch to each toe, strong regularly placed nails, thick and firm pads. Dog must stand true, i.e. equally on all parts of the foot.

TAIL Continues line of spine, but slightly curved, without kinks or twists, not carried too high, or touching ground when at rest.

GAIT/MOVEMENT Should be free and flowing. Stride should be long, with the drive coming from the hindquarters when viewed from the side. Viewed from in front or behind, the legs and feet should move parallel to each other with the distance apart being the width of the shoulder and hip joints respectively.

COAT
SMOOTH-HAIRED: Dense, short and smooth. Hair on underside of tail coarse in texture. Skin loose and supple, but fitting closely all over without dewlap and little or no wrinkle.
LONG-HAIRED: Soft and straight, or only slightly waved; longest under neck, on underparts of body, and behind legs, where it forms abundant feathering, on tail where it forms a flag. Outside of ears well feathered. Coat flat, and not obscuring outline. Too much hair on feet undesirable.
WIRE-HAIRED: With exception of jaw, eyebrows, chin and ears, the whole body should be covered with a short, straight, harsh coat with dense undercoat, beard on the chin, eyebrows bushy, but hair on ears almost smooth. Legs and feet well but neatly furnished with harsh coat.

COLOUR All colours allowed but (except in dapples which should be evenly marked all over) no white permissible, save for a small patch on chest which is permitted but not desirable. Nose and nails black in all colours except chocolate/tan and chocolate/dapple, where brown permitted.

SIZE Ideal weight: 9-12 kg (20-26 lb).

MINIATURES Ideal weight: 4.5 kg (10 lb). It is of the utmost importance that judges should not award prizes to animals over 5.0 kg (11 lb).

FAULTS Any departure from the foregoing points should be considered a fault and the seriousness with which the fault should be regarded should be in exact proportion to its degree.

NOTE Male animals should have two apparently normal testicles fully descended into the scrotum.

BELOW: *Miniature Wire-haired Dachshund*

DEERHOUND

THERE CAN BE FEW DOGS WHICH command the affection of people who have never owned a single specimen of the breed more than does the Deerhound, known at one time as the Scottish Deerhound. The combination of elegance of proportion with a down-to-earth, workmanlike look makes this fellow an object of admiration. Better acquaintance only serves to confirm first impressions.

Mystery surrounds the origins of the breed but there are grounds for thinking the Deerhound may have been taken to Scotland by Phoenician traders. Certainly there were running hounds there when the Romans arrived. He has hunted the red deer for a thousand years and although today more accustomed to the showring, he has remained similar in type over the centuries.

Dignity and humour, affection and loyalty, all play their part in his temperament, and he delights in exercise.

As he is less bulky than many breeds which reach his height, he takes up a lot less floor space than one might expect even if his true environment really ought to be in front of the log fire in a baronial hall.

GENERAL APPEARANCE Resembles a rough-coated greyhound of larger size and bone.

ABOVE: *The Deerhound Brutus of Bridgesollers, bred in 1925 and painted by Cecil Aldin (1870–1935).*

CHARACTERISTICS The build suggests the unique combination of speed, power and endurance necessary to pull down a stag, but general bearing is one of gentle dignity.

TEMPERAMENT Gentle and friendly. Obedient and easy to train because eager to please. Docile and good-tempered, never suspicious, aggressive or nervous. Carries himself with quiet dignity.

HEAD AND SKULL Broadest at ears, tapering slightly to eyes, muzzle tapering more decidedly to nose, lips level. Head long, skull flat rather than round, with very slight rise over eyes, with no stop. Skull coated with moderately long hair, softer than rest of coat. Nose slightly aquiline and black. In lighter-coloured dogs black muzzle preferred. Good moustache of rather silky hair and some beard.

EYES Dark. Generally dark brown or hazel. Light eyes undesirable. Moderately full with a soft look in repose, but keen, far-away look when dog is roused. Rims black.

EARS Set-on high and in repose folded back. In excitement raised above head without losing the fold and in some cases semi-erect. A big thick ear hanging flat to the head or a prick ear most undesirable. Ear soft, glossy and like a mouse's coat to the touch; the smaller the better, no long coat or fringe. Ears black or dark coloured.

MOUTH Jaws strong, with a perfect, regular and complete scissor bite, i.e. upper teeth closely overlapping lower teeth and set square to jaws.

NECK Very strong with good reach sometimes disguised by mane. Nape of neck very prominent where head is set-on, no throatiness.

FOREQUARTERS Shoulders well laid, not too far apart. Loaded and straight shoulders undesirable. Forelegs straight, broad and flat, a good broad forearm and elbow being desirable.

BODY Body and general formation that of a greyhound of larger size and bone. Chest deep rather than broad, not too narrow and flat-sided. Loin well arched and drooping to tail. Flat topline undesirable.

HINDQUARTERS Drooping, broad and powerful, hips set wide apart. Hindlegs well bent at stifle with great length from hip to hock. Bone broad and flat.

FEET Compact and well knuckled. Nails strong.

TAIL Long, thick at root, tapering and reaching almost to ground. When standing, dropped perfectly straight down or curved. Curved when moving, never lifted above line of back. Well covered with hair; on upper side thick and wiry, on underside longer, and towards end a slight fringe is not objectionable. A curl or ring tail undesirable.

GAIT/MOVEMENT Easy, active and true, with a long stride.

COAT Shaggy, but not overcoated. Woolly coat unacceptable. The correct coat is thick, close-lying, ragged; harsh or crisp to the touch. Hair on body, neck and quarters harsh and wiry about 7 cm (3 in) to 10 cm (4 in) long; that on head, breast and belly much softer. A slight hairy fringe on inside of fore- and hindlegs.

COLOUR Dark blue-grey, darker and lighter greys or brindles and yellows, sandy-red or red fawns with black points. A white chest, white toes and a slight white tip to stern are permissible but the less white the better, since it is a self-coloured dog. A white blaze on head or white collar unacceptable.

SIZE Height: dogs: minimum desirable height at withers 76 cm (30 in); bitches: 71 cm (28 in). Weight: dogs: about 45.5 kg (100 lb); bitches: about 36.5 kg (80 lb).

FAULTS Any departure from the foregoing points should be considered a fault and the seriousness with which the fault should be regarded should be in exact proportion to its degree.

NOTE Male animals should have two apparently normal testicles fully descended into the scrotum.

ELKHOUND

A VERY SOLID DOG FOR A HOUND, BUT he needs to be able to cope with his traditional prey the elk. A Spitz type with prick ears and curly tail, he is a friendly dog, but his loud voice acts a deterrent to unwanted visitors.

The breed stems from Norway. Skeletons have been found dating back to the Stone Age which are not unlike the dog of today.

Officially described as grey of various shades, he is far from being a dull-looking dog, having black tips to his longer outer coat as well as a distinctive shoulder stripe running from the withers. From the grooming angle the coat is easy to maintain in good shape and can become thoroughly dirty on a country ramble without causing the house-proud too much anxiety.

He enjoys all the exercise offered by an active family, but will be content to live a less strenuous life if his owners are less energetic. He must not be allowed to get too lazy, however, as he is capable, as are most hounds, of putting on weight to excess.

GENERAL APPEARANCE Powerful; compact body; square outline and proud carriage; coat close and abundant but not open; upstanding pointed ears; tail tightly curled over back.

CHARACTERISTICS A hardy hunting Spitz with a bold energetic disposition.

TEMPERAMENT Friendly, intelligent and independent without any sign of nervousness.

HEAD AND SKULL Wedge-shaped, comparatively broad between ears; stop, not large; forehead and back of head slightly arched; foreface broad at root (not pinched in), evenly tapering whether seen from above or side, never pointed; bridge of nose straight and approximately the length of forehead; tight-fitting skin on head, no wrinkle.

EYES Not prominent, slightly oval, medium size, dark brown, giving frank, fearless and friendly expression.

EARS Set high, small, firm and erect, pointed and very mobile; slightly taller than width at base; when alert, outer edge should be vertical.

MOUTH Jaws strong with perfect, regular scissor bite, i.e. upper teeth closely overlapping lower teeth and set square to the jaws.

NECK Medium length, powerful, carrying the head high; a rich ruff on close-fitting skin but no dewlap.

FOREQUARTERS Legs straight with good, not coarse, bone and strong pasterns; shoulders sloping; elbows closely set in.

BODY Powerful; short, strong back; loin short and wide with very little tuck-up; chest deep and broad; well curved ribs; topline straight and level; distance from brisket to ground not less than half the height at withers.

HINDQUARTERS Legs firm, strong and powerful; little but definite bend at stifle and hock; straight when viewed from behind.

FEET Comparatively small, slightly oval; tightly closed, well arched toes with protective hair between thick pads; turning neither in nor out. Nails firm and strong.

TAIL Strong, set-on high; thickly coated without plume; tightly curled, preferably over the centre line of back.

GAIT/MOVEMENT Demonstrates agility and endurance; stride at the trot even and effortless, back remaining level; as speed of trot increases, front and rear legs converge equally in straight lines towards a centre line beneath body.

COAT Close, abundant, weather-resistant; soft, dense, woolly undercoat and coarse, straight outer coat; short and smooth on head and front of legs, slightly longer on back of front legs, longest on neck, back of thighs and tail; not trimmed.

COLOUR Grey of various shades, with black tips to outer coat; lighter on chest, stomach, legs, underside of tail, buttocks and in a harness mark; ears and foreface dark; a dark line from eye to ear desirable; undercoat pure pale grey. Any pronounced variation from the grey colour, sooty colour on lower legs, spectacles or white markings undesirable.

SIZE Ideal height at shoulder: dogs: 52 cm (20½ in); bitches: 49 cm (19½ in). Weight approx 23 kg (50 lb) and 20 kg (43 lb) respectively.

FAULTS Any departure from the foregoing points should be considered a fault and the seriousness with which the fault should be regarded should be in exact proportion to its degree.

NOTE Male animals should have two apparently normal testicles fully descended into the scrotum.

FINNISH SPITZ

BRIGHT RED DOGS OF TYPICAL SPITZ shape, unusual in that they hunt small birds and give considerable tongue while doing so. Increasing in popularity steadily, as well they might; the breed temperament is lively and friendly resulting in an active companion for the family requiring exercise.

The Finnish Spitz is the national dog of Finland with a written standard going back to 1812. A number of national patriotic songs include mentions of the breed.

Originally the Finnish Spitz tracked larger game such as bear and elk, but now is used mainly to seek out capercaillie and black grouse. The strength of the game bird population has a direct effect on the strength of the breed, registrations dropping in years which are bad for the birds.

Straight-legged, compactly, but not heavily, bodied, the Finnish Spitz is a square shaped breed with sparkle and charm. The middle-length coat is semi-erect, stiffer on neck and back, and particularly prominent in the ruff of the male.

Easy to maintain, the coat, although not short, cleans quickly with the aid of a sponge. Equally happy in all weathers, the Finnish Spitz considers that his place is not outside in the kennel, but indoors with his friends.

GENERAL APPEARANCE Dog considerably larger and carrying more coat than the bitch. Bearing bold. Whole appearance, particularly eyes, ears and tail, indicates liveliness. Compact, hard-conditioned hunting dog with medium bone and no suggestion of coarseness.

CHARACTERISTICS Eagerness to hunt, courage tempered with caution, fidelity and intelligence.

TEMPERAMENT Alert, lively, friendly but independent.

HEAD AND SKULL Head medium-sized and clean-cut. Longer than broad. Forehead slightly arched, stop moderate. Muzzle narrow, seen from above and from sides, evenly tapering. Nose pitch black. Lips black, tightly closed and thin.

EYES Medium-sized, lively, preferably dark. Almond-shaped with black rims, set slightly aslant, with outer corners tilted upwards.

EARS Small, cocked, sharply pointed. Fine in texture and mobile.

MOUTH Jaws strong with perfect regular scissor bite, i.e. upper teeth closely overlapping lower teeth and set square to the jaws.

NECK Muscular, of medium length, with no excess of skin or fat. In males may appear shorter due to dense ruff.

FOREQUARTERS Strong and straight.

BODY Almost square in outline. Back straight and strong. Chest deep. Belly slightly drawn up.

HINDQUARTERS Strong. Only moderate turn of stifle. Hock of medium angulation.

FEET Preferably round. Hind dewclaws always removed. Removal of front dewclaws optional.

TAIL Plumed, curves vigorously from its root in an arch, forward downward and backward, then pressing down against thigh, with its tip extending to middle part of thigh. Extended, the bone of tail usually reaches to hock joint.

GAIT/MOVEMENT Light and springy, quick and graceful, with drive.

COAT On head and front of legs short and close, on body and back of legs longish, semi-erect, stiffer on neck and back. Outer coat on shoulders considerably longer and coarser,

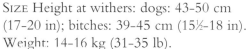

particularly in males. On back of thighs and on tail hair longer and denser. No trimming allowed, not even of whiskers. Undercoat short, soft and dense.

COLOUR On back reddish-brown or red gold, preferably bright. Hairs on inner sides of ears, cheeks, under muzzle, on breast, abdomen, behind shoulders, inside legs, back of thighs, underside of tail, of lighter shades. Undercoat also a lighter colour, making whole coat glow. Narrow white stripe not exceeding 1.5 cm in width on breast permitted. Black hairs on lips and sparse separate black pointed hairs on back and tail permitted. Puppies may have black hairs which decrease with age, black on tail persisting longer.

SIZE Height at withers: dogs: 43-50 cm (17-20 in); bitches: 39-45 cm (15½-18 in). Weight: 14-16 kg (31-35 lb).

FAULTS Any departure from the foregoing points should be considered a fault and the seriousness with which the fault should be regarded should be in exact proportion to its degree.

NOTE Male animals should have two apparently normal testicles fully descended into the scrotum.

FOXHOUND

(INTERIM)

THE TRADITIONAL HANDSOME Foxhound has rarely been regarded as a household pet; indeed the Kennel Club removed the breed standard from its official issue in the mid-1980s. In the United States of America the breed has been treated as a genuine show-dog over the years in small numbers but is only occasionally seen in the showring in Britain.

Most adult foxhounds are maintained in kennels in packs by one or other of the hunts; the puppies are 'walked' through their growing period by hunt-supporters in order that they should become part-socialised. As a breed they have to be recognised as being relatively large and determined; discipline is not their strong-point. They are registered with The Kennel Club irregularly on the basis of reciprocal agreements with masters of recognised hunts. The breed may well make a greater impact in the showring in the future.

GENERAL APPEARANCE Well balanced, powerful and clean cut.

CHARACTERISTICS Stamina and endurance, natural ability to hunt.

TEMPERAMENT Friendly and not aggressive.

HEAD AND SKULL Well balanced, skull flat of medium width. Muzzle long and square with large nostrils. Slight stop, moderately developed flews.

EYES Medium size, hazel or brown. Keen expression.

EARS Leathers pendant, carried close to head, high set.

MOUTH Jaws strong with a perfect, regular and complete scissor bite, i.e. upper teeth closely overlapping lower teeth and set square to the jaws.

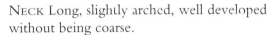

NECK Long, slightly arched, well developed without being coarse.

FOREQUARTERS Shoulders well laid back, muscular without being loaded. Forelegs long, straight and well boned down to feet, pastern strong.

BODY Chest deep, ribs well sprung. Back broad and level. Strong over loins.

HINDQUARTERS Powerful and muscular. Stifles well bent. Hocks well let down. Well boned down to feet.

FEET Round, tight and strong. Well padded. Nails strong. Dewclaws optional.

TAIL Well set-on high. Carried gaily but never curled over back.

GAIT/MOVEMENT Free-striding, tireless with the ability to gallop. Good drive behind with no indication to roll.

COAT Short and dense. Weatherproof.

COLOUR Any recognised hound colour and markings.

SIZE Height: approx 58-64 cm (23-25 in).

FAULTS Any departure from the foregoing points should be considered a fault and the seriousness with which the fault should be regarded should be in exact proportion to its degree.

NOTE Male animals should have two apparently normal testicles fully descended into the scrotum.

GRAND BASSET GRIFFON VENDEEN

(INTERIM)

ARRIVING FROM FRANCE IN 1990, the 'Grand', as his devotees call him, is described as 'low to ground', hence the Basset in his full name which is customarily shortened to its initials of GBGV. He hunts rabbit and hare and uses his very efficient nose to keep him on track. He is perhaps somewhat taller than he appears from a distance and is not just a different form of the Petit Basset.

He is a chap with a sense of humour and delights in joining in with every human activity, although, being a true hound, he has a tendency to be hard of hearing when it suits him! He is a canine escapologist; his owner's garden requires an intensity of attention to boundary maintenance.

He needs regular grooming of an unfussy nature.

He eats well and uncritically; he has a prodigious voice; he has stamina.

This is a breed which will recruit many disciples; both existing breeders and future devotees will need to ensure that it is not spoilt by too much popularity in its early years here.

GENERAL APPEARANCE Well balanced, medium height hound. Rough coated with a familiar and intelligent look and noble bearing.

CHARACTERISTICS A strong, active hound capable of a day's hunting, with a good voice freely used.

TEMPERAMENT Happy and outgoing, but thoughtful and not easily agitated; independent, yet willing to please.

HEAD AND SKULL A noble head. Skull domed and not too wide. Well cut away under the eyes; stop clearly defined; occipital bone well developed. Long, square muzzle. Slight roman nose. Underjaw strong, well developed. Nose black, large with wide nostrils. Eyes surmounted by long eyebrows standing forward but not to obscure eyes, lips covered with long hair forming beard and moustache.

EYES Large, dark, showing no white, with a friendly, intelligent expression. Haw not visible.

EARS Supple narrow and fine, covered with long hair, folding inwards ending in an oval shape; reaching to at least the end of the nose; set-on low, not above the line of the eye.

MOUTH Jaws strong with perfect, regular and complete scissor bite, i.e. upper teeth closely overlapping lower teeth and set square to the jaws.

NECK Long and strong, set into well laid shoulders, thicker at base; without throatiness, carrying the head proudly.

FOREQUARTERS Shoulders clean and well laid back; elbows close to the body, never turning out. Forelegs straight, thick and well boned. Pasterns strong and slightly sloping. Knuckling over is unacceptable.

BODY Deep brisket, ribs moderately rounded, extending well back. Back of good length and level topline with slight rise over well muscled loins.

HINDQUARTERS Heavy boned, strong and muscular with moderate bend of stifle. Heavily muscled thighs and well defined second thigh.

FEET Big and tight padded. Pads firm and solid. Nails strong and short.

TAIL Good length, set-on high, strong at the base, tapering regularly, well furnished with hair of good length; carried proudly like the blade of a sabre or slightly turned in, but never falling back over the loins.

GAIT/MOVEMENT Free with great drive. Front action straight and reaching well forward; hind action easy and elastic, hocks turning neither in nor out.

COAT Rough and long without exaggeration, with a flat structure, never silky or woolly, fringing not too abundant, thick undercoat. Hounds should be shown untrimmed.

COLOUR White with any combination of lemon, orange, tricolour or grizzle markings.

SIZE Height: 39-43 cm (15½-17 in); 2 cm (¾ in) above the upper limit permissible.

FAULTS Any departure from the foregoing points should be considered a fault and the seriousness with which the fault should be regarded should be in exact proportion to its degree.

NOTE Male animals should have two apparently normal testicles fully descended into the scrotum.

GRAND BLEU DE GASCOIGNE

(INTERIM)

THE GRAND BLEU IS AN ARISTOCRAT among hounds, being tall and possessed of a long head with very characteristic markings. He owns a powerful baying voice which will certainly persuade the neighbours that there is a new presence among them.

The basic colour is white with black patches, and black-mottled all over, producing a blue tinge from which the Bleu name is derived.

He gives the impression that he is sad, a quality to which a French canine historian alluded in describing his 'majestic allure and aristocratic melancholy'. Like all hounds, Bleus are hunters, once of wolves, and in modern times, of hares. They do not gallop aimlessly after their quarry so much as pursue it unremittingly. They live in a world of scent and need understanding owners, sensitive to the concept that they are not as easily trained as are gundogs or the herding breeds.

The breed failed to find favour as a hunting dog in Great Britain once the wolf was extinct. His introduction as a show dog is very recent. The attracion is his size combined with elegance. It is to be hoped that his excellence at following a cold scent is not lost in the show breeding programmes of British breeders.

They are best maintained in outside kennels with their own runs. Definitely a breed for the connoisseur, not for the masses!

GENERAL APPEARANCE One of the larger French hunting hounds with aristocratic long head, characteristic head markings and distinctive colour.

CHARACTERISTICS Highly developed sense of smell and deep bay.

TEMPERAMENT Gentle and kind.

HEAD AND SKULL Large, long and distinguished. Occiput pronounced. Slight stop, loose skin covering head and forming one or two wrinkles along cheeks, lips pendulous and well pigmented. Black palate.

EYES Dark chestnut colour, not prominent. Sad, trusting expression.

EARS Set low, fine, curled inward reaching at least to tip of nose.

MOUTH Jaws strong, with a perfect, regular and complete scissor bite, i.e. upper teeth closely overlapping lower teeth and set square to the jaws.

NECK Medium length, rounded, carrying dewlap.

FOREQUARTERS Strong, straight and well boned. Elbows close to body, shoulders well laid and muscular.

BODY Chest well developed, being long, wide and deep. Ribs moderately rounded; back rather long and muscular. Flanks deep and wide.

HINDQUARTERS Broad and well muscled. Hocks low to ground, set wide apart and parallel. Sloping croup. Prominent hip bones.

FEET Long, oval, deep and well padded.

TAIL (Stern) Well set-on, rather thick, fairly long and carried sickle fashion.

GAIT/MOVEMENT Loose-limbed and long-striding.

COAT Smooth, weather resistant and not too short.

COLOUR Black marked on a white base but covered entirely with black mottling which gives a blue appearance. Two black marks are found on head, covering each ear, enveloping eyes and stopping at cheeks. Blaze also mottled, but a small black mark is often found on skull, a characteristic of the breed. Above each eye a spot of tan gives breed 'four-eyed' effect. Tan marks also found on cheeks, lips, inside ears, on legs and under tail. Some hounds completely mottled, but always have required tan marks.

SIZE Height: dogs: 63.5-70 cm (25-27½ in); bitches: 60-65 cm (23½-25½ in).

FAULTS Any departure from the foregoing points should be considered a fault and the seriousness with which the fault should be regarded should be in exact proportion to its degree.

NOTE Male animals should have two apparently normal testicles fully descended into the scrotum.

GREYHOUND

THE EXPERTS, ALTHOUGH NOT unanimous, consider that the Greyhound could have had its origins in the Middle East. Drawings of Greyhound-type dogs have been found on walls in Ancient Egyptian tombs, dating as far back as 4000 BC. Though dogs of the type spread through Europe over the years, it was in Britain that they were developed to a standard.

The prototype of the so-called sighthounds, or gazehounds, the Greyhound is well known to many people who have never been anywhere near a dog show and probably wouldn't even know that Greyhounds were ever exhibited. The show animal is somewhat bigger than his racing cousin while the coursing version, which hunts the live hare as opposed to the electric,

is, if anything, slightly smaller, giving him greater manoeuvrability. The racing Greyhound was developed from that which was used for coursing and only the cheetah tops the Greyhound for speed. One racing Greyhound was clocked at over 45 mph.

The Greyhound comes in virtually every colour with or without white. He is obviously possessed of an insatiable instinct to chase and kill, and this is a trait to be remembered when there are small dogs and cats about! With the human race there is no such problem – he is gentle, affectionate and faithful.

Easy to keep clean and shining with a minimum of polishing with a hound-glove; not big eaters; in fact a breed which makes a grand companion in a household where the family has the time and energy to give the dog adequate exercise.

GENERAL APPEARANCE Strongly built, upstanding, of generous proportions, muscular power and symmetrical formation, with long head and neck, clean well laid shoulders, deep chest, capacious body, arched loin, powerful quarters, sound legs and feet, and a suppleness of limb, which emphasise in a marked degree its distinctive type and quality.

CHARACTERISTICS Possessing remarkable stamina and endurance.

TEMPERAMENT Intelligent, gentle, affectionate and even-tempered.

HEAD AND SKULL Long, moderate width, flat skull, slight stop. Jaws powerful and well chiselled.

EYES Bright, intelligent, oval and obliquely set. Preferably dark.

EARS Small, rose-shape, of fine texture.

MOUTH Jaws strong with a perfect, regular and complete scissor bite, i.e. upper teeth closely overlapping lower teeth and set square to the jaws.

NECK Long and muscular, elegantly arched, well let into shoulders.

FOREQUARTERS Shoulders oblique, well set back, muscular without being loaded, narrow and cleanly defined at top. Forelegs, long and straight, bone of good substance and quality. Elbows free and well set under shoulders. Pasterns moderate length, slightly sprung. Elbows, pasterns and toes inclining neither in nor out.

BODY Chest deep and capacious, providing adequate heart room. Ribs deep, well sprung and carried well back. Flanks well cut up. Back rather long, broad and square. Loins powerful, slightly arched.

HINDQUARTERS Thighs and second thighs wide and muscular, showing great propelling power. Stifles well bent. Hocks well let down, inclining neither in nor out. Body and hindquarters, features of ample proportions and well coupled, enabling adequate ground to be covered when standing.

FEET Moderate length, with compact, well knuckled toes and strong pads.

TAIL Long, set-on rather low, strong at root, tapering to point, carried low, slightly curved.

GAIT/MOVEMENT Straight, low-reaching, free stride enabling the ground to be covered at great speed. Hindlegs coming well under body giving great propulsion.

COAT Fine and close.

COLOUR Black, white, red, blue, fawn, fallow, brindle or any of these colours broken with white.

SIZE Ideal height: dogs: 71-76 cm (28-30 in); bitches: 68-71 cm (27-28 in).

FAULTS Any departure from the foregoing points should be considered a fault and the seriousness with which the fault should be regarded should be in exact proportion to its degree.

NOTE Male animals should have two apparently normal testicles fully descended into the scrotum.

HAMILTONSTOVARE

(INTERIM)

THIS HANDSOME, STYLISH DOG COMES from Sweden, where he is the most popular of the hound breeds. He carries the name of Count Hamilton who created the breed in the late 1800s. The count was a connoisseur of hounds and founder of the Swedish Kennel Club. His foundation dog and bitch for the Hamiltonstovare were basically of English Foxhound breeding crossed with German hounds.

The Hamilton is a hunting dog which is not used in packs but which hunts singly, more suited to the country than the town, and will spend hours in the fields. Should he get out on his own he will be far too engrossed to come back to a quick whistle, but will eventually return in his own good time.

His richly coloured black, tan and white coat combined with his elegant head carriage add to his attraction. His coat is easy to care for. A dog who likes to work, he makes a happy, easy-going friend and companion.

GENERAL APPEARANCE Well proportioned, giving impression of great strength and stamina. Tricoloured.

CHARACTERISTICS Handsome, upstanding dog of striking colouring. Hardy and sound.

TEMPERAMENT Typical even-tempered hound.

HEAD AND SKULL Head longish, rectangular, with slightly arched and moderately broad skull. Occiput not too prominent. Stop well defined but not over pronounced. Jowls not too heavy. Muzzle fairly long, large and rectangular. Bridge of nose straight and parallel to line of skull. Nose always black, well developed with large nostrils. Upper lips full but not too overhanging.

EYES Clear and dark brown with tranquil expression.

EARS Set fairly high, when drawn alongside jaw, ears extend to approximately half-way along muzzle and should be raised only slightly above skull when responding to call. Soft with straight fall and fore edge not folded out.

MOUTH Jaws strong, with a perfect, regular and complete scissor bite, i.e. upper teeth closely overlapping lower teeth and set square to the jaws.

NECK Long and powerful, merging well into shoulders, skin on neck supple and close fitting.

FOREQUARTERS Shoulders muscular and well laid back. When viewed from front forelegs appear straight and parallel. Upper foreleg long and broad and set at a right angle to shoulder blade. Elbows set close in to body.

BODY Back straight and powerful. Croup slightly inclined, long, broad with well defined muscles. Chest deep. Ribs moderately sprung, back ribs proportionately long. Belly slightly tucked up.

HINDQUARTERS Strong and parallel when viewed from behind. Well angulated, muscle well developed and broad when seen from side.

FEET Short and hard. Pads firm and pointing straight forward. Dewclaws only allowed on front legs.

TAIL Set-on high, in an almost straight continuation of line of back. Held in straight position or curving slightly in sabre-like shape. Fairly wide at base and narrowing off towards tip. In length reaches hock.

GAIT/MOVEMENT Free-striding and long-reaching. Hindlegs showing drive. Not moving close behind.

COAT Coat consists of two layers. Undercoat short, close and soft, especially thick during winter. Upper coat strongly weather-resistant lying close to body. On underside of tail, ordinary hair quite long but not forming a fringe. Ample hair between pads.

COLOUR Upper side of neck, back, sides of trunk and upper side of tail black. Head and legs, as well as side of neck, trunk and tail brown. Blaze on upper part of muzzle, underside of neck, breast and tip of tail, together with feet, white. A mixture of black and brown undesirable, as is any preponderance of any of the three permissible colours.

SIZE Ideal size 57 cm (22½ in) for dogs with a permitted variation in height of between 50 and 60 cm (19½ – 23½ in), and 53 cm (21 in) for bitches with a permitted variation of 46-57 cm (18-22½ in).

FAULTS Any departure from the foregoing points should be considered a fault, and the seriousness with which the fault should be regarded should be in exact proportion to its degree.

NOTE Male animals should have two apparently normal testicles fully descended into the scrotum.

HOUND

47

IBIZAN HOUND

A TYPICAL MEDITERRANEAN HOUND, with tall ears, as depicted on Egyptian tombs and pottery since time immemorial. A relentless hunter, who can shut his ears to all human entreaty when on the chase. Not a breed for the town-dweller, who is usually not able to provide adequate exercise with a reasonable degree of freedom for him to gallop.

The breed's ability to jump considerable heights gives him a justified reputation as an escapologist. Temperamentally aloof with strangers but devoted to owners. The smooth coat is easy to keep clean and even the rough-coated variety sponges down quickly. The breed feels the cold if left outside in a British winter.

Though the breed takes his name from the island of Ibiza, he probably arrived there by way of early trading ships, such as those of the Phoenicians. The breed has been known not only on Ibiza but also on the neighbouring island of Formentera for something like 5,000 years.

GENERAL APPEARANCE Tall, narrow, finely built, large erect ears.

CHARACTERISTICS Agile, tireless, controlled hunter. Retrieves to hand, has ability to jump great heights without take-off run.

TEMPERAMENT Reserved with strangers, not nervous or aggressive. Dignified, intelligent and independent.

HEAD AND SKULL Fine, long, flat skull with prominent occipital bone. Stop not well defined, slightly convex muzzle, length of which from eyes to tip of nose equals length from eyes to occiput. Nose flesh-coloured, should protrude beyond teeth, jaws very strong and lean.

EYES Clear amber, expressive. Almond-shaped; not prominent, large or round.

EARS Large, thin, stiff, highly mobile, erect when dog is alert, in a continuous line with arch of neck when viewed in profile; base set-on level with eyes. Drop ears unacceptable.

MOUTH Perfectly even white teeth; scissor bite, i.e. upper teeth closely overlapping lower teeth and set square to the jaws. Thin lips with no dewlap.

NECK Very lean, long, muscular and slightly arched.

FOREQUARTERS Rather steep, short shoulder blades, long straight legs, erect pasterns of good length.

BODY Level back sloping slightly from the pin bones to rump. Long, flat ribcage. Short coupled with well tucked-up waist, breast bone very prominent. Depth measured between bottom of ribcage and elbow 7-8 cm (2½-3 in).

HINDQUARTERS Long, strong, straight and lean, no great angulation, long second thigh, turning neither in nor out.

FEET Well arched toes, thick pads, light-coloured claws. Front feet may turn slightly outwards. Dewclaws should not be removed in front. No hind dewclaws.

TAIL Long, thin, low set, reaching well below the hock; when passed between legs and round flank reaches spine; may be carried high when excited, but not curled within itself or low over back.

GAIT/MOVEMENT A suspended trot, which is a long far-reaching stride, with a slight hover before placing foot to ground.

COAT Smooth or rough always hard, close, dense. Longer under tail and at back of legs. Hunting scars should not be penalised.

COLOUR White, chestnut or lion solid colour, or any combination of these.

SIZE In country of origin varies between 56 and 74 cm (22-29 in), but balance is overriding factor.

FAULTS Any departure from the foregoing points should be considered a fault and the seriousness with which the fault should be regarded should be in exact proportion to its degree.

NOTE Male animals should have two apparently normal testicles fully descended into the scrotum.

IRISH WOLFHOUND

STANDING VERY NEARLY A YARD HIGH at the shoulder, the Wolfhound is not only the tallest of all the hounds, but he is the biggest breed of them all. In addition he is well built in all departments, any tendency to lightness of head, limbs or body being frowned on by his devotees.

In spite of his size, he is one of the most gentle of dogs, with an expression which combines pride and calm, but which can occasionally light up with genial mischief as his dark eyes flash. Everything about the Wolfhound is large, but one of his greatest attributes is his perfection of balance, his rough, harsh coat fitting his image perfectly.

Originally the Wolfhound could be found with either a smooth or rough coat though in early years there was probably great variance of type. After the last wolf was killed in Ireland, before 1800, the breed almost died out and was further affected by the big famine of Ireland in 1840. There followed a restoration of the breed by 1870 and a breed club was in being by 1885.

The Wolfhound never appears to hurry, but he can cover a lot of ground and obviously is a dog which needs space and reasonable exercise. He also needs food in fair quantity, especially in his growing years, when his rapid increase in size requires attention to a high calibre diet if his huge frame is to be properly developed.

A delightful dog but not to be taken on lightly.

GENERAL APPEARANCE Of great size, strength, symmetry and commanding appearance, very muscular, yet gracefully built.

CHARACTERISTICS Of great power, activity, speed and courage.

TEMPERAMENT Gentle, kind and friendly nature.

HEAD AND SKULL Head long, carried high, the frontal bones of forehead very slightly raised and very little indentation between eyes. Skull not too broad. Muzzle long and moderately pointed. Nose and lips black.

EYES Dark. Elliptical (regular oval) and full. Eyelids black.

EARS Small, rose-shaped, of fine velvet texture. Preferably dark in colour, not hanging close to face.

MOUTH Jaws strong with a perfect, regular and complete scissor bite, i.e. upper teeth closely overlapping lower teeth and set square to the jaws. Level bite tolerated but not desirable.

NECK Rather long, very strong and muscular, well arched, without dewlap or loose skin about throat.

FOREQUARTERS Shoulders muscular, giving breadth of chest, set sloping. Elbows well under, turned neither in nor out. Leg and forearm muscular, and whole leg strong and straight.

BODY Chest very deep. Breast wide. Back, long rather than short. Loins arched. Belly well drawn up.

HINDQUARTERS Muscular thighs and second thighs, long and strong, good bend of stifle with hocks well let down and turning neither in nor out.

FEET Moderately large and round, turned neither in nor out. Toes well arched and closed. Nails very strong and curved.

TAIL Long and slightly curved, of moderate thickness and well covered with hair, carried low with an upward sweep towards the extremity.

GAIT/MOVEMENT Easy and active.

COAT Rough and harsh on body, legs and head; especially wiry and long over eyes and under jaw.

COLOUR Recognised colours are grey, brindle, red, black, pure white, fawn, wheaten and steel grey.

SIZE Minimum height for dogs: 79 cm (31 in); bitches: 71 cm (28 in). Minimum weight: 54.5 kg (120 lb) for dogs, 40.9 kg (90 lb) for bitches. Great size, including height of shoulder and proportionate length of body, is to be aimed at, and it is desired to firmly establish a breed that shall average from 81-86 cm (32-34 in) in dogs.

FAULTS Any departure from the foregoing points should be considered a fault and the seriousness with which the fault should be regarded should be in exact proportion to its degree.

NOTE Male animals should have two apparently normal testicles fully descended into the scrotum.

NORWEGIAN LUNDEHUND

(INTERIM)

A REMARKABLE SMALL DOG HAILING from islands off the coast of Norway; he only appeared in Great Britain during the 1990s.

He is a Spitz in type; he is unusual in having six toes on each of his four feet. This is apparently as a result of selective adaptation and enables him to climb cliffs on which Puffins are nesting. The Lundehund manages to climb up and persuade the sitting birds to leave their nests and eggs unprotected.

As a breed the Lundehund is good-natured and lively.

GENERAL APPEARANCE Small, Spitz type dog, rectangular in shape. Comparatively lightly made.

CHARACTERISTICS At least six toes on each foot, ear orifice capable of closing.

TEMPERAMENT Alert, energetic, lively, not nervous or aggressive.

HEAD AND SKULL Clean, wedge shaped. Skull slightly domed; of medium width. Protruding bony ridges over eyes. Pronounced stop. Muzzle of medium length and width.

EYES Slightly slanting, not protruding. Medium to dark brown.

EARS Triangular, medium size, carried erect, very mobile. Feature of the breed that cartilage ends meet in upper part of ear and can shut when the dog raises its ears half way.

MOUTH Jaws strong, with a perfect, regular and complete scissor bite, i.e. upper teeth closely over-lapping lower teeth and set square to the jaws.

NECK Clean cut, medium length and strong.

FOREQUARTERS Legs straight and strong; shoulders moderately sloping.

BODY Rectangular, strong, straight back, slightly sloping croup. Medium width of chest, spacious and relatively deep. Long ribcage not barrelled. Slight tuck-up of belly.

HINDQUARTERS Narrow in stance. Strong, moderately angulated. Muscular first and second thighs.

FEET These are a unique characteristic of the breed. Oval in shape. Forefeet and hindfeet slightly turned out, with at least six toes on each. Forefeet – five of the toes on forefeet should be on the ground. Hindfeet – turning out with four of the toes on the ground.

TAIL Set-on high. Medium short with dense coat but no flag. Hanging or carried in a ring but not tightly curled.

GAIT/MOVEMENT Springy. Characteristic loose action of front legs. Hindlegs moving parallel.

COAT Dense, rough outer coat with soft undercoat. Short on head and front of legs. Longer on neck and thighs.

COLOUR Reddish brown to fallow with black tips to hairs preferred. Black or grey. All with white markings. White with dark markings. Mature dogs usually carrying more distinct black in outer coat.

SIZE Height: dogs: 35-38 cm (14-15 in); bitches: 32-35 cm (12½-14 in). Weight: dogs: approx 7 kg (15½ lb); bitches: approx 6 kg (13 lb).

FAULTS Any departure from the foregoing points should be considered a fault and the seriousness with which the fault should be regarded should be in exact proportion to its degree.

NOTE Male animals should have two apparently normal testicles fully descended into the scrotum.

OTTERHOUND

FROM EVERY VIEWPOINT THE Otterhound is a large dog with a truly rugged appearance. Built to gallop when on land, his main function has always been to spend his working day in water. It is generally felt that his ancestry includes a French influence combined with original English hound strains.

His rough double coat is extremely weather-resistant, but this means that he can bring a deal of the countryside into the home when he returns from the long rambles which he enjoys.

He is a kindly fellow with a typical loud baying call which he can use to good effect when he needs to indicate that he has found a prey that interests him, though today his primary purpose of hunting otters is banned.

An Otterhound has keen scenting ability. When following the scent of an otter on land the scent is called a drag and in water a wash. An Otterhound can follow a drag for up to twelve hours and when following a wash may swim for five hours. In addition to his oily coat he has webbed feet.

A dog for the energetic, but not for the house-proud.

GENERAL APPEARANCE Large, straight-limbed and sound, rough-coated with majestic head, strong body and loose, long-striding action. Rough double coat and large feet essential. Free moving.

CHARACTERISTICS Big, strong hound primarily built for long day's work in water but able to gallop on land.

TEMPERAMENT Amiable and even-tempered.

HEAD AND SKULL Clean, very imposing, deep rather than wide, clean cheekbones, skull nicely domed, neither coarse nor overdone, rising from distinct though not exaggerated stop to slight peak at occiput. No trace of scowl or bulge on forehead, expression being open and amiable.

Muzzle strong, deep; with good wide nose, wide nostrils. Distance from nose end to stop slightly shorter than from stop to occiput. Plenty of lip and flew, but not exaggerated. Whole head except for nose well covered with rough hair, ending in slight moustache and beard.

EYES Intelligent, moderately deep-set eye; haw showing only slightly. Eye colour and rim pigment variable according to coat colour (a blue and tan hound may have hazel eyes). Yellow eye undesirable.

EARS Unique feature of the breed. Long, pendulous, set-on level with corner of eye; easily reaching nose when pulled forward, with characteristic fold. Leading edge folding or rolling inwards giving curious draped appearance – an essential point not to be lost. Well covered and fringed with hair.

MOUTH Jaws strong, large, well placed teeth with perfect, regular scissor bite, i.e. upper teeth closely overlapping lower teeth and set square to the jaws.

NECK Long, powerful, set smoothly into well laid back, clean shoulders. Slight dewlap permissible.

FOREQUARTERS Well laid shoulders. Forelegs strongly boned, straight from elbow to ground. Pasterns strong and slightly sprung.

BODY Chest deep with well sprung, fairly deep, oval ribcage. Ribs carried well back allowing plenty of heart and lung room; neither too wide nor too narrow. Body very strong, with level topline and broad back. Loin short and strong.

HINDQUARTERS Very strong; well muscled when viewed from an angle, standing neither too wide nor too narrow behind. Hind angulation moderate; hocks well let down, turning neither in nor out. Thighs and second

thighs heavily muscled. In natural stance, hindlegs from hock to ground perpendicular.

FEET Large, round, well knuckled, thick padded, turning neither in nor out. Compact but capable of spreading hindfeet only slightly smaller than forefeet. Web must be in evidence.

TAIL (Stern) Set high, carried up when alert or moving, never curling over back and may droop when standing. Thick at base, tapering to point; bone reaching to hock and carried straight or in a slight curve. Hair under tail rather longer and more profuse than that on upper surface.

GAIT/MOVEMENT Very loose and shambling at walk, springing immediately into a loose, very long-striding, sound, active trot. Gallop smooth and exceptionally long-striding.

COAT Long 4–8 cm (1½–3 in), dense, rough, harsh and waterproof but not wiry; of broken appearance. Softer hair on head and lower legs natural. Undercoat evident and there may be a slight oily texture in top and undercoat. Not trimmed for exhibition. Presentation should be natural.

COLOUR All recognised hound colours permissible: whole coloured, grizzle, sandy, red, wheaten, blue; these may have slight white markings on head, chest, feet and tail tip. White hounds may have slight lemon, blue or badger pied markings. Black and tan, blue and tan, black and cream, occasional liver, tan and liver, tan and white. Colours not permissible: liver and white, a white-bodied hound with black and tan patches distinctly separate. Pigment should harmonise though not necessarily blend with coat colour; for example a tan hound may have a brown nose and eye rims. A slight butterfly nose permissible.

SIZE Approximate height at shoulder: dogs: 67 cm (27 in); bitches: 60 cm (24 in)

FAULTS Any departure from the foregoing points should be considered a fault and the seriousness with which the fault should be regarded should be in exact proportion to its degree.

NOTE Male animals should have two apparently normal testicles fully descended into the scrotum.

PETIT BASSET GRIFFON VENDEEN

THE LENGTH OF THE BREED'S NAME HAS led to this chap being known to all and sundry by his initials, as the 'PBGV'; nicknames are often applied to favourites and it is a measure of his charm that, though he is still relatively rare since he was introduced to Britain from home in Western France in 1969, many devotees of other breeds will smile when he walks in the showring.

Though low to the ground as denoted by the term 'basset', he is a balanced dog, is extremely active and demonstrates soundness on the move. A typical hound, he is most at home in the country, preferably with his beard and moustaches picking up the dead leaves as he sweeps the ground after his prey. His long eyebrows impart a faintly comical look, and this is confirmed in his happy, extrovert temperament.

A breed for the healthy, fun-loving family; not needing a great deal of polishing with a duster, but more of the curry-comb or the vacuum cleaner.

GENERAL APPEARANCE Well balanced, short legged, compact hound. Rough-coated with alert outlook and lively bearing.

CHARACTERISTICS Strong, active hound capable of a day's hunting, with a good voice freely used.

TEMPERAMENT Happy, extrovert, independent, yet willing to please.

HEAD AND SKULL Medium in length, not too wide, oval in shape when viewed from front. Well cut away under eyes; stop clearly defined; occipital bone well developed. Muzzle slightly shorter than from stop to occipital point. Under jaw strong and well developed. Nose black, large with wide nostrils. Eyes surmounted by long eyebrows standing forward but not to obscure eyes; lips covered with long hair forming beard and moustache.

EYES Large, dark, showing no white, with friendly intelligent expression. Red of lower eyelid not showing.

EARS Supple, narrow and fine, covered with long hair, folding inwards, ending in an oval shape; reaching to end of nose; set-on low, not above line of eye.

MOUTH Jaws strong with a perfect, regular and complete scissor bite, i.e. upper teeth closely overlapping lower teeth and set square to the jaws. Level bite acceptable.

NECK Long and strong, set into well laid shoulders; without throatiness; carrying head proudly.

FOREQUARTERS Shoulders clean and sloping; elbows close to body. Forelegs straight, a slight crook acceptable; thick and well boned. Pasterns strong and slightly sloping. Knuckling over highly undesirable.

BODY Chest deep with prominent sternum; ribs moderately rounded extending well back. Back of medium length; level topline with slight arching over strong loins.

HINDQUARTERS Strong and muscular with good bend of stifle. Well defined second thigh. Hocks short and well angulated.

FEET Hard, tight-padded, not too long. Nails strong and short.

TAIL Of medium length; set-on high, strong at base, tapering regularly, well furnished with hair; carried proudly like the blade of a sabre.

GAIT/MOVEMENT Free at all paces, with great drive. Front action straight and reaching well forward; hocks turning neither in nor out.

COAT Rough, long without exaggeration and harsh to the touch, with thick undercoat, never silky or woolly. Shown untrimmed.

COLOUR White with any combination of lemon, orange, tricolour or grizzle markings.

SIZE Height: 33-38 cm (13-15 in).

FAULTS Any departure from the foregoing points should be considered a fault and the seriousness with which the fault should be regarded should be in exact proportion to its degree.

NOTE Male animals should have two apparently normal testicles fully descended into the scrotum.

PHARAOH HOUND

ANYONE WHO HAS EVER LOOKED AT the pottery or paintings in the tombs of Ancient Egypt will recognise the Pharaoh Hound of modern times. Indeed, it is quite remarkable that breed-type can have lasted through literally thousands of years. The obvious elegance of outline of the breed makes it easy to understand the degree to which this classic dog was venerated by the Pharaohs of old.

The Pharaoh Hound became a native of Malta, an island colonised by the Phoenicians around 1,000 BC. They almost certainly took their dogs with them and it was from that island that the first imports came, with the breed finally establishing itself in Britain in the 1970s. The most striking feature of the Pharaoh Hound is his shining, glossy coat of rich tan verging on red. The erect ears, the amber eyes with their keen gaze, and the athletic enthusiasm make him a dog who appeals to lovers of the aesthetic, but his ability to hunt both by scent and sight makes him much more than an object of beauty. He really is a working hound and as such needs an owner who is ready and able to give him both exercise and affection.

His short coat makes him easy to maintain in prime condition, but equally makes it necessary to prevent him being exposed to intense cold without proper protection.

GENERAL APPEARANCE Medium-sized, of noble bearing with clean-cut lines. Graceful yet powerful. Very fast with free, easy movement and alert expression.

CHARACTERISTICS An alert keen hunter, hunting by scent and sight using its ears to a marked degree when working close.

TEMPERAMENT Alert, intelligent, friendly, affectionate and playful.

HEAD AND SKULL Skull long, lean and well chiselled. Foreface slightly longer than skull. Only slight stop. Top of skull parallel with foreface, whole head representing a blunt wedge when viewed in profile and from above.

EYES Amber-coloured, blending with coat; oval, moderately deep-set, with keen, intelligent expression.

EARS Medium-high-set; carried erect when alert, but very mobile; broad at base, fine and large.

MOUTH Powerful jaws with strong teeth. Scissor bite, i.e. upper teeth closely overlapping lower teeth and set square to the jaws.

NOSE Flesh-coloured only, blending with coat.

NECK Long, lean, muscular and slightly arched. Clean throat line.

FOREQUARTERS Shoulders strong, long and well laid back. Forelegs straight and parallel. Elbows well tucked in. Pasterns strong.

BODY Lithe with almost straight topline. Slight slope down from croup to root of tail. Deep brisket extending down to point of elbow. Ribs well sprung. Moderate cut up. Length of body from breast to haunch bone slightly longer than height at withers.

HINDQUARTERS Strong and muscular. Moderate bend of stifle. Well developed second thigh. Limbs parallel when viewed from behind.

FEET Strong, well knuckled and firm, turning neither in nor out. Paws well padded. Dewclaws may be removed.

TAIL Medium-set – fairly thick at base and tapering (whip-like), reaching just below point of hock in repose. Carried high and curved when dog is in action. Tail should not be tucked between legs. A screw tail undesirable.

GAIT/MOVEMENT Free and flowing; head held fairly high and dog should cover ground well without any apparent effort. Legs and feet should move in line with body; any tendency to throw feet sideways, or high stepping 'hackney' action highly undesirable.

COAT Short and glossy, ranging from fine and close to slightly harsh; no feathering.

COLOUR Tan or rich tan with white markings allowed as follows: white tip on tail strongly desired. White on chest (called 'The Star'). White on toes. Slim white blaze on centre line of face permissible. Flecking or white other than above undesirable.

SIZE Dogs: 56-63 cm (22 25 in); bitches 53-61 cm (21-24 in).

FAULTS Any departure from the foregoing points should be considered a fault and the seriousness with which the fault should be regarded should be in exact proportion to its degree.

NOTE Male animals should have two apparently normal testicles fully descended into the scrotum.

RHODESIAN RIDGEBACK

THE RHODESIAN RIDGEBACK, REGARDED by the Kennel Union of Southern Africa as the native dog, is one of possibly only two dogs in the world to have a ridge of hair 'growing the wrong way' down its spine. The other known example is in Thailand and early specimens of this dog may have been taken to Africa by dog traders and over time passed the peculiarity of reverse hair to native dogs.

The Ridgeback is an agile dog, powerful and speedy. His original purpose in Rhodesia (now Zimbabwe) was assisting big game hunters in the pursuit of their quarry, which often included lions. The ridge is a feature of the breed and there are two crowns either side of the ridge just behind the shoulders.

These days the Ridgeback is used in his native Africa as a guard dog. He is an excellent family dog, good with children, affectionate, and very loyal and protective to his family.

GENERAL APPEARANCE Handsome, strong, muscular and active dog, symmetrical in outline, capable of great endurance with fair amount of speed. Mature dog is handsome and upstanding.

CHARACTERISTICS Peculiarity is the ridge on back formed by hair growing in opposite direction to the remainder of coat; ridge must be regarded as the escutcheon of breed. Ridge clearly defined, tapering and symmetrical, starting immediately behind shoulders and continuing to haunch, and containing two identical crowns only, opposite each other, lower edges of crowns not extending further down ridge than one-third of its length. Up to 5 cm (2 in) is a good average for width of ridge.

TEMPERAMENT Dignified, intelligent, aloof with strangers but showing no aggression or shyness.

HEAD AND SKULL Of fair length, skull flat, rather broad between ears, free from wrinkles when in repose. Stop reasonably well defined.

Nose black or brown in keeping with colour of dog. Black nose accompanied by dark eyes, brown nose by amber eyes. Muzzle long, deep and powerful. Lips clean and close fitting.

EYES Set moderately well apart, round, bright and sparkling with intelligent expression, colour harmonising with coat colour.

EARS Set rather high, medium size, rather wide at base, gradually tapering to a rounded point. Carried close to head.

MOUTH Jaws strong, with a perfect, regular and complete scissor bite, i.e. upper teeth closely overlapping lower teeth and set square to the jaws. Well developed teeth, especially canines.

NECK Fairly long, strong and free from throatiness.

FOREQUARTERS Shoulders sloping, clean and muscular. Forelegs perfectly straight, strong, heavy in bone; elbows close to body.

BODY Chest not too wide, very deep and capacious; ribs moderately well sprung, never barrel-ribbed. Back powerful; loins strong, muscular and slightly arched.

HINDQUARTERS Muscles clean, well defined; good turn of stifle; hocks well let down.

FEET Compact, well arched toes; round, tough, elastic pads, protected by hair between toes and pads.

TAIL Strong at root, not inserted high or low, tapering towards end, free from coarseness. Carried with a slight curve upwards, never curled.

GAIT/MOVEMENT Straight forward, free and active.

COAT Short and dense, sleek and glossy in appearance but neither woolly nor silky.

COLOUR Light wheaten to red wheaten. Head, body, legs and tail of uniform colour. Little white on chest and toes permissible, but excessive white hairs here, on belly or above paws undesirable. Dark muzzle and ears permissible.

SIZE Dogs: 63 cm (25 in) desirable minimum height at withers; 67 cm (27 in) desirable maximum height at withers; bitches: 61 cm (24 in) desirable minimum height at withers; 66 cm (26 in) desirable maximum height at withers.

FAULTS Any departure from the foregoing points should be considered a fault and the seriousness with which the fault should be regarded should be in exact proportion to its degree.

NOTE Male animals should have two apparently normal testicles fully descended into the scrotum.

SALUKI

THIS GRACEFUL, DIGNIFIED DOG HAS always been a much prized possession of the Arabs. His highly developed hunting instinct, and the speed with which he moves over all types of terrain, suit him well for work in the Middle East, where sheikhs have carefully kept records of his breeding and hunting abilities for hundreds of years.

Though this is a very old breed it was not seen in Britain until 1840 and was not officially recognised until 1923. Two possibilities for the origin of the name are that it was taken from the long-gone Arabian city of Saluk or from the town of Seleukia in ancient Syria.

The Saluki is not really the ideal pet for the average family – he can be naughty in the house if left alone, and he very easily becomes bored. He is highly strung, very sensitive, very intelligent, and extremely affectionate to those he loves.

GENERAL APPEARANCE Gives impression of grace, symmetry and of great speed and endurance, coupled with strength and activity. Expression dignified and gentle with faithful, far-seeing eyes.

CHARACTERISTICS Of great quality with unique shaped foot necessary for hunting natural terrain.

TEMPERAMENT Reserved with strangers but not nervous or aggressive. Dignified, intelligent and independent.

HEAD AND SKULL Head long and narrow, skull moderately wide between ears, not domed, stop not pronounced, whole showing great quality. Nose black or liver.

EYES Dark to hazel, bright, large and oval, not prominent.

EARS Long and mobile, not too low-set, covered with long silky hair, hanging close to skull. Bottom tip of leather reaches to corner of mouth when brought forward. Provided ear is covered with silky hair, which may grow only from top half, the standard is complied with but longer hair also correct.

MOUTH Teeth and jaws strong with a perfect, regular and complete scissor bite, i.e. upper teeth closely overlapping lower teeth and set square to the jaws.

NECK Long, supple and well muscled.

FOREQUARTERS Shoulders sloping and set well back, well muscled without being coarse. Chest deep and moderately narrow, when viewed from front not an inverted V. Forelegs straight and long from elbow to wrist. Pasterns strong and slightly sloping. Not round boned. Humerus sloping slightly backwards.

BODY Back fairly broad, muscles slightly arched over loin, but never roach-backed. Brisket long and deep, not barrel-ribbed or slab-sided, with good cut up. Sufficient length of loin important.

HINDQUARTERS Strong hip bones set wide apart. Stifle moderately bent with well developed first and second thigh. Hocks low to ground.

FEET Strong and supple of moderate length, toes slightly webbed, long and well arched, two inner toes considerably longer than two outer toes on all four feet. Not splayed out or cat-footed and feathered between toes. Front feet point forward at very slight angle when standing.

TAIL Set-on low from long and gently sloping pelvis. Carried naturally in curve. Well feathered on underside but not bushy. In adults not carried above line of back except in play. Tip reaching to hock.

GAIT/MOVEMENT Light, lifting, effortless, showing both reach and drive, body lifting off ground with long, flat strides, not flinging itself forward. No hackney action or plodding.

COAT Smooth, of silky texture, feathering on legs and back of thighs and between hock and heel. Puppies may have slight woolly feathering on thigh and shoulder. Feathering on throat permissible but not desirable. Smooth variety as above but without feathering.

COLOUR White, cream, fawn, golden red, grizzle, silver grizzle, deer grizzle, tricolour (white, black and tan), black and tan and variations of these colours, i.e. black fringed fawn, black fringed red not brindle.

SIZE Dogs: 58.4-71.1 cm (23-28 in) at shoulders; bitches: proportionately smaller.

FAULTS Any departure from the foregoing points should be considered a fault and the seriousness with which the fault should be regarded should be in exact proportion to its degree.

NOTE Male animals should have two apparently normal testicles fully descended into the scrotum.

SEGUGIO ITALIANO

(INTERIM)

A TALL HOUND WITH A SHORT COAT which can be either harsh or smooth; it has a range of colours from cream to red but can also be black and tan.

A very active dog of middle size and considerable stamina, one which has not been in the country for any great length of time. In his native Italy the breed is used to flush boar rather than actually catch his prey; as boars are not available in great numbers in modern Italy, he is used to find hares and spring them to the gun.

Temperamentally this is a quiet breed which tends towards the cautious, though the dog's natural intelligence makes him relatively trainable.

GENERAL APPEARANCE Medium-sized, lightly built, square in outline.

CHARACTERISTICS Keen nose, active, versatile hunting dog of great endurance.

TEMPERAMENT Gentle, affectionate and even-tempered.

HEAD AND SKULL Elongated; narrow, slightly arched skull; well defined occiput; very slight stop. Skin taut, no wrinkles. Nose black, bridge slightly curved. Nostrils wide.

EYES Oval, large and dark. Tight lids.

EARS Fine, low-set, triangular. Length reaching to tip of nose, hanging close to cheek.

MOUTH Jaws strong with a perfect, regular and complete scissor bite, i.e. upper teeth closely overlapping lower teeth and set square to the jaws. Lips black; level.

NECK Medium length, lean, slightly arched, well set-on.

FOREQUARTERS Shoulders long and well laid back. Forelegs straight and powerful, pasterns slightly sloping. Elbows set close to body.

BODY Deep chested and well let down. Ribs moderately well sprung. Back short, muscular and rising slightly over loin.

HINDQUARTERS Thighs muscular and well developed. Well bent hocks. Limbs parallel when viewed from behind.

FEET Tight, oval. Pads and nails black.

TAIL Set high, strong, thin, tapering. When moving, carried high in a sabre curve.

GAIT/MOVEMENT Straight forward, free and active.

COAT Coarsehaired: Harsh, dense, wiry, close lying. Length: 5 cm (2 in) maxiumum.

Shorthaired: Smooth, thick, shiny.

COLOUR Black/tan or any shade from deep red to wheaten. White markings on head, chest, feet and tip of tail permissible.

SIZE Dogs: 52-59 cm (20½-23 in); bitches: 48-56 cm (19-22 in).

FAULTS Any departure from the foregoing points should be considered a fault and the seriousness with which the fault should be regarded should be in exact proportion to its degree.

NOTE Male animals should have two apparently normal testicles fully descended into the scrotum.

SLOUGHI

(INTERIM)

THIS IS A BREED WHICH EMANATES from the deserts and mountains of North Africa, having existed there for many centuries as a typical working sighthound. Like many hunters he tends to be a trifle stand-offish with strangers, but is affectionate to those he knows and trusts.

The name Sloughi dates back to the Middle Ages and the dog may have as one of his ancestors a type of wolfhound which existed centuries ago in North Africa, particularly the Sahara Desert region, and which, in turn, originated as far away as Saudi Arabia. Though the breed has been on the European show scene for a number of years, it is only since the latter part of the twentieth century that the Sloughi has been known in Britain.

He has not achieved much in the way of popularity in Britain and this may be due partly to the fact that the phrase in the breed standard which asks for the haunches to be prominent has persuaded some devotees to assume that this was to be interpreted as suggesting that the dog should carry no spare weight at all. As a result the dividing line between lightness of build and unappealing thinness has at times been hard to distinguish.

Another breed which is easy to keep clean, his tough, fine coat is most frequently sable or fawn, but he is also seen as brindle, white or even black with tan points.

A tall dog, he has long, thin oval feet, supporting his none too broad or deep chest, on long, well muscled legs.

GENERAL APPEARANCE Elegant yet racy with a frame marked by its muscular leanness.

CHARACTERISTICS Clean, quiet and decorative. Desert variety of moderate height, slender, light, graceful and elegant. Mountain counterpart more compact with stronger bone but otherwise identical. Both types may be bred from same litter.

TEMPERAMENT Affectionate towards owner and indifferent to strangers.

HEAD AND SKULL Without being heavy, head fairly strong but with lines not excessively angular. Skull flat, fairly broad, clearly rounded at rear and curving harmoniously into sides. Eyes sockets barely protruding. Marked frontal bone and pronounced occiput. Muzzle in shape of wedge, refined without exaggeration; about equal in length to skull. Stop barely visible. Nose and lips black or very dark brown.

EYES Large, dark and set well into orbit. Triangular, slightly on slant; expression gentle, a little sad and wistful. In light-coated animals (off-white, sable, fawn, Isabella) eyes usually burnt topaz or dark amber.

EARS Not too large, triangular in shape but with rounded tips; flat. Usually folding down and carried close to head, set level with or slightly above eye but may be carried away from the skull or sometimes even thrown backwards.

MOUTH Jaws strong with a perfect, regular and complete scissor bite, i.e. upper teeth closely over-lapping lower teeth and set square to the jaws.

NECK Strong yet very elegant in proportion to body. Moderately long with good arch. Skin slightly loose, making fine pleats under throat.

FOREQUARTERS Shoulders well laid and clearly visible. Legs round with flat bone and well muscled.

BODY Chest not too broad; in depth reaching barely to level of elbow. Good tuck-up. Topline almost level and relatively short, but slightly longer in bitches. Croup bony and very oblique. Haunches prominent.

HINDQUARTERS Loins broad and slightly arched. Thighs of good length to stifle. Hocks well let down with good angulation.

FEET Thin, of elongated, oval shape, harefoot. Nails strong, black or dark.

TAIL Fine and well set-on, without fringes or long hair. Strong curve at end which reaches at least to point of hock. When moving, tail never carried higher than level of back.

GAIT/MOVEMENT Free and flowing, capable of great speed.

COAT Hair tough and fine.

COLOUR Sable or fawn in all shades, with or without a black mask. Also permissible a coat more or less dark, white, brindle, black with tan points; brindle pattern on fawn background on head, feet and sometimes breast. Dark coats with a white patch on chest undesirable. Parti-colours not permissible. Solid black or white undesirable.

SIZE Height: 60-70 cm (23½-27½ in). Ideal height for dogs: 68 cm (27 in); bitches: 65 cm (25½ in).

FAULTS Any departure from the foregoing points should be considered a fault and the seriousness with which the fault should be regarded should be in exact proportion to its degree.

NOTE Male animals should have two apparently normal testicles fully descended into the scrotum.

WHIPPET

THERE CAN BE FEW BREEDS WITH MORE delightful charm than the dainty Whippet. Size tends to vary in different countries, although the standard requires an animal standing around the 51 centimetre (20 inch) mark, but no matter the size, the essence is in the balance of muscularity with neatness, power with elegance. Carrying a short, fine coat, cleanliness is the Whippet's hallmark and it is easy to get him tidy enough for the house within a very short time after returning from a country walk in winter.

The description of his temperament in the official standard, 'gentle' and 'affectionate' is a considerable understatement; he loves the company of mankind and is equally at home in castle or cottage. Light enough to pick up when necessary, but spirited enough to spend a day on exercise, with a tremendous turn of speed over short distances, he represents one of the most deservingly popular of all the sporting dogs.

Many have found great pleasure in owning racing Whippets, especially in the north-east of England. As races often had to be in alleyways between the houses, the dogs developed into 'straight racers'. Some could cover just over 180 metres (200 yards) in as little as 12 seconds.

GENERAL APPEARANCE Balanced combination of muscular power and strength with elegance and grace of outline. Built for speed and work. All forms of exaggeration should be avoided.

CHARACTERISTICS An ideal companion. Highly adaptable in domestic and sporting surroundings.

TEMPERAMENT Gentle, affectionate, even disposition.

HEAD AND SKULL Long and lean, flat on top tapering to muzzle with slight stop, rather wide between the eyes, jaws powerful and clean-cut, nose black, in blues a bluish colour permitted, in livers a nose of the same colour, in whites or parti-colour a butterfly nose permissible.

EYES Oval, bright, expression very alert.

EARS Rose-shaped, small, fine in texture.

MOUTH Jaws strong with a perfect regular and complete scissor bite, i.e. upper teeth closely overlapping lower teeth and set square to the jaws.

NECK Long, muscular, elegantly arched.

FOREQUARTERS Shoulders oblique and muscular, blades carried up to top of spine, where they are clearly defined. Forelegs straight and upright, front not too wide, pasterns strong with slight spring, elbows set well under body.

BODY Chest very deep with plenty of heart room, brisket deep, well defined, broad back, firm, somewhat long, showing definite arch over loin but not humped. Loin giving impression of strength and power, ribs well sprung, muscled on back.

HINDQUARTERS Strong, broad across thighs, stifles well bent, hocks well let down, well developed second thighs, dog able to stand over a lot of ground and show great driving power.

FEET Very neat, well split up between toes, knuckles well arched, pads thick and strong.

TAIL No feathering. Long, tapering, when in action carried in a delicate curve upward but not over back.

GAIT/MOVEMENT Free, hindlegs coming well under body for propulsion. Forelegs thrown

well forward lower over the ground, true coming and going. General movement not to look stilted, high stepping, short or mincing.

COAT Fine, short, close in texture.

COLOUR Any colour or mixture of colours.

SIZE Height: dogs: 47–51 cm (18½–20 in); bitches: 44–47 cm (17–18½ in).

FAULTS Any departure from the foregoing points should be considered a fault and the seriousness with which the fault should be regarded should be in exact proportion to its degree.

NOTE Male animals should have two apparently normal testicles fully descended into the scrotum.

BELOW: *Field Trial Champion Sulhamstead Valla D'Or, an Irish Setter, by Cecil Aldin (1870–1935). This pastel drawing was bequeathed to The Kennel Club by Mrs Florence Neagle, a Vice President, who died in 1988. The dog was bred by E A Whitworth in May 1926.*

- FIELD - TRIAL - CHAMPION -
SULHAMSTEAD - VALLA - D'OR

BRACCO ITALIANO

THE BRACCO OBVIOUSLY STEMS FROM the old practice of mating the hounds with gundogs in order to produce a type of pointing animal with extra stamina. He is one of that group of multi-purpose dogs, so popular in the countries of mainland Europe, which hunt, point and retrieve.

As the breed only arrived in Great Britain for the first time in the early 1990s it is not yet possible to assess the Bracco's value; he is certainly an attractive, upstanding creature with an easy-clean, glossy coat; rated by his fan club as a hard worker, he has the gentle temperament typical of this talented sub-group.

GENERAL APPEARANCE Strong, powerful, muscular, robust and lean.

CHARACTERISTICS Attentive with jaunty bearing.

TEMPERAMENT Docile and gentle.

HEAD AND SKULL Long, angular; occiput pronounced. Well developed zygomatic arch. Slight stop. Nose flesh-coloured or chestnut. Wide nostrils.

EYES Oval, neither deep set nor protruding. Shades of amber. Intelligent, attentive expression.

EARS Well developed, supple, slightly rounded tip. Set rather forward, slightly higher than eye level, carried close to cheek. Leathers extend to end of muzzle.

MOUTH Jaws strong, with perfect, regular and complete scissor bite, i.e. upper teeth closely overlapping lower teeth and set square to the jaws.

NECK Short in proportion to body. Powerful. Slight dewlap.

FOREQUARTERS Shoulders long, sloping, muscular and well laid back. Forelegs straight, firm, held close to chest; elbows well tucked in.

BODY Well sprung ribs, good depth of brisket. Back strong.

HINDQUARTERS Long, well muscled. Hocks well let down.

FEET Sturdy, oval feet. Slightly extended toes, covered in fine, short hair. Single dewclaws preferred, double accepted.

TAIL Medium length, strong at base, slightly tapered. Carried below horizontal at rest; slightly raised when dog is moving.

GAIT/MOVEMENT Strong, smooth and driving. Parallel movement fore and aft; no hackney action.

COAT Fine, dense, short and glossy.

COLOUR Orange and white, orange roan, chestnut and white or chestnut roan.

SIZE Height at withers: 55-67 cm (22-27 in).

FAULTS Any departure from the foregoing points should be considered a fault and the seriousness with which the fault should be regarded should be in exact proportion to its degree.

NOTE Male animals should have two apparently normal testicles fully descended into the scrotum.

BRITTANY

NOWN AT ONE TIME AS THE BRITTANY Spaniel, this dog is a relative newcomer from France. He is one of the Hunt, Point and Retrieve breeds, and as such has already proved himself in Kennel Club field trials. His square shape gives him an unusual, clipped style of movement, and though he is a fairly light-built dog, he is capable of carrying hare or pheasant.

Though the Brittany is a spaniel, the French spaniels are really more like small setters and dogs similar to the Brittany have been used for a long time, working in a style rather like a pointer or setter. The breed is not dissimilar to the old couching dogs of Europe, especially some of the all-purpose gundogs to be found in Germany.

A busy dog, he is easy to train, has an affectionate, easy-going attitude to life, and will no doubt increase in popularity in Britain as he has in the United States. His dense, fine coat is not difficult to keep clean.

GENERAL APPEARANCE Workmanlike, compact, lively, squarely built.

CHARACTERISTICS Energetic, intelligent, hunt-point-retriever.

TEMPERAMENT Affectionate and eager to please.

HEAD AND SKULL Medium length, rounded with the median line slightly visible. Stop well defined but not too deep. Occiput not pronounced but can be felt. Muzzle about two thirds the length of the skull, tapered but not snipy. Nostrils open and well shaped.

EYES Expressive, brown to dark brown in harmony with coat colour, never light or hard in expression. Well set in.

EARS Drop ear, set high, rather short, lightly fringed and vine-shaped covered with slightly wavy hair.

MOUTH Jaws strong with a perfect regular scissor bite, i.e. upper teeth closely overlapping lower teeth and set square to the jaws. Lips tight, upper lip slightly overlapping lower.

NECK Medium length, clean and well set into shoulders.

FOREQUARTERS Sloping and well set-on shoulders. Forelegs straight with good muscle. Moderately well boned. Feathered.

BODY Chest deep, descending to the level of elbow. Ribs well rounded. Back short with loin short and strong with slight slope from withers to croup and from croup to hindquarters.

HINDQUARTERS Strong and broad, flanks well rounded, moderate bend of stifle. Hocks well let down. Feathered to mid-thigh.

FEET Small, compact with a little hair between toes.

TAIL Naturally tailless, short or customarily docked. Carried level with back.

GAIT/MOVEMENT Brisk, short-striding, straight and true.

COAT Body coat rather flat, dense, fairly fine and slightly wavy.

COLOUR Orange/white, liver/white, black/white, tricolour, or roan of any of any of these colours. Nose dark or harmony with coat colour.

SIZE Ideal height: dogs 48-50 cm (19-20 in); bitches 47-49 cm (18-19 in).

FAULTS Any departure from the foregoing points should be considered a fault and the seriousness with which the fault should be regarded should be in exact proportion to its degree.

NOTE Male animals should have two apparently normal testicles fully descended into the scrotum.

ENGLISH SETTER

ONE OF THE MOST GLAMOROUS OF ALL breeds, the English Setter has the ability to attract not only those who admire a stylish worker, but also those who want a dog capable of being a cheerful companion.

His coat has an overall basis of white, flecked generously with black, lemon or liver, with the black or liver occasionally intermingled with tan into a tricolour. The flecking is referred to by the cognoscenti as 'belton', thus lemon belton or orange belton. A longish, fairly lean head on a slightly arched neck, well set shoulders and firm straight bone, a deep chest, and strong muscular hindquarters are the hallmarks of a handsome breed which must combine elegance, quality and stamina under a silky, easily groomed coat.

Development of the English Setter into the breed as we know it today began around the mid 1800s. The breed was shown at the first dog show in Newcastle in 1859.

GENERAL APPEARANCE Of medium height, clean in outline, elegant in appearance and movement.

CHARACTERISTICS Very active with a keen game sense.

TEMPERAMENT Intensely friendly and good-natured.

HEAD AND SKULL Head carried high, long and reasonably lean, with well defined stop. Skull oval from ear to ear, showing plenty of brain room, a well defined occipital protuberance. Muzzle moderately deep and fairly square, from stop to point of nose should equal length of skull from occiput to eyes, nostrils wide and jaws of nearly equal length, flews not too pendulous; colour of nose black or liver, according to colour of coat.

EYES Bright, mild and expressive. Colour ranging between hazel and dark brown, the darker the better. In liver beltons only, a lighter eye acceptable. Eyes oval and not protruding.

EARS Moderate length, set-on low, and hanging in neat folds close to cheek, tip velvety, upper part clothed in fine silky hair.

MOUTH Jaws strong, with a perfect, regular and complete scissor bite, i.e. upper teeth closely overlapping lower teeth and set square to the jaws. Full dentition desirable.

NECK Rather long, muscular and lean, slightly arched at crest, and clean-cut where it joins head, towards shoulder larger and very muscular, never throaty nor pendulous below throat, but elegant in appearance.

FOREQUARTERS Shoulders well set back or oblique, chest deep in brisket, very good depth and width between shoulder blades, forearms straight and very muscular with rounded bone, elbows well let down close to body, pasterns short, strong, round and straight.

BODY Moderate length, back short and level with good round widely sprung ribs and deep in back ribs, i.e. well ribbed up.

HINDQUARTERS Loins wide, slightly arched, strong and muscular, legs well muscled including second thigh, stifles well bent and thighs long from hip to hock, hock inclining neither in nor out and well let down.

FEET Well padded, tight with close, well arched toes protected by hair between them.

TAIL Set almost in line with back, medium length, not reaching below hock, neither curly nor ropy, slightly curved or scimitar-shaped but with no tendency to turn upwards: flag or feathers hanging in long pendant flakes. Feather commencing slightly below the root, and

increasing in length towards middle, then gradually tapering towards end, hair long, bright, soft and silky, wavy but not curly. Lively and slashing in movement and carried in a plane not higher than level of back.

GAIT/MOVEMENT Free and graceful action, suggesting speed and endurance. Free movement of the hock showing powerful drive from hindquarters. Viewed from rear, hip, stifle and hock joints in line. Head naturally high.

COAT From back of head in line with ears slightly wavy, not curly, long and silky as is coat generally, breeches and forelegs nearly down to feet well feathered.

COLOUR Black and white (blue belton), orange and white (orange belton), lemon and white (lemon belton), liver and white (liver belton) or tricolour, that is blue belton and tan or liver belton and tan, those without heavy patches of colour on body but flecked (belton) all over preferred.

SIZE Height: dogs 65-68 cm (25½-27 in); bitches: 61-65 cm (24-25½ in).

FAULTS Any departure from the foregoing points should be considered a fault and the seriousness with which the fault should be regarded should be in exact proportion to its degree.

NOTE Male animals should have two apparently normal testicles fully descended into the scrotum.

GERMAN SHORT-HAIRED POINTER

SINCE THE END OF THE 1939-45 WAR there has been an influx of breeds from the Continent, and none has been more successfully introduced to both the shooting and showing scenes than the German Short-haired Pointer (GSP). The first of the Hunt, Point and Retrieve (HPR) breeds to arrive, the GSP has on several occasions won that coveted award in the world of the gundog, the Dual Championship, a dog which is able to beat all comers in the field and in the showring.

The GSP stems from dogs known collectively as bird dogs. The basis for the breed was almost certainly the kennels of Prince Albrecht zu Somsbrauenfels, who owned Schweisshunds, a breed of good but slowish working hounds with outstanding ability to scent game, which were crossed with traditional English Pointer stock.

The breed comes in either black or liver or both colours may be spotted or ticked with white, the coat being short, flat and coarse to the feel. As a result, he is a very easy dog to keep clean and wholesome even in the foulest weathers.

Medium-sized, trainable and friendly, he combines grace, energy and stamina in a neat frame.

GENERAL APPEARANCE Noble, steady dog showing power, endurance and speed, giving the immediate impression of an alert and energetic dog whose movements are well co-ordinated. Of medium size, with a short back standing over plenty of ground. Grace of outline, clean-cut head, long sloping shoulders, deep chest, short back, powerful hindquarters, good bone composition, adequate muscle, well carried tail and taut coat.

CHARACTERISTICS Dual purpose Pointer/ Retriever, very keen nose, perseverance in searching and initiative in game finding, excellence in field, a naturally keen worker, equally good on land and water.

TEMPERAMENT Gentle, affectionate and even-tempered. Alert, biddable and very loyal.

HEAD AND SKULL Clean-cut, neither too light nor too heavy, well proportioned to body. Skull sufficiently broad and slightly round. Nasal bone rising gradually from nose to forehead (this more pronounced in dogs) and never possessing a definite stop, but when viewed from side a well defined stop effect due to position of eyebrows. Lips falling away almost vertically from somewhat protruding nose and continuing in a slight curve to corner of mouth. Lips well developed, not overhung. Jaws powerful and sufficiently long to enable the dog to pick up and carry game. Dish-faced and snipy muzzle undesirable. Nose solid brown or black depending on coat colour. Wide nostrils, well opened and soft.

EYES Medium size, soft and intelligent, neither protruding nor too deep-set. Varying in shades of brown to tone with coat. Light eye undesirable. Eyelids should close properly.

EARS Broad and set high; neither too fleshy nor too thin, with a short, soft coat; hung close to head, no pronounced fold, rounded at tip and reaching almost to corner of mouth when brought forward.

MOUTH Teeth sound and strong. Jaws strong, with a perfect, regular and complete scissor bite, i.e. upper teeth closely overlapping lower teeth and set square to the jaws.

NECK Moderately long, muscular and slightly arched, thickening towards shoulders. Skin not fitting too loosely.

FOREQUARTERS Shoulders sloping and very muscular, top of shoulder blades close; upper arm bones, between shoulder and elbow, long. Elbows well laid back, neither pointing outwards nor inwards. Forelegs straight and lean, sufficiently muscular and strong, but not coarse-boned. Pasterns slightly sloping.

BODY Chest must appear deep rather than wide but in proportion to rest of body; ribs deep and well sprung, never barrel-shaped nor flat; back ribs reaching well down to tuck-up of loins. Chest measurement immediately behind elbows smaller than about a hand's breadth behind elbows, so that upper arm has freedom of movement. Firm, short back, not arched. Loin wide and slightly arched; croup wide and sufficiently long, neither too heavy nor too sloping starting on a level with back and sloping gradually towards tail. Bones solid and strong. Skin should not fit loosely or fold.

HINDQUARTERS Hips broad and wide, falling slightly towards tail. Thighs strong and well muscled. Stifles well bent. Hocks square with body and slightly bent, turning neither in nor out. Pasterns nearly upright.

FEET Compact, close-knit, round to spoon-shaped, well padded, turning neither in nor out. Toes well arched with strong nails.

TAIL Starts high and thick growing gradually thinner, customarily docked to medium length by two-fifths to half its length. When quiet, tail carried down; when moving, horizontally; never held high over back or bent.

GAIT/MOVEMENT Smooth, lithe gait essential. As gait increases from walk to a faster speed, legs converge beneath body (single tracking). Forelegs reach well ahead, effortlessly covering plenty of ground with each stride and followed by hindlegs, which give forceful propulsion.

COAT Short, flat and coarse to touch, slightly longer under tail.

COLOUR Solid liver, liver and white spotted, liver and white spotted and ticked, liver and white ticked, solid black and white same variations (not tricolour).

SIZE Dogs: minimum height 58 cm (23 in) at withers, maximum height 64 cm (25 in) at withers. Bitches: minimum height 53 cm (21 in) at withers, maximum height 59 cm (23 in) at withers.

FAULTS Any departure from the foregoing points should be considered a fault and the seriousness with which the fault should be regarded should be in exact proportion to its degree.

NOTE Male animals should have two apparently normal testicles fully descended into the scrotum.

GERMAN WIRE-HAIRED POINTER

ANOTHER HUNT, POINT AND RETRIEVE breed from the Continent, introduced to the British scene more recently than his Short-haired cousin. The GWP is increasing in popularity particularly with those who require a dog for the rough shoot. His thick, harsh outer coat measuring up to 4 centimetres (1½ inches) long protects him from the ravages of thorn and bramble, while not being so long as to make him impractical in foul weather as a household companion. He is only 2 or 3 centimetres (an inch or so) taller than the Shorthaired, but he does give the impression of being larger and heavier.

Easily trained and friendly, he has a tough, cheerful appearance, making him as good a family dog as he is a worker. His colour is liver and white, solid liver, or black and white, but not, for preference, solid black.

Bristly-coated gundogs have always interested the Germans and in the late 1800s there were several varieties. It was exactly this wide variation which led eventually to the setting up of separate organisations. So the GWP came into existence and today Wirehaireds lead the registration for all hunting dogs in Germany.

GENERAL APPEARANCE Medium-sized hunting dog, with wire hair completely covering skin. Overall should be slightly longer in body, compared to shoulder height.

CHARACTERISTICS Powerful, strong, versatile hunting dog, excels in both field and water. Loyal, intelligent, sound temperament and alert.

TEMPERAMENT Gentle, affectionate and even-tempered. Alert, biddable and very loyal.

HEAD AND SKULL Balanced in proportion to body. Skull sufficiently broad and slightly rounded. Moderate stop, skull and muzzle of equal length with no overhanging lips. Nose liver or black.

EYES Medium-sized oval, hazel or darker, with eyelids closing properly, not protruding nor too deep-set.

EARS Medium-sized in relation to head, set high, when brought forward should reach corner of lips.

MOUTH Teeth and jaws strong, with perfect, regular and complete scissor bite, i.e. upper teeth closely overlapping lower teeth and set square to the jaws, with full dentition.

NECK Strong and of adequate length, skin tightly fitting.

FOREQUARTERS Shoulders sloping and very muscular with top of shoulder blades not too close; upper arm bones between shoulder and elbow long. Elbows close to body, neither pointing outwards nor inwards. Forelegs straight and lean, sufficiently muscular and strong but not coarse-boned. Pasterns slightly sloping, almost straight but not quite.

BODY Chest must appear deep rather than wide but not out of proportion to the rest of the body; ribs deep and well sprung, never barrel-shaped nor flat, back rib reaching well down to tucked-up loins. Chest measurement immediately behind elbows smaller than that of about a hand's breadth behind elbows so that upper arm has freedom of movement. Firm back, not arched, with slightly falling back line.

HINDQUARTERS Hips broad and wide, croup falling slightly towards tail. Thighs strong and well muscled. Stifles well bent. Hocks square with body, turning neither in nor out. Pasterns nearly upright. Bone strong but not coarse.

FEET Compact, close-knit, round to oval-shaped, well padded, should turn neither in nor out. Toes well arched, heavily nailed.

TAIL Starts high and thick growing gradually thinner. Customarily docked to approximately two-fifths of original length. When quiet, tail should be carried down; when moving horizontally, never held high over back or bent. Tail set following continuation of back line.

GAIT/MOVEMENT Smooth, covering plenty of ground with each stride, driving hind action, elbows turning neither in nor out. Definitely not a hackney action.

COAT Outer coat thicker and harsh, no longer than 3.8 cm (1½ in) long with a dense undercoat (undercoat more prevalent in winter than summer). It should not hide body shape but it should be long enough to give good protection. Coat should lie close to the body. Hair on head and ears thick and short, but not too soft. Bushy eyebrows, full but not overlong beard.

COLOUR Liver and white, solid liver, black and white. Solid black and tricoloured highly undesirable.

SIZE Ideal height at shoulder: dogs: 60-67 cm (24-26 in); bitches: 56-62 cm (22-24 in). Weight: dogs: 25-34 kg (55-75 lb); bitches: 20.5-29 kg (45-64 lb).

FAULTS Any departure from the foregoing points should be considered a fault and the seriousness with which the fault should be regarded should be in exact proportion to its degree.

NOTE Male animals should have two apparently normal testicles fully descended into the scrotum.

GORDON SETTER

THIS IS A BIG DOG BUILT ON THE LINES of a heavy-weight hunter. He comes in one colour pattern, black and tan; he gives the impression of being built to work steadily and without glamour, all day and every day, and as such attracts those who need a dog which will do his job without fuss.

The Gordon, as his name implies, hails from the estates of the Dukes of Gordon, and has a long history of honest trainability, which endears him to those who appreciate a kindly, intelligent dog capable of enjoying all the exercise which a household can give him.

His heavy coat will require regular attention to keep it clear of mud and thorns. Its length and weight mean that it takes time to dry but, properly maintained, the coat will gleam and shine.

GENERAL APPEARANCE Stylish dog, with galloping lines. Consistent with its build which can be compared to a weight-carrying hunter. Symmetrical in conformation throughout.

CHARACTERISTICS Intelligent, able and dignified.

TEMPERAMENT Bold, outgoing, of a kindly even disposition.

HEAD AND SKULL Head deep rather than broad, but broader than muzzle, showing brain room. Skull slightly rounded, broadest between ears. Clearly defined stop, length from occiput to stop slightly longer than from stop to nose. Below and above eyes lean, cheeks as narrow as leanness of head allows. Muzzle fairly long with almost parallel lines, neither pointed, nor snipy. Flews not pendulous, clearly defined lips. Nose large, broad, nostrils open and black. Muzzle not quite as deep as its length.

EYES Dark brown, bright. Neither deep nor prominent, set sufficiently under brows, showing keen, intelligent expression.

EARS Medium size, thin. Set low, lying close to head.

MOUTH Jaws strong with a perfect, regular and complete scissor bite, i.e. upper teeth closely over-lapping lower teeth and set square to the jaws.

NECK Long, lean, arched, without throatiness.

FOREQUARTERS Shoulder blades long, sloping well back, wide flat bone, close at withers, not loaded. Elbows well let down, and close to body. Forelegs flat-boned, straight, strong; upright pasterns.

BODY Moderate length, deep brisket, ribs well sprung. Back ribs deep. Loins wide, slightly arched. Chest not too broad.

HINDQUARTERS From hip to hock long, broad and muscular, hock to heel short, strong, stifles well bent, straight from hock joint to ground. Pelvis tending to horizontal.

FEET Oval, close-knit, well arched toes, plenty of hair between. Well padded toes, deep heel cushions.

TAIL Straight or slightly scimitar, not reaching below hocks. Carried horizontally or below line of back. Thick at root, tapering to fine point. Feather or flag starting near root, long, straight, growing shorter to point.

GAIT/MOVEMENT Steady, free-moving and true, with plenty of drive behind.

COAT On head, front of legs, tips of ears short and fine, moderate length; flat and free from curl or wave on all other parts of body. Feather on upper portion of ears long and silky; on backs of legs long, fine, flat and straight, fringes on belly may extend to chest and throat. As free as possible from curl or wave.

COLOUR Deep, shining coal black, without rustiness, with markings of chestnut red, i.e. lustrous tan. Black pencilling on toes and black streak under jaw permissible. 'Tan markings': two clear spots over eyes not over 2 cm (¾ in) in diameter. On sides of muzzle, tan not reaching above base of nose, resembling a stripe around clearly defined end of muzzle from one side to other. Also on throat, two large, clear spots on chest. On inside hindlegs and inside thighs, showing down front of stifle and broadening out to outside of hindlegs from hock to toes. On forelegs, up to elbows behind, and to knees or little above, in front. Around vent. Very small white spot on chest permissible. No other colour permissible.

SIZE Height: dogs: 66 cm (26 in); bitches: 62 cm (24½ in). Weight: dogs: 29.5 kg (65 lb); bitches: 25.5 kg (56 lb).

FAULTS Any departure from the foregoing points should be considered a fault and the seriousness with which the fault should be regarded should be in exact proportion to its degree.

NOTE Male animals should have two apparently normal testicles fully descended into the scrotum.

HUNGARIAN VIZSLA

MEDIUM-SIZED AND ELEGANTLY BUILT, he is an outstanding all-purpose gundog combining an excellent nose with stable pointing, good retrieving, and a positive enjoyment of working in water. He has great stamina and is happy to work in all weathers. He has an aristocratic air, with a lively but equable temperament. His short, coarse, easy to care for coat is richly coloured in russet gold.

An intelligent dog, with a good memory which makes him easy to train, he is responsive to intelligent handling. He is a very popular pet in his native Hungary where he adapts to living quarters of all sizes.

It is from the central plains of Hungary that the breed comes, though one school of thought believes it reached there with invaders from farther east. The breed suffered as a result of war in Europe and much of today's modern stock has been developed from dogs taken out of Hungary by emigrants.

GENERAL APPEARANCE Medium-sized, of distinguished appearance, robust and medium boned.

CHARACTERISTICS Lively, intelligent, obedient, sensitive, very affectionate and easily trained. Bred for hunting fur and feather, pointing and retrieving from land and water.

TEMPERAMENT Lively, gentle-mannered and demonstratively affectionate, fearless and with well developed protective instinct.

HEAD AND SKULL Head lean and noble. Skull moderately wide between ears with median line down forehead and a moderate stop. Skull a little longer than muzzle. Muzzle, although tapering, well squared at the end. Nostrils well developed, broad and wide. Jaws strong and powerful. Lips covering jaws completely and neither loose nor pendulous. Nose brown.

EYES Neither deep nor prominent, of medium size, a shade darker in colour than coat. Slightly oval in shape, eyelids fitting tightly. Yellow or black eye undesirable.

EARS Moderately low-set, proportionately long with a thin skin and hanging down close to cheeks. Rounded 'V' shape; not fleshy.

MOUTH Sound and strong white teeth. Jaws strong with perfect, regular and complete scissor bite, i.e. upper teeth closely overlapping lower teeth and set square to the jaws. Full dentition desirable.

NECK Strong, smooth and muscular; moderately long, arched and devoid of dewlap.

FOREQUARTERS Shoulders well laid and muscular, elbows close to body and straight, forearm long, pasterns upright.

BODY Back level, short, well muscled, withers high. Chest moderately broad and deep with prominent breast bone. Distance from withers to lowest part of chest equal to distance from chest to ground. Ribs well sprung and belly with a slight tuck-up beneath loin. Croup well muscled.

HINDQUARTERS Straight when viewed from rear, thighs well developed with moderate angulation, hocks well let down.

FEET Rounded with toes short, arched and tight. Cat-like foot is required, harefoot undesirable. Nails short, strong and a shade darker in colour than coat, dewclaws should be removed.

TAIL Moderately thick, rather low-set, customarily one-third docked. When moving carried horizontally.

GAIT/MOVEMENT Graceful, elegant with a lively trot and ground-covering gallop.

COAT Short, straight, dense, smooth and shiny, feeling greasy to the touch.

COLOUR Russet gold, small white marks on chest and feet, though acceptable, undesirable.

SIZE Height at withers: dogs: 57-64 cm (22½-25 in); bitches: 53-60 cm (21-23½ in). Weight: 20-30 kg (48½-66 lb).

FAULTS Any departure from the foregoing points should be considered a fault and the seriousness with which the fault should be regarded should be in exact proportion to its degree.

NOTE Male animals should have two apparently normal testicles fully descended into the scrotum.

HUNGARIAN WIRE-HAIRED VIZSLA

(INTERIM)

A TRULY HANDSOME HUNT, POINT AND Retrieve breed in the same glowing colour as the better-known smooth-coated Vizsla, the Wirehaired Vizsla has been making a mini-revival in Great Britain since 1991.

Same weight and height as his cousin, but with a harsh jacket; he also has somewhat bushy eyebrows, which render his facial expression perhaps a trifle sterner. In point of fact, he has very much the same style of behaviour as the smooth-coated breed, and he is accepted as a good-worker in the shooting world.

GENERAL APPEARANCE Medium-sized, of distinguished appearance, robust and well boned, without losing elegance.

CHARACTERISTICS Lively, intelligent, obedient, sensitive, very affectionate and easily trained. Bred for hunting fur and feather, pointing and retrieving from land and water.

TEMPERAMENT Lively, gentle-mannered and demonstratively affectionate, fearless and with well developed protective instinct.

HEAD AND SKULL Head lean and noble. Skull moderately wide between ears with median line down forehead and a moderate stop. Skull a little longer than muzzle. Muzzle, although tapering, well squared at the end. Nostrils well developed, broad and wide. Jaws strong and powerful. Lips covering jaws completely and neither loose nor pendulous. Nose brown.

EYES Neither deep nor prominent, of medium size, a shade darker in colour than coat. Slightly oval in shape, eyelids fitting tightly. Yellow or black eye undesirable.

EARS Moderately low-set, proportionately long with a thin skin and hanging down close to cheeks. Rounded 'V'; shape; not fleshy.

MOUTH Sound and strong white teeth. Jaws strong with perfect, regular and complete scissor bite, i.e. upper teeth closely overlapping lower teeth and set square to the jaws. Full dentition desirable.

NECK Strong, smooth and muscular; moderately long, arched and devoid of dewlap.

FOREQUARTERS Shoulders well laid and muscular, elbows close to body and straight, forearm long, pasterns upright.

BODY Back level, short, well muscled, withers high. Chest moderately broad and deep with prominent breast bone. Distance from withers to lowest part of chest equal to distance from chest to ground. Ribs well sprung and belly with slight tuck-up beneath loin. Croup well muscled.

HINDQUARTERS Straight when viewed from rear, thighs well developed with moderate angulation, hocks well let down.

FEET Rounded with toes short, arched and tight. Cat-like foot is required, harefoot undesirable. Nails short, strong and a shade darker in colour than coat, dewclaws should be removed.

TAIL Moderately thick, rather low-set, customarily one-third docked. When moving carried horizontally.

GAIT/MOVEMENT Graceful, elegant with a lively trot and ground-covering gallop.

COAT Lustreless. Hair on head short and harsh, longer on muzzle, forming beard. Pronounced eyebrows. Longer and finer on ears. Longer over body, fitting closely to neck and trunk. Short harsh hair fitting closely and smoothly to forelimbs.

COLOUR Russet gold. Small white marks on chest and feet should not be penalised.

SIZE Height: dogs: 57-64 cm (22½ – 25 in); bitches 53-60 cm (21-23½ in)

FAULTS Any departure from the foregoing points should be considered a fault and the seriousness with which the fault should be regarded should be in exact proportion to its degree.

NOTE Male animals should have two apparently normal testicles fully descended into the scrotum.

IRISH RED AND WHITE SETTER

THIS BREED DERIVES FROM THE SAME root-stock as the Irish Setter, and may even have been his predecessor. Recently reintroduced to Great Britain, he is similar to the Irish, but differs in having a more powerful, broader head, and having a less prominent peak to the back of the skull. He is also heavier in body, and is described as athletic rather than racy.

A good-natured dog capable of joining in family pursuits, he sports an easily maintained coat of medium length, and this is basically white with solid red patches.

He is not a difficult dog to feed, is not large, and is steadily increasing in popularity.

As with the solid red Irish Setter, the Red and White does not have specific height or weight requirements in the Kennel Club standard and some are known to stand up to 68.5 centimetres (27 inches) and weigh around 32 kilograms (70 pounds). Records provide several references to the breed being kept in prominent kennels of the seventeenth and eighteenth centuries, one of which was owned by the Lord Rossmore of Monaghan. Even today the Red and White is occasionally known as the Rossmore Setter.

GENERAL APPEARANCE Strong and powerful, without lumber; athletic rather than racy.

CHARACTERISTICS Biddable, highly intelligent, good worker.

TEMPERAMENT Happy, good-natured and affectionate.

HEAD AND SKULL Head broad in proportion to body, with good stop. Skull domed without occipital protuberance as in Irish Setters, fairly square, clean muzzle.

EYES Hazel or dark brown, round, slight prominence, and without haw.

EARS Set level with eyes and well back, lying close to head.

MOUTH Jaws strong with a perfect, regular scissor bite, i.e. upper teeth closely overlapping lower teeth and set square to the jaws.

NECK Moderately long, very muscular, but not too thick, slightly arched, free from throatiness.

FOREQUARTERS Shoulders well laid back. Elbows free, turning neither in nor out. Strong, oval bone, well muscled, sinewy, pasterns slightly sloping.

BODY Strong and muscular, deep chest and well sprung ribs. Back and quarters very muscular and powerful. Bone strong, well built up with muscle and sinew.

HINDQUARTERS Wide and powerful. Legs from hip to hock long and muscular, from hock to heel short and strong. Stifle well bent, hocks well let down turning neither in nor out.

FEET Close-knit, well feathered between toes.

TAIL Strong at root, tapering to fine point, with no appearance of ropiness; not reaching below

hock. Well feathered, carried level with back or below in lively manner.

GAIT/MOVEMENT Long, free-striding, effortless with drive.

COAT Finely textured with good feathering. Slight wave permissible but never curly.

COLOUR Clearly parti-coloured, i.e. base colour pearl white, solid red patches. Mottling or flecking but no roaning permitted around

face and feet and up foreleg to elbow and up hindleg to hock.

FAULTS Any departure from the foregoing points should be considered a fault and the seriousness with which the fault should be regarded should be in exact proportion to its degree.

NOTE Male animals should have two apparently normal testicles fully descended into the scrotum.

IRISH SETTER

THE IRISH SETTER MUST RANK AMONGST the most glamorous of all the breeds of dog. Immensely popular with all manner of people, he is ideal as a centre of attraction for the glossy advertisement, with his rich chestnut coat gleaming as only that of a healthy athlete can. A moderate amount of white on his chest is not uncommon, and will not disqualify him for the showring.

His air of the devil-may-care is totally genuine and his friendly, affectionate nature makes him a good household dog ready for all the fun and frolic a family will hand him.

Despite his racy outlines, he needs to be powerful in his hindquarters, and well boned throughout. Given the chance he will demonstrate that underneath the glamour there is a worker willing to give of his best.

Popularity of the solid Reds increased from about the late 1800s when they had become among the top-winning dogs and a breed club for the Irish (Red) Setter was formed in 1882, pushing the Red and White into something of a decline, which now has been reversed. Like the Red and White there are no specific height or weight restrictions in the standard and specimens can be found up to 68.5 centimetres (27 inches) or at 32 kilograms (70 pounds) weight.

GENERAL APPEARANCE Must be racy, balanced and full of quality. In conformation, proportionate.

CHARACTERISTICS Most handsome, and refined in looks, tremendously active with untiring readiness to range and hunt under any conditions.

TEMPERAMENT Demonstrably affectionate.

HEAD AND SKULL Head long and lean, not narrow or snipy, not coarse at the ears. Skull oval (from ear to ear) having plenty of brain room and well defined occipital protuberance. From occiput to stop and from stop to tip of nose to be parallel and of equal length, brows raised showing stop. Muzzle moderately deep, fairly square at end. Jaws of nearly equal length, flews not pendulous, nostrils wide. Colour of nose dark mahogany, dark walnut or black.

EYES Dark hazel to dark brown, not too large, preferably like an unshelled almond in shape, set level (not obliquely) under brows showing kind, intelligent expression.

EARS Of moderate size, fine in texture, set-on low, well back and hanging in a neat fold close to head.

MOUTH Jaws strong, with a perfect, regular and complete scissor bite, i.e. upper teeth closely overlapping lower teeth and set square to the jaws.

NECK Moderately long, very muscular but not too thick, slightly arched and free from all tendency to throatiness, setting cleanly without a break of topline into shoulders.

FOREQUARTERS Shoulders fine at points, deep and sloping well back. Forelegs straight and sinewy having plenty of bone, with elbows free, well let down and not inclined either in or out.

BODY Chest as deep as possible, rather narrow in front. Ribs well sprung leaving plenty of lung room and carried well back to muscular loin, slightly arched. Firm straight topline gently sloping downwards from withers.

HINDQUARTERS Wide and powerful. Hindlegs from hip to hock long and muscular, from hock to heel short and strong. Stifle and hock joints well bent and not inclined either in or out.

FEET Small, very firm; toes strong, close together and arched.

TAIL Of moderate length proportionate to size of body, set-on just below the level of the back, strong at root tapering to a fine point and carried as nearly as possible on a level with or below the back.

GAIT/MOVEMENT Free-flowing, driving movement with true action when viewed from front or rear, and in profile, showing perfect co ordination.

COAT On head, front of legs and tips of ears, short and fine; on all other parts of body and legs of moderate length, flat and as free as possible from curl or wave. Feathers on upper portion of ears long and silky; on back of fore- and hindlegs long and fine. Fair amount of hair on belly, forming a nice fringe which may extend on to chest and throat. Feet well feathered between toes. Tail to have fringe of moderately long hair decreasing in length as it approaches point. All feathering to be as straight and flat as possible.

COLOUR Rich chestnut with no trace of black. White on chest, throat, chin or toes, or small star on forehead or narrow streak or blaze on nose or face not to disqualify.

FAULTS Any departure from the foregoing points should be considered a fault and the seriousness with which the fault should be regarded should be in exact proportion to its degree.

NOTE Male animals should have two apparently normal testicles fully descended into the scrotum.

ITALIAN SPINONE

AN ALL-PURPOSE GUNDOG RECENTLY brought into Great Britain, and already showing a fair degree of popularity with those who want a hardy worker in the field, or a faithful, patient companion in the house. There is quite possibly a bit of hound in his make-up, and he is adaptable enough to put up a good performance as a guard dog if he is asked to do so.

Though the Spinone did not achieve championship status in Britain until 1994 it is a very old breed whose true origins are somewhat difficult to put together. It is thought that the breed has a lot of blood of native hounds of Italy mixed with that of the French Griffons. Another of the Hunt, Point and Retrieve breeds from the Continent, he is noted for his good scenting and soft mouth and is especially successful as a worker in rough woodland or marshes.

An easy dog to train, he will fit into the family pattern. His thick, somewhat wiry coat is simple to keep in good order, so that he does not cause a great deal of mess on returning from a walk across farm land, or a day on the rough shoot.

His colour is basically white all over, with a variable amount of orange or brown which can be speckled or patched. He is unusual in having a slight slope in his back from his withers and then back up again towards the croup.

GENERAL APPEARANCE Solid, squarely built, strong bone and well muscled. Kind and earnest expression.

CHARACTERISTICS Intrepid and untiring, very hardy, adaptable to any terrain including water. All-purpose gundog.

TEMPERAMENT Faithful, intelligent, patient and affectionate.

HEAD AND SKULL Head long, skull flat, lean; sides gently sloping and very slightly rounded, equal in length from well developed occiput to stop as from gently sloping stop to tip of nose. Median furrow pronounced. Nose large, spongy in appearance, protruding over rather thin lips.

EYES Large, fairly round and open, eyelids close fitting. Deep yellow in white, and white and orange; ochre in brown roans.

EARS Set-on level with corner of eye, long, but not more than 5 cm (2 in) below jaw line, pendulous, forward edge touching cheek. Triangular in shape, slightly rounded at tip, covered with thick short hair, longer and denser at edges.

MOUTH Jaws powerful with a perfect, regular and complete scissor bite, i.e. upper teeth closely overlapping lower teeth and set square to the jaws. Lips rather thin.

NECK Strong, muscular, fairly short, merging into shoulder, slight, divided dewlap.

FOREQUARTERS Shoulders strong, well muscled and well laid back. Points of shoulder set well apart. Forelegs straight, bone oval; strong, well defined tendons. Pasterns slightly sloping when viewed from side, elbows turning neither in nor out.

BODY Length equal to height at withers, chest broad, open, well let down. Brisket reaching at least to level of elbows. Front of sternum comes well forward below points of shoulders. Ribs open, well sprung. Topline, a very slight slope from raised withers to well muscled loins, slight rise from loin to broad and muscular croup, croup sloping.

HINDQUARTERS Thighs long, broad, muscular and strong. Hocks well let down. Metatarsals vertical on extension of buttock line. Tendons clearly visible.

FEET Front compact, round. Hindfeet slightly oval. Toes arched, covered with short thick hair especially between toes. Nails strong, arched. Pads hard. Pigmented according to coat colours. Never black. Dewclaws on all four feet.

TAIL Thick at base, set-on as a continuation of croup line, carried horizontally or down, customarily docked to half its length.

GAIT/MOVEMENT Free, relaxed and capable of fast trot.

COAT Tough, thick, slightly wiry, close fitting, length 3.8-6 cm (1½-2½ in) on body, shorter on nasal bridge, ears and head, even shorter on front of legs and feet. Eyebrows consist of longer stiffer hair; even longer but softer hair covers cheeks and upper lips forming moustache and beard. Skin thick and leathery.

COLOUR White, white with orange markings; solid white peppered orange, white with brown markings, white speckled with brown (brown roan), with or without large brown markings. Pigment of skin, eyelids, nose, lips and pads fleshy red in white dogs, deeper in white/orange and brown roan dogs.

SIZE Height: dogs: 60-70 cm (23½-27½ in); bitches: 59-65 cm (23-25½ in). Weight: dogs: 34 39 kg (70-82 lb); bitches: 29-34 kg (62-71 lb).

FAULTS Any departure from the foregoing points should be considered a fault and the seriousness with which the fault should be regarded should be in exact proportion to its degree.

NOTE Male animals should have two apparently normal testicles fully descended into the scrotum.

Kooikerhondje

GUNDOG

94

THIS COMPACTLY SMALL BREED, WHICH hails from the Netherlands, is blessed with a spectacular coat of clear red-orange splodges on a white background. His eye-catching coat is effectively used to attract swimming ducks and seduce them along streams into netting traps. The whole effect is aided and abetted by the gaily carried, well-feathered tail waving aloft.

For those not involved in duck hunting, he can be a cheerful and neat companion; he enjoys human company, especially the energetic variety. He has not been in Great Britain all that long, but could well be a success story in the making.

GENERAL APPEARANCE Parti-coloured dog with a nearly square body with length slightly more than height at shoulders. High head carriage.

CHARACTERISTICS/TEMPERAMENT Friendly, good-natured and alert.

HEAD AND SKULL Length of skull about equal to muzzle with a moderate stop. Muzzle not too deep, lips tight-fitting, well filled under the eye. Nose black.

EYES Deep brown, almond-shaped, alert expression.

EARS Medium-sized, set just above eye level; pendant, hanging close to the cheeks. Long feathered, dark tips preferred.

MOUTH Jaws strong with a perfect, regular and complete scissor bite, i.e. upper teeth closely overlapping lower teeth and set square to the jaw.

NECK Short and well muscled.

FOREQUARTERS Shoulders well laid back. Forelegs straight; not too heavily feathered.

BODY Strong, level back, deep chest with good spring of rib.

HINDQUARTERS Strong and broad, flanks well rounded, stifle slightly angulated, feathered to mid-thigh.

FEET Small and tight. Slightly hare-shaped.

TAIL Carried on level with back or slightly above; not curled, reaching the hock. Well feathered with white plume.

GAIT/MOVEMENT Jaunty and springy.

COAT Medium long, slightly waved or straight; not curled, close fitting. Hair not too fine, well developed undercoat.

COLOUR Clear orange-red coloured patches on white. White blaze preferred.

SIZE Height: 35-40 cm (14-16 in).

FAULTS Any departure from the foregoing points should be regarded as a fault and the seriousness with which the fault should be regarded should be in exact proportion to its degree.

NOTE Male animals should have two apparently normal testicles fully descended into the scrotum.

LARGE MUNSTERLANDER

THE INFLUX OF BREEDS OF GUNDOG from the Continent since the early 1950s has introduced a number of multi-purpose dogs to our rough shooting scene. None has been more strikingly handsome than this tall black-headed, white-and black-bodied breed from Munster in Germany, which was first registered by The Kennel Club in 1971. Since then, he has proved himself both an effective worker and a family companion. A biddable dog, he gives the impression that he enjoys life and would like you to enjoy it too.

His coat is long and dense, with a good deal of feathering on his legs and under his tail; he also has a fair amount of hair between his toes, so he can bring a heap of the great outdoors into the parlour if allowed to make an unhindered entrance straight from the shooting field, or the country ramble.

Now that docking is optional he is very rarely docked, which seems eminently sensible in something so well plumed. The Munsterlander does well in obedience competition and is good with children.

GENERAL APPEARANCE Alert and energetic, with strong muscular body, having good movement with drive.

CHARACTERISTICS Multi-purpose gundog, ideal for the rough shooter. Excellent nose, staying power, and works equally well on land and in water. A keen worker, easily taught.

TEMPERAMENT Loyal, affectionate and trustworthy.

HEAD AND SKULL Well proportioned to body, elongated. Skull sufficiently broad, slightly rounded, with no pronounced occiput. Strong jaw muscles, well formed black nose, wide soft nostrils, slight rise from the nasal bone to the forehead but no pronounced stop. Lips slightly rounded, and well fitting.

EYES Intelligent, medium size, dark brown, not deep-set or protruding. No haw showing.

EARS Broad and set high, lying flat and close to the head, with a rounded tip. Hair on the ears should be long, extending beyond the tip.

MOUTH Strong and sound, with well developed teeth, with a perfect, regular and complete scissor bite, i.e. upper teeth closely overlapping lower teeth and set square to the jaws.

NECK Strong, muscular, slightly arched, joining the shoulder and chest smoothly.

FOREQUARTERS Chest wide and with good depth of brisket. Shoulders laid well back, forelegs straight, pasterns strong.

BODY Firm strong back, short-coupled, slightly higher at the shoulders, sloping smoothly towards the croup and tail. Wide, well muscled loin. Wide croup. Ribs well sprung, deep and reaching well up to the loins. Taut abdomen, slightly tucked up.

HINDQUARTERS Hips broad. Well muscled thighs, well turned stifles, hocks well let down. Dewclaws should be removed.

FEET Tight, moderately rounded and well knuckled with dense hair between the toes, well padded. Nails black and strong.

TAIL Well set-on, in line with the back. Base thick, tapering evenly towards the tip, well feathered. It should be carried horizontally or curved slightly upwards. Docking of tip of tail optional.

GAIT/MOVEMENT Free, long-striding, springy gait.

COAT Hair long and dense, but not curly or coarse. Well feathered on front and hindlegs and on tail, more so in dogs than in bitches. Hair must lie short and smooth on the head.

COLOUR Head solid black, white blaze, snip or star allowed. Body white or blue roan with black patches, flecked, ticked, or combination of these.

SIZE Height: dogs: 60-65 cm (23½-25½ in); bitches 58-63 cm (23-25 in). Weight: dogs: approx 25-29 kg (55-65 lb); bitches: approx 25 kg (55 lb).

FAULTS Any departure from the foregoing points should be considered a fault and the seriousness with which the fault should be regarded should be in exact proportion to its degree.

NOTE Male animals should have two apparently normal testicles fully descended into the scrotum.

NOVA SCOTIA DUCK TOLLING RETRIEVER

(INTERIM)

CANADA IS THE COUNTRY OF ORIGIN OF several well-known breeds of dog; the Nova Scotia Duck Tolling Retriever (the Toller to his intimates) is yet another Canadian native; he arrived in Britain as recently as 1988, and has made steady progress ever since.

His method of work may appear strange to many; his task is to use his waving, white-tipped tail to lure waterfowl to within range of the guns and then retrieve them, especially from water. He is blessed with the canine equivalent of web-feet which enables him to swim powerfully. He is not difficult to groom.

He has been selected over the generations for his intelligence and trainability; as a result he makes an ideal and enthusiastic family companion for the active household; he enjoys agility and flyball; he performs well as a tracker and in obedience. As he is also handsome, he has attracted the attention of a wide circle of friends, who are dedicated to maintaining him as the athlete he is.

GENERAL APPEARANCE Medium-sized, compact. Powerful, well muscled. A heavily feathered tail, constantly moving.

CHARACTERISTICS Jumps and plays to lure waterfowl into decoy. Retrieves dead and wounded birds. Strong swimmer.

TEMPERAMENT Kind, confident, intelligent, easy to train. Playful.

HEAD AND SKULL Clean-cut skull, slightly wedge shaped. Broad, slightly rounded. Occiput not prominent. Cheeks flat. Moderate stop. Muzzle tapers from stop to nose. Nostrils well developed. Nose flesh-coloured or black.

EYES Medium size, almond-shaped, well set apart. Alert expression. Brown to amber. Eye rims flesh-coloured or black.

EARS Triangular, medium size, set high and well back on skull. Base held very slightly erect; well feathered at back of fold, hair shorter at rounded tips.

MOUTH Jaws strong with a perfect, regular and complete scissor bite, i.e. upper teeth closely overlapping lower teeth and set square to the jaws. Teeth sound and strong. Softness of mouth essential. Lips tight fitting, flesh-coloured or black.

NECK Medium length, strongly muscled, well set-on, no indication of throatiness.

FOREQUARTERS Shoulders well laid back, muscular, medium length. Elbows close to body. Forelegs straight and strong. Pasterns strong, slightly sloping.

BODY Deep chested, ribs well sprung, brisket reaches to elbow. Back short, level topline. Loins strong and muscular. Moderate tuck-up.

HINDQUARTERS Well muscled. Stifles well bent, hocks well let down, turning neither in nor out.

FEET Medium-sized, round, tight. Toes well arched and strongly webbed. Pads thick, blending with coat colour.

TAIL Set-on, slightly sloping towards croup. Broad at base, well feathered; reaching the hock. Carried below level of back at rest; when alert, curves over, not touching back.

GAIT/MOVEMENT Impression of power, springy, jaunty with good reach of forelegs and strong rear drive; parallel movement fore and aft. Single tracks at speed; head carried almost level with back.

COAT Straight, repellent, double coat of medium length and softness with a softer, dense undercoat. Slight wave on back allowed. Feathering at throat, behind ears and at back of thighs. Forelegs moderately feathered.

COLOUR All shades of red or orange with lighter feathering under tail. White marks are permissible on tip of tail, feet and chest, or as blaze. Lack of white not to be penalised.

SIZE Ideal height: dogs: 48-51 cm (19-20 in); bitches: 45-48 cm (18-19 in).

FAULTS Any departure from the foregoing points should be considered a fault and the seriousness with which the fault should be regarded should be in exact proportion to its degree.

NOTE Male animals should have two apparently normal testicles fully descended into the scrotum.

POINTER

THE POINTER IS SAID TO HAVE originated in Spain, but he has undoubtedly become a truly English breed over the last two or three centuries. During this time he has been employed by shooting men in his traditional role of indicating the presence and position of sitting game. He combines a distinctive elegance with a sleek muscularity which enables him to cover great areas of ground at considerable speed. His movement, though specifically not that of a hackney, is characterised by his habit of carrying his head reasonably high as he tests the air, until it is lowered to the characteristic point as he indicates his quarry.

His smooth, hard coat should have a definite sheen and be either lemon, orange, liver or black, all with white. Possibly his most distinguishing feature is the slight concavity on the top of his muzzle, giving his nose a tip-tilted appearance.

A clean dog, of even temperament, capable of fitting into a family circle, but obviously most at home on the moors in his true element. To be good the Pointer needs superb scenting powers, speed over the ground and steadiness on point, a quality which was vital in the days of the slow-loading flintlock weapons when having found game the Pointer had to hold it until the hunter and his gun could catch up.

GENERAL APPEARANCE Symmetrical and well built all over, general outline a series of graceful curves. A strong but lissom appearance.

CHARACTERISTICS Aristocratic. Alert with appearance of strength, endurance and speed.

TEMPERAMENT Kind, even disposition.

HEAD AND SKULL Skull of medium breadth, in proportion to length of foreface, stop well defined, pronounced occipital bone. Nose and eye rims dark, but may be lighter in the case of a lemon and white coloured dog. Nostrils wide, soft and moist. Muzzle somewhat concave, ending on level with nostrils, giving a slightly dish-faced appearance. Slight depression under eyes, check bones not prominent, well developed soft lip.

EYES Same distance from occiput as from nostrils, bright and kindly in expression. Either hazel or brown according to colour of coat. Neither bold nor staring, not looking down the nose.

EARS Leathers thin, set-on fairly high, lying close to head, of medium length, slightly pointed at tips.

MOUTH Jaws strong, with perfect, regular and complete scissor bite, i.e. upper teeth closely overlapping lower teeth and set square to the jaws.

NECK Long, muscular, slightly arched, springing cleanly from shoulders and free from throatiness.

FOREQUARTERS Shoulders long, sloping and well laid back. Chest just wide enough for plenty of heart room. Brisket well let down, to level with elbows. Forelegs straight and firm, with good oval bone, with back sinews strong and visible. Knee joint flat with front leg and protruding very little on inside. Pasterns lengthy, strong and resilient. Slightly sloping.

BODY Well sprung ribs carried well back gradually falling away at strong, muscular and slightly arched loins. Short-coupled. Haunch bones well spaced and prominent, not above level of back.

HINDQUARTERS Very muscular. Well turned stifles. Good expanse of first and second thigh. Hocks well let down.

FEET Oval, well knit, arched toes, well cushioned.

TAIL Medium length, thick at root, tapering gradually to a point. Well covered with close hair, carried on a level with back, with no upward curl. In movement, tail should lash from side to side.

GAIT/MOVEMENT Smooth, covering plenty of ground. Driving hind action, elbows neither in nor out. Definitely not a hackney action.

COAT Fine, short, hard and evenly distributed, perfectly smooth and straight with decided sheen.

COLOUR Usual colours are lemon and white, orange and white, liver and white, and black and white. Self colours and tricolours are also correct.

SIZE Desirable heights at withers: dogs: 63-69 cm (25-27 in); bitches: 61-66 cm (24-26 in).

FAULTS Any departure from the foregoing points should be considered a fault and the seriousness with which the fault should be regarded should be in exact proportion to its degree.

NOTE Male animals should have two apparently normal testicles fully descended into the scrotum.

CHESAPEAKE BAY RETRIEVER

(INTERIM)

THERE IS NO DOUBT WHATSOEVER about the origin of this breed. All the books ever written about the Chesapeake Bay are agreed on a tale about two puppies being rescued from a wrecked ship off the coast on the eastern seaboard of Maryland. They were reputed, some two centuries ago, to have been Newfoundland in type, were discovered to love water and so were crossed with local retriever types, probably including the Curly Coat. The result was the ultimate in natural waterproof dog.

Basically a duck-dog, he is at his very best in water, the colder the better; the oiliness and thickness of the coat is so efficient that a thorough shake restores him to a slightly moist feel in no time at all.

Undoubted courage, inexhaustible energy, strength of muscle and affection tinged with independence, all go to produce a dog for the energetic family. Not a breed for the lazy.

He eats in quantities sufficient for a dog of his size and 'work-rate', which means he likes his food.

Grooming is simple and elementary; a stiff brush and a chamois-leather will cover all his requirements.

GENERAL APPEARANCE Well proportioned, active worker with a distinctive coat and intelligent expression. Strong muscular appearance.

CHARACTERISTICS Independent, affectionate and courageous, with a great love of water. Makes a good guardian and companion, especially with children.

TEMPERAMENT Bright and happy disposition, alert and intelligent and showing a willingness to work.

HEAD AND SKULL Broad and round with medium stop. Medium-short muzzle, pointed but not sharp. Lips thin, not pendulous. Nostrils well developed. Nose and lips of colour to harmonise with coat.

EYES Medium size, very clear, of yellow or amber colour and set wide apart.

EARS Small, well set up on head, hanging loosely and of medium leather.

MOUTH Jaws strong with a perfect, regular and complete scissor bite, i.e. upper teeth closely overlapping lower teeth and set square to the jaws. Level bite tolerated.

NECK Of medium length with a strong muscular appearance tapering from head to shoulders.

FOREQUARTERS Forelegs straight, with good bone of equal length to depth of body and showing good muscle. Shoulders well laid back, long in blade with upper arm of equal length placing legs well under body with no restriction of movement. Strong. Pasterns slightly bent. Dewclaws may be removed.

BODY Chest strong, deep and broad, with well sprung ribs. Body of medium length, short but not cobby. Flanks well tucked-up. Back well coupled and powerful. Topline not roached, but rather approaching hollowness.

HINDQUARTERS Should be as high or a trifle higher than shoulders. Powerful to supply power for swimming. Stifles well angulated. Good hindquarters are an essential requirement for this breed. Hocks of medium length. Dewclaws, if any, must be removed from the hindlegs.

FEET Of good size, harefeet well webbed. Toes well rounded and close.

TAIL Should extend to hock. Medium heavy at base and strong. Should be straight or slightly curved. Moderate feathering is permissible.

GAIT/MOVEMENT Powerful with no restriction of movement. Correct conformation will lend to single track movement.

COAT AND TEXTURE A distinctive feature. Coat should be thick and reasonably short, not over 3.8 cm (1½ in) long, with harsh oily outer coat and dense, fine woolly undercoat covering whole body; hairs having tendency to wave on neck, shoulders, back and loins. Hair on face and legs only should be very short and straight. Moderate feathering on stern and tail permissible. Curly coat not permissible. Texture of coat very important as dog is used for working under all sorts of adverse weather conditions, often working in ice and snow. Oil in harsh coat and woolly undercoat of extreme value. The coat should resist water.

COLOUR Dead grass (straw to bracken), sedge (red gold), or any shade of brown. White spots on chest, toes and belly permissible. The smaller the spot the better. Self-coloured dogs preferred. Colour of coat and its texture must be given every consideration when judging.

SIZE Height: dogs: 58.5-66 cm (23-26 in); bitches: 53.5-60.9 cm (21-24 in). Oversized or undersized dogs highly undesirable.

FAULTS Any departure from the foregoing points should be considered a fault and the seriousness with which the fault should be regarded should be in exact proportion to its degree.

NOTE Male animals should have two apparently normal testicles fully descended into the scrotum.

CURLY COATED RETRIEVER

ONE OF THE MOST DISTINCTIVE features about this dog is his coat the colour of which is either black or liver. His body, ears and tail are covered with tight, crisp curls, whilst his face and muzzle are smooth haired. His coat is waterproof and, even after a swim, he shakes himself a few times and is practically dry. This unique coat does require specialised treatment to keep it at its best.

He has a remarkable ability to mark the fall of game and remember locations, and is brilliant at retrieving the wounded duck, hiding in water or rushes. However, a good nose, combined with intelligence, endurance and strength, gives him the ability to retrieve most game. Friendly, but despite this he is a good guard dog. He needs plenty of exercise, and is essentially an outdoor type.

The breed is around 200 years old, having evolved from crosses of water spaniels and varieties of retrievers and, say some, pointers. Cross breeding with Poodles is believed to have been used to tighten the curl in the coat. It was at its most popular as a shooting dog in the latter part of the nineteenth century and many Curlies were exported to New Zealand and Australia to hunt birds.

GENERAL APPEARANCE Strong, upstanding dog with a degree of elegance. Distinctive coat.

CHARACTERISTICS Intelligent, steady, reliable.

TEMPERAMENT Bold, friendly, self-confident and independent. May seem aloof.

HEAD AND SKULL Head wedge-shaped in both side and front profiles. In proportion to body size. Slight stop. Foreface and skull equal length. Planes of skull and muzzle parallel. Nose black in blacks and brown in livers.

EYES Large, not prominent, oval-shaped, obliquely set. Dark brown in blacks, in livers brown tone to blend with coat colour.

EARS Rather small, set slightly above level of eye; lying close to head, covered with small curls.

MOUTH Jaws strong, with perfect, regular and complete scissor bite, i.e. upper teeth closely overlapping lower teeth and set square to the jaws.

NECK Strong and slightly arched, of medium length, free from throatiness and flowing freely into well laid back shoulders.

FOREQUARTERS Shoulders well laid back and muscular. Upper arm and shoulder blade approximately equal length. Forelegs straight with strong pasterns and set well under body.

BODY Chest deep with well sprung ribs, oval in cross section with brisket reaching elbow. Forechest visible. Ribs extend well back into short, deep and powerful loin. Slight tuck-up to flank. Topline strong and level. Slightly longer from withers to root of tail than from withers to ground.

HINDQUARTERS Strong, muscular. Moderate turn of stifle. Hocks well let down and well bent.

FEET Round, tight and well-arched toes.

TAIL Flows from topline. Should reach approximately to hock; carried straight on a level with topline when moving.

GAIT/MOVEMENT Effortless, powerful gait with good extension and drive. Parallel movement. At speed, legs tend to converge.

COAT Body coat a thick mass of small, tight, crisp curls lying close to skin, extending from occiput to tip of tail; without undercoat or bare patches. Elsewhere hair smooth.

COLOUR Black or liver.

SIZE Ideal height at withers: dogs: 67.5 cm (27 in); bitches: 62.5 cm (25 in).

FAULTS Any departure from the foregoing points should be considered a fault and the seriousness with which the fault should be regarded should be in exact proportion to its degree.

NOTE Male animals should have two apparently normal testicles fully descended into the scrotum.

FLAT COATED RETRIEVER

THE FLAT COAT IS A SLOW MATURING dog retaining his delightful puppy-like qualities for several years. An extrovert, always happy and eager to please with an incessantly wagging tail, and full of good humour and bonhomie.

A tireless worker in the field, he is an excellent water dog and a natural swimmer. He loves human companionship and is definitely not the dog to be shut up on his own, when his Houdini-like qualities will soon become apparent in his endeavour to reunite himself with friends and family. His deep bark makes him a good guard dog, giving warning of any strangers or intruders. He is in his element in the country and was at one time popularly known as the gamekeepers' dog, attracting attention when widely used in the late 1800s on the large shooting estates. Mr Sewallis Evelyn Shirley, founder of The Kennel Club and its chairman from 1873 to 1899, helped stabilise the breed type.

GENERAL APPEARANCE A bright, active dog of medium size with an intelligent expression, showing power without lumber, and raciness without weediness.

CHARACTERISTICS Generously endowed with natural gundog ability, optimism and friendliness demonstrated by enthusiastic tail action.

TEMPERAMENT Confident and kindly.

HEAD AND SKULL Head long and nicely moulded. Skull flat and moderately broad with a slight stop between eyes, in no way accentuated, avoiding a down- or dish-faced appearance. Nose of good size, with open nostrils. Jaws long and strong, capable of carrying a hare or pheasant.

EYES Medium size, dark brown or hazel, with a very intelligent expression (a round prominent eye highly undesirable). Not obliquely placed.

EARS Small and well set-on, close to side of head.

MOUTH Jaws strong with a perfect, regular and complete scissor bite, i.e. upper teeth closely overlapping lower teeth and set square to the jaws. Teeth sound and strong.

NECK Head well set in neck, the latter reasonably long and free from throatiness, symmetrically set and obliquely placed in shoulders, running well into the back to allow for easy seeking of trail.

FOREQUARTERS Chest deep and fairly broad, with well defined brisket, on which elbows should move cleanly and evenly. Forelegs straight, with bone of good quality throughout.

BODY Foreribs fairly flat. Body well ribbed up, showing a gradual spring and well arched in centre but rather lighter towards quarters. Loin short and square. Open couplings highly undesirable.

HINDQUARTERS Muscular. Moderate bend of stifle and hock, latter well let down. Should stand true all round. Cow-hocks highly undesirable.

FEET Round and strong with toes close and well arched. Soles thick and strong.

TAIL Short, straight and well set-on, gaily carried, but never much above level of back.

GAIT/MOVEMENT Free and flowing, straight and true as seen from front and rear.

COAT Dense, of fine to medium texture and good quality, as flat as possible. Legs and tail well feathered. Full furnishings on maturity complete the elegance of a good dog.

COLOUR Black or liver only.

SIZE Preferred height: dogs: 59-61.5 cm (23-24 in); bitches: 56.5-59 cm (22-23 in). Preferred weight in hard condition: dogs: 27-36 kg (60-80 lb); bitches: 25-32 kg (55-70 lb).

FAULTS Any departure from the foregoing points should be considered a fault and the seriousness with which the fault should be regarded should be in exact proportion to its degree.

NOTE Male animals should have two apparently normal testicles fully descended into the scrotum.

GOLDEN RETRIEVER

ONE OF THE MOST POPULAR DOGS IN the world. Bred as its name suggests to retrieve game in the shooting field, the breed has adapted to so many roles that there is virtually nothing he doesn't do, with the obvious exception of being a professional guard dog – a task for which his friendly temperament makes him quite unsuited. He has been a guide dog, a drug and explosives detecting dog, a tracker, an obedience competitor, in addition to the job he does so universally and well, simply being an energetic, fun-loving member of the family.

Easy to train to basic obedience or higher standards; rarely a choosy feeder; a thick coat which is reasonably easy to keep clean; it is no surprise that the breed has risen in popularity over the decades, now occupying a place in the top three or four as far as The Kennel Club's registration system is concerned.

For many years there was confusion over the origin of the breed but nowadays it is accepted as an undeniable fact that it was the first Lord Tweedmouth who began Golden Retrievers as a definite breed. 'Yellow' Retrievers had existed for many years in the Border Country between England and Scotland and at first Goldens were registered and shown as Flatcoats, being defined only by colour until 1913. They took their present name in 1920.

GENERAL APPEARANCE Symmetrical, balanced, active, powerful, level mover; sound with kindly expression.

CHARACTERISTICS Biddable, intelligent and possessing natural working ability.

TEMPERAMENT Kindly, friendly and confident.

HEAD AND SKULL Balanced and well chiselled, skull broad without coarseness; well set-on neck, muzzle powerful, wide and deep. Length of foreface approximately equals length from well defined stop to occiput. Nose preferably black.

EYES Dark brown, set well apart, dark rims.

EARS Moderate size, set-on approximate level with eyes.

MOUTH Jaws strong, with a perfect, regular and complete scissor bite, i.e. upper teeth closely overlapping lower teeth and set square to the jaws.

NECK Good length, clean and muscular.

FOREQUARTERS Forelegs straight with good bone, shoulders well laid back, long in blade with upper arm of equal length placing legs well under body. Elbows close fitting.

BODY Balanced, short-coupled, deep through heart. Ribs deep, well sprung. Level topline.

HINDQUARTERS Loin and legs strong and muscular, good second thighs, well bent stifles. Hocks well let down, straight when viewed from rear, neither turning in nor out. Cow-hocks highly undesirable.

FEET Round and cat-like.

TAIL Set-on and carried level with back, reaching to hocks, without curl at tip.

GAIT/MOVEMENT Powerful with good drive. Straight and true in front and rear. Stride long and free with no sign of hackney action in front.

COAT Flat or wavy with good feathering, dense water-resisting undercoat.

COLOUR Any shade of gold or cream, neither red nor mahogany. A few white hairs, on chest only, permissible.

SIZE Height at withers: dogs: 56-61 cm (22-24 in); bitches: 51-56 cm (20-22 in).

FAULTS Any departure from the foregoing points should be considered a fault and the seriousness with which the fault should be regarded should be in exact proportion to its degree.

NOTE Male animals should have two apparently normal testicles fully descended into the scrotum.

LABRADOR RETRIEVER

THE LABRADOR IS ONE OF THE BEST ALL-round dogs in the world. Not only used for retrieving game, he has also made his mark in the world of guide dogs, and as a 'sniffer' dog for drug and arms detection. It is popularly thought that he originated on the coast of Greenland where fishermen were seen to use a dog of similar appearance to retrieve fish.

An excellent water dog, his weather-resistant coat and unique tail, likened to that of an otter because of its shape, emphasise this trait. A real gentleman, he adores children, has a kind and loving nature, and a confident air. The big city is not really his scene; a bit of a country squire at heart, he comes into his own in rural surroundings.

Comparatively speaking, the Labrador is not a very old breed, its breed club having been formed in 1916 and the Yellow Labrador Club having been founded in 1925. It was in field trialling that the Labrador found early fame, having been originally introduced to these shores in the late 1800s by Col Peter Hawker and the Earl of Malmesbury. It was a dog called Malmesbury Tramp which was described by Lorna, Countess Howe as one of the 'tap roots' of the modern Labrador.

GENERAL APPEARANCE Strongly built, short-coupled, very active; broad in skull; broad and deep through chest and ribs; broad and strong over loins and hindquarters.

CHARACTERISTICS Good-tempered, very agile. Excellent nose, soft mouth; keen love of water. Adaptable, devoted companion.

TEMPERAMENT Intelligent, keen and biddable, with a strong will to please. Kindly nature, with no trace of aggression or undue shyness.

HEAD AND SKULL Skull broad with defined stop; clean-cut without fleshy cheeks. Jaws of medium length, powerful not snipy. Nose wide, nostrils well developed.

EYES Medium size, expressing intelligence and good temper; brown or hazel.

EARS Not large or heavy, hanging close to head and set rather far back.

MOUTH Jaws and teeth strong with a perfect, regular and complete scissor bite, i.e. upper teeth closely overlapping lower teeth and set square to the jaws.

NECK Clean, strong, powerful, set into well placed shoulders.

FOREQUARTERS Shoulders long and sloping. Forelegs well boned and straight from elbow to ground when viewed from either front or side.

BODY Chest of good width and depth, with well sprung barrel ribs. Level topline. Loins wide, short-coupled and strong.

HINDQUARTERS Well developed, not sloping to tail; well turned stifle. Hocks well let down, cow-hocks highly undesirable.

FEET Round, compact; well arched toes and well developed pads.

TAIL Distinctive feature, very thick towards base, gradually tapering towards tip, medium length, free from feathering, but clothed thickly all round with short, thick dense coat, thus giving 'rounded' appearance described as 'Otter' tail. May be carried gaily but should not curl over back.

GAIT/MOVEMENT Free, covering adequate ground; straight and true in front and rear.

COAT Distinctive feature, short, dense without wave or feathering, giving fairly hard feel to the touch; weather-resistant undercoat.

COLOUR Wholly black, yellow or liver/ chocolate. Yellows range from light cream to red fox. Small white spot on chest permissible.

SIZE Ideal height at withers: dogs: 56-57 cm (22-22½ in); bitches: 54-56 cm (21½-22 in).

FAULTS Any departure from the foregoing points should be considered a fault and the seriousness with which the fault should be regarded should be in exact proportion to its degree.

NOTE Male animals should have two apparently normal testicles fully descended into the scrotum.

AMERICAN COCKER SPANIEL

DERIVED IN THE LAST CENTURY IN America from the Cocker Spaniel, ostensibly to retrieve quail, the American Cocker has very striking differences from his English forebear. The prominent rounding of his skull is most distinctive, as are the full eyes set to look straight forward. His back appears short, and slopes slightly from withers to tail. His most characteristic attribute is his coat which, while being short on his head, is longer on the body, and becomes profuse on legs and abdomen. The breed standard does require that it should not be so excessive as to affect his function as a sporting dog, but it has to be said that he usually appears in the showring with a great deal of coat, which is unlikely to find favour in the field. However, he is a cheerful fellow, and makes a highly successful family dog; he is on the small side of 38 centimetres (15 inches) and does not need much food, though he needs careful grooming.

GENERAL APPEARANCE Serviceable-looking dog with refined chiselled head, strong, well boned legs, well up at the shoulder, compact sturdy body, wide muscular quarters, well balanced.

CHARACTERISTICS Merry, free, sound, keen to work.

TEMPERAMENT Equable with no suggestion of timidity.

HEAD AND SKULL Well developed and rounded, neither flat nor domed. Eyebrows and stop clearly defined. Median line distinctly marked to rather more than half-way up crown. Area surrounding eye socket well chiselled. Distance from tip of nose to stop approximately one-half distance from stop up over crown to base of skull. Muzzle broad, deep, square, even jaws. Nose well developed. Nostrils black in black and tans, black or brown in buffs, browns, brown and tans, roans and parti-colours.

EYES Eyeballs round, full and looking directly forward. Shape of eye rims gives a slightly almond appearance. Neither weak nor goggled. Expression intelligent, alert, soft and appealing. Colour of iris dark brown to black in blacks, black and tans, buffs and creams, and in the darker shades of parti-colours and roans. In reds and browns, dark hazel; in parti-colours and roans of lighter shades, not lighter than hazel; the darker the better.

EARS Lobular, set-on line no higher than lower part of eyes, leather fine and extending to nostrils, well clothed with long silky, straight or wavy hair.

MOUTH Jaws strong with a perfect, regular and complete scissor bite, i.e. upper teeth closely overlapping lower teeth and set square to the jaws.

NECK Long, muscular and free from throatiness. Rising strongly and slightly arched.

FOREQUARTERS Shoulders deep, clean-cut and sloping without protrusion, so set that upper points of withers at an angle permitting wide spring of ribs. Forelegs straight, strongly boned and muscular, set close to body well under scapulae. Elbows well let down, turning neither in nor out. Pasterns short and strong.

BODY Height at withers approximating length from withers to set-on of tail. Chest deep. Lowest point no higher than elbows, front sufficiently wide for adequate heart and lung space, yet not so wide as to interfere with straight forward movement of forelegs. Ribs deep and well sprung throughout. Body short in couplings and flank, with depth at flank somewhat less than at last rib. Back strong, sloping evenly and slightly downwards from withers to set of tail. Hips wide with quarters well rounded and muscular. Body appearing short, compact and firmly knit together, giving impression of strength. Never appearing long and low.

HINDQUARTERS Strongly boned, muscled with good angulation at stifle and powerful, clearly defined thighs. Stifle joint strong without slippage. Hocks strong, well let down; when viewed from behind, hindlegs parallel when in motion or at rest.

FEET Compact, not spreading, round and firm, with deep, strong, tough pads and hair between toes; facing truly forward.

TAIL Customarily docked by three-fifths of tail. Set-on and carried on a line with topline of back or slightly higher, never straight up and never so low as to indicate timidity. When dog in motion merry tail action.

GAIT/MOVEMENT Co-ordinated, smooth and effortless, covering ground well.

COAT On head, short and fine; on body, medium length, with enough undercoating to give protection. Ears, chest, abdomen and legs well feathered, but not so excessive as to hide body lines or impede movement and function as a sporting dog. Texture most important. Coat silky, flat or slightly wavy. Excessive coat, curly, woolly or cotton texture undesirable.

COLOUR

BLACKS: Jet black; shadings of brown or liver in sheen of coat undesirable. Black and tan and brown and tan (classified under solid colours) having definite tan markings on jet black or brown body. Tan markings distinct and plainly visible and colour of tan may be from lightest cream to darkest red colour. Amount of tan markings restricted to ten per cent or less of colour of specimen; tan markings in excess of ten per cent undesirable. Tan markings not readily visible in ring or absence of tan markings in any of specified locations undesirable. Tan markings located as follows:

1. A clear spot over each eye.
2. On sides of muzzle and on cheeks.
3. On underside of ears.
4. On all feet and legs.
5. Under tail.
6. On chest, optional, presence or absence permissible.

Tan on muzzle which extends upwards and joins over muzzle highly undesirable. Any solid colour other than black of uniform shades. Lighter colouring of feathering permissible. In all above solid colours a small amount of white on chest and throat while not desirable, permissible, but white in any other location highly undesirable.

PARTI-COLOURS: Two or more definite colours appearing in clearly defined markings essential. Primary colour which is ninety per cent or more highly undesirable; secondary colour or colours which are limited solely to one location also highly undesirable. Roans are classified as parti-colours and may be of any usual roaning patterns. Tricolours, any of above colours combined with tan markings. Tan markings preferably located in same pattern as for black and tan.

SIZE Ideal height: (the word approximate leaves too much to chance) dogs: 36.25-38.75 cm (14¼-15¼ in); bitches: 33.75-36.25 cm (13¼-14¼ in).

FAULTS Any departure from the foregoing points should be considered a fault and the seriousness with which the fault should be regarded should be in exact proportion to its degree.

NOTE Male animals should have two apparently normal testicles fully descended into the scrotum.

CLUMBER SPANIEL

SAID TO HAVE COME IN THE FIRST PLACE from France over two hundred years ago, the Clumber was brought to Great Britain by the Duke of Newcastle, and bred at his family home of Clumber Park in Nottinghamshire.

It is obvious at a glance that he is a very heavy dog, and his pace of working is more leisurely than that of other Spaniels. He has been allowed to become ever heavier in the past fifty years or so, and though the top weight for dogs now stands at 36 kilograms (80 pounds), it would appear that some are in excess of even this figure.

His background colouring of plain white with lemon or orange markings, especially on head and ears, makes him an attractive dog, and his kind, steady nature complements his looks exactly. However, lovers of the breed should make certain that his great size does not encourage any weakness in his hindquarters.

He has an eye shape which permits the showing of a little haw, but this should never be excessive.

A delightful dog, he deserves greater popularity, happily lending himself to family life. He is a well-mannered companion.

GENERAL APPEARANCE Well balanced, heavily boned, active with a thoughtful expression, overall appearance denoting strength.

CHARACTERISTICS Stoical, great-hearted, highly intelligent with a determined attitude enhancing his natural ability. A silent worker with an excellent nose.

TEMPERAMENT Steady, reliable, kind and dignified; more aloof than other Spaniels, showing no tendency towards aggression.

HEAD AND SKULL Square, massive, medium length, broad on top with decided occiput; heavy brows; deep stop. Heavy, square muzzle with well developed flews. No exaggeration in head and skull.

EYES Clean, dark amber, slightly sunk, some haw showing but without excess. Full light eyes highly undesirable.

EARS Large, vine leaf-shaped, well covered with straight hair. Hanging slightly forward, feather not to extend below leather.

MOUTH Jaws strong, with a perfect, regular and complete scissor bite, i.e. upper teeth closely overlapping lower teeth and set square to the jaws.

NECK Fairly long, thick, powerful.

FOREQUARTERS Shoulders strong, sloping, muscular; legs short, straight, well boned, strong.

BODY Long, heavy, near to ground. Chest deep. Well sprung ribs. Back straight, broad, long. Muscular loin, well let down in flank.

HINDQUARTERS Very powerful and well developed. Hocks low, stifles well bent and set straight.

FEET Large, round, well covered with hair.

TAIL Set low, well feathered, carried level with back.

GAIT/MOVEMENT Rolling gait attributable to long body and short legs. Moving straight fore and aft, with effortless drive.

COAT Abundant, close, silky and straight. Legs and chest well feathered.

COLOUR Plain white body preferred, with lemon markings; orange permissible. Slight head markings and freckled muzzle.

SIZE Ideal weight: dogs: 36 kg (80 lb); bitches: 29.5 kg (65 lb).

FAULTS Any departure from the foregoing points should be considered a fault and the seriousness with which the fault should be regarded should be in exact proportion to its degree.

NOTE Male animals should have two apparently normal testicles fully descended into the scrotum.

COCKER SPANIEL

THE MOST POPULAR OF THE SPANIEL family, the Cocker is an active, happy, small dog, who quickly adapts himself to his surroundings. He is highly intelligent and affectionate, and is in his element foraging around fields and hedgerows. He also employs his retrieving instincts around the house, and can often be found with a toy or slipper in his mouth, his tail wagging furiously, waiting for praise.

He originated as the 'cocking spaniel', and derived this name from flushing woodcock. Easy to train – his main aim in life is to please his owner – he is a busy little dog who enjoys plenty of exercise, and thrives on human companionship.

As with a number of gundog breeds there is a difference between those used for work and those used for show. The show Cocker is a sturdier, heavier version of his work counterpart and is but one of a variety of spaniels divided because of their size and usefulness. Cockers were recognised as a separate breed from Field and Springer Spaniels soon after the formation of The Kennel Club in 1873.

GENERAL APPEARANCE Merry, sturdy, sporting; well balanced; compact; measuring approximately same from withers to ground as from withers to root of tail.

CHARACTERISTICS Merry nature with ever-wagging tail, shows a typical bustling movement, particularly when following scent, fearless of heavy cover.

TEMPERAMENT Gentle and affectionate, yet full of life and exuberance.

HEAD AND SKULL Square muzzle, with distinct stop set midway between tip of nose and occiput. Skull well developed, cleanly chiselled, neither too fine nor too coarse. Cheek bones not prominent. Nose sufficiently wide for acute scenting power.

EYES Full, but not prominent. Dark brown or brown, never light, but in the case of liver, liver roan and liver and white, dark hazel to harmonise with coat; with expression of intelligence and gentleness but wide awake, bright and merry; rims tight.

EARS Lobular, set low on a level with eyes. Fine leathers extending to nose tip. Well clothed with long, straight, silky hair.

MOUTH Jaws strong with a perfect, regular and complete scissor bite, i.e. upper teeth closely overlapping lower teeth and set square to the jaws.

NECK Moderate in length, muscular. Set neatly into fine sloping shoulders. Clean throat.

FOREQUARTERS Shoulders sloping and fine. Legs well boned, straight, sufficiently short for concentrated power. Not too short to interfere with tremendous exertions expected from this grand, sporting dog.

BODY Strong, compact. Chest well developed and brisket deep; neither too wide nor too narrow in front. Ribs well sprung. Loin short, wide with firm, level topline gently sloping downwards to tail from end of loin to set-on of tail.

HINDQUARTERS Wide, well rounded, very muscular. Legs well boned, good bend of stifle, short below hock, allowing for plenty of drive.

FEET Firm, thickly padded, cat-like.

TAIL Set-on slightly lower than line of back. Must be merry in action and carried level, never cocked up. Customarily docked but never too short to hide, nor too long to interfere with the incessant merry action when working.

GAIT/MOVEMENT True through action with great drive covering ground well.

COAT Flat, silky in texture, never wiry or wavy, not too profuse and never curly. Well feathered forelegs, body and hindlegs above hocks.

COLOUR Various. In self-colours no white allowed except on chest.

SIZE Height approximately: dogs 39–41 cm (15½–16 in); bitches: 38–39 cm (15–15½ in). Weight approximately: 12.75–14.5 kg (28–32 lb).

FAULTS Any departure from the foregoing points should be considered a fault and the seriousness with which the fault should be regarded should be in exact proportion to its degree.

NOTE Male animals should have two apparently normal testicles fully descended into the scrotum.

ENGLISH SPRINGER SPANIEL

THE NAME, 'SPRINGER', IS DERIVED from the use of this type of Spaniel to startle the birds into the air so that they spring upwards. The English Springer, with his black and white or liver and white markings, is the traditional dog for the rough-shooter – a dog capable of working tirelessly all day; ready to enter water even when he has to break ice to do it.

Like so many of the gundog breeds, his cheerful extrovert nature has endeared him to the general public, and he is in great demand as an energetic companion for a growing family. His thick coat is tough and weather-resistant, but like so many Spaniels his lengthy ear flaps need to be kept well trimmed if he is not to suffer from uninvited seeds and twigs getting inside the more sensitive depths of the ears themselves.

Official breed status was accorded the English Springer in 1902. He took his present name in 1900 after formerly being known for many years as the Norfolk Spaniel.

GENERAL APPEARANCE Symmetrically built, compact, strong, merry, active. Highest on leg and raciest in build of all British land Spaniels.

CHARACTERISTICS Breed is of ancient and pure origins, oldest of sporting gundogs; original purpose was finding and springing game for net, falcon or greyhound. Now used to find, flush and retrieve game for gun.

TEMPERAMENT Friendly, happy disposition, biddable. Timidity or aggression highly undesirable.

HEAD AND SKULL Skull of medium length, fairly broad, slightly rounded, rising from foreface, making a brow or stop, divided by fluting between eyes, dying away along forehead towards occipital bone which should not be prominent. Cheeks flat. Foreface of proportionate length to skull, fairly broad and deep, well chiselled below eyes, fairly deep and square in flew. Nostrils well developed.

EYES Medium size, almond-shaped, not prominent nor sunken, well set in (not showing haw), alert, kind expression. Dark hazel. Light eyes undesirable.

EARS Lobular, good length and width, fairly close to head, set in line with eye. Nicely feathered.

MOUTH Jaws strong, with a perfect, regular and complete scissor bite, i.e. upper teeth closely overlapping lower teeth and set square to the jaws.

NECK Good length, strong and muscular, free from throatiness, slightly arched, tapering towards head.

FOREQUARTERS Forelegs straight and well boned. Shoulders sloping and well laid. Elbows set well to body. Strong flexible pasterns.

BODY Strong, neither too long nor too short. Chest deep, well developed. Well sprung ribs. Loin muscular, strong with slight arch and well coupled.

HINDQUARTERS Hindlegs well let down. Stifles and hocks moderately bent. Thighs broad, muscular, well developed. Coarse hocks undesirable.

FEET Tight, compact, well rounded, with strong, full pads.

TAIL Set low, never carried above level of back. Well feathered with lively action. Customarily docked.

GAIT/MOVEMENT Strictly his own. Forelegs swing straight forward from shoulder, throwing feet well forward in an easy free manner. Hocks driving well under body, following in line with forelegs. At slow movement may have a pacing stride typical of this breed.

COAT Close, straight and weather-resisting, never coarse. Moderate feathering on ears, forelegs, body and hindquarters.

COLOUR Liver and white, black and white, or either of these colours with tan markings.

SIZE Approximate height: 51 cm (20 in).

FAULTS Any departure from the foregoing points should be considered a fault and the seriousness with which the fault should be regarded should be in exact proportion to its degree.

NOTE Male animals should have two apparently normal testicles fully descended into the scrotum.

FIELD SPANIEL

A PRODUCT OF CROSSING THE ONE-TIME Sussex Springer and the Cocker Spaniel in the late nineteenth century, the Field Spaniel is somewhat longer in the back than his height at the withers. His muzzle is long and lean, which gives him a characteristic appearance. He can be black, liver or roan with tan markings, and his coat has a high gloss of real quality.

It is interesting to note the very definite statement which his devotees have written into his breed standard to the effect that he is not suitable for the city.

Not a popular breed by modern standards, he makes a good companion for the country dweller. Twice the breed nearly disappeared, firstly when fashion fads all but ruined the breed in the early 1900s and, secondly, when in the 1950s breed numbers were so small that The Kennel Club withdrew championship status, this being restored in 1969 only after determined efforts by breeders to maintain the breed.

GENERAL APPEARANCE Well balanced, noble, upstanding sporting Spaniel built for activity and endurance.

CHARACTERISTICS Ideal for rough shooting or companion for the country dweller. Not suitable for city.

TEMPERAMENT Unusually docile, active, sensitive, independent.

HEAD AND SKULL Conveys the impression of high breeding, character and nobility. Well chiselled, occiput well defined, lean beneath eyes. A thickness here gives coarseness to whole head. Slightly raised eyebrows. Moderate stop. Nose well developed with good open nostrils. Muzzle long and lean, neither snipy nor squarely cut. In profile curving gradually from nose to throat.

EYES Wide open but almond-shaped with tight lids showing no haw. Grave and gentle in expression. Dark hazel in colour.

EARS Moderately long and wide, set low and well feathered.

MOUTH Jaws strong with a perfect, regular and complete scissor bite, i.e. upper teeth closely overlapping lower teeth and set square to the jaws.

NECK Long, strong and muscular enabling dog to retrieve his game without undue fatigue.

FOREQUARTERS Shoulders long and sloping and well laid back. Legs of moderate length. Straight, flat bone.

BODY Chest deep and well developed. Ribs moderately well sprung. Length of ribcage is two-thirds of the body length. Back and loin strong, level and muscular.

HINDQUARTERS Strong, muscular; stifles moderately bent. Hocks well let down.

ABOVE: *Field Spaniel by Margaret Collyer (fl. 1897–1910).*

FEET Tight, round with strong pads and not too small.

TAIL Set-on low and never carried above the level of the back. Nicely feathered, with lively action. Customarily docked by one-third.

GAIT/MOVEMENT Long, unhurried stride with great drive from the rear. Short, stumping action undesirable.

COAT Long, flat, glossy and silky in texture. Never curly, short or wiry. Dense and weatherproof. Abundant feathering on chest, under body and behind legs, but clean from hock to ground.

COLOUR Black, liver or roan. Any one of these with tan markings. In self-coloured dogs white or roan on chest permissible. Clear black/white or liver/white unacceptable.

SIZE Height: approximately 45.7 cm (18 in) at the shoulders. Weight: between 18-25 kg (40-55 lb).

FAULTS Any departure from the foregoing points should be considered a fault and the seriousness with which the fault should be regarded should be in exact proportion to its degree.

NOTE Male animals should have two apparently normal testicles fully descended into the scrotum.

IRISH WATER SPANIEL

THE TALLEST OF ALL THE SPANIELS, the Irish Water Spaniel is a breed of great antiquity. He delights in water, and is an admirable and enthusiastic retriever. He derives considerable intelligence from the Poodle, which has obviously played a significant part in his ancestry. Although tall, he is always well balanced. A dark liver in colour, his coat is composed of dense, tight ringlets, which cover every bit of him except his muzzle, the front of his neck and the major portion of his tail.

The Irish Water Spaniel is something of an enigma: although in Britain he is shown as a Spaniel he works in field trials as a retriever. The breed attracted attention when show classes were first put on for him at Birmingham in 1862.

He is blessed with an affectionate disposition, and a distinct sense of humour. He is not a big eater for his size, and makes both a good worker in the field, especially for a wildfowler, and a lovable family dog, revelling in all the exercise that is on offer.

GENERAL APPEARANCE Smart, upstanding, strongly built, compact.

CHARACTERISTICS Enduring, versatile gundog for all types of shooting, particularly in wildfowling.

TEMPERAMENT Initially aloof, staunch and affectionate; with an endearing sense of humour and a stable disposition.

HEAD AND SKULL Head of good size. Skull high in dome; of good length and width allowing adequate brain capacity. Muzzle long, strong, somewhat square with gradual stop. Face smooth, nose large and well developed, dark liver colour, overall an impression of fineness.

EYES Comparatively small, almond-shaped, medium to dark brown, intelligent and alert.

EARS Long, oval-shaped; set low, hanging close to cheeks.

MOUTH Jaws strong, with a perfect, regular and complete scissor bite, i.e. upper teeth closely overlapping lower teeth and set square to the jaws.

NECK Strongly set into shoulders, powerful, arching and long enough to carry the head well above level of back.

FOREQUARTERS Shoulders powerful and sloping; chest deep, reasonable width and curvature between forelegs. Forelegs well boned and straight.

BODY Ribs carried well back, so well sprung behind shoulder as to give a barrel shape. Back short, broad and level, strongly coupled to hindquarters. Loins deep and wide.

HINDQUARTERS Powerful; well angulated stifle and low-set hock.

FEET Large, round and spreading, well covered with hair over and between toes.

TAIL Short, not reaching to hock joint, straight, thick at root and tapering to a fine point. Low-set, straight and below level of back. 7.5-10 cm (3-4 in) of tail root covered by close curls which stop abruptly. The remainder bare or covered by short straight, fine hairs.

GAIT/MOVEMENT Moves freely and soundly, with reach and drive; characteristic rolling motion accentuated by barrel-shaped ribcage.

COAT On body, dense, tight, crisp ringlets, free from woolliness. Hair having natural oiliness. Forelegs covered down to feet with curls or ringlets. Abundant all round, though shorter in front. Below hocks, hindlegs should be smooth in front and with curls or ringlets behind down to feet. On skull covering of long curls forming a pronounced 'top-knot', growing in a well defined peak to a point between the eyes. Ears covered with long twisted curls. Neck covered with curls similar to those on body. Throat smooth, the smooth hair forming a V-shaped patch from back of lower jaw to breast bone.

COLOUR Rich, dark liver with purplish tint or bloom peculiar to the breed and sometimes referred to as puce-liver.

SIZE Height: dogs: 53-58 cm (21-23 in); bitches: 51-56 cm (20-22 in).

FAULTS Any departure from the foregoing points should be considered a fault and the seriousness with which the fault should be regarded should be in exact proportion to its degree.

NOTE Male animals should have two apparently normal testicles fully descended into the scrotum.

SUSSEX SPANIEL

A HEAVILY BUILT DOG WITH A RICH golden-liver coat which is abundant and flat, the Sussex Spaniel is an old breed of great substance. He is somewhat unusual among gundogs in that he tends to give tongue when working.

He has a wider head than many Spaniels, and his rather wrinkled brows give him a frowning look; but that is as far as the frown goes because he is a kindly dog as capable of being a family dog in a country household as he is of crashing his way through thick cover.

His mode of progression is characterised by a distinct roll, and, in fact, he does give the impression of being a loose-framed dog, but with massively boned limbs and powerful muscles.

This is another breed which deserves more general acclaim than has been his lot of recent years.

GENERAL APPEARANCE Massive, strongly built. Active, energetic dog, whose characteristic movement is a decided roll, and unlike that of any other Spaniel.

CHARACTERISTICS Natural working ability, gives tongue at work in thick cover.

TEMPERAMENT Kindly disposition, aggression highly undesirable.

HEAD AND SKULL Skull wide, showing moderate curve from ear to ear, neither flat nor apple-headed with centre indentation and a pronounced stop. Brows frowning; occiput decided, but not pointed. Nostrils well developed and liver in colour. Well balanced head.

EYES Hazel colour, fairly large, not full, but soft expression and not showing much haw.

EARS Thick, fairly large and lobular, set moderately low, just above eye level. Lying close to skull.

MOUTH Jaws strong, with a perfect, regular and complete scissor bite, i.e. upper teeth closely overlapping lower teeth and set square to the jaws.

NECK Long, strong, and slightly arched, not carrying head much above level of back. Slight throatiness, but well marked frill.

FOREQUARTERS Shoulders sloping and free; arms well boned and muscular. Knees large and strong, pasterns short and well boned. Legs rather short and strong.

BODY Chest deep and well developed; not too round and wide. Back and loin well developed and muscular in both width and depth. The back ribs must be deep. Whole body strong and level with no sign of waistlines from withers to hips.

HINDQUARTERS Thighs strongly boned and muscular; hocks large and strong, legs short and strong with good bone. Hindlegs not appearing shorter than forelegs or over angulated.

FEET Round, well padded, well feathered between toes.

TAIL Set low and never carried above level of back. Lively actioned. Customarily docked to a length of from 12.75-17.75 cm (5-7 in).

GAIT/MOVEMENT True fore and aft with distinctive roll.

COAT Abundant and flat with no tendency to curl and ample undercoat for weather resistance. Ears covered with soft, wavy hair, but not too profuse. Forequarters and hindquarters moderately well feathered. Tail thickly clothed with hair but not feathered.

COLOUR Rich golden liver and hair shading to golden at tip; gold predominating. Dark liver or puce undesirable.

SIZE Ideal height at withers 38–41 cm (15–16 in). Weight approximately 23 kg (50 lb).

FAULTS Any departure from the foregoing points should be considered a fault and the seriousness with which the fault should be regarded should be in exact proportion to its degree.

NOTE Male animals should have two apparently normal testicles fully descended into the scrotum.

WELSH SPRINGER SPANIEL

THERE IS OBVIOUSLY A FAMILY LIKENESS between the two breeds of Springer Spaniel but any suggestion that the Welsh originated from the English is liable to call down the wrath of the Principality on the speaker's head. The Welsh is somewhat smaller, and has a finer head, but his temperament is equally kindly, especially of latter years. His popularity has increased steadily, and he has become a favourite household dog in much the same fashion as other Spaniels.

Standardisation of the breed coincided with both that of the Cocker and the English Springer and, like the English Springer, the Welsh was recognised by The Kennel Club in 1902.

The rich, dark red of his coat on its white background appears to have become more and more striking in the same period. His proper purpose in life is to spring or 'start' game and his fame as a worker has, of right, spread from his homeland.

He is slightly lighter in build than the English Springer, and he is, if anything, easier to keep clean in wet weather.

ABOVE: *Champion Longmynd Myfanwy Spaniel and Champion Longmynd Megan painted in 1906 by Maud Earl. These litter sisters won numerous certificates.*

GENERAL APPEARANCE Symmetrical, compact, not leggy, obviously built for endurance and hard work. Quick and active mover, displaying plenty of push and drive.

CHARACTERISTICS Very ancient and distinct breed of pure origin. Strong, merry and very active.

TEMPERAMENT Kindly disposition, not showing aggression or nervousness.

HEAD AND SKULL Skull of proportionate length, slightly domed, clearly defined stop, well chiselled below eyes. Muzzle of medium length, straight, fairly square. Nostrils well developed, flesh-coloured to dark.

EYES Hazel or dark, medium size, not prominent, or sunken, or showing haw.

EARS Set moderately low and hanging close to cheeks. Comparatively small and gradually narrowing towards tip and shaped somewhat like a vine leaf.

MOUTH Jaws strong with a perfect, regular and complete scissor bite, i.e. upper teeth closely overlapping lower teeth and set square to the jaws.

NECK Long, muscular, clean in throat, neatly set into sloping shoulders.

FOREQUARTERS Forelegs of medium length, straight, well boned.

BODY Not long. Strong and muscular. Deep brisket, well sprung ribs. Length of body should be proportionate to length of leg. Loin muscular and slightly arched. Well coupled.

HINDQUARTERS Strong and muscular, wide and fully developed with deep second thighs. Hindlegs well boned, hocks well let down, stifles moderately angled, neither turning in nor out.

FEET Round, with thick pads. Firm and cat-like, not large or spreading.

TAIL Well set-on and low, never carried above level of back, customarily docked. Lively in action.

GAIT/MOVEMENT Smooth, powerful, ground-covering action; driving from rear.

COAT Straight or flat, silky texture, dense, never wiry or wavy. Curly coat highly undesirable. Forelegs and hindlegs above hocks moderately feathered, ears and tail lightly feathered.

COLOUR Rich red and white only.

SIZE Approximate height: dogs: 48 cm (19 in) at withers; bitches: 46 cm (18 in) at withers.

FAULTS Any departure from the foregoing points should be considered a fault and the seriousness with which the fault should be regarded should be in exact proportion to its degree.

NOTE Male animals should have two apparently normal testicles fully descended into the scrotum.

WEIMARANER

ANOTHER OF THE MULTI-PURPOSE Hunt, Point and Retrieve dogs from the Continent. Striking in his grey coloration and his light eyes, the Weimaraner has increased in popularity with the shooting fraternity. At the same time, he has moved into the companion animal realm where he finds a lot of friends. In his early days in Britain there were occasions where his temperament was somewhat stand-offish, but this is showing a definite improvement nowadays.

The Weimaraner is a tall, rangy dog somewhat larger than the other members of his group. The colours of his eyes, from shades of amber into blue-grey, are very different from the great majority of breeds, but they tone in with the very unusual grey of the short sleek coat. Grooming, as with most smooth-coated dogs, is relatively simple. There is a longer-coated variety with hair length up to 5 centimetres (2 inches), but this type has not become popular.

The powerful stride of a Weimaraner, like that in many thoroughbreds, gives those who recognise it a great deal of pleasure. The breed takes its name from the German court of Weimar, where it found much favour, and there is a Van Dyck painting of a dog of the Weimaraner type dated in the early 1600s though the depicted dog is more hound-like in appearance.

GENERAL APPEARANCE Medium-sized, grey with light eyes. Presents a picture of power, stamina and balance.

CHARACTERISTICS Hunting ability of paramount concern.

TEMPERAMENT Fearless, friendly, protective, obedient and alert.

HEAD AND SKULL Moderately long, aristocratic; moderate stop, slight median line extending back over forehead. Rather prominent occipital bone. Measurement from top of nose to stop equal to measurement from stop to occipital prominence. Flews moderately deep, enclosing powerful jaw. Foreface straight, and delicate at the nostrils. Skin tightly drawn. Nose grey.

EYES Medium-sized, round. Shades of amber or blue-grey. Placed far enough apart to indicate good disposition, not too protruding or deeply set. Expression keen, kind and intelligent.

EARS Long, lobular, slightly folded, set high. When drawn alongside jaw, should end approximately 2.5 cm (1 in) from point of nose.

MOUTH Jaws strong with a perfect, regular and complete scissor bite, i.e. upper teeth closely overlapping lower teeth and set square to the jaws. Lips and gums of pinkish, flesh colour. Complete dentition highly desirable.

NECK Clean-cut and moderately long.

FOREQUARTERS Forelegs straight and strong. Measurement from elbow to ground equal to distance from elbow to top of withers.

BODY Length of body from highest point of withers to roof of tail should equal the measurement from the highest point of withers to ground. Topline level, with slightly sloping croup. Chest well developed, deep. Shoulders well laid. Ribs well sprung, ribcage extending well back. Abdomen firmly held, moderately tucked-up flank. Brisket should drop to elbow.

HINDQUARTERS Moderately angulated, with well turned stifle. Hocks well let down, turned neither in nor out. Musculation well developed.

FEET Firm, compact. Toes well arched, pads close, thick. Nails short, grey or amber in colour. Dewclaws customarily removed.

TAIL Customarily docked so that remaining tail covers scrotum in dogs and vulva in bitches. Thickness of tail in proportion to body, and should be carried in a manner expressing confidence and sound temperament. In long-haired, tip of tail may be removed.

GAIT/MOVEMENT Effortless, ground covering, indicating smooth co-ordination. Seen from rear, hindfeet parallel to front feet. Seen from side, topline remains strong and level.

COAT Short, smooth and sleek. In long-haired variety, coat from 2.5-5 cm (1-2 in) long on body, somewhat longer on neck, chest and belly. Tail and back of limbs, feathered.

COLOUR Preferably silver grey, shades of mouse or roe grey permissible; blending to lighter shade on head and ears. Dark eel stripe frequently occurs along back. Whole coat gives an appearance of metallic sheen. Small white mark permissible on chest. White spots resulting from injuries not penalised.

SIZE Height at withers: dogs: 61-69 cm (24-27 in); bitches: 56-64 cm (22-25 in).

FAULTS Any departure from the foregoing points should be considered a fault and the seriousness with which the fault should be regarded should be in exact proportion to its degree.

NOTE Male animals should have two apparently normal testicles fully descended into the scrotum.

BELOW: The Pick of the Kennel *by Arthur Wardle (1864–1949) depicts a West Highland White Terrier, a Scottish Terrier and a Cairn Terrier. In the nineteenth century West Highland White and Cairn Terriers were exhibited in classes for Scottish Terriers at dog shows.*

TERRIER GROUP

AIREDALE TERRIER

THE AIREDALE IS ALSO KNOWN AS THE King of Terriers: he is the largest of all the terrier breeds and encompasses all the characteristics of this group of dogs. A native of Great Britain, from the county of Yorkshire, it is reputed that the Airedale Show gave the breed its name. Many 'Waterside Terriers' from the valleys of the rivers Wharfe, Calder and Aire were exhibited at this show, making up a large entry.

He is an excellent family dog, particularly good with children and always ready to join in their games. Not aggressive by nature but protective of his family, he is a devoted companion ready for a walk at any time or even a ride in the car. His double coat is waterproof and a daily brush and comb will keep him looking smart. However, he will shed his coat twice a year and on these occasions it is advisable to have him professionally stripped. Provided he has daily exercise he is suitable for either town or country life.

The Airedale has remarkable scenting powers and has been used in Africa, India and Canada for tracking, has aided the Red Cross in times of war and has seen service with police and in the armed forces of both Britain and Russia.

GENERAL APPEARANCE Largest of the Terriers, a muscular, active, fairly cobby dog, without suspicion of legginess or undue length of body.

CHARACTERISTICS Keen of expression, quick of movement, on the tiptoe of expectation at any movement. Character denoted and shown by expression of eyes, and by carriage of ears and erect tail.

TEMPERAMENT Outgoing and confident, friendly, courageous and intelligent. Alert at all times, not aggressive but fearless.

HEAD AND SKULL Skull long and flat, not too broad between ears, and narrowing slightly to eyes. Well balanced, with no apparent difference in length between skull and foreface. Free from wrinkles, with stop hardly visible; cheeks level and free from fullness. Foreface well filled up before eyes, not dish-faced or falling away quickly below eyes, but a delicate chiselling prevents appearance of wedginess or plainness. Upper and lower jaws deep, powerful, strong and muscular, as strength of foreface is greatly desired. No excess development of the jaws to give a rounded or bulging appearance to the cheeks, as 'cheekiness' is undesirable. Lips tight, nose black.

EYES Dark in colour, small, not prominent, full of terrier expression, keenness and intelligence. Light or bold eye highly undesirable.

EARS V-shaped with a side carriage, small but not out of proportion to size of dog. Top line of folded ear slightly above level of skull. Pendulous ears or ears set too high undesirable.

MOUTH Teeth strong. Jaws strong. Scissor bite, i.e. upper teeth closely overlapping lower teeth and set square to the jaws preferable, but vice-like bite acceptable. An overshot or undershot mouth undesirable.

NECK Clean, muscular, of moderate length and thickness, gradually widening towards shoulders, and free from throatiness.

FOREQUARTERS Shoulders long, well laid back, sloping obliquely, shoulder blades flat. Forelegs perfectly straight, with good bone. Elbows perpendicular to body, working free of sides.

BODY Back short, strong, straight and level, showing no slackness. Loins muscular. Ribs well sprung. In short-coupled and well ribbed-up dogs there is little space between ribs and hips. When dog is long in couplings some slackness will be shown here. Chest deep (i.e. approximately level with elbows) but not broad.

HINDQUARTERS Thighs long and powerful with muscular second thigh, stifles well bent, turned neither in nor out. Hocks well let down, parallel with each other when viewed from behind.

FEET Small, round and compact, with a good depth of pad, well cushioned, and toes moderately arched, turning neither in nor out.

TAIL Set-on high and carried gaily, not curled over back. Good strength and substance. Customarily docked. Tip approximately at the same height as top of skull.

GAIT/MOVEMENT Legs carried straight forward. Forelegs move freely, parallel to the sides. When approaching, forelegs should form a continuation of the straight line of the front, feet being same distance apart as elbows. Propulsive power is furnished by hindlegs.

COAT Hard, dense and wiry, not so long as to appear ragged. Lying straight and close, covering body and legs; outer coat hard, wiry and stiff, undercoat shorter and softer. Hardest coats are crinkling or just slightly waved; curly or soft coat highly undesirable.

COLOUR Body saddle black or grizzle as is top of the neck and top surface of tail. All other parts tan. Ears often a darker tan, and shading may occur round neck and side of skull. A few white hairs between forelegs acceptable.

SIZE Height about 58-61 cm (23-24 in) for dogs, taken from top of shoulder, and bitches about 56-59 cm (22-23 in).

FAULTS Any departure from the foregoing points should be considered a fault and the seriousness with which the fault should be regarded should be in exact proportion to its degree.

NOTE Male animals should have two apparently normal testicles fully descended into the scrotum.

AUSTRALIAN TERRIER

HIS ORIGINS IN AUSTRALIA ARE SAID TO have been along similar lines to the Australian Silky Terrier, from the Toy Group, and to have been developed in the nineteenth century by Australians using native British terrier breeds. The likely antecedents of the Australian Terrier are Scottish and North of England terriers taken out by early settlers.

The Australian Terrier gained approval in Britain in 1936 and is a cheerful, lively little dog.

He is smart, but with a rugged 'hard-bitten' appearance, partly derived from the expression and size of his dark, keen eyes. He has a 'ready for anything' approach to life and enjoys exercise and plenty of play. He makes a good house-dog, and is watchful and vociferous at the approach of strangers.

The Australian Terrier is a very popular breed in the country from which he derives his name, and comes in two distinct colours – blue and tan, and all red. As puppies the blue and tan often carry a blue-black coat, which changes in colour when the puppy is about nine months old. The 'Aussie' is a good all-round family dog.

GENERAL APPEARANCE A sturdy low-set dog rather long in proportion to height. Untrimmed, harsh coat with definite ruff around neck extending to breast bone, assists hard bitten and rugged appearance.

CHARACTERISTICS Strong terrier character; alertness, activity and soundness. Essentially a working terrier, it is equally suited as a

companion dog owing to its loyalty and even disposition.

TEMPERAMENT Friendly, extrovert, obedient and anxious to please. Lives happily in town or country. Not aggressive but courageous if attacked.

HEAD AND SKULL Head long with flat skull of moderate width, full between eyes, with slight but definite stop. Muzzle strong but powerful, of equal length to that of skull, which should be covered with a soft, silky 'top-knot'. Nose black, of moderate size, leather extending to bridge of muzzle.

EYES Small with keen expression and of dark brown colour, set well apart and not prominent.

EARS Small, erect, pointed, well carried, set-on moderately wide, free from long hair and sensitive in their use (puppies under six months excepted).

MOUTH Jaws strong and punishing, scissor bite, i.e. upper teeth closely overlapping lower teeth and set square to the jaws.

NECK Long, slightly arched, shapely and strong, blending into long, well laid shoulders.

FOREQUARTERS Forelegs well boned and perfectly straight, parallel when viewed from front. Pasterns strong without slope, slightly feathered to knee.

BODY Long in proportion to height, strongly constructed, with well sprung ribs and chest of moderate depth and width. Level topline. Loins strong. Flanks deep.

HINDQUARTERS Moderate length of quarters, broad with strong muscular thighs, stifles well turned and hocks well bent and let down. Viewed from behind, parallel, neither too wide nor too close.

FEET Small, well padded, toes closely knit and moderately arched, turned neither in nor out, with strong black or dark toenails.

TAIL Customarily docked, set high, and carried erect, but not over back.

GAIT/MOVEMENT Free, springy and forceful. When viewed from front, forelegs move truly without looseness of shoulder, elbows or pasterns. Hindquarters have drive and power, with free movement of stifles and hocks. Seen from rear, legs from hocks to ground parallel, neither too close nor too wide.

COAT Body coat consists of harsh, straight, dense top coat, approximately 6.35 cm (2½ in) long with short, soft-textured undercoat. Muzzle, lower legs and feet free from hair.

COLOUR
a) Blue, steel blue or dark grey blue, with rich tan (not sandy) on face, ears, under body, lower legs and feet and around the vent (puppies excepted). The richer the colour and more clearly defined the better. 'Top-knot' blue or silver of a lighter shade than head colour.
 b) Clear sandy or red, smuttiness or dark shading undesirable. 'Top-knot' a lighter shade.

SIZE Height: approx 25.5 cm (10 in) at withers. Weight: approx 6.34 kg (14 lb).

FAULTS Any departure from the foregoing points should be considered a fault and the seriousness with which the fault should be regarded should be in exact proportion to its degree.

NOTE Male animals should have two apparently normal testicles fully descended into the scrotum.

BEDLINGTON TERRIER

THIS UNIQUE BREED HAS A LAMB-LIKE look about it, but don't be fooled, he is a terrier through and through. A North Country dog, originally his role was to catch rabbits for the family pot, and a sporting dog he still remains.

It is claimed that the Bedlington can boast a longer traceable pedigree than any other terrier and once was known as the Rothbury Terrier, hailing from the former mining areas of the North of England. His fame spread outside his native region and an association was started for the breed in 1877.

One of the features peculiar to this breed is the coat which is described as 'linty', and his neat outline does require regular trimming. Although his expression is mild he is quite capable of fending for himself, but will not seek a scrap. He is a tough little dog, good in the house, and makes a delightful family pet.

GENERAL APPEARANCE A graceful, lithe, muscular dog, with no signs of either weakness or coarseness. Whole head pear or wedge-shaped, and expression in repose mild and gentle.

CHARACTERISTICS Spirited and game, full of confidence. An intelligent companion with strong sporting instincts.

TEMPERAMENT Good-tempered, having an affectionate nature, dignified, not shy or nervous. Mild in repose but full of courage when roused.

HEAD AND SKULL Skull narrow, but deep and rounded; covered with profuse silky 'top-knot' which should be nearly white. Jaw long and tapering. There must be no 'stop', the line from occiput to nose end straight and unbroken. Well filled up beneath eye, close fitting lips, without flew. Nostrils large and well defined.

EYES Small, bright and deep-set. Ideal eye has appearance of being triangular. Blues a dark eye; blue and tans have lighter eye with amber lights, livers and sandies a light hazel eye.

EARS Moderately sized, filbert-shaped, set-on low, and hanging flat to cheek. Thin and velvety in texture; covered with short fine hair with fringe of whitish silky hair at tip.

MOUTH Teeth large and strong. Scissor bite, i.e. upper teeth closely overlapping lower teeth and set square to the jaws.

NECK Long and tapering, deep base with no tendency to throatiness. Springs well up from shoulders, and head carried rather high.

FOREQUARTERS Forelegs straight, wider apart at chest than at feet. Pasterns long and slightly sloping without weakness. Shoulders flat and sloping.

BODY Muscular and markedly flexible. Chest deep and fairly broad. Flat ribbed, deep through brisket which reaches to elbow. Back has natural arch over loin creating a definite tuck-up of underline. Body slightly greater in length than height.

HINDQUARTERS Muscular and moderate length, arched loin with curved topline immediately above loins. Hindlegs have appearance of being longer than forelegs. Hocks strong and well let down, turning neither in nor out.

FEET Long harefeet with thick and well closed up pads.

TAIL Moderate length, thick at root, tapering to a point and gracefully curved. Set-on low, never carried over back.

GAIT/MOVEMENT Capable of galloping at high speed and have appearance of being able to do

so. Action very distinctive, rather mincing, light and springy in slower paces and slight roll when in full stride.

COAT Very distinctive. Thick and linty, standing well out from skin, but not wiry. A distinct tendency to twist, particularly on head and face.

COLOUR Blue, liver or sandy with or without tan. Darker pigment to be encouraged. Blues and blue and tans must have black noses; livers and sandies must have brown noses.

SIZE Height: about 41 cm (16 in) at withers. This allows for slight variation below in the case of a bitch and above in the case of a dog. Weight: 8.2–10.4 kg (18–23 lb).

FAULTS Any departure from the foregoing points should be considered a fault and the seriousness with which the fault should be regarded should be in exact proportion to its degree.

NOTE Male animals should have two apparently normal testicles fully descended into the scrotum.

BORDER TERRIER

Looking at a typical border terrier one gets the impression that if nature were left to itself and dogs just bred naturally without man selecting the matings, the end result would be something very much along this dog's lines. In fact he's just the sort of dog one would expect to have his origins in the border between England and Scotland.

The breed standard is terse and to the point; it outlines exactly the qualities which are required for a dog that is expected to go to ground after a fox. He needs a powerful pair of jaws, good bone but not heavy, and a chest which is not too wide for him to get out of any earth he enters. He also needs to have the stamina to keep up with a horse, in order that he will be there when he's needed. He is basically a worker, but is perfectly capable of being an active member of a family, having a temperament which combines good nature with a terrier's gameness.

The Border was once known as the Reedwater or the Coquetdale Terrier, after the localities of his early days. His present name was adopted around 1880, probably because he was worked with the Border Foxhounds. But it was forty more years before the breed was recognised by The Kennel Club, in 1920.

GENERAL APPEARANCE Essentially a working terrier.

CHARACTERISTICS Capable of following a horse, combining activity with gameness.

TEMPERAMENT Active and game as previously stated.

HEAD AND SKULL Head like that of an otter but moderately broad in skull, with short, strong muzzle. Black nose preferable, but liver- or flesh-coloured one not a serious fault.

EYES Dark with a keen expression.

EARS Small, V-shaped; of moderate thickness, and dropping forward close to the cheek.

MOUTH Scissor bite, i.e. upper teeth closely overlapping lower teeth and set square to the jaws. Level bite acceptable. Undershot or overshot a major fault and highly undesirable.

NECK Of moderate length.

FOREQUARTERS Forelegs straight, not too heavy in bone.

BODY Deep, narrow, fairly long. Ribs carried well back, but not oversprung, as a terrier should be capable of being spanned by both hands behind the shoulder. Loins strong.

HINDQUARTERS Racy

FEET Small with thick pads.

TAIL Moderately short; fairly thick at base, then tapering. Set high, carried gaily, but not curled over back.

GAIT/MOVEMENT Has the soundness to follow a horse.

COAT Harsh and dense; with close undercoat. Skin must be thick.

COLOUR Red, wheaten, grizzle and tan, or blue and tan.

SIZE Weight: dogs: 5.9-7.1 kg (13-15½ lb); bitches: 5.1-6.4 kg (11½-14 lb).

FAULTS Any departure from the foregoing points should be considered a fault and the seriousness with which the fault should be regarded should be in exact proportion to its degree and its effect on the terrier's ability to work.

NOTE Male animals should have two apparently normal testicles fully descended into the scrotum.

BULL TERRIER

NO ONE COULD MISTAKE A BULL Terrier for anything else. He stands on firm, powerful legs, staring straight at you, built on lines reminiscent of the bull from which his name is partly derived. But for all his somewhat forbidding presence, he is in fact a kindly chap, loving the human race, even if he is none too sure about his attitude to the dog next door. Handled properly he will live in peace with his neighbour but he does need a firm hand if he is to fit effectively into modern civilisation.

It was a certain James Hinks who first standardised the breed type in the 1850s, selecting the egg-shaped head. The breed was first shown in its present form at Birmingham in 1862. The Bull Terrier Club was formed in 1887.

Most people would regard him as being basically white all over, with an occasional piratical patch over one eye, but he does come in other hues, including brindle, red, fawn and tricolour.

The truly interesting thing about him is that his standard says quite deliberately, 'There are neither weight nor height limits, but there should be the impression of maximum substance for size of dog consistent with quality and sex'.

GENERAL APPEARANCE Strongly built, muscular, well balanced and active with a keen, determined and intelligent expression.

CHARACTERISTICS The Bull Terrier is the gladiator of the canine race, full of fire and courageous. A unique feature is a downfaced, egg-shaped head. Irrespective of size, dogs should look masculine and bitches feminine.

TEMPERAMENT Of even temperament and amenable to discipline. Although obstinate, is particularly good with people.

HEAD AND SKULL Head long, strong and deep right to end of muzzle, but not coarse. Viewed from front egg-shaped and completely filled, its surface free from hollows or indentations. Top of skull almost flat from ear to ear. Profile curves gently downwards from top of skull to tip of nose which should be black and bent downwards at tip. Nostrils well developed and under-jaw deep and strong.

EYES Appearing narrow, obliquely placed and triangular, well sunken, black or as dark brown as possible so as to appear almost black, and with a piercing glint. Distance from tip of nose to eyes perceptibly greater than that from eyes to top of skull. Blue or partly blue undesirable.

EARS Small, thin and placed close together. Dog should be able to hold them stiffly erect, when they point straight upwards.

MOUTH Teeth sound, clean, strong, of good size, regular with perfect, regular and complete scissor bite, i.e. upper teeth closely overlapping lower teeth and set square to the jaws. Lips clean and tight.

NECK Very muscular, long, arched, tapering from shoulders to head and free from loose skin.

FOREQUARTERS Shoulders strong and muscular without loading. Shoulder blades wide, flat and held closely to chest wall and have a very pronounced backward slope of front edge from bottom to top, forming almost a right angle with upper arm. Elbows held straight and strong, pasterns upright. Forelegs have strongest type of round, quality bone, dog should stand solidly upon them and they should be perfectly parallel. In mature dogs length of foreleg should be approximately equal to depth of chest.

BODY Body well rounded with marked spring of rib and great depth from withers to brisket, so that latter nearer ground than belly. Back short,

strong with backline behind withers level, arching or roaching slightly over broad, well muscled loins. Underline from brisket to belly forms a graceful upward curve. Chest broad when viewed from front.

HINDQUARTERS Hindlegs in parallel when viewed from behind. Thighs muscular and second thighs well developed. Stifle joint well bent and hock well angulated with bone to foot short and strong.

FEET Round and compact with well arched toes.

TAIL Short, set-on low and carried horizontally. Thick at root, it tapers to a fine point.

GAIT/MOVEMENT When moving appears well knit, smoothly covering ground with free, easy strides and with a typical jaunty air. When trotting, movement parallel, front and back, only converging towards centre line at faster speeds, forelegs reaching out well and hindlegs moving smoothly at hip, flexing well at stifle and hock, with great thrust.

COAT Short, flat, even and harsh to touch with a fine gloss. Skin fitting dog tightly. A soft textured undercoat may be present in winter.

COLOUR For White, pure white coat. Skin pigmentation and markings on head not to be penalised. For Coloured, colour predominates; all other things being equal, brindle preferred. Black, brindle, red, fawn and tricolour acceptable. Tick markings in white coat undesirable. Blue and liver highly undesirable.

SIZE There are neither weight nor height limits, but there should be the impression of maximum substance for size of dog consistent with quality and sex.

FAULTS Any departure from the foregoing points should be considered a fault and the seriousness with which the fault should be regarded should be in exact proportion to its degree.

NOTE Male animals should have two apparently normal testicles fully descended into the scrotum.

MINIATURE BULL TERRIER

THE STANDARD is the same as that of the Bull Terrier with the exception of the following:

SIZE Height should not exceed 35.5 cm (14 in). There should be an impression of substance to size of dog. There is no weight limit. Dog should at all times be balanced.

CAIRN TERRIER

SCOTTISH IN ANCESTRY, THIS SMALL, sturdy terrier is in every way a game little dog. He is very natural with a slightly shaggy, but not unkempt, appearance, and his double waterproof coat takes very little effort to look after. He has a particularly expressive head set off by dark, sparkling eyes which give a good indication of his character. With his small prick ears and shaggy eyebrows his expression can change from mischievousness to one of gentle devotion very quickly.

He loves people, is an able swimmer and a great hunter. Ready for any activity, he makes an ideal companion for a family, fitting in well with any lifestyle.

The first time a dog of this breed was exhibited was in 1909 and three years later the Cairn was recognised by The Kennel Club with challenge certificates on offer. Yet, in spite of this comparatively recent emergence in our showring, dogs of the Cairn type can be traced back some five hundred years and the breed's development runs parallel with that of the Skye, West Highland White and Scottish Terriers. In fact, when first exhibited in 1909, it was known as the Short-haired Skye Terrier.

GENERAL APPEARANCE Agile, alert, of work-manlike, natural appearance. Standing well forward on forepaws. Strong quarters. Deep in rib, very free in movement. Weather-resistant coat.

CHARACTERISTICS Should impress as being active, game and hardy.

TEMPERAMENT Fearless and gay disposition; assertive but not aggressive.

HEAD AND SKULL Head small, but in proportion to body. Skull broad; a decided indentation between the eyes with a definite stop. Muzzle powerful, jaw strong but not long or heavy. Nose black. Head well furnished.

EYES Wide apart, medium in size, dark hazel. Slightly sunk with shaggy eyebrows.

EARS Small, pointed, well carried and erect, not too closely set nor heavily coated.

MOUTH Large teeth. Jaws strong, with perfect, regular and complete scissor bite, i.e. upper teeth closely overlapping lower teeth and set square to the jaws.

NECK Well set-on, not short.

FOREQUARTERS Sloping shoulders, medium length of leg, good but not too heavy bone. Forelegs never out at elbow. Legs covered with harsh hair.

BODY Back level, medium length. Well sprung deep ribs; strong supple loin.

HINDQUARTERS Very strong muscular thighs. Good, but not excessive, bend of stifle. Hocks well let down inclining neither in nor out when viewed from the rear.

FEET Forefeet larger than hind, may be slightly turned out. Pads thick and strong. Thin, narrow or spreading feet and long nails objectionable.

TAIL Short, balanced, well furnished with hair but not feathery. Neither high nor low set, carried gaily but not turned down towards back.

GAIT/MOVEMENT Very free-flowing stride. Forelegs reaching well forward. Hindlegs giving strong propulsion. Hocks neither too close nor too wide.

COAT Very important. Weather-resistant. Must be double-coated, with profuse, harsh, but not coarse, outer coat; undercoat short, soft and close. Open coats objectionable. Slight wave permissible.

COLOUR Cream, wheaten, red, grey or nearly black. Brindling in all these colours acceptable. Not solid black, or white, or black and tan. Dark points, such as ears and muzzle, very typical.

SIZE Approx 28-31 cm (11-12 in) at withers, but in proportion to weight – ideally 6-7.5 kg (14-16 lb).

FAULTS Any departure from the foregoing points should be considered a fault and the seriousness with which the fault should be regarded should be in exact proportion to its degree.

NOTE Male animals should have two apparently normal testicles fully descended into the scrotum.

CESKY TERRIER

(INTERIM)

TERRIER

144

THE NATIONAL DOG OF THE CZECH Republic, the Ceski ('sesk-i') is a gentle character for a terrier breed. He stands as tall as 35.5 centimetres (14 inches) at the withers and is slightly longer in the back than he is high.

He requires regular trimming of his somewhat silky coat along back and body, especially if he is to be an inmate of a family household. Well-groomed, his black, grey or silver coat can exhibit a well-shone look.

He is non-aggressive and somewhat chary of strangers, but is relatively biddable as a companion. He has only been registered in the United Kingdom since 1990, so is not available in numbers as yet, but could become popular.

GENERAL APPEARANCE A sturdy low-set dog, rather long in proportion to height.

CHARACTERISTICS Very agile working terrier, hardy and tough, plenty of stamina.

TEMPERAMENT Not aggressive, friendly and companionable.

HEAD AND SKULL Relatively long. Skull slightly arched; slight but distinct stop. Head forms a blunt, long, but not too broad triangle when viewed from above. Nostrils large. Nose black in grey-blue dogs; liver in light brown dogs.

EYES Medium-sized, rather deep-set, friendly. In blue-grey dogs – black or brown; in light brown dogs – light to dark brown.

EARS Medium size, triangular, high-set, pendulous, carried close to cheeks.

MOUTH Perfect, regular and complete scissor bite, i.e. upper teeth closely overlapping lower teeth and set square to the jaws.

NECK Medium long, slightly arched and powerful. Slightly loose skin at throat.

FOREQUARTERS Muscular, well laid shoulders. Elbows free moving. Forelegs straight, strong-boned.

BODY Medium long. Level back, slight rise over the loins. Brisket more rounded than deep. Ideal chest circumference 40-45 cm (15½-17½ in). Ribs well-sprung. Loins long, broad and muscular. Moderate tuck-up.

HINDQUARTERS Strong, muscular upper thighs, short lower thighs. High-set, strongly developed hock. Hind legs stand parallel.

FEET Round, arched and well padded. Forefeet larger than hindfeet.

TAIL Long, medium-set. At rest, hangs with tip slightly raised. Carried slightly upwards when dog is moving.

GAIT/MOVEMENT Propulsive movement. Brisk and vigorous with plenty of drive. Parallel movement fore and aft.

COAT Wavy with silky sheen. Clipped except on upper part of head, legs, ribcage and belly. Eyebrows prominent. Transition between clipped and unclipped must be gradual. Hair on back and neck should be no more than 1.5 cm (½ in) long.

COLOUR Grey-blue or light brown. Yellow and grey markings allowed on cheeks, underside of muzzle, neck, breast, lower parts of legs and under tail. White collar or tail tip permissible. Skin on grey-blue dog – grey; on light brown dog – flesh-coloured.

SIZE Height: 28-35.5 cm (11-14 in).
Ideal weight: dogs: 8 kg (17½ lb); bitches: 7 kg (15½ lb).

FAULTS Any departure from the foregoing points should be considered a fault and the seriousness with which the fault should be regarded should be in exact proportion to its degree.

NOTE Male animals should have two apparently normal testicles fully descended into the scrotum.

DANDIE DINMONT TERRIER

THOSE WHO HAVE READ SIR WALTER Scott's *Guy Mannering* will recognise the name Dandie Dinmont. This fictional character gave the breed its name. The colours by which these dogs are known, mustard and pepper, were adopted from the names of Mannering's dogs. The Dandie looks sedate but can move extraordinarily quickly. He is a most intelligent chap with a will of his own, and he is not the most obedient of pets.

Devoted to children, he can melt the hardest of hearts with his soulful expression and enjoys, and asks for, plenty of attention.

The breed comes from the same root stock as many others from the north of England and the borders between England and Scotland. The Dandie was developed in the 1600s for badger and otter hunting.

GENERAL APPEARANCE Distinctive head with beautiful silky covering, with large, wise, intelligent eyes offsetting long, low, weaselly body. Short, strong legs; weatherproof coat.

CHARACTERISTICS Game, workmanlike terrier.

TEMPERAMENT Independent, highly intelligent, determined, persistent, sensitive, affectionate and dignified.

HEAD AND SKULL Head strongly made, large but in proportion to dog's size, muscles showing extraordinary development, especially the maxillary. Skull broad, narrowing towards eye, measuring about the same from inner corner of eye to back of skull, as from ear to ear. Forehead well domed; head covered with very soft, silky hair not confined to mere 'top-knot'. Cheeks gradually tapering towards deep and strongly made muzzle. Muzzle in proportion to skull as three is to five. Top of muzzle has triangular bare patch pointing backwards to eyes from nose about an inch broad. Nose black.

EYES Rich dark hazel; set wide apart and low, large, bright, full and round but not protruding.

EARS Pendulous, set well back, wide apart, low on skull, hanging close to cheeks with very slight projection at base; broad at junction of head and tapering almost to a point, fore part of ear coming almost straight down from its junction with head to tip. Cartilage and skin of ear very thin. Length of ear, from 7.5-10 cm (3-4 in). Ears harmonise in colour with body colour. In a pepper dog, covered with soft, straight, dark hair (in some cases almost black). In a mustard dog, hair mustard in colour, a shade darker than body but not black. Both should have a thin feather of light hair starting about 5 cm (2 in) from the tip, and of nearly the same colour and texture as 'top-knot', giving ear appearance of a distinct point. This may not appear until after the age of two years.

MOUTH Jaws strong with a perfect, regular and complete scissor bite, i.e. upper teeth closely overlapping lower teeth and set square to the jaws. Any deviation highly undesirable. Teeth very strong, especially canines which are extraordinary in size for a small dog. Canines fit well against each other, to give greatest available holding and punishing power. Inside of mouth black or dark-coloured.

NECK Very muscular, well developed and strong, showing great power. Well set into shoulders.

FOREQUARTERS Shoulders well laid back but not heavy. Forelegs short with immense muscular development and bone, set wide apart and chest coming well down between them. Forearms to follow line of chest with feet pointing forward or slightly outward when standing. Bandy legs highly undesirable.

BODY Long, strong and flexible; ribs well sprung and round, chest well developed and well let down between forelegs; back rather low at shoulders having slight downward curve and corresponding arch over loins, slight gradual drop from top of loin to root of tail. Backbone well muscled.

HINDQUARTERS Hindlegs a little longer than forelegs; set rather wide apart, but not spread out in an unnatural manner; thighs well developed. Stifles angulated, hocks well let down. Dewclaws, if present, customarily removed.

FEET Round and well padded. Hindfeet smaller than forefeet. Nails dark but varying in shade according to colour of body. Flat or open feet highly undesirable.

TAIL Rather short from 20-25 cm (8-10 in), rather thick at root, getting thicker for about 10 cm (4 in) and tapering off to a point. Not twisted or curled in any way but with a curve like a scimitar, the tip when excited being in a perpendicular line with root of tail, set neither too high nor too low. When not excited carried gaily a little above body level.

GAIT/MOVEMENT Strong, straight impulsion from rear, giving a fluent free and easy stride, reaching forward at the front. A stiff, stilted, hopping or weaving gait highly undesirable.

COAT Very important feature of the breed. Double coat with a soft linty undercoat and a harder top coat, not wiry but giving a crisp feel to the hand. The coat should not 'shed' down the back, but should lie in pencils caused by the harder hair coming through the softer undercoat. The forelegs have feather about 5 cm

(2 in) long. Upper side of tail covered with wiry hair, underside not so wiry with neat feathering of softer hair.

COLOUR Pepper or mustard.
PEPPER: Ranges from dark bluish black to light silvery grey; intermediate shades preferred. Body colour coming well down shoulder and hips gradually merging into colour of legs and feet which varies according to body colour from rich tan to pale fawn. Profuse silvery white 'top-knot'.
MUSTARD: Varies from reddish brown to pale fawn. Profuse creamy white 'top-knot', legs and feet of darker shade than head.

In both colours feather on forelegs rather lighter than hair on fore part of leg. Some white hair on chest and white nails permissible. White feet undesirable. Hair on underside of tail lighter than on upper side which should be darker colour than body.

SIZE Weight: 8-11 kg (18-24 lb) for dogs in good working condition. The lower weights preferred.

FAULTS Any departure from the foregoing points should be considered a fault and the seriousness with which the fault should be regarded should be in exact proportion to its degree.

NOTE Male animals should have two apparently normal testicles fully descended into the scrotum.

SMOOTH FOX TERRIER

THE FOX TERRIER IN BOTH FORMS, Smooth and Wire, is known throughout the world but is from British origins and probably owes its existence to the same types of dog which produced both the Bull Terrier and the Black and Tan (now Manchester) Terrier. Uniformity of type was established in the late 1800s and the original standard for the Fox Terrier drawn up in 1876.

An active, lively breed, likened in the standard to a short-backed, well made hunter, covering a lot of ground. One of the most lively and alert of terriers, refinement to his present show excellence has not allowed him to become one whit unsound. Capable of standing up to any amount of exercise, always ready to deal with rats, rabbits, and, of course, foxes. Not the dog to let loose on a hillside covered with sheep, but ideal for family life in town or, properly controlled, in the country. Small enough to be carried if necessary, but tough enough to appeal to the man in the household.

GENERAL APPEARANCE Active and lively, bone and strength in small compass, never cloddy or coarse. Neither leggy nor too short in the leg, standing like a well made, short-backed hunter, covering a lot of ground.

CHARACTERISTICS Alert, quick of movement, keen of expression, on tiptoe of expectation.

TEMPERAMENT Friendly, forthcoming and fearless.

HEAD AND SKULL Skull flat, moderately narrow, gradually decreasing in width to eyes. A little stop apparent, cheeks never full, jaws, upper and lower, strong and muscular, falling away only slightly below eyes. This portion of foreface moderately chiselled out, so as not to go down in a straight line like a wedge. Nose black.

EYES Dark, small and rather deeply set, as near as possible circular in shape. Expression bright and intelligent.

EARS Small, V-shaped and dropping forward close to cheek, not hanging by side of head. Fold of ear above level of skull. Leather of moderate thickness.

MOUTH Jaws strong with a perfect, regular and complete scissor bite, i.e. upper teeth closely overlapping lower teeth and set square to the jaws.

NECK Clean and muscular, without throatiness, of fair length and gradually widening to shoulders.

FOREQUARTERS Shoulders long and sloping, well laid back, fine at points, cleanly cut at withers. Legs from any angle must be straight showing little or no appearance of an ankle in front. They should be strong in bone throughout.

BODY Chest deep, not broad. Back short, level and strong without slackness. Loin powerful, very slightly arched. Foreribs moderately sprung, back ribs deep.

HINDQUARTERS Strong and muscular, quite free from droop or crouch; thighs long and powerful, hocks well let down, good turn of stifle.

FEET Small, round and compact. Soles hard and tough, toes moderately arched, and turning neither in nor out.

TAIL Customarily docked. Set-on rather high and carried gaily, but not over back, or curled. Of good strength.

GAIT/MOVEMENT Fore- and hindlegs carried straight forward and parallel. Elbows move perpendicular to body, working free of sides, stifles neither turning in nor out and hocks not close. Good drive coming from well flexing hindquarters.

COAT Straight, flat, smooth, hard, dense and abundant. Belly and underside of thighs not bare.

COLOUR White should predominate, all white, white with tan, black and tan or black markings. Brindle, red or liver markings highly undesirable.

SIZE Weight: dogs: 7.3–8.2 kg (16–18 lb); bitches: 6.8–7.7 kg (15–17 lb).

FAULTS Any departure from the foregoing points should be considered a fault and the seriousness with which the fault should be regarded should be in exact proportion to its degree.

NOTE Male animals should have two apparently normal testicles fully descended into the scrotum.

WIRE FOX TERRIER

A NATIVE BREED, THE WIRE FOX TERRIER is a classy dog, and really looks his best when nicely trimmed. He is a long-lived breed with an expected life span of well over ten years. Alert, very active, somewhat vociferous, he is a bold dog, originally known as the Rough-haired Terrier, when he was used for sporting pursuits.

It is probable that the rough coat was developed before that of the Smooth Fox Terrier but, strangely, the appearance of the Wire Fox Terrier in the showring was some twenty years later than that of the Smooth. A strain of rough-coat terriers was kept for fifty-five years by the Revd Jack Russell, who gave his name to another terrier breed.

Cheerful and happy, he makes an excellent children's playmate and family pet. A great show dog, enjoying popularity and success in this field throughout the world.

GENERAL APPEARANCE Active and lively, bone and strength in small compass, never cloddy or coarse. Conformation to show perfect balance; in particular this applies to the relative proportions of skull and foreface, and similarly height at withers and length of body from shoulder point to buttocks appear approximately equal. Standing like a short-backed hunter covering a lot of ground.

CHARACTERISTICS Alert, quick of movement, keen of expression, on tiptoe of expectation at slightest provocation.

TEMPERAMENT Friendly, forthcoming and fearless.

HEAD AND SKULL Topline of skull almost flat, sloping slightly and gradually decreasing in width towards eyes. Little difference in length between skull and foreface. If foreface is noticeably shorter head looks weak and unfinished. Foreface gradually tapering from eye to muzzle and dipping slightly at its juncture with forehead but not dished or falling away quickly below eyes where it should be full and well made up. Excessive bony or muscular development of jaws undesirable and unsightly. Full and rounded contour of cheeks undesirable. Nose black.

EYES Dark, full of fire and intelligence, moderately small, not prominent. As near circular in shape as possible. Not too far apart nor too high in skull nor too near ears. Light eyes highly undesirable.

EARS Small, V-shaped, of moderate thickness, flaps neatly folded over and dropping forward close to cheeks. Topline of folded ears well above level of skull. Prick, tulip or rose ears highly undesirable.

MOUTH Jaws strong with perfect, regular and complete scissor bite, i.e. upper teeth closely overlapping lower teeth and set square to the jaws.

NECK Clean, muscular, of fair length, free from throatiness, broadening to shoulders, presenting a graceful curve when viewed from side.

FOREQUARTERS Seen from front, shoulders slope steeply down from junction with neck towards points which should be fine; viewed from side, long and well laid back and sloping obliquely backwards. Withers always clean-cut. Chest deep, not broad. Viewed from any direction, legs straight, bone strong right down to feet. Elbows perpendicular to body, working free of sides, carried straight when moving.

BODY Back short, level and strong without slackness, loin muscular, slightly arched. Brisket deep, front ribs moderately arched, rear ribs deep, well sprung. Very short-coupled.

HINDQUARTERS Strong, muscular and free from droop or crouch. Thighs long and powerful. Stifles well bent, turning neither in

nor out. Hocks well let down, upright and parallel when viewed from rear. Combination of short second thigh and straight stifle highly undesirable.

FEET Round, compact with small, tough and well cushioned pads, toes moderately arched. Turning neither in nor out.

TAIL Customarily docked. Set high, carried erect not over back nor curled. Of good strength and fair length.

GAIT/MOVEMENT Fore- and hindlegs move straight forward and parallel. Elbows move perpendicular to body, working free of sides. Stifles turning neither in nor out. Good drive coming from well flexing hindquarters.

COAT Dense, very wiry texture, 2 cm (¾ in) on shoulder to 4 cm (1½ in) on withers, back, ribs and quarters with undercoat of short, softer hair. Back and quarters harsher than sides. Hair on

jaws crisp and of sufficient length to impart appearance of strength to foreface. Leg hair dense and crisp.

COLOUR White predominates with black, black and tan or tan markings. Brindle, red, liver or slate-blue marking undesirable.

SIZE Height at withers not exceeding 39 cm (15½ in) in dogs, bitches slightly less. Ideal weight in show condition 8.25 kg (18 lb) for dogs, bitches slightly less.

FAULTS Any departure from the foregoing points should be considered a fault and the seriousness with which the fault should be regarded should be in exact proportion to its degree.

NOTE Male animals should have two apparently normal testicles fully descended into the scrotum.

GLEN OF IMAAL TERRIER

(INTERIM)

A BREED WHICH ORIGINATES FROM County Wicklow, Ireland, and which has been through some hard times in recent years, is only now making something of a comeback. A tough, small dog, the Glen of Imaal Terrier has a mixture of the game and the gentle about him. He appears on first impression to be a rather rough chap, and his harsh coat of blue, wheaten or brindle tends to confirm this, but he is in fact a good family companion, not nearly as noisy as many small terriers. However, his gutteral bark would deter most intruders.

Despite his build, he is very much more active than one would expect.

The breed was not formally recognised until 1930 and The Irish Kennel Club first put on classes for it in 1933. Until the banning of badger trials in 1966 the Glen had to earn a certificate at a trial as well as winning in the showring before he could be called 'champion'. Though the test is no longer necessary the Glen is still thought of as a working dog whose bowed front legs were desirable to give the dog what was termed a 'mechanical advantage' when digging.

GENERAL APPEARANCE Medium-sized with medium length coat, great strength with impression of maximum substance for the size of dog. Body longer than high.

CHARACTERISTICS Active, agile and silent when working. Native of County Wicklow and named after the Glen of Imaal.

TEMPERAMENT Game and spirited with great courage when called upon, otherwise gentle and docile.

HEAD AND SKULL Of good width and fair length with powerful foreface. Muzzle to taper towards nose. Well defined stop. Nose black.

EYES Brown, medium size, round and set well apart. Light eyes undesirable.

EARS Small, rose or half pricked when alert, thrown back when in repose. Full drop or prick undesirable.

MOUTH Jaws strong, with a perfect, regular and complete scissor bite, i.e. upper teeth closely overlapping lower teeth and set square to the jaws. Teeth of good size.

NECK Very muscular and of moderate length.

FOREQUARTERS Shoulders broad, muscular and well laid back. Forelegs short, bowed and well boned.

BODY Deep and of medium length, slightly longer than height at withers. Well sprung ribs with neither flat nor barrel appearance. Chest wide and strong. Topline slightly rising to a strong loin.

HINDQUARTERS Strong, well muscled, with good thighs and good bend of stifle. Hocks turned neither in nor out.

FEET Compact and strong with rounded pads. Front feet to turn out slightly from pastern.

TAIL Strong at root, well set-on and carried gaily. Docking optional.

GAIT/MOVEMENT Free in action. Covers the ground effortlessly with good drive behind.

COAT Medium length, of harsh texture with soft undercoat. Coat may be tidied to present a neat outline.

COLOUR Blue, brindle and wheaten (all shades).

SIZE 35-36 cm (14 in) at the shoulder is maximum height for dogs and bitches.

FAULTS Any departure from the foregoing points should be considered a fault and the seriousness with which the fault should be regarded should be in exact proportion to its degree.

NOTE Male animals should have two apparently normal testicles fully descended into the scrotum.

IRISH TERRIER

A DAREDEVIL AT HEART, RECKLESS AND sometimes foolhardy where canine opponents are concerned, the Irish Terrier has the softest, most gentle and loving disposition. He is totally reliable with youngsters and has a sympathetic attitude to the moods and foibles of adults.

This long-legged terrier is good-looking with a harsh red coat, and a graceful racy outline is coupled with a delightful sense of humour.

Once called the Irish Red Terrier to distinguish the breed from other terriers in Ireland, the Irish Terrier may well be the oldest of them all. The breed was first shown in Ireland in 1875 when there was still variation in size and type, and was also the first of all the native Irish terriers to receive recognition by The Kennel Club in England, back in the nineteenth century.

GENERAL APPEARANCE An active, lively and wiry appearance; plenty of substance but free of clumsiness. Neither cloddy nor cobby but showing a graceful racy outline.

CHARACTERISTICS There is a heedless, reckless pluck about the Irish Terrier which is characteristic and, coupled with the headlong dash, blind to all consequences, with which he rushes at his adversary, has earned for the breed the proud epithet of 'the Daredevils'. When 'off duty' they are characterised by a quiet caress-inviting appearance, and when one sees them endearingly, timidly pushing their heads into their masters' hands, it is difficult to realise that on occasions, at the 'set-on', they can prove that they have the courage of a lion, and will fight to the last breath in their bodies. They develop an extraordinary devotion for their masters and have been known to track them almost incredible distances.

TEMPERAMENT Good-tempered, notably with humans; it being admitted, however, that he is perhaps a little too ready to resent interference on the part of other dogs.

HEAD AND SKULL Head long; skull flat, and rather narrow between ears, narrowing towards eye; free from wrinkles; stop hardly visible except in profile. Jaw strong and muscular, but not too full in cheek, and of good length. Foreface not dished or falling away quickly between eyes, delicately chiselled. Lips well fitting and externally almost black in colour. Nose black.

EYES Dark, small, not prominent. A light or yellow eye highly undesirable.

EARS Small and V-shaped, of moderate thickness, set well on head, and dropping forward closely to cheek. Top of folded ear well above level of skull. Ear must be free of fringe, and hair thereon shorter and darker in colour than body.

MOUTH Teeth even, strong and free from discoloration. Jaws strong, with perfect, regular scissor bite, i.e. upper teeth closely overlapping lower teeth and set square to the jaws.

NECK Fair length and gradually widening towards shoulders, well carried and free of throatiness. Generally a slight fringe at each side of neck, running nearly to corner of ear.

FOREQUARTERS Shoulders fine, long and well laid back. Legs moderately long, well set from shoulders, perfectly straight, with plenty of bone and muscle; elbows working freely clear of sides; pasterns short and straight, hardly noticeable, the forelegs moving straight forward when travelling.

BODY Chest deep and muscular, neither full nor wide. Body moderately long; back strong and straight, with no appearance of slackness behind shoulders; loin muscular and slightly arched; ribs fairly sprung, rather deep than round, and well ribbed back.

HINDQUARTERS Strong and muscular, thighs powerful, hocks well let down, stifles moderately bent. Hindlegs move straight forward when travelling, hocks not turned outwards. Hair on legs dense and crisp.

FEET Strong, tolerably round, moderately small, toes arched, neither turned out nor in; black toenails most desirable. Pads sound and free from cracks or horny excrescences.

TAIL Customarily docked to about three quarters; free of fringe or feather, but well covered with rough hair, set-on pretty high, carried gaily, but not over back or curled.

GAIT/MOVEMENT Fore- and hindlegs carried straight forward and parallel. Elbows move perpendicular to body, working free of sides, stifles neither turning in nor out.

COAT Harsh and wiry, having broken appearance, free of softness or silkiness, not so long as to hide the outline of body particularly in hindquarters, straight and flat, no shagginess and free of lock or curl. At base of these stiff hairs is growth of finer and softer hair, usually termed the undercoat. Hair on foreface crisp and only sufficiently long to impart appearance of additional strength. Hair on legs dense and crisp.

COLOUR 'Whole-coloured', most preferable colours being red, red/wheaten, or yellow/red. Small amount of white on chest acceptable, white on feet highly undesirable. Black shading highly undesirable.

SIZE Ideal height: dogs: 48 cm (19 in); bitches: 46 cm (18 in).

FAULTS Any departure from the foregoing points should be considered a fault and the seriousness with which the fault should be regarded should be in exact proportion to its degree.

NOTE Male animals should have two apparently normal testicles fully descended into the scrotum.

KERRY BLUE TERRIER

THE COAT IS QUITE A FEATURE OF THIS breed; puppies are born black and can take up to eighteen months to change to blue. The coat itself is soft and silky, resembling astrakhan, and does not shed.

An extrovert at heart, the Kerry is a compact, spirited dog, determined but adaptable. He makes a good house pet, kind with people but an excellent guard. Coming from a rustic Irish background he is understandably fond of outdoor pursuits, likes water, and is easily trained.

Actual origins of the breed are obscure but there are references to a blackish-blue dog native to County Kerry which may have been the root stock. It was possibly mated to a dog which swam ashore from a wrecked ship in the Bay of Tralee in the 1700s. The breed reached its peak in the 1920s when there were four breed clubs in Ireland and the Kerry Blue made up more than 25 per cent of Irish Kennel Club registrations.

GENERAL APPEARANCE Upstanding, well knit and proportioned, well developed and muscular body.

CHARACTERISTICS Compact, powerful Terrier, showing gracefulness and an attitude of alert determination, with definite terrier style and character throughout.

TEMPERAMENT Disciplined gameness.

HEAD AND SKULL Well balanced, long, proportionally lean, with slight stop and flat over the skull. Foreface and jaw very strong, deep and punishing; nose black; nostrils of due proportion.

EYES Dark as possible. Small to medium with keen Terrier expression.

EARS Small to medium and V-shaped; carried forward but not too high.

MOUTH Gums and roof of mouth dark with perfect, regular scissor bite, i.e. upper teeth closely overlapping lower teeth and set square to the jaws.

NECK Strong and reachy, running into sloping shoulders.

FOREQUARTERS Shoulders flat as possible with elbows carried close to body while standing or moving. Legs straight, bone powerful. Front straight, neither too wide nor too narrow.

BODY Short-coupled with good depth of brisket and well sprung ribs. Deep chest. Topline level.

HINDQUARTERS Large and well developed, stifle bent and hocks close to ground giving perfect freedom of hind action.

FEET Round and small. Nails black.

TAIL Set-on high and carried erect. Customarily docked.

GAIT/MOVEMENT Free and powerful. Fore- and hindlegs moving straight and parallel, stifles turning neither in nor out.

COAT Soft and silky, plentiful and wavy.

COLOUR Any shade of blue with or without black points. Tan permissible in puppies, also a dark colour up to the age of 18 months. A small white patch on chest should not be penalised.

SIZE Ideal height: dogs: 46–48 cm (18–19 in) at shoulder; bitches: slightly less. The most desirable weight for a fully developed dog is 15–16.8 kg (33–37 lb), and bitches should weigh proportionately less, but 15.9 kg (35 lb) is the most desirable weight to aim for.

FAULTS Any departure from the foregoing points should be considered a fault and the seriousness with which the fault should be regarded should be in exact proportion to its degree.

NOTE Male animals should have two apparently normal testicles fully descended into the scrotum.

LAKELAND TERRIER

A CHEERFUL LITTLE RASCAL, HARDY AND agile, he comes from England's Lake District where once his ancestors were known by the names of their area of origin, and eventually linked under the all-embracing name of Lakeland. Courageous, affectionate, tireless, lovable and naughty; all of these epithets fit him well.

Small enough to tuck under your arm, he is tough enough to spend a whole day running in the countryside. He belongs to the trimmed breeds, but apart from professional care twice a year his coat is easy to keep tidy on a day-to-day basis.

The breed was not known as Lakeland until a club was formed in 1912 and The Kennel Club formally recognised the breed in 1921.

One famed Lakeland was Champion Stingray of Derrybah who was Best in Show at Crufts in 1967 and then became Best in Show at America's Westminster show the following year. A trophy recognising this dual achievement is housed at The Kennel Club in London, having been presented by the American Kennel Club in acknow-ledgment of Stingray being the only dog to have won both these prestigious shows.

TERRIER

159

GENERAL APPEARANCE Smart, workmanlike, well balanced and compact.

CHARACTERISTICS Gay, fearless demeanour, keen of expression, quick of movement, on the tiptoe of expectation.

TEMPERAMENT Bold, friendly and self-confident.

HEAD AND SKULL Well balanced. Skull flat and refined. Jaws powerful and muzzle broad but not too long. Length of head from stop to tip of nose not exceeding that from occiput to stop. Nose black, except in liver-coated dogs when the nose will be liver.

EYES Dark or hazel. Slanting eyes undesirable.

EARS Moderately small, V-shaped and carried alertly. Set neither too high nor too low on head.

MOUTH Teeth even with perfect, regular scissor bite, i.e. upper teeth closely overlapping lower teeth and set square to the jaws.

NECK Reachy, slightly arched, free from throatiness.

FOREQUARTERS Shoulders well laid back. Forelegs straight, well boned.

BODY Chest reasonably narrow. Back strong, moderately short and well coupled.

HINDQUARTERS Strong and muscular. Thighs long and powerful with well turned stifles. Hocks low to ground and straight.

FEET Small, compact, round and well padded.

TAIL Customarily docked. Well set-on, carried gaily but not over back or curled.

GAIT/MOVEMENT Fore- and hindlegs carried straight forward and parallel. Elbows move perpendicular to body, working free of sides, stifles turning neither in nor out. Good drive coming from well flexing hindquarters.

COAT Dense, harsh and weather-resisting with good undercoat.

COLOUR Black and tan, blue and tan, red, wheaten, red grizzle, liver, blue or black. Small tips of white on feet and chest undesirable but permissible. Mahogany or deep tan not typical.

SIZE Height not exceeding 37 cm (14½ in) at shoulder. Average weight: dogs: 7.7 kg (17 lb); bitches: 6.8 kg (15 lb).

FAULTS Any departure from the foregoing points should be considered a fault and the seriousness with which the fault should be regarded should be in exact proportion to its degree.

NOTE Male animals should have two apparently normal testicles fully descended into the scrotum.

MANCHESTER TERRIER

A GOOD-LOOKING BLACK AND TAN DOG with the advantage of a smooth coat. His name denotes his origin, and it is likely that there is some Whippet in his ancestry. Elegant and graceful, he was bred as a ratter and can still be relied upon to despatch vermin quickly and efficiently.

Rat killing reached its peak in the mid-1800s and what dog shows there were, at that time, were usually held in public houses. In Manchester, especially, these became a weekly feature and soon this terrier had classes of his own, eventually taking the name Manchester Terrier.

In spite of his background there is nothing sharp about him with humans – he is a sporting companion, very agile and not aggressive. He becomes devoted to his family and fits into any environment, be it town or country.

GENERAL APPEARANCE Compact, elegant and sound with substance.

CHARACTERISTICS Keen, alert, gay and sporting.

TEMPERAMENT Discerning and devoted.

HEAD AND SKULL Long skull, flat and narrow, level and wedge-shaped, without showing cheek muscles, well filled up under eyes, with tapering, tight-lipped mouth.

EYES Small, dark and sparkling. Almond-shaped, not prominent.

EARS Small and V-shaped, carried well above topline of head and hanging close to head above eyes.

MOUTH Jaws level, with perfect, regular scissor bite, i.e. upper teeth closely overlapping lower teeth and set square to the jaws.

NECK Fairly long and tapering from shoulder to head and slightly arched at crest; free from throatiness.

FOREQUARTERS Shoulders clean and well sloped. Front narrow and deep. Forelegs quite straight, set-on well under dog; and proportionate length to body.

BODY Short with well sprung ribs, slightly arched over the loin and cut up behind ribs.

HINDQUARTERS Strong and muscular, well bent at stifle. Hindlegs neither cow-hocked nor with feet turned in.

FEET Small, semi-harefooted and strong with well arched toes.

TAIL Short and set-on where arch of back ends, thick where it joins body, tapering to a point, carried not higher than level of back.

GAIT/MOVEMENT Straight, free and balanced with good-reaching forequarters and driving power in hindquarters.

COAT Close, smooth, short and glossy, of firm texture.

COLOUR Jet black and rich mahogany tan distributed as follows: on head, muzzle tanned to nose, nose and nasal bone jet black. Small tan spot on each cheek and above each eye, under-jaw and throat tanned with distinct tan V. Legs from knee downward tanned with exception of toes which shall be pencilled with black, a distinct black mark (thumbmark) immediately above feet. Inside hindlegs tanned but divided with black at stifle joint. Under tail tanned, vent tanned by marking as narrow as possible so that it is covered by tail. A slight tan mark on each side of chest. Tan outside hindlegs, commonly called breeching, is undesirable. In all cases black should not run into tan or vice versa, but division between colours clearly defined.

SIZE Ideal height at shoulder: dogs: 40–41 cm (16 in); bitches: 38 cm (15 in).

FAULTS Any departure from the foregoing points should be considered a fault and the seriousness with which the fault should be regarded should be in exact proportion to its degree.

NOTE Male animals should have two apparently normal testicles fully descended into the scrotum.

NORFOLK TERRIER AND NORWICH TERRIER

A TYPICAL SHORT-LEGGED TERRIER WITH a sound, compact body, the Norfolk has been used not only on fox and badger, but on rats as well. He has a delightful disposition, is totally fearless but is not one to start a fight.

As a worker he does not give up in the face of a fierce adversary underground, and his standard's reference to the acceptability of 'honourable scars from fair wear and tear' is a good indication of the type of dog the breeders require.

Of recent years, the docking of part of his tail has become optional, but even in its unshortened state it should be thick at the root and should taper towards the tip.

The Norfolk Terrier's ears should drop forward at the tip, whereas those of his older cousin, the Norwich Terrier, should stand erect when the dog is at attention.

The Norfolk and the Norwich take their names, obviously, from the county and the city, though turning the clock back to the early and mid-1800s there was no such distinction, this being just a general farm dog. Glen of Imaals, red Cairn Terriers and Dandie Dinmonts are among the breeds behind these East Anglian terriers and from the resultant red progeny emerged the present Norfolk and Norwich.

BELOW: *Norfolk Terrier*

Norfolk Terrier

GENERAL APPEARANCE Small, low, keen dog, compact and strong, short back, good substance and bone. Honourable scars from fair wear and tear permissible.

CHARACTERISTICS One of the smallest of terriers, a 'demon' for his size. Lovable disposition, not quarrelsome, hardy constitution.

TEMPERAMENT Alert and fearless.

HEAD AND SKULL Skull broad, only slightly rounded with good width between ears. Muzzle wedge-shaped and strong; length of muzzle about one-third less than measurement from occiput to bottom of well defined stop.

EYES Oval-shaped and deep-set, dark brown or black. Expression alert, keen and intelligent.

EARS Medium size, V-shaped, slightly rounded at tip, dropping forward close to cheek.

MOUTH Tight-lipped, strong jaw, teeth strong and rather large; perfect scissor bite, i.e. upper teeth closely overlapping lower teeth and set square to the jaws.

NECK Strong and of medium length.

FOREQUARTERS Clean, well laid back shoulder blade, approximating in length to upper arm. Front legs short, powerful and straight.

BODY Compact, short back, level topline, well sprung ribs.

HINDQUARTERS Well muscled, good turn of stifle, hocks well let down and straight when viewed from rear; great propulsion.

FEET Round with thick pads.

TAIL Docking of tail optional.
a) Medium docked, set level with topline and carried erect.

b) Tail of moderate length to give a general balance to the dog, thick at the root and tapering towards the tip, as straight as possible, carried jauntily, but not excessively gay.

GAIT/MOVEMENT True, low and driving. Moving straight forward from shoulder. Good rear angulation showing great powers of propulsion. Hindlegs follow track of forelegs, moving smoothly from hips. Flexing well at stifle and hock. Topline remaining level.

COAT Hard, wiry, straight, lying close to body. Longer and rougher on neck and shoulders. Hair on head and ears short and smooth, except for slight whiskers and eyebrows. Excessive trimming undesirable.

COLOUR All shades of red, wheaten, black and tan or grizzle. White marks or patches undesirable but permissible.

SIZE Ideal height at withers 25-26 cm (10 in).

FAULTS Any departure from the foregoing points should be considered a fault and the seriousness with which the fault should be regarded should be in exact proportion to its degree.

NOTE Male animals should have two apparently normal testicles fully descended into the scrotum.

NORWICH TERRIER

GENERAL APPEARANCE Small, low, keen dog, compact and strong with good substance and bone. Honourable scars from fair wear and tear not to be unduly penalised.

CHARACTERISTICS One of the smallest of the terriers. Lovable disposition, not quarrelsome, tremendously active with hardy constitution.

TEMPERAMENT Gay and fearless.

HEAD AND SKULL Muzzle wedge-shaped and strong. In length two-thirds of measurement from occiput to bottom of well defined stop. Slightly rounded, wide skull, good width between ears.

EYES Small, oval-shaped, dark, full of expression, bright and keen.

EARS Erect, set well apart on top of skull. Medium size with pointed tips. Perfectly erect when aroused, can be laid back when not at attention.

MOUTH Tight-lipped, jaws clean and strong. Rather large, strong teeth with perfect, regular scissor bite, i.e. upper teeth closely overlapping lower teeth and set square to the jaws.

NECK Strong of good length, commensurate with correct overall balance, flowing into well laid shoulders.

FOREQUARTERS Legs short, powerful and straight; elbows close to body. Pasterns firm and upright.

BODY Short back, compact with good depth. Ribcage long and well sprung with short loin. Level topline.

HINDQUARTERS Broad, strong and muscular, well turned stifle. Low-set hock with great propulsion.

FEET Rounded, well padded and cat-like. Pointing straight forward standing and moving.

TAIL Docking optional.
a) Medium docked. Set high, completing perfectly level topline. Carried erect.
b) Tail of moderate length to give a general balance to dog, thick at root and tapering towards tip, as straight as possible, carried jauntily, not excessively gay, completing perfectly level topline.

GAIT/MOVEMENT Forelegs should move straight forward when travelling; hindlegs follow in their track; hocks parallel and flexing to show pads.

COAT Hard, wiry, straight, lying close to body, thick undercoat. Longer and rougher on neck forming a ruff to frame face. Hair on head and ears short and smooth, except for slight whiskers and eyebrows.

COLOUR All shades of red, wheaten, black and tan or grizzle. White marks or patches are undesirable.

SIZE Ideal height at withers 25-26 cm (10 in).

FAULTS Any departure from the foregoing points should be considered a fault and the seriousness with which the fault should be regarded should be in exact proportion to its degree.

NOTE Male animals should have two apparently normal testicles fully descended into the scrotum.

PARSON JACK RUSSELL TERRIER

(INTERIM)

FOR MANY YEARS, GREAT CONTROVERSY has existed in the ranks of the terrier fanciers over a type of terrier called somewhat vaguely 'the Jack Russell'. The Kennel Club became involved in this affair as a result of applications from a considerable number of devotees of a strain of Fox Terrier bred by a Victorian hunting parson, the Revd John Russell.

This strain is particularly well described as ideally standing 35 centimetres (14 inches) high at the withers and weighing 6.4 kilograms (14 pounds). He can be smooth or rough-coated; in either jacket he is a happy, lively animal, equally at home while working or playing among a household.

'The Parson' is not truly suited to a town life unless given a fair degree of freedom and exercise. He is too intelligent to be left on his own for long periods; he will get bored and could easily become destructive as well as aggravating the neighbours with uncontrolled barking.

GENERAL APPEARANCE Workmanlike, active and agile; built for speed and endurance.

CHARACTERISTICS Essentially a working terrier with ability and conformation to go to ground and run with hounds.

TEMPERAMENT Bold and friendly.

HEAD AND SKULL Flat, moderately broad, gradually narrowing to the eyes. Shallow stop. Length from nose to stop slightly shorter than from stop to occiput. Nose black.

EYES Almond-shaped, fairly deep-set, dark, keen expression.

EARS Small, V-shaped, dropping forward, carried close to head, fold not to appear above top of skull.

MOUTH Jaws strong, muscular. Teeth with a perfect, regular and complete scissor bite, i.e. upper teeth closely overlapping lower teeth and set square to the jaws.

NECK Clean, muscular, of good length, gradually widening to shoulders.

FOREQUARTERS Shoulders long and sloping, well laid back, cleanly cut at withers. Legs strong, must be straight with joints turning neither in nor out. Elbows close to body, working free of the sides.

BODY Chest of moderate depth, capable of being spanned behind the shoulders by average-size hands. Back strong and straight. Loin slightly arched. Well balanced, length of back from withers to root of tail equal to height from withers to ground.

HINDQUARTERS Strong, muscular with good angulation and bend of stifle. Hocks short and parallel giving plenty of drive.

FEET Compact with firm pads, turning neither in nor out.

TAIL Strong, straight, set-on high. Customarily docked with length complementing the body while providing a good handhold.

GAIT/MOVEMENT Free, lively, well co-ordinated; straight action front and behind.

COAT Naturally harsh, close and dense, whether rough or smooth. Belly and undersides coated. Skin must be thick and loose.

COLOUR Entirely white or predominantly white with markings which are tan, lemon or black, or any combination of these colours, preferably confined to the head or root of tail.

SIZE Height: minimum 33 cm (13 in), ideally 35 cm (14 in) at withers for dogs, and minimum

30 cm (12 in), ideally 33 cm (13 in) at withers for bitches.

FAULTS Any departure from the foregoing points should be considered a fault and the seriousness with which the fault should be regarded should be in exact proportion to its degree.

NOTE Male animals should have two apparently normal testicles fully descended into the scrotum.

SCOTTISH TERRIER

TERRIER

168

A POPULAR SHORT-LEGGED DOG FROM the Highlands, sturdy and low-slung. More often thought of as black, he can have a striking wheaten or brindle-coloured coat. His public image is often that of a dour Scot, but to his family and friends he is affectionate and cheerful. Happy to curl up in a favourite armchair, he will soon rouse himself at the slightest sound, when his dark eyes will glint with protectiveness as he prepares to guard his house and home.

The Scottish Terrier Club was formed in 1882, a year after the first standard for the breed was drawn up, and just three years after the start of the breed as we know it today by Capt Gordon Murray. He was strongly supported by the founder and first chairman of The Kennel Club, Mr Sewallis Evelyn Shirley.

GENERAL APPEARANCE Thick-set, of suitable size to go to ground, short-legged, alert in carriage and suggestive of great power and activity in small compass. Head gives impression of being long for size of dog. Very agile and active in spite of short legs.

CHARACTERISTICS Loyal and faithful. Dignified, independent and reserved, but courageous and highly intelligent.

TEMPERAMENT Bold, but never aggressive.

HEAD AND SKULL Long without being out of proportion to size of dog. Length of skull enabling it to be fairly wide and yet retain narrow appearance. Skull nearly flat and cheek bones not protruding. Foreface strongly constructed and deep throughout. Skull and

foreface of equal length. Slight but distinct stop between skull and foreface just in front of eye. Nose large and, in profile, line from nose towards chin appears to slope backwards.

EYES Almond-shaped, dark brown, fairly wide apart, set deeply under eyebrows with keen, intelligent expression.

EARS Neat, fine texture, pointed, erect and set-on top of skull but not too close together. Large, wide-based ears highly undesirable.

MOUTH Teeth large with perfect, regular scissor bite, i.e. upper teeth closely overlapping lower teeth and set square to the jaws.

NECK Muscular and of moderate length.

FOREQUARTERS Head carried on muscular neck of moderate length showing quality, set into long sloping shoulders, brisket well in front of straight, well boned forelegs to straight pasterns. Chest fairly broad and hung between forelegs which must not be out at the elbow nor placed under body.

BODY Well rounded ribs flattening to deep chest and carried well back. Back proportionately short and very muscular. Topline of body straight and level, loin muscular and deep, powerfully coupling ribs to hindquarters.

HINDQUARTERS Remarkably powerful for size of dog. Big, wide buttocks, deep thighs and well bent stifles. Hocks short, strong, turning neither in nor out.

FEET Good size, well padded, toes well arched and close-knit, forefeet slightly larger than hindfeet.

TAIL Moderate length giving general balance to dog, thick at root and tapering towards tip. Set-on with upright carriage or slight bend.

GAIT/MOVEMENT Smooth and free, straight both back and front with drive from behind and level gait throughout.

COAT Close-lying, double coat; undercoat short, dense and soft; outer coat harsh, dense and wiry, together making a weather-resisting covering.

COLOUR Black, wheaten or brindle of any shade.

SIZE Height at withers 25.4-28 cm (10-11 in); weight 8.6-10.4 kg (19-23 lb).

FAULTS Any departure from the foregoing points should be considered a fault and the seriousness with which the fault should be regarded should be in exact proportion to its degree.

NOTE Male animals should have two apparently normal testicles fully descended into the scrotum.

SEALYHAM TERRIER

ABOUT 150 YEARS AGO A CERTAIN Capt John Owen Tucker Edwardes, who lived at Sealyham, Pembrokeshire, South Wales, decided to promote his idea of the perfect terrier. From a mix of the Welsh Corgi, the Dandie Dinmont, the West Highland White, the Bull Terrier and the Wire Fox Terrier among others he produced the dog which was to become the Sealyham.

Edwardes culled weaklings and it was the survival of the fittest, all of whom had to pass tough tests of tackling rats and other vermin. Edwardes died in 1891 and a Fred Lewis took up promotion of the breed, which was shown for the first time in 1903. A breed club was formed in 1908 and the Sealyham received Kennel Club recognition in 1911.

Though his origins are rural Welsh he can be as much at home in the town as in the country. Supple, active, ready to romp and play, he makes an intelligent and charming companion, happy to be with you or able to make his own amusement, whichever the occasion demands. Perhaps he is not really an ideal indoor pet for the pernickety and homeproud as his short legs and low-to-the-ground body do tend to collect mud on a wet day. However, for those prepared to spend a few minutes cleaning him up on such occasions he will pay considerable dividends.

GENERAL APPEARANCE Free-moving, active, balanced and of great substance in small compass. General outline oblong, not square.

CHARACTERISTICS Sturdy, game and workmanlike.

TEMPERAMENT Alert and fearless but of friendly disposition.

HEAD AND SKULL Skull slightly domed and wide between ears. Cheek bones not prominent. Punishing square jaw, powerful and long. Nose black.

EYES Dark, well set, round, of medium size. Dark, pigmented eye rims preferred but unpigmented tolerated.

EARS Medium-sized, slightly rounded at tip and carried at side of cheek.

MOUTH Teeth level and strong with canines fitting well into each other and long for size of dog. Jaws strong with regular scissor bite, i.e. upper teeth closely overlapping lower teeth and set square to the jaws.

NECK Fairly long, thick and muscular on well laid shoulders.

FOREQUARTERS Forelegs short, strong and as straight as possible consistent with chest being well let down. Point of shoulder in line with point of elbow which should be close to side of chest.

BODY Medium in length, level and flexible with ribs well sprung. Chest broad and deep, well let down between forelegs.

HINDQUARTERS Notably powerful for size of dog. Thighs deep and muscular with well bent stifle. Hocks strong, well bent and parallel to each other.

FEET Round and cat-like with thick pads. Feet pointing directly forward.

TAIL Set in line with back and carried erect. Quarters should protrude beyond set of tail. Customarily docked.

GAIT/MOVEMENT Brisk and vigorous with plenty of drive.

COAT Long, hard and wiry top coat with weather-resistant undercoat.

COLOUR All white or white with lemon, brown, blue or badger pied markings on head and ears. Much black and heavy ticking undesirable.

SIZE Height should not exceed 31 cm (12 in) at shoulder. Ideal weight: dogs approx 9 kg (20 lb); bitches approx 8.2 kg (18 lb). General conformation, overall balance, type and substance are main criteria.

FAULTS Any departure from the foregoing points should be considered a fault and the seriousness with which the fault should be regarded should be in exact proportion to its degree.

NOTE Male animals should have two apparently normal testicles fully descended into the scrotum.

SKYE TERRIER

ONE OF THE OLDEST SCOTTISH BREEDS; he is distrustful of strangers, but devoted and loyal to family and friends, is courageous but not aggressive. His long coat makes him a very glamorous dog, but he does require weekly brushing and occasional bathing to keep him in good condition. He makes a good watchdog and house-dog, and a great plus is that his coat rarely sheds. Being low to ground, mud does stick to his furnishings, but can quickly and easily be brushed out when dry.

Although the majority of Skye Terriers are prick-eared, there is also a variety known as 'drop-eared', and then the ears hang flat against the skull. The Skye was once known as the Terrier of the Western Isles, evolving into what we now call the Skye Terrier, with a mix of breeds behind him, including Cairn Terrier prototypes. One of the most famed of the breed was Greyfriars Bobby who, in Edinburgh, around 1858 took up a vigil at his master's grave in Greyfriars Churchyard until he too died. Greyfriars Bobby was buried in unconsecrated ground in the churchyard and his devotion is commemorated by a memorial plaque in the street and by a tablet on his grave.

GENERAL APPEARANCE Long, low and profusely coated, twice as long as high. Moves with seemingly effortless gait. Strong in quarters, body and jaw.

CHARACTERISTICS Elegant and dignified.

TEMPERAMENT A 'one-man' dog, distrustful of strangers, never vicious.

HEAD AND SKULL Long and powerful, strength not sacrificed for extreme length. Moderate width at back of skull, tapering gradually with slight stop to strong muzzle. Nose black.

EYES Brown, preferably dark brown, medium in size, close-set and full of expression.

EARS Prick or drop. When prick, gracefully feathered, not large, erect at outer edges and slanting towards each other at inner edge, from peak to skull. When drop, larger, hanging straight, lying flat and close at front.

MOUTH Jaws strong and level with perfect, regular scissor bite, i.e. upper teeth closely overlapping lower teeth and set square to the jaws.

NECK Long and slightly crested.

FOREQUARTERS Shoulders broad, close to body, chest deep, legs short and muscular.

BODY Long and low, back level. Ribcage oval, deep and long. Short loin. Sides appear flattish due to straight-falling coat.

HINDQUARTERS Strong, full, well developed and well angulated. Legs short, muscular and straight when viewed from behind. No dewclaws.

FEET Forefeet larger than hind, pointing truly forward. Pads thick, nails strong.

TAIL When hanging, upper part pendulous and lower half thrown back in a curve. When raised, a prolongation of incline of back, not rising higher or curling up. Gracefully feathered.

GAIT/MOVEMENT Legs proceed straight forward when travelling. When approaching, forelegs form a continuation of straight line of front, feet being same distance apart as elbows. Principal propelling power is furnished by hindlegs which travel straight forward. Forelegs moving well forward, without too much lift. Whole movement termed free, active and effortless and gives a more or less fluid picture.

COAT Double. Undercoat short, close, soft and woolly. Outer coat long, hard, straight, flat and free from curl. Hair on head shorter, softer, veiling forehead and eyes. Mingling with side locks, surrounding ears like a fringe and allowing their shape to appear.

COLOUR Black, dark or light grey, fawn, cream, all with black points. Any self-colour allowing shading of same colour and lighter undercoat, so long as nose and ears are black. A small white spot on chest permissible.

SIZE Ideal height: 25-26 cm (10 in); length from tip of nose to tip of tail 103 cm (41½ in). Bitches slightly smaller in same proportions.

FAULTS Any departure from the foregoing points should be considered a fault and the seriousness with which the fault should be regarded should be in exact proportion to its degree.

NOTE Male animals should have two apparently normal testicles fully descended into the scrotum.

SOFT COATED WHEATEN TERRIER

AS ONE WOULD EXPECT FROM HIS origin, he has a typical happy-go-lucky Irish outlook. He loves children, and thrives on human companionship. Extrovert and exuberant, he is willing to go anywhere at any time. He requires a little patience to train, but is eager to please.

His coat, when natural, needs very little care; described as the colour of ripening wheat, it is soft and silky, and suits his jaunty approach to life. A sturdy dog, who is hardy and unexaggerated in any way, he makes an excellent house pet.

GENERAL APPEARANCE Medium-sized, compact, upstanding terrier well covered with a soft, wheaten-coloured, natural coat that falls in loose curls or waves. An active, short-coupled dog, strong and well built; well balanced in structure and movement, not exaggerated in any way. Standing four square with head and tail up, giving the appearance of a happy dog, full of character.

CHARACTERISTICS A natural terrier with strong sporting instincts, hardy and of strong constitution.

TEMPERAMENT Good-tempered, spirited and game. Full of confidence and humour; a delightful, affectionate, intelligent companion.

HEAD AND SKULL Flat, moderately long and profusely covered with coat which falls forward over the eyes. Skull of medium width but not coarse. Stop well defined, cheek bones not prominent. Distance from eye to nose not longer, and preferably shorter, than the distance from the eyes to occiput. Jaws strong and punishing, muzzle square with no suggestion of snipiness. Topline of muzzle absolutely straight and parallel with skull. Nose black and large for size of dog. Head in general powerful, without being coarse.

EYES Clear, bright dark hazel. Medium size set under strong brow. Eye rims black.

EARS V-shaped and folded at level of skull. Forward edge drops down slightly forward to lie closely along cheek, back edge standing slightly away from side of head. Leathers thin, small to medium in size, covered with coat and fringe.

MOUTH Lips tight and black. Teeth large. Jaws strong with a perfect, regular and complete scissor bite, i.e. upper teeth closely overlapping lower teeth and set square to the jaws.

NECK Moderately long, strong, muscular and slightly arched. Without throatiness. Gradually widening toward, and running cleanly into shoulders.

FOREQUARTERS Shoulders long, well laid back, and sloping inwards from points to withers. Not loose, fine, but muscular. Viewed from any angle, the forelegs perfectly straight. Good bone and muscle. Pasterns strong and springy. Chest moderately wide. Dewclaws on the front legs may be removed.

BODY Compact, with powerful short loins. Back strong and level. Ribs well sprung without roundness, providing deep chest with relatively short coupling. Length of back from point of withers to base of tail should measure about the same as, or slightly less than, from point of withers to ground.

HINDQUARTERS Thighs strong and muscular. Hindlegs well developed with powerful muscle and well bent stifles. Hocks well let down and turning neither in nor out. Dewclaws on the hindlegs should be removed.

FEET Strong and compact, turned neither in nor out. Good depth of pad. Toenails black.

TAIL Customarily docked. Tail of fully grown dog about 10-13 cm (4-5 in) long. Set-on high,

carried gaily but never over back. Not curled and not too thick.

GAIT/MOVEMENT Free, graceful and lively. Well co-ordinated with long, low strides. Reach in front and good drive behind; straight action fore and aft. Head and tail carried high, the backline remaining level.

COAT Soft and silky. Neither woolly nor wiry. Loosely waved or curly, but if curly, curls large, light and loose. The coat should not stand off but flow and fall naturally. Coat abundant all over body and especially profuse on head and legs. Length of leg coat sufficient to give good balance to the length of coat on head and body. There is no seasonal change in the length or texture of the mature coat. Over-trimming or stylising should be penalised. For show purposes the coat may be tidied to present a neat outline. Coat colour and texture do not stabilise until about 24 months and should be given some latitude in young dogs.

COLOUR A good clear wheaten. A shade of ripening wheat. A white coat and red coat equally objectionable. Dark shading on ears not untypical. Often a slight fluctuation in the intensity of colour in mature coat, but overall effect should be light wheaten. Dark overall colour and the even darker markings, often present in the immature coat, should clear by about 18-24 months.

SIZE Height: dogs approx 46-49 cm (18-19½ in) measured at the withers; bitches slightly less. Weight: dogs approx 16-20.5 kg (35-45 lb); bitches somewhat less.

FAULTS Any departure from the foregoing points should be considered a fault and the seriousness with which the fault should be regarded should be in exact proportion to its degree.

NOTE Male animals should have two apparently normal testicles fully descended into the scrotum.

STAFFORDSHIRE BULL TERRIER

TERRIER

176

ONE OF THE MOST POPULAR OF ALL THE terriers, the Staffordshire is renowned for his courage, which unfortunately can lead him into bad ways with other dogs owing to his great tendency to 'get his retaliation in first'. With the human race he is kindness itself. He is descended from a cross between the Bulldog and a terrier, and thus combines the temperaments of the two breeds. Fortunately, his genuine love of children is well known.

Despite his historical connection with fighting, he has become a great favourite in the showring, but this has not been allowed to affect his traditional rugged looks.

GENERAL APPEARANCE Smooth-coated, well balanced, of great strength for his size. Muscular, active and agile.

CHARACTERISTICS Traditionally of indomitable courage and tenacity. Highly intelligent and affectionate, especially with children.

TEMPERAMENT Bold, fearless and totally reliable.

HEAD AND SKULL Short, deep though with broad skull. Very pronounced cheek muscles, distinct stop, short foreface, nose black.

EYES Dark preferred but may bear some relation to coat colour. Round, of medium size, and set to look straight ahead. Eye rims dark.

EARS Rose or half pricked, not large or heavy. Full, drop or pricked ears highly undesirable.

MOUTH Lips tight and clean. Jaws strong, teeth large, with a perfect, regular and complete scissor bite, i.e. upper teeth closely overlapping lower teeth and set square to the jaws.

NECK Muscular, rather short, clean in outline gradually widening towards shoulders.

FOREQUARTERS Legs straight and well boned, set rather wide apart, showing no weakness at the pasterns, from which point feet turn out a little. Shoulders well laid back with no looseness at elbow.

BODY Close-coupled, with level topline, wide front, deep brisket, well sprung ribs; muscular and well defined.

HINDQUARTERS Well muscled, hocks well let down with stifles well bent. Legs parallel when viewed from behind.

FEET Well padded, strong and of medium size. Nails black in solid-coloured dogs.

TAIL Medium length, low-set, tapering to a point and carried rather low. Should not curl much and may be likened to an old-fashioned pump handle.

GAIT/MOVEMENT Free, powerful and agile with economy of effort. Legs moving parallel when viewed from front or rear. Discernible drive from hindlegs.

COAT Smooth, short and close.

COLOUR Red, fawn, white, black or blue, or any one of these colours with white. Any shade of brindle or any shade of brindle with white. Black and tan or liver colour highly undesirable.

SIZE Desirable height at withers 35.5-40.5 cm (14-16 in), these heights being related to the weights. Weight: dogs: 12.7-17 kg (28-38 lb); bitches: 11-15.4 kg (24-34 lb).

FAULTS Any departure from the foregoing points should be considered a fault and the seriousness with which the fault should be regarded should be in exact proportion to its degree.

NOTE Male animals should have two apparently normal testicles fully descended into the scrotum.

WELSH TERRIER

A BREED WITH A TRULY WORKING background, the Welsh Terrier is perhaps rather less exuberant than some of the other members of his group. As such, he tends to make a very satisfactory house-dog with a love of family companionship. He is a dog with a cheerful spirit and is good with children. Like so many of his cousins, he was originally used in hunting the fox, badger and even otter.

He is a neat, workmanlike dog with a tight wiry coat normally of black and tan, which is relatively easy to maintain in a clean state with a normal degree of trimming.

The Welsh and Lakeland Terriers, which have considerable similarity, may well have had a common origin prior to the Roman invasion of Britain when their Celtic owners retreated to the Welsh mountains and the Lake District.

GENERAL APPEARANCE Smart, workmanlike, well balanced and compact.

CHARACTERISTICS Affectionate, obedient and easily controlled.

TEMPERAMENT Happy and volatile, rarely of shy nature. Game and fearless but definitely not aggressive although at all times able to hold his own when necessary.

HEAD AND SKULL Flat, of moderate width between ears. Jaws powerful, clean-cut, rather deep and punishing. Stop not too defined, medium length from stop to end of nose. Nose black.

EYES Small, well set in, dark, expression indicative of temperament. A round, full eye undesirable.

EARS V-shaped, small, leathers not too thin, set-on fairly high, carried forward and close to cheek.

MOUTH Jaws strong with perfect, regular scissor bite, i.e. upper teeth closely overlapping lower teeth and set square to the jaws.

NECK Moderate length and thickness, slightly arched and sloping gracefully into shoulders.

FOREQUARTERS Shoulders long, sloping and well set back. Legs straight and muscular, possessing ample bone, with upright and powerful pasterns.

BODY Back short and well ribbed up, loin strong, good depth and moderate width of chest.

HINDQUARTERS Strong, thighs muscular, of good length, with hocks well bent, well let down and with ample bone.

FEET Small, round and cat-like.

TAIL Well set-on but not carried too gaily. Customarily docked.

GAIT/MOVEMENT Fore- and hindlegs carried straight forward and parallel. Elbows move perpendicular to body, working free of sides, stifles turning neither in nor out.

COAT Wiry, hard, very close and abundant. Single coat undesirable.

COLOUR Black and tan for preference, or black grizzle and tan, free from black pencilling on toes. Black below hocks most undesirable.

SIZE Height at shoulder not exceeding 39 cm (15½ in). Weight 9-9.5 kg (20-21 lb).

FAULTS Any departure from the foregoing points should be considered a fault and the seriousness with which the fault should be regarded should be in exact proportion to its degree.

NOTE Male animals should have two apparently normal testicles fully descended into the scrotum.

WEST HIGHLAND WHITE TERRIER

ONE OF THE MOST POPULAR OF THE terrier breeds, this small dog has a cheerful, outgoing personality. He makes an ideal companion and playmate for youngsters as he is full of fun and virtually tireless. Always ready for a walk in snow or shine, and small enough to pick up and take anywhere. The right size for house or flat, he really is an all-purpose pet.

His harsh coat requires regular brushing and combing and it is as well to have him professionally trimmed two or three times a year if you wish to keep his smart appearance.

GENERAL APPEARANCE Strongly built; deep in chest and back ribs; level back and powerful quarters on muscular legs and exhibiting in a marked degree a great combination of strength and activity.

CHARACTERISTICS Small, active, game, hardy, possessed of no small amount of self-esteem with a varminty appearance.

TEMPERAMENT Alert, gay, courageous, self-reliant but friendly.

HEAD AND SKULL Skull slightly domed; when handled across forehead presents a smooth contour. Tapering very slightly from skull at level of ears to eyes. Distance from occiput to eyes slightly greater than length of foreface. Head thickly coated with hair, and carried at right angle or less, to axis of neck. Head not to be carried in extended position. Foreface gradually tapering from eye to muzzle. Distinct stop formed by heavy, bony ridges immediately above and slightly overhanging eye, and slight indentation between eyes. Foreface not dished nor falling away quickly below eyes, where it is well made up. Jaws strong and level. Nose black and fairly large, forming smooth contour with rest of muzzle. Nose not projecting forward.

EYES Set wide apart, medium in size, not full, as dark as possible. Slightly sunk in head, sharp and intelligent, which, looking from under heavy eyebrows, impart a piercing look. Light-coloured eyes highly undesirable.

EARS Small, erect and carried firmly, terminating in sharp point, set neither too wide nor too close. Hair short and smooth (velvety), should not be cut. Free from any fringe at top. Round-pointed, broad, large or thick ears or too heavily coated with hair most undesirable.

MOUTH As broad between canine teeth as is consistent with varminty expression required. Teeth large for size of dog, with regular scissor bite, i.e. upper teeth closely overlapping lower teeth and set square to the jaws.

NECK Sufficiently long to allow proper set-on of head required, muscular and gradually thickening towards base allowing neck to merge into nicely sloping shoulders.

FOREQUARTERS Shoulders sloping backwards. Shoulder blades broad and lying close to chest wall. Shoulder joint placed forward, elbows well in, allowing foreleg to move freely, parallel to axis of body. Forelegs short and muscular, straight and thickly covered with short, hard hair.

BODY Compact. Back level, loins broad and strong. Chest deep and ribs well arched in upper half presenting a flattish side appearance. Back ribs of considerable depth and distance from last rib of quarters as short as compatible with free movement of body.

HINDQUARTERS Strong, muscular and wide across top. Legs short, muscular and sinewy. Thighs very muscular and not too wide apart. Hocks bent and well set in under body so as to be fairly close to each other when standing or moving. Straight or weak hocks most undesirable.

FEET Forefeet larger than hind, round, proportionate in size, strong, thickly padded and covered with short harsh hair. Hindfeet are smaller and thickly padded. Under surface of pads and all nails preferably black.

TAIL 12.5-15 cm (5-6 in) long, covered with harsh hair, no feathering, as straight as possible, carried jauntily, not gay or carried over back. A long tail undesirable, and on no account should tails be docked.

GAIT/MOVEMENT Free, straight and easy all round. In front, legs freely extended forward from shoulder. Hind movement free, strong and close. Stifle and hocks well flexed and hocks drawn under body giving drive. Stiff, stilted movement behind and cow-hocks highly undesirable.

COAT Double-coated. Outer coat consists of harsh hair, about 5 cm (2 in) long, free from any curl. Undercoat, which resembles fur, short, soft and close. Open coats most undesirable.

COLOUR White.

SIZE Height at withers approx 28 cm (11 in).

FAULTS Any departure from the foregoing points should be considered a fault and the seriousness with which the fault should be regarded should be in exact proportion to its degree.

NOTE Male animals should have two apparently normal testicles fully descended into the scrotum.

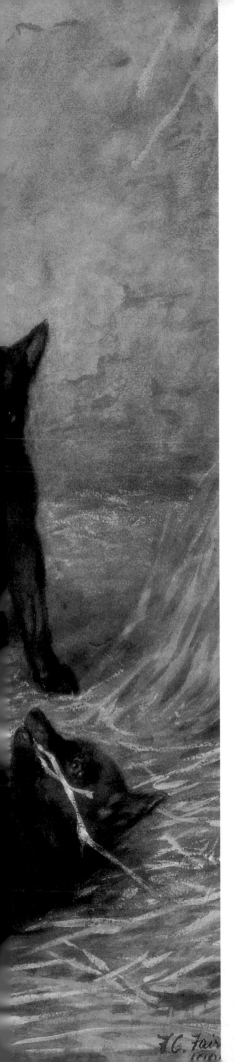

UTILITY GROUP

LEFT: *A Schipperke with puppies (1900), painted in oil on canvas by Frances L Fairman (1836–1923). The artist was an active member of The Ladies Kennel Association and especially interested in oriental breeds – although this dog comes from Flanders.*

BOSTON TERRIER

UTILITY

184

A REAL YANKEE-DOODLE-DANDY. Although he owes a little of his ancestry to the British Bulldog, the breed actually came into being in the late nineteenth century in the eastern states of America. His short, square muzzle identifies him as a 'Bull breed' and his small erect ears combined with his well-defined colouring add to his smart appearance. Dapper and classy he is a real eye-catcher when out and about.

The Boston is derived from original pit fighting dogs and is one of the few breeds 'made in the USA'. It was in 1893 that a mix of bull and terrier types produced the first pair of dogs which were to become the foundation of the Boston Terrier.

He is good-tempered and a happy house-dog – if a little boisterous. His short coat is easy to care for and his sense of intelligence is highly developed.

GENERAL APPEARANCE Smooth-coated, short-headed, compactly built, short-tailed, well balanced dog of medium size, brindle in colour, evenly marked with white. Body rather short and well knit; limbs strong and neatly turned; tail short and no feature so prominent that the dog appears badly proportioned. Dog must convey an impression of determination, strength and activity, with style of a high order; carriage easy and graceful.

CHARACTERISTICS Lively and intelligent.

TEMPERAMENT Determined and strong willed.

HEAD AND SKULL Skull square, flat on top, free from wrinkles; cheeks flat; brow abrupt, stop well defined. Muzzle short, square, wide and deep with no tendency to taper in proportion to skull; free from wrinkles; shorter in length than in width and depth, approximately one-third of length of skull; width and depth carried out well to end; muzzle from stop to end of nose on a line parallel to top of skull; nose black, wide with

well defined line between nostrils. Jaws broad and square. Flews of good depth, not pendulous, completely covering teeth when mouth closed. Head in proportion to size of dog.

EYES Wide apart, large and round, dark in colour; expression alert, kind and intelligent. Eyes set square in skull, outside corners on a line with cheeks when viewed from front.

EARS Carried erect; small, thin, situated as near corner of skull as possible.

MOUTH Teeth short and regular, bite even, or sufficiently undershot to square muzzle.

NECK Of fair length, slightly arched, carrying head gracefully; neatly set into shoulders.

FOREQUARTERS Shoulders sloping, legs set moderately wide apart on line with point of shoulders; straight in bone and well muscled; pasterns short and strong. Elbows turning neither in nor out.

BODY Deep with good width of chest; back short; ribs deep and well sprung, carried well back to loins; loins short and muscular; rump curving slightly to set-on of tail; flank very slightly cut up; body appears short but not chunky.

HINDQUARTERS Legs set true, good turn of stifle, hocks well let down; turning neither in nor out; thighs strong and well muscled.

FEET Round, small, compact, turning neither in nor out; toes well arched.

TAIL Set-on low; short, fine, tapering, straight or screw; devoid of fringes or coarse hair, never carried above horizontal.

GAIT/MOVEMENT Easy and graceful. Sure-footed, straight-gaited, forelegs and hindlegs moving straight ahead with perfect rhythm. Each step indicating grace and power.

COAT Short, smooth, lustrous and fine in texture.

COLOUR Brindle with white markings; brindle must show throughout body distinctly; black with white markings but brindles with white markings preferred. Ideal markings; white muzzle, even white blaze over head, collar, breast, part of whole of forelegs, and hindlegs below hocks.

SIZE Weight not exceeding 11.4 kg (25 lb) divided by classes as follows: Lightweight: under 6.8 kg (15 lb); Middleweight: 6.8 kg (15 lb) and under 9.1 kg (20 lb); Heavyweight: 9.1 kg (20 lb) and under 11.4 kg (25 lb).

FAULTS Any departure from the foregoing points should be considered a fault and the seriousness with which the fault should be regarded should be in exact proportion to its degree.

NOTE Male animals should have two apparently normal testicles fully descended into the scrotum.

BULLDOG

ONE OF OUR OLDEST INDIGENOUS breeds, known as the national dog of Great Britain, and associated throughout the world with British determination and the legendary John Bull.

The Bulldog was first classified as such in the 1630s though there is earlier mention of similar types referred to as bandogs, a term reserved today for a type of fighting dog. Used originally for bull-baiting, the Bulldog also fought its way through the dog pits but after 1835 began to evolve into the shorter-faced, more squat version we now know. It entered the showring in 1860 and the ensuing years saw a big personality change.

A delightfully ugly dog with a pugilistic expression, which belies a loving, affectionate nature to family and friends. He has a reputation for tenacity and is very courageous, strong and powerful. A little bit stubborn by nature, but good-tempered with children, of whom he is also fiercely protective. The impression he gives of being slow and sluggish is completely contradicted by the great bursts of speed which he can and does produce when the occasion demands.

His mood can be dignified, humorous or comical, and he has many endearing ways.

GENERAL APPEARANCE Smooth-coated, thick-set, rather low in stature, broad, powerful and compact. Head massive, fairly large in proportion to size but no point so much in excess of others as to destroy the general symmetry, or make the dog appear deformed, or interfere with its powers of motion. Face short, muzzle broad, blunt and inclined upwards. Body short, well knit, limbs stout, well muscled and in hard condition. Hindquarters high and strong but somewhat lighter in comparison with heavy foreparts. Bitches not so grand or well developed as dogs.

CHARACTERISTICS Conveys impression of determination, strength and activity.

TEMPERAMENT Alert, bold, loyal, dependable, courageous, fierce in appearance, but possessed of affectionate nature.

HEAD AND SKULL Skull large in circumference, should measure round (in front of ears) approximately height of dog at shoulder. Viewed from front appears very high from corner of lower jaw to apex of skull; also very broad and square. Cheeks well rounded and extended sideways beyond eyes. Viewed from side, head appears very high and short from back to point of nose. Forehead flat with skin upon and about head, loose and wrinkled, neither prominent nor overhanging face. Projections of frontal bones prominent, broad, square and high; deep, wide indentation between eyes. From stop, a furrow both broad and deep extending to middle of skull being traceable to apex. Face from front of cheek bone to nose, short, skin wrinkled. Muzzle short, broad, turned upwards and very deep from corner of eye to corner of mouth. Nose and nostrils large, broad and black, under no circumstances liver colour, red or brown; top set back towards eyes. Distance from inner corner of eye (or from centre of stop between eyes) to extreme tip of nose not exceeding length from tip of nose to edge of underlip. Nostrils large and wide with well defined vertical straight line between. Flews (chops) thick, broad, pendant and very deep, hanging completely over lower jaws at sides, not in front joining underlip in front and quite covering teeth. Jaws broad, massive and square, lower jaw projecting considerably in front of upper and turning up. Viewed from front, the various properties of the face must be equally balanced on either side of an imaginary line down centre.

EYES Seen from front, situated low down in skull, well away from ears. Eyes and stop in same straight line, at right angles to furrow. Wide apart, but outer corners within the outline of cheeks. Round in shape, of moderate size, neither sunken nor prominent, in colour very dark – almost black – showing no white when looking directly forward.

EARS Set high – i.e. front edge of each ear (as viewed from front) joins outline of skull at top corner of such outline, so as to place them as wide apart, as high and as far from eyes as possible. Small and thin. 'Rose ear' correct, i.e. folding inwards back, upper or front inner edge curving outwards and backwards, showing part of inside of burr.

MOUTH Jaws broad and square with six small front teeth between canines in an even row. Canines wide apart. Teeth large and strong, not seen when mouth closed. When viewed from front, under jaw directly under upper jaw and parallel.

NECK Moderate in length (rather short than long), very thick, deep and strong. Well arched at back, with much loose, thick and wrinkled skin about throat, forming dewlap on each side, from lower jaw to chest.

FOREQUARTERS Shoulders broad, sloping and deep, very powerful and muscular giving appearance of being 'tacked on' body. Brisket capacious, round and very deep from top of shoulders to lowest part where it joins chest. Well let down between forelegs. Large in diameter, round behind forelegs (not flat-sided, ribs well rounded). Forelegs very stout and strong, well developed, set wide apart, thick, muscular and straight, presenting rather bowed outline, but bones of legs large and straight, not bandy nor curved and short in proportion to hindlegs, but not so short as to make back appear long, or detract from dog's activity and so cripple him. Elbows low and standing well away from ribs. Pasterns short, straight and strong.

BODY Chest wide, laterally round, prominent and deep. Back short, strong, broad at shoulders, comparatively narrower at loins. Slight fall to back close behind shoulders (lowest part) whence spine should rise to loins (top higher than top of shoulder), curving again more suddenly to tail, forming arch (termed roach back) – a distinctive characteristic of breed. Body well ribbed up behind with belly tucked up and not pendulous.

HINDQUARTERS Legs large and muscular, longer in proportion than forelegs, so as to elevate loins. Hocks slightly bent, well let down; legs long and muscular from loins to hock; short, straight, strong lower part. Stifles round and turned slightly outwards away from body. Hocks thereby made to approach each other and hindfeet to turn outwards.

FEET Fore, straight and turning very slightly outward; of medium size and moderately round. Hind, round and compact. Toes compact and thick, well split up, making knuckles prominent and high.

TAIL Set-on low, jutting out rather straight and then turning downwards. Round, smooth and devoid of fringe or coarse hair. Moderate in length – rather short than long – thick at root, tapering quickly to a fine point. Downward carriage (not having a decided upward curve at end) and never carried above back.

GAIT/MOVEMENT Peculiarly heavy and constrained, appearing to walk with short, quick steps on tips of toes, hindfeet not lifted high, appearing to skim ground, running with one or other shoulder rather advanced.

COAT Fine texture, short, close and smooth (hard only from shortness and closeness, not wiry).

COLOUR Whole or smut (i.e. whole colour with black mask or muzzle). Only whole colours (which should be brilliant and pure of their sort) viz., brindles, reds with their various shades, fawns, fallows, etc., white and pied (i.e. combination of white with any of the foregoing colours). Dudley, black and black with tan highly undesirable.

SIZE Dogs: 25 kg (55 lb); bitches: 22.7 kg (50 lb).

FAULTS Any departure from the foregoing points should be considered a fault and the seriousness with which the fault should be regarded should be in exact proportion to its degree.

NOTE Male animals should have two apparently normal testicles fully descended into the scrotum.

CANAAN DOG

(INTERIM)

A RECENT RE-INTRODUCTION TO THE United Kingdom, the Canaan Dog is generally accepted as the national breed of Israel. A few have been registered here in past decades, but it is only in the last few years that the breed has begun to be exhibited at shows.

He stands up to 61 centimetres (24 inches) at the shoulder, which means he is at the upper end of the medium-sized dogs. He has his origins in the feral dog of the Middle East, the pariah dog, and selective breeding is evolving a distinct breed type. The current interim breed standard is based closely on that of the Fédération Cynologique Internationale (FCI), but there is some disagreement on the subject by those who consider themselves to be the founders of the current UK revival.

Suffice it to say that he is an effective guarding dog, alert and versatile, and that no doubt, as time goes on, he will settle to a definite British pattern.

GENERAL APPEARANCE Medium-sized, well balanced, strong and square. Marked distinction between sexes.

CHARACTERISTICS Agile, alert and highly intelligent.

TEMPERAMENT Confident and vigilant. Aloof with strangers. Steady and loyal to owners.

HEAD AND SKULL Well proportioned, wedge-shaped of medium length, appearing broader due to low-set ears. Skull somewhat flattened between ears. Stop shallow but defined. Length from muzzle to stop approximately equal to length from stop to occiput. Nose black. Lips tight and well pigmented.

EYES Dark, almond-shaped and obliquely set with black rims.

EARS Medium-sized, erect and set low with broad base and rounded tip.

MOUTH Jaws strong with a perfect, regular and complete scissor bite, i.e. upper teeth closely overlapping lower teeth and set square to the jaws; level bite acceptable.

NECK Muscular, well arched, of medium length without throatiness.

FOREQUARTERS Well laid muscular shoulder, elbows close to body. Medium-boned. When viewed from the front forelegs straight. Pasterns slightly sloping.

BODY Square, withers well developed, back level, loins muscular, chest deep and of moderate breadth, ribs well sprung. Belly well tucked up.

HINDQUARTERS Powerful, broad muscular thighs, hocks well let down. Legs straight when viewed from behind.

FEET Strong, round and cat-like with hard pads.

TAIL Set high, thick brush carried curled over back when trotting or excited.

GAIT/MOVEMENT Energetic and natural trot.

COAT Outer coat dense, harsh and straight of short to medium length. Undercoat close and profuse according to season.

COLOUR Sandy to red-brown, white, black, or spotted, with or without a symmetrical black mask. White markings permitted on all colours. Grey, brindle, black and tan or tricolour undesirable.

SIZE Height: 50-60 cm (20-24 in). Weight: 18-25 kg (40-55 lb).

FAULTS Any departure from the foregoing points should be considered a fault and the seriousness with which the fault should be regarded should be in exact proportion to its degree.

NOTE Male animals should have two apparently normal testicles fully descended into the scrotum.

CHOW CHOW

THE ANCESTRY OF THE CHOW IS attributed to China where he was kept as a guard dog, and also used for hunting. He made his way to England sometime during the late eighteenth century. He is unique with his stiff, stilted movement and bluish-black tongue, and such is his appearance that he cannot be mistaken for any other breed. He is aloof, stand-offish, and extremely loyal to his owner, with a tendency to be a one-man dog. Not noisy, but when roused he is well able to defend home and owner.

The Rough Chow has a coat which is abundant, thick, and stands off from the body. It requires about five minutes' daily grooming to keep it in good condition. The Smooth Chow has a woolly undercoat with a short top coat of plush texture. Although red is the most popular colour for both varieties, followed by black, they can also be seen in the most lovely whole blue, or shades of fawn.

The Chow has been known in China for upwards of 2000 years and is related to Spitz dogs of the Nordic type, also containing something of the mastiff. Because of China's 'closed door' policy to the rest of the world Chows did not begin to appear in other countries until around 1800 and were not really noticed in Britain until the 1920s, with a number being shown at Crufts in 1925.

GENERAL APPEARANCE Active, compact, short-coupled and essentially well balanced, leonine in appearance, proud, dignified bearing; well knit frame; tail carried well over back.

CHARACTERISTICS Quiet dog, good guard, bluish-black tongue; unique in its stilted gait.

TEMPERAMENT Independent, loyal, yet aloof.

HEAD AND SKULL Skull flat, broad; stop not pronounced, well filled out under eyes. Muzzle moderate in length, broad from eyes to end (not pointed at end like a fox). Nose, large and wide in all cases, black (with exception of cream and near white in which case a light-coloured nose permissible, and in blues and fawns a self-coloured nose).

EYES Dark, oval-shaped, medium-sized and clean. A matching coloured eye permissible in blues and fawns. Clean eye, free from entropion, never being penalised for sake of mere size.

ABOVE: *Premier Champion Chow VIII, painted in 1899 by Frances L Fairman, won 62 Firsts, nine Championships and six Premier Championships and Specials.*

EARS Small, thick, slightly rounded at tip, carried stiffly and wide apart but tilting well forward over eyes and slightly towards each other, giving peculiar characteristic scowling expression of the breed. Scowl never to be achieved by loose wrinkled skin of head.

MOUTH Teeth strong and level, jaws strong, with a perfect, regular and complete scissor bite, i.e. upper teeth closely overlapping lower teeth and set square to the jaws. Tongue bluish-black. Roof of mouth and flews black (blue-black), gums preferably black.

NECK Strong, full, not short, set well on shoulders and slightly arched.

FOREQUARTERS Shoulders muscular and sloping. Forelegs perfectly straight, of moderate length, with good bone.

BODY Chest broad and deep. Ribs well sprung but not barrelled. Back short, level and strong. Loins powerful.

HINDQUARTERS Hindlegs muscular, hocks well let down, with minimal angulation, essential to produce characteristic stilted gait. From hocks downwards to appear straight, hocks never flexing forward.

FEET Small, round, cat-like, standing well on toes.

TAIL Set high, carried well over back.

GAIT/MOVEMENT Short and stilted. Forelegs and hindlegs moving parallel to each other and straight forward.

COAT Either rough or smooth.
ROUGH: profuse, abundant, dense, straight and stand-off. Outer coat rather coarse in texture, with soft woolly undercoat. Especially thick round neck forming mane or ruff and with good culottes or breechings on back of thighs.

SMOOTH: coat short, abundant, dense, straight, upstanding, not flat, plush-like in texture.

Any artificial shortening of the coat which alters the natural outline or expression should be penalised.

COLOUR Whole coloured black, red, blue, fawn, cream or white, frequently shaded but not in patches or parti-coloured (underpart of tail and back of thighs frequently of a lighter colour).

SIZE Dogs: 48-56 cm (19-22 in) at shoulder. Bitches: 46-51 cm (18-20 in) at shoulder.

FAULTS Any departure from the foregoing points should be considered a fault and the seriousness with which the fault should be regarded should be in exact proportion to its degree.

NOTE Male animals should have two apparently normal testicles fully descended into the scrotum.

DALMATIAN

THE DALMATIAN HAS A VERY distinctive appearance, being either black spotted, or liver spotted, the spots standing out well on the pure white background colour of his coat. As a puppy he is born pure white, making it impossible to know whether his spots will be black or liver.

The breed was very popular in Britain during the Regency period, and was known as the 'carriage dog', as he was used to run under or beside all types of carriages, from those of the gentry to the mail coach. The Dalmatian also used to run ahead of the horse-drawn fire engines of London, earning itself the name 'Firehouse Dog'. When running with carriages or coaches it was termed 'Marathon Runner' and is a breed of incredible endurance, travelling over long distances at a moderate speed. An excellent companion and house-dog, he has a sporting side to his nature, with a good nose and a soft mouth. An active, agile dog, strong and muscular, who enjoys plenty of exercise, he is more suited to country life than the town.

GENERAL APPEARANCE A distinctively spotted dog, balanced, strong, muscular and active. Symmetrical in outline, free from coarseness and lumber.

CHARACTERISTICS A carriage dog of good demeanour, capable of great endurance and a fair turn of speed.

TEMPERAMENT Outgoing and friendly, not shy or hesitant, free from nervousness and aggression.

HEAD AND SKULL Of fair length, skull flat, reasonably broad between ears, moderately well defined in front of ears. Moderate amount of stop. Entirely free from wrinkle. Muzzle long, powerful, never snipy; lips clean, fitting jaw moderately closely. Nose in black spotted variety always black, in liver spotted variety always brown.

EYES Set moderately well apart, medium size, round, bright and sparkling, with intelligent expression. Colour, dark in black spotted, amber in liver spotted. Eye rims preferably completely black in black spotted, and liver brown in liver spotted.

EARS Set-on rather high, moderate size, rather wide at base, gradually tapering to rounded point. Fine in texture, carried close to head. Marking well broken up, preferably spotted.

MOUTH Jaws strong, with a perfect, regular and complete scissor bite, i.e. upper teeth closely overlapping lower teeth and set square to the jaws.

NECK Fairly long, nicely arched, light and tapering. Entirely free from throatiness.

FOREQUARTERS Shoulders moderately oblique, clean and muscular. Elbows close to body. Forelegs perfectly straight with strong round bone down to feet, with slight spring at pastern joint.

BODY Chest not too wide but deep and capacious with plenty of lung and heart room. Ribs well sprung, well defined withers, powerful level back, loin strong, clean, muscular and slightly arched.

HINDQUARTERS Rounded, muscles clean with well developed second thigh, good turn of stifle, hocks well defined.

FEET Round, compact, with well arched toes, cat-like, round, tough, elastic pads. Nails black or white in black spotted variety, in liver spotted, brown or white.

TAIL Length reaching approximately to hock. Strong at insertion gradually tapering towards end, never inserted too low or too high, free from coarseness and carried with a slight upward curve, never curled. Preferably spotted.

GAIT/MOVEMENT Great freedom of movement. Smooth, powerful, rhythmic action with long stride. Viewed from behind, legs move in parallel, hindlegs tracking the fore. A short stride and paddling action incorrect.

COAT Short, hard, dense; sleek and glossy in appearance.

COLOUR Ground colour pure white. Black spotted, dense black spots, and liver spotted, liver brown spots; not running together but round and well defined. In size one-pence to fifty-pence piece. Spots as well distributed as possible. Spots on extremities smaller than those on body. Patches, tricolours and lemon spots highly undesirable. Bronzing on spots undesirable in adults.

SIZE Overall balance of prime importance. Ideal height: dogs: 58.4–61 cm (23–24 in); bitches: 55.9–58.4 cm (22–23 in).

FAULTS Any departure from the foregoing points should be considered a fault and the seriousness with which the fault should be regarded should be in exact proportion to its degree.

NOTE Male animals should have two apparently normal testicles fully descended into the scrotum.

FRENCH BULLDOG

A COMPACTLY BUILT DOG WHO, IN SPITE of his name, is believed to be at least partly of British origin. He is a descendant of the Toy Bulldog which was bred during the nineteenth century and exported to France where the breed became popular. In fact, English lacemakers from the Midlands who went to work in France took small Bulldogs with them. This stock is believed to have mixed with short-faced bull-baiting dogs from other European countries. This 'new' breed was brought to England and first shown around 1900, with a French Bulldog club being formed in 1903.

The bat ear is a distinctive feature of this breed and adds to the droll expression. He is very intelligent, always ready for fun, has an affectionate disposition, is not noisy and has a short, easy-to-keep-clean coat, making him an ideal house pet. Although he has a jolly, engaging personality and is very vivacious he is not a boisterous dog. Comfort means a lot to him and he will happily live in house or flat as an integral part of the family. This attractive medium-to-small-sized dog is bred in three colours – brindle, pied and fawn.

GENERAL APPEARANCE Sturdy, compact, solid, small dog with good bone, short, smooth coat. No point exaggerated, balance essential.

CHARACTERISTICS Full of courage, yet with clown-like qualities. Bat ears and short undocked tail essential features of the breed.

TEMPERAMENT Vivacious, deeply affectionate, intelligent.

HEAD AND SKULL Head square, large and broad but in proportion to dog's size. Skull nearly flat between ears, domed forehead, loose skin forming symmetrical wrinkles. Muzzle broad, deep and set well back, muscles of cheeks well developed; nose and lips black. Stop well defined. Lower jaw deep, square, broad, slightly undershot and well turned up. Nose extremely short, black and wide, with open nostrils and line between well defined. Lips thick, meeting each other in centre, completely hiding teeth. Upper lip covers lower on each side with plenty of cushion, never so exaggerated as to hang too much below level of lower jaw.

EYES Preferably dark and matching. Moderate size, round, neither sunken nor prominent, showing no white when looking straight forward; set wide apart and low down in skull.

EARS 'Bat ears', of medium size, wide at base, rounded at top; set high, carried upright and parallel, a sufficient width of skull preventing them being too close together; skin soft and fine, orifice as seen from the front, showing entirely.

MOUTH Slightly undershot. Teeth sound and regular, but not visible when the mouth is closed. Tongue must not protrude.

NECK Powerful, with loose skin at throat, but not exaggerated. Well arched and thick, but not too short.

FOREQUARTERS Legs set wide apart, straight-boned, strong, muscular and short.

BODY Short, cobby, muscular and well rounded with deep, wide brisket; roach back; strong; wide at shoulders and narrowing at loins; good 'cut up', ribs well sprung.

HINDQUARTERS Legs strong, muscular and longer than forelegs, thus raising loins above shoulders. Hocks well let down.

FEET Small, compact and placed in continuation of line of leg, with absolutely sound pasterns. Hindfeet rather longer than the forefeet. Toes compact; well knuckled; nails short, thick and preferably black.

TAIL Undocked, very short, set low, thick at root, tapering quickly towards tip, either straight or kinked, never curling over back nor carried gaily.

GAIT/MOVEMENT Free and flowing.

COAT Texture fine, smooth, lustrous, short and close.

COLOUR Brindle, pied or fawn. Tan, mouse and grey/blue highly undesirable.
BRINDLE: a mixture of black and coloured hairs. May contain white provided brindle predominates.
PIED: white predominates over brindle. Whites are classified with pieds for show purposes; but their eyelashes and eye rims should be black. In pieds the white should be clear with definite brindle patches and no ticking or black spots.
FAWN: may contain brindle hairs but must have black eyelashes and eye rims.

SIZE Ideal weight: dogs: 12.7 kg (28 lb); bitches: 10.9 kg (24 lb). Soundness not to be sacrificed to smallness.

FAULTS Any departure from the foregoing points should be considered a fault and the seriousness with which the fault should be regarded should be in exact proportion to its degree.

NOTE Male animals should have two apparently normal testicles fully descended into the scrotum.

GERMAN SPITZ

THERE HAVE BEEN GERMAN SPITZ BREEDS for many years, varying in size from the tiniest at about 2.3 kilograms (5 pounds) in weight to the largest in the 20 kilogram (45 pound) range. Recently accepted versions in two sizes by shoulder measurement have been introduced to The Kennel Club's list of breeds.

The Klein variety should measure between 23 and 29 centimetres (9 and 11½ inches), while the Mittel stands between 30 and 38 centimetres (12 and 15 inches). Otherwise the two should be identical in shape and characteristics. Interestingly, there are no restrictions on colour.

The Geman Spitz is an independent character with a happy outlook on life. His harsh outer coat coupled with his thick undercoat insulates him against all weathers. His high-set, well curled tail and his brisk movement give him an air of considerable importance in his bearing. Not a difficult breed to maintain as long as his grooming is thorough. He makes an ideal pet quite capable of living with old and young alike.

GENERAL APPEARANCE Compact, short-coupled and well knit with an almost square outline. Firm condition, the profuse coat not disguising any lack of substance.

CHARACTERISTICS The German Spitz is intelligent, active and alert. Its buoyancy, independence and devotion to the family are the breed characteristics.

TEMPERAMENT Happy, equable disposition, showing confidence, with no sign of nervousness or aggression.

HEAD AND SKULL Medium-large, broad and nearly flat skull when viewed from above and narrowing in a wedge shape to the nose. Stop moderately defined; muzzle approximately half length of head. Cheeks clean. Flews tight, no trace of lippiness.

NOSE Black in black, white, black/white parti-colours, black/tan bi-colours. Self-colour as compatible with coat colour in other colour varieties. Never parti-colour or pink.

EYES Medium size, oval-shaped and obliquely set. Not too wide apart. Always dark with black rims in blacks, whites, black/white parti-colours, black/tan bi-colours. As dark as compatible with coat colour in other colour varieties.

EARS Small, triangular and set rather high. Perfectly erect.

MOUTH A perfect, regular and complete scissor bite, i.e. upper teeth closely overlapping lower teeth and set square to the jaws. Black lips in blacks, whites, black/white in parti-colours, black/tan bi-colours. Colour as compatible with coat colour in other colour varieties.

NECK Clean, moderately short and well set into the shoulders.

FOREQUARTERS Moderately sloping shoulder; upper arm of sufficient length to ensure elbow is vertically below point of withers. Moderate forechest. Elbows equidistant between ground and withers, turning neither in nor out. Well-boned, straight legs. Pasterns strong and flexible.

BODY Length from point of shoulder to point of buttock equal to height at withers; short, well-developed loin. Moderate tuck-up. Well ribbed up and rounded. Distance from brisket to ground not less than half the height from ground to withers. Topline level.

HINDQUARTERS Moderate angulation with hocks moderately well let down. Neither cow-hocked nor wide behind.

FEET Small, rounded, cat-like, with well arched toes.

TAIL High-set, curled right up from root, lying curled over back.

GAIT/MOVEMENT Moving without exaggeration from any angle. Straight coming and going. Viewed from side, effortless, brisk action, retaining topline.

COAT Double coat consisting of a soft woolly undercoat and a long harsh-textured perfectly straight top coat covering the whole of the body. Very abundant around neck and forequarters with a frill of profuse off-standing straight hair extending over the shoulders. Forelimbs well feathered tapering from elbows to pasterns. Hindlimbs feathered to hocks. Ears covered with soft, short hair. Hair on the face smooth and short. Tail profusely covered with long spreading hair. This is not a trimmed breed and evidence of trimming and shaping, other than tidying of the feet, anal area and legs below the hocks, unacceptable.

COLOUR All colour varieties and markings acceptable. Butterfly pigment not permitted with any colour.

SIZE: Height: Klein: 23-29 cm (9-11½ in)
Mittel: 30-38 cm (12-15 in)
Dogs masculine, bitches feminine.

FAULTS Any departure from the foregoing points should be considered a fault and the seriousness with which the fault should be regarded should be in exact proportion to its degree.

NOTE Male animals should have two apparently normal testicles fully descended into the scrotum.

JAPANESE AKITA

THE MOST POPULAR BREED IN HIS native Japan, a large, upstanding, dignified dog, whose proud head carriage and stance is enhanced by his small, triangular ears and dark eyes. His strong body is balanced by his large, full tail curling to meet his back.

The Akita Inu (meaning 'large dog') traces its origins back many centuries to the polar regions from where Spitz-type dogs found their way to the northern mountainous areas of Japan. The largest and most powerful were used for breeding and the Akita emerged some three hundred years ago. He was developed originally as a fighting dog but diverted into hunting for black bear, wild boar and deer.

He comes in a variety of brilliant and clear colours often set off by a facial mask or blaze. His impressive appearance is matched by his strength and character, which is reserved and quiet but dominant over other dogs. He makes an excellent guard, but would probably not be the best companion for an audacious terrier. Devoted and protective towards his owners, he is also very affectionate.

GENERAL APPEARANCE Large, powerful, alert, with much substance and heavy bone.

CHARACTERISTICS Large, broad head, with relatively small eyes and erect ears carried forward in line with back of neck; large, curled tail, in balance with head.

TEMPERAMENT Dignified, courageous, aloof; tends to show dominance over other dogs.

HEAD AND SKULL Large, in balance with body, skull flat, forehead broad, defined stop and clear furrow. Head forms blunt triangle when viewed from above, free from wrinkle. Muzzle broad and strong, cheeks well developed. Nose large

and black, bridge straight. Lips tight and black. In white dogs flesh-colour pigmentation is permissible on nose and lips. Length from nose to stop is to length from stop to occiput as 2 is to 3.

EYES Relatively small, almond-shaped, clean, moderately set apart and dark brown. Eye rims dark and tight.

EARS Relatively small, thick, triangular, not low-set, carried forward over eyes in line with back of neck, firmly erect. Moderately set apart; slightly rounded at tips.

MOUTH Jaws strong, with a perfect, regular and complete scissor bite, i.e. upper teeth closely overlapping lower teeth and set square to the jaws.

NECK Thick and muscular, comparatively short, widening gradually toward shoulders. Pronounced crest blends with back of skull.

FOREQUARTERS Shoulders strong and powerful, moderately laid back. Elbows very tight. Forelegs well boned and straight when viewed from front. Pasterns inclining at approximately 15 degrees.

BODY Longer than high, as 10 is to 9 in males, 11 to 9 in bitches. Chest wide and deep, depth of brisket is one-half height of dog at shoulder. Well developed forechest. Level back, firmly muscled loin, moderate tuck-up. Skin pliant but not loose.

HINDQUARTERS Strong and muscular, well developed thighs, moderate turn of stifle. Strong hocks, with only moderate angulation, well let down, turning neither in nor out.

FEET Thick, well knuckled and very tight, turning neither in nor out. Pads hard. Nails hard. Dewclaws on hindlegs customarily removed.

TAIL Large and full, set high, carried over back, full or double curl, always dipping to or below level of back. On a three-quarter curl tail, tip dips down flank. Root large and strong. Hair coarse, straight and full with no appearance of a plume. Sickle or uncurled tail highly undesirable.

GAIT/MOVEMENT Resilient and vigorous with strides of moderate length. Back remains firm and level. Hindlegs move in line with front legs, whilst gaiting will single track.

COAT Outer coat coarse, straight, and standing off body. Undercoat soft and dense. Coat at withers and rump is approximately 5 cm (2 in), slightly longer than on rest of body, more profuse on tail. No indication of ruff or feathering.

COLOUR Any colour including white, brindle or pinto. Colours are brilliant and clear. Markings are well defined with or without mask or blaze.

SIZE Height at withers: dogs: 66–71 cm (26–28 in); bitches: 61–66 cm (24–26 in).

FAULTS Any departure from the foregoing points should be considered a fault and the seriousness with which the fault should be regarded should be in exact proportion to its degree.

NOTE Male animals should have two apparently normal testicles fully descended into the scrotum.

JAPANESE SHIBA INU

(INTERIM)

UTILITY

202

A RECENT NEWCOMER FROM JAPAN AND still only registered on the 'Imported Breed Register', the Shiba Inu is a neat, tidy Spitz-style dog, and one that shows every sign of becoming popular. Shiba Inu literally means 'small dog' and, ideally, should look like a smaller version of the Akita. Shibas originate in the mountainous inland areas of Japan, their work being that of a hunting dog, mainly of ground game though occasionally called on to help track larger game such as boar and deer.

A very alert, small dog, he gives the impression of being interested in everything going on around him. His size makes him ideal as a pet in such a highly populated country as Japan, where he is one of the most popular dogs. On first sight one expects that he could be a somewhat yappy animal, but in fact he tends to watch and study rather than shout the odds.

The thick, dense undercoat keeps him very warm and copes with rain very efficiently. Colourwise, most of the specimens so far seen here are red, but the standard allows him to be black, black and tan, or brindle, as well as white with red or grey.

A breed to watch as its genetic base increases with more imports coming in from Japan and elsewhere.

GENERAL APPEARANCE Small, well balanced, sturdy dog of Spitz type. Very slightly longer than height at withers.

CHARACTERISTICS Lively and friendly.

TEMPERAMENT Bright, active, keen and alert, also docile and faithful.

HEAD AND SKULL Head appears as a blunt triangle when viewed from above. Broad skull, cheeks well developed. Definite stop with slight furrow. Muzzle straight, of good depth, tapering gradually. Lips tight. Black nose preferred but flesh-coloured acceptable in white dogs.

EYES Relatively small, almond, set well apart and dark brown.

EARS Small, triangular, pricked and inclining slightly forward.

MOUTH Jaws strong with a perfect, regular and complete scissor bite, i.e. upper teeth closely overlapping lower teeth and set square to the jaws.

NECK Medium length, thick and muscular.

FOREQUARTERS Shoulders moderately sloping. Elbows set close to the body. Forearms straight. Pasterns slightly sloping.

BODY Withers high and well developed. Short, level back. Deep chest. Moderate spring of rib. Belly well tucked up.

HINDQUARTERS Long upper thigh, short strong second thigh. Hocks strong and parallel when seen from rear, turning neither in nor out. Well developed. Slight but definite bend of stifle.

FEET Cat-like with firm, tight, well knuckled toes. Pads firm and elastic. Dark nails preferred.

TAIL Set-on high. Thick and carried curled or curved as a sickle.

GAIT/MOVEMENT Light, quick and energetic.

COAT Hard, straight outer coat with soft, dense undercoat. Hair on tail slightly longer.

COLOUR Red, black, black and tan or brindle. White with red or grey tinge.

SIZE Height: dogs: 39.5 cm (15½ in); bitches: 36.5 cm (14½ in approx) with allowance of 1.5 cm (¾ in) either way.

FAULTS Any departure from the foregoing points should be considered a fault and the seriousness with which the fault should be regarded should be in exact proportion to its degree.

NOTE Male animals should have two apparently normal testicles fully descended into the scrotum.

JAPANESE SPITZ

YET ANOTHER OF THE GROWING ARMY of Spitz breeds being seen in the UK in ever increasing numbers. In a mere ten years registrations have risen from nought to one hundred and fifty per year, and are growing fast. This is hardly surprising as his startlingly white coat and bold, affectionate nature make him an attractive household pet. In addition he is never lost for a word and will indicate the presence of invaders in a forceful manner.

Like many of his type, his profuse stand-off coat and his thick underlay need hearty attention on a regular basis, but this does not mean that a new owner is condemning himself to hard labour for life.

A small, nimble dog, he demands neither excessive feeding nor much exercise. This is a lap-sized Spitz-type breed descended from Nordic long-haired dogs. It was taken to Japan early in the twentieth century and, after its arrival there, was bred to reduce its size. The breed was then exported to Sweden where it was readily accepted, and in 1970 some were brought from Sweden to England.

GENERAL APPEARANCE Profuse, pure white, stand-off coat. Pointed muzzle, triangular-shaped ears standing erect. Bushy tail curled over back. Overall quality of body firm and strong, full of flexibility. Ratio of height to length, 10:11.

CHARACTERISTICS Affectionate, companionable. Slightly chary at first meeting with strangers.

TEMPERAMENT Alert, intelligent, bold and lively.

HEAD AND SKULL Head medium size, without coarseness; moderately broad, slightly rounded. Skull broadest at occiput; well defined stop; forehead not protruding. Muzzle pointed, neither too thick nor too long. Lips firm, tightly closed, black. Nose round, small and black.

EYES Dark, moderate size, oval-shaped, set rather obliquely and not too wide apart; black eye rims.

EARS Small, angular, standing erect. Set high, facing forward, not too wide apart.

MOUTH Jaws strong with perfect, regular and complete scissor bite, i.e. upper teeth closely overlapping lower teeth and set square to the jaws.

NECK Strong, arched and of moderate length.

FOREQUARTERS Well proportioned and balanced. Shoulders well laid. Forelegs straight; elbows firm and tight; pasterns slightly sloping.

BODY Chest broad and deep. Ribs powerfully sprung; belly moderately firm with good tuck-up. Back straight and short. Loins broad and firm. Croup slightly arched.

HINDQUARTERS Well proportioned and balanced. Muscular, moderately angulated. Hindlegs parallel to each other viewed from rear.

FEET Small, round, cat-like and well cushioned. Pads black, nails preferably dark.

TAIL Moderate length, root set high, curled over back.

GAIT/MOVEMENT Light, nimble, active, energetic and very smooth.

COAT Outer coat straight and stand-off. Profuse, short, dense undercoat, soft in texture. Shorter on face, ears, front of fore- and hindlegs and below hocks. Remainder of body covered with long coat. Mane on neck and shoulders reaching down to brisket. Tail profusely covered with long hair.

COLOUR Pure white.

SIZE Height at shoulder: dogs: 30–36 cm (12–14 in); bitches slightly smaller.

FAULTS Any departure from the foregoing points should be considered a fault and the seriousness with which the fault should be regarded should be in exact proportion to its degree.

NOTE Male animals should have two apparently normal testicles fully descended into the scrotum.

KEESHOND

KNOWN AS THE DUTCH BARGE DOG, the Keeshond is a typical prick-eared, curly-tailed Spitz, full of activity and occasionally of noise. Quite capable of letting visitors know that their arrival has been detected, he is then only too ready to greet them as long-lost friends. Much easier to groom than his thick, long double coat would suggest, the Keeshond is hardy, loves his exercise and easily withstands the most Arctic temperatures.

He will take all the exercise you want to give him, is easy to feed and will give a great deal of companionship to all ages, from children and teenagers to the elderly.

Keeshonds take their name from the Dutch patriot, Cornelius de Gysalaer, who was nicknamed 'Kees'. His dog became the symbol of the Dutch Patriot party members who followed him, but his party fell and people turned their back on the breed, which went into decline. Nearly a hundred and fifty years later, in 1920, through the interest of Baroness von Hardenbroek, good specimens were found and once more the Keeshond prospered. It was seen not only in Holland but also in England and America in the 1930s.

GENERAL APPEARANCE Short, compact body, confident carriage. Fox-like head with small pointed ears, alert expression, large ruff, well feathered tail curled over back.

CHARACTERISTICS Sturdy, intelligent and adaptable, ideal companion, good guard, shows boldly.

TEMPERAMENT Bold, alert, friendly with marked guarding tendency.

HEAD AND SKULL Well proportioned, wedge-shaped when seen from above; from side showing definite stop. Dark muzzle equal to length of flat skull. Neither coarse nor snipy. Nose black.

EYES Dark, medium size, almond-shaped, obliquely set. Well defined 'spectacles' shown as a delicately pencilled black line slanting from outer corner of eye to lower corner of ear, coupled with distinct marking and shading forming expressive short eyebrows.

EARS Dark, small, ivy-leafed in shape. Erect, velvety texture. Well set-on head, neither too wide nor meeting.

MOUTH Jaws strong, with a perfect, regular and complete scissor bite, i.e. upper teeth closely overlapping lower teeth and set square to the jaws. Lips black.

NECK Moderately long and arched, covered with thick, profuse coat forming large ruff.

FOREQUARTERS Shoulders well sloped. Straight front of medium width with good bone.

BODY Short, compact; length from withers to tail equal to height at withers, well sprung in rib. Good depth of brisket.

HINDQUARTERS Strong muscled, hindlegs straight when viewed from behind. Hock showing slight angulation when viewed from side, profuse light-coloured trousers down to hocks.

FEET Well padded, round, cat-like, tight, cream in colour; black nails.

TAIL Moderately long, high-set, tightly curled over back, double curl highly desirable. Light plume on top where curled, with black tip, carried closely at all times.

GAIT/MOVEMENT Clean, brisk, straight and sharp.

COAT Harsh, off-standing, straight. Dense ruff, well feathered on forelegs and profuse trousers, not feathered below hock. Soft, thick, light-coloured (not tawny) undercoat. Never silky, wavy or woolly, nor forming a parting on back.

COLOUR A mixture of grey and black. Undercoat very pale grey or cream (not tawny). All shades of grey acceptable, body hairs black-tipped. Shoulder markings well defined and all markings definite. Forelegs and hocks cream with no black below wrist or hock. Pencilling acceptable.

SIZE Ideal height: dogs: 45.7 cm (18 in); bitches: 43.2 cm (17 in).

FAULTS Any departure from the foregoing points should be considered a fault and the seriousness with which the fault should be regarded should be in exact proportion to its degree.

NOTE Male animals should have two apparently normal testicles fully descended into the scrotum.

LEONBERGER

THE LEONBERGER HAILS FROM THE German town of Leonberg. Produced originally by crossing the Newfoundland with the St. Bernard, he is naturally a powerful dog, though not as massive as either of the breeds from which he came.

The breed was created in 1840 by the then mayor of Leonberg, Heinrich Essig, to honour his town. He was helped by monks from the Hospice of St. Bernard who sent him dogs. In return, Essig helped the monastery, whose St. Bernards had suffered in both numbers and quality, by sending the monks some of his crosses.

A good guarding breed, he is of generally equable temper and could well establish himself here. This is in spite of the fact that in 1918, after the end of the First World War, records stated that only five Leonbergers remained alive. Careful breeding began to restore the breed but it again suffered in the Second World War, after which only eight could be found. It took twenty-five more years to see the breed firmly re-established.

His well feathered, pendant ears, his black mask and his medium-textured coat give him an attractive appearance. He moves in a deliberate, firm fashion, and never appears to be in a hurry.

GENERAL APPEARANCE Strong and muscular.

CHARACTERISTICS Faithful, intelligent, amenable, good watchdog. Web-footed.

TEMPERAMENT Equable, self-confident, neither timid nor aggressive.

HEAD AND SKULL Tolerably wide skull; moderately deep. Broad, not too short, square muzzle. Slight stop, no wrinkles.

EYES Medium size, dark with intelligent, good-natured expression; showing no haw.

EARS Set-on high, close to head but not too far back. Wide as long, rounded at tips, well feathered and pendant.

MOUTH Lips black and well fitting with no open corners. Jaws strong, with a perfect, regular and complete scissor bite, i.e. upper teeth closely overlapping lower teeth and set square to the jaws.

NECK Strong, moderately long. No dewlap.

FOREQUARTERS Shoulders well laid, elbows close to chest; forelegs straight and well boned.

BODY Slightly longer than height at withers. Strong back and loins. Chest deep, ribs well sprung but not barrelled.

HINDQUARTERS Strong and muscular. Hindlegs well angulated and parallel when viewed from behind. Hind dewclaws removed.

FEET Tight, rounded and webbed. Pads black.

TAIL Well furnished, carried at half mast, never too high nor over back.

GAIT/MOVEMENT Strong and firm.

COAT Medium soft to hard, fairly long, lying close to body despite good undercoat. Slightly wavy but never curled. Very evident mane at throat and chest.

COLOUR Light yellow, golden to red-brown preferably with black mask. Dark or even black points on coat permissible. Small white star on chest and white hair on toes permissible. Hair at throat, on forelegs and underside of tail may be somewhat brighter.

SIZE Height at withers: dogs: 72-80 cm (28¾-32 in): bitches: 65-75 cm (26-30 in).

FAULTS Any departure from the foregoing points should be considered a fault and the seriousness with which the fault should be regarded should be in exact proportion to its degree.

NOTE Male animals should have two apparently normal testicles fully descended into the scrotum.

UTILITY

209

LHASA APSO

THIS BREED COMES FROM TIBET WHERE many live at high altitudes and the climate can be severe. He has to be a hardy little dog to withstand these conditions, and this has had a great influence on his development. His long, hard coat with its dense undercoat acts as insulation during winter, and the fall of hair over his eyes protects them from the wind, dust and glare. An Apso in full coat is a most impressive sight. It is not difficult to keep his coat in good condition, though grooming is necessary, for it will become matted if not properly cared for.

The Apso is one of several Eastern breeds to come to the West. The first Apsos arrived in Britain in the early 1920s and were being shown in London soon after. When they were first seen in Britain they were confused with other shaggy Oriental dogs and all were labelled 'Lhasa Terriers'. Later a distinction was made, especially between the Apso and the Tibetan Terrier which is thought to have been behind the early Apsos. A breed club for the Lhasa Apso was established in Britain in 1933.

He is of an independent nature, and can be quite stubborn, chary of strangers, but very loving and affectionate to friends and family. He will happily walk for miles over any terrain and makes a charming, very attractive pet, with his jaunty movement and proud head carriage, all set off by a beautifully plumed tail.

GENERAL APPEARANCE Well balanced, sturdy, heavily coated.

CHARACTERISTICS Gay and assertive.

TEMPERAMENT Alert, steady but somewhat aloof with strangers.

HEAD AND SKULL Heavy head furnishings with good fall over eyes, good whiskers and beard. Skull moderately narrow, falling away behind eyes, not quite flat, but not domed or apple-headed. Straight foreface with medium stop. Nose black. Muzzle about 4 cm (1½ in), but not square; length from tip of nose roughly one-third total length from nose to back of skull.

EYES Dark. Medium size, frontally placed, oval, neither large nor full, nor small and sunk. No white showing at base or top.

EARS Pendant, heavily feathered.

MOUTH Upper incisors close just inside lower, i.e. reverse scissor bite. Incisors in a broad and as straight a line as possible. Full dentition desirable.

NECK Strong and well arched.

FOREQUARTERS Shoulders well laid back. Forelegs straight, heavily furnished with hair.

BODY Length from point of shoulders to point of buttocks greater than height at withers. Well ribbed. Level topline. Strong loin. Balanced and compact.

HINDQUARTERS Well developed with good muscle. Good angulation. Heavily furnished with hair. Hocks when viewed from behind parallel and not too close together.

FEET Round, cat-like with firm pads. Well feathered.

TAIL High-set, carried well over back but not like a pot-hook. Often a kink at end. Well feathered.

GAIT/MOVEMENT Free and jaunty.

COAT Top coat long, heavy, straight, hard, neither woolly nor silky. Moderate undercoat.

COLOUR Golden, sandy, honey, dark grizzle, slate, smoke, parti-colour, black, white or brown. All equally acceptable.

SIZE Ideal height: dogs: 25.4 cm (10 in) at shoulder; bitches slightly smaller.

FAULTS Any departure from the foregoing points should be considered a fault and the seriousness with which the fault should be regarded should be in exact proportion to its degree.

NOTE Male animals should have two apparently normal testicles fully descended into the scrotum.

MINIATURE SCHNAUZER

A SMART, SMALL DOG WITH A WIRY coat. The breed was derived from the Schnauzer and, it is believed, the Affenpinscher. Of German origin, the breed comes in three colours – pepper and salt, black, and black and silver – and its eyebrows and whiskers enhance its distinctive appearance. The breed's handy size makes this a popular town dog. Schnauzers are robust, hardy and agile, are very alert and will always warn of the approach of strangers to their property. Daily grooming with a wire glove on the body and a comb through their whiskers and leg hair keeps them in good shape. They do require stripping twice a year.

There are, in fact, three sizes of the Schnauzer: the Miniature, a Standard version and the Giant Schnauzer. The Standard version was the earliest of the three, the Miniature being developed later and making its debut in the showring in 1899.

GENERAL APPEARANCE Sturdily built, robust, sinewy, nearly square (length of body equal to height at shoulders). Expression keen and attitude alert. Correct conformation is of more importance than colour or other purely 'beauty' points.

CHARACTERISTICS Well balanced, smart, stylish and adaptable.

TEMPERAMENT Alert, reliable and intelligent. Primarily a companion dog.

HEAD AND SKULL Head strong and of good length, narrowing from ears to eyes and then gradually forward toward end of nose. Upper part of the head (occiput to the base of forehead) moderately broad between ears. Flat, creaseless forehead; well muscled but not too strongly developed cheeks. Medium stop to accentuate prominent eyebrows. Powerful muzzle ending in a moderately blunt line, with bristly, stubby moustache and chin whiskers. Ridge of nose straight and running almost parallel to extension of forehead. Nose black with wide nostrils. Lips tight but not overlapping.

EYES Medium-sized, dark, oval, set forward, with arched bushy eyebrows.

EARS Neat, V-shaped, set high and dropping forward to temple.

MOUTH Jaws strong with perfect, regular and complete scissor bite, i.e. upper teeth closely over-lapping lower teeth and set square to the jaws.

NECK Moderately long, strong and slightly arched; skin close to throat; neck set cleanly on shoulders.

FOREQUARTERS Shoulders flat and well laid. Forelegs straight viewed from any angle. Muscles smooth and lithe rather than prominent; bone strong, straight and carried well down to feet; elbows close to body and pointing directly backwards.

BODY Chest moderately broad, deep with visible strong breast bone reaching at least to height of elbow, rising slightly backward to loins. Back strong and straight, slightly higher at shoulder than at hindquarters, with short, well developed loins. Ribs well sprung. Length of body equal to height from top of withers to ground.

HINDQUARTERS Thighs slanting and flat but strongly muscled. Hindlegs (upper and lower thighs) at first vertical to the stifle; from stifle to hock, in line with the extension of the upper neck line; from hock, vertical to ground.

FEET Short, round, cat-like, compact with closely arched toes, dark nails, firm black pads, feet pointing forward.

TAIL Set-on and carried high, customarily docked to three joints.

GAIT/MOVEMENT Free, balanced and vigorous, with good reach in forequarters and good driving power in hindquarters. Topline remains level in action.

COAT Harsh, wiry and short enough for smartness, dense undercoat. Clean on neck and shoulders, ears and skull. Harsh hair on legs. Furnishings fairly thick but not silky.

COLOUR All pepper and salt colours in even proportions, or pure black, or black and silver. That is, solid black with silver markings on eyebrow, muzzle, chest and brisket and on the forelegs below the point of elbow, on inside of hindlegs below the stifle joint, on vent and under tail.

SIZE Ideal height: dogs: 35.6 cm (14 in); bitches: 33 cm (13 in). Too small, toyish appearing dogs are not typical and undesirable.

FAULTS Any departure from the foregoing points should be considered a fault and the seriousness with which the fault should be regarded should be in exact proportion to its degree.

NOTE Male animals should have two apparently normal testicles fully descended into the scrotum.

POODLES

THERE ARE THREE SIZES OF POODLE – Toy, Miniature and Standard – all in a wide range of beautiful solid colours. The Poodle's coat does not shed, but regular grooming is essential. For the fashion-conscious there are many different styles in which he can be clipped. A dandy at heart, he will always show his appreciation when his toilette has been completed.

He is a clown by nature who gives amusement and devotion to his owners. Because he is capable of learning quickly, and enjoys showing off, the French circus utilised his abilities, and the Poodle became a popular entertainer. Today these characteristics stand him in good stead in the showring. Extremely versatile, he excels in obedience, has a history as a water and retrieving dog, and was adept at searching out the gourmet's delight of truffles. In fact there seems no end to his talents.

All three varieties of Poodle have their country of origin listed as France but Germany is believed to have been their actual home, the breed entering France with German soldiers. It came from the marshes of Germany and at one time the Poodle was well established as a water retriever. The French certainly know the Poodle as a duck dog and the smaller Poodles were used to sniff out truffles.

Interest in the breed was heightened by the courts of Europe where they became very popular as pet dogs, especially the two smaller varieties. Early show Poodles were exhibited with a corded coat.

Lighthearted, with a happy nature, elegant, friendly and high-spirited, his sporting and home-loving instincts all combine to make him the ideal companion.

OPPOSITE: *Miniature Poodle*
BELOW: *Standard Poodle*

GENERAL APPEARANCE Well balanced, elegant looking with very proud carriage.

CHARACTERISTICS Distinguished by a special type of clip for show activity and by a type of coat which does not moult.

TEMPERAMENT Gay-spirited and good-tempered.

HEAD AND SKULL Long and fine with slight peak. Skull not broad, moderate stop. Foreface strong, well chiselled, not falling away under eyes; cheek bones and muscle flat. Lips tight-fitting. Chin well defined but not protruding. Head in proportion to size of dog.

EYES Almond-shaped, dark, not set too close together, full of fire and intelligence.

EARS Leathers long and wide, set low, hanging close to face.

MOUTH Jaws strong with perfect, regular, complete scissor bite, i.e. upper teeth closely overlapping lower teeth and set square to the jaws. A full set of 42 teeth is desirable.

NECK Well proportioned, of good length and strong to admit of the head being carried high and with dignity. Skin fitting tightly at the throat.

FOREQUARTERS Well laid back shoulders, strong and muscular. Legs set straight from shoulders, well muscled.

BODY Chest deep and moderately wide. Ribs well sprung and rounded. Back short, strong, slightly hollowed; loins broad and muscular.

HINDQUARTERS Thighs well developed and muscular; well bent stifles, hocks well let down; hindlegs turning neither in nor out.

LEFT: *Toy Poodle*

FEET Tight, proportionately small, oval in shape, turning neither in nor out, toes arched, pads thick and hard, well cushioned. Pasterns strong.

TAIL Set-on rather high, carried at slight angle away from body, never curled or carried over back, thick at root. Customarily docked.

GAIT/MOVEMENT Sound, free and light movement essential with plenty of drive.

COAT Very profuse and dense; of good harsh texture. All short hair close, thick and curly. It is strongly recommended that the traditional lion clip be adhered to.

COLOUR All solid colours. White and creams to have black nose, lips and eye rims, black toenails desirable. Browns to have dark amber eyes, dark liver nose, lips, eye rims and toenails. Apricots to have dark eyes with black points or deep amber eyes with liver points. Blacks, silvers and blues to have black nose, lips, eye rims and toenails. Creams, apricots, browns, silvers and blues may show varying shades of the same colour up to 18 months. Clear colours preferred.

SIZE
POODLES (STANDARD): over 38 cm (15 in).
POODLES (MINIATURE): height at shoulder should be under 38 cm (15 in) but not under 28 cm (11 in).
POODLES (TOY): height at shoulder should be under 28 cm (11 in).

FAULTS Any departure from the foregoing points should be considered a fault and the seriousness with which the fault should be regarded should be in exact proportion to its degree.

NOTE Male animals should have two apparently normal testicles fully descended into the scrotum.

SCHIPPERKE

ONE OF THE SMALLER SPITZ BREEDS, the Schipperke has a very typical dense, harsh coat, and though most frequently seen as a black dog, he does appear in solid cream or fawn as a solid colour. In the past, his tail, if present, has been customarily removed to produce a smooth rump; however, recently some have been allowed to retain their tails and this is becoming more popular and acceptable.

A very compact breed, he originates from the canals of Belgium and Holland, where he guarded the barges most efficiently. He still has the ability to detect and deter strangers thus making him a most acceptable house-dog.

His tight-fitting coat makes him an easy dog to keep clean, and his brisk pace on his neat, tight feet ensures that he will enjoy all the exercise his family can give him.

The breed, though associated with Holland and Belgium, comes from the province known as Flanders, where at one time the breed was extremely popular with shoemakers. On Sundays the tradesmen would parade them. The Schipperke can be credited with the first one-breed dog show, put on by guild workmen in 1690.

GENERAL APPEARANCE Small, cobby, active dog, with sharp, foxy expression.

CHARACTERISTICS Intensely lively and alert.

TEMPERAMENT Amenable, intelligent and faithful.

HEAD AND SKULL Skull not round, but fairly broad, flat, with little stop. Muzzle moderate in length, fine but not weak, well filled under eyes. Nose black and small.

EYES Dark brown, more oval than round, not full; bright, most expressive.

EARS Moderate length, not too broad at base, tapering to a point. Carried stiffly erect and strong enough not to be bent otherwise than lengthways.

MOUTH Jaws strong, with perfect, regular and complete scissor bite, i.e. upper teeth closely overlapping lower teeth and set square to the jaws.

NECK Strong and full, rather short, set broad on shoulders, slightly arched.

FOREQUARTERS Shoulders muscular and sloping. Legs perfectly straight, well under the body, bone in proportion to the body.

BODY Chest broad and deep in brisket. Back short, straight and strong. Loins powerful, well drawn up from brisket.

HINDQUARTERS Fine compared with forequarters; muscular and well developed thighs; well rounded rump. Legs strong, muscular, hocks well let down.

FEET Small, cat-like, and standing well on the toes.

TAIL Customarily docked.

GAIT/MOVEMENT Short, brisk stride, moving true fore and aft.

COAT Abundant, dense and harsh; smooth on head, ears and legs; lying close on back and side; erect and thick round neck, forming a mane and frill; with good culottes on the back of thighs.

COLOUR Usually black but other whole colours permissible.

SIZE Weight about 5.4 to 7.3 kg (12–16 lb).

FAULTS Any departure from the foregoing points should be considered a fault and the seriousness with which the fault should be regarded should be in exact proportion to its degree.

NOTE Male animals should have two apparently normal testicles fully descended into the scrotum.

SCHNAUZER

THE MIDDLE-SIZED MEMBER OF THE Schnauzer family, suitable for those who want something a little larger than the Miniature, but not quite as big as the Giant. He is known in America as the Standard Schnauzer.

The home country for the Schnauzer is Germany, where the standard version filled many roles: ratter, drovers' dog, stock tender and guard in the house and stables. He was even used to pull carts to market, making him the all-round farm dog. The first standard for the medium size Schnauzer was produced in 1880.

A good-looking, robust dog, well muscled and with a harsh, wiry coat in either black, or salt and pepper, which means shades of grey. His coat needs a lot of attention to keep him looking smart and tailored. He has

a lively nature, is a good house-dog and guard, and enjoys obedience work. Gentle, patient and trustworthy with children, he needs plenty of exercise, and is the ideal companion for an active person.

GENERAL APPEARANCE Sturdily built, robust, sinewy, nearly square (length of body equal to height at shoulders). Expression keen and attitude alert. Correct conformation is of more importance than colour or purely 'beauty' points.

CHARACTERISTICS Strong, vigorous dog capable of great endurance.

TEMPERAMENT Alert, reliable and intelligent. Primarily a companion dog.

HEAD AND SKULL Head strong and of good length, narrowing from ears to eyes and then gradually forward toward end of nose. Upper part of the head (occiput to the base of the forehead) moderately broad between ears. Flat, creaseless forehead; well muscled but not too strongly developed cheeks. Medium stop to accentuate prominent eyebrows. Powerful muzzle ending in a moderately blunt line, with bristly, stubby moustache and chin whiskers. Ridge of nose straight and running almost parallel to extension of forehead. Nose black with wide nostrils. Lips tight but not overlapping.

EYES Medium-sized, dark, oval, set forward with arched bushy eyebrows.

EARS Neat, V-shaped, set high and dropping forward to temple.

MOUTH Jaws strong, with a perfect, regular and complete scissor bite, i.e. upper teeth closely overlapping lower teeth and set square to the jaws.

NECK Moderately long, strong, and slightly arched; skin close to throat; neck set cleanly on shoulders.

FOREQUARTERS Shoulders flat and well laid. Forelegs straight viewed from any angle. Muscles smooth and lithe rather than prominent; bone strong, straight and carried well down to feet; elbows close to body and pointing directly backward.

BODY Chest moderately broad; deep with visible, strong breastbone reaching at least to height of elbow and rising slightly backward to loins. Back strong and straight, slightly higher at shoulder than at hindquarters, with short, well developed loins. Ribs well sprung. Length of body equal to height from top of withers to ground.

HINDQUARTERS Thighs slanting and flat but strongly muscled. Hindlegs (upper and lower thighs) at first vertical to the stifle; from stifle to hock in line with the extension of the upper neck line; from hock, vertical to ground.

FEET Short, round, cat-like, compact with closely arched toes, dark nails, firm black pads, feet pointing forward.

TAIL Set-on and carried high, customarily docked to three joints.

GAIT/MOVEMENT Free, balanced and vigorous, with good reach in forequarters and good driving power in hindquarters. Topline remains level in action.

COAT Harsh, wiry and short enough for smartness. Closer on neck and shoulders; clean on throat, skull and ears. Harsh hair on legs. Dense undercoat essential.

COLOUR Pure black (white markings on head, chest and legs undesirable) or pepper and salt. Pepper and salt shades range from dark iron grey to light grey: good pigmentation. Hairs banded dark/light/dark. Facial mask to harmonise with corresponding coat colour.

SIZE Ideal height at withers: dogs: 48.3 cm (19 in); bitches 45.7 cm (18 in). Any variations of more than 2.5 cm (1 in) in these heights undesirable.

FAULTS Any departure from the foregoing points should be considered a fault and the seriousness with which the fault should be regarded should be in exact proportion to its degree.

NOTE Male animals should have two apparently normal testicles fully descended into the scrotum.

SHAR PEI

(INTERIM)

DEVOTEES OF THIS RECENTLY introduced native of China will tell you that the 'h' in his name is not pronounced and that there is no plural. These unusual features are only the start of the differences from other dogs which the breed exhibits, but the early specimens brought here from America tended to give a very unfortunate impression. They were generally short in the leg, had excessively wrinkled skins even as adults, and suffered almost 100 per cent from entropion, or inward rolling of the eyelids, leading to discomfort to the eyes and necessitating frequent veterinary attention. Fortunately, the influence of the breeders who were not wedded to the 'get-rich-quick' principle has resulted in a dog with a longer leg, a better-fitting skin and better eyelids.

One of his most distinctive features is the truly bristly feel to his coat, which may be black, red, or fawn/cream. The inside of his mouth should be black in the darker varieties. However, despite his frowning expression, he is blessed with an affectionate view of mankind.

The breed's original use was as a hunter, a herder and a guard dog. Its guarding qualities prompted local residents to misuse it as a fighting dog. Its wrinkled skin and deep-set eyes helped the Shar Pei to escape serious damage. There is a mastiff link behind the Shar Pei, which is one of the world's really ancient breeds.

GENERAL APPEARANCE Alert, active, compact, short-coupled, squarely built. Dogs larger and more powerful than bitches.

CHARACTERISTICS Loose skin, frowning expression.

TEMPERAMENT Calm, independent, very affectionate, and devoted to people.

HEAD AND SKULL Rather large in proportion to body, skull flat, broad, moderate stop. Fine wrinkles on forehead and cheeks continuing to form dewlaps. Muzzle distinctive feature of breed; moderately long, broad from eyes to point of nose without any suggestion of tapering. Lips and top of muzzle well padded, causing slight bulge at base of nose. When viewed from front, bottom jaw appears wider than top due to padding of lips. Nose large, wide, preferably black but any colour conforming to general coat colour permissible.

EYES Dark, medium size, almond-shaped with frowning expression. Lighter colour permissible in cream and light fawn dogs. Function of eyeball or lid in no way disturbed by surrounding skin, folds or hair. Any sign of irritation of eyeball, conjunctiva or eyelids highly undesirable. Free from entropion.

EARS Very small, rather thick, equilaterally triangular in shape, slightly rounded at tip, with tips pointing towards eyes, set well forward over eyes, wide apart and close to skull. Pricked ears highly undesirable.

MOUTH Bluish-black tongue preferred, pink-spotted permissible. Solid pink tongue undesirable. Flews, roof of mouth and gums preferably black; lighter colours permissible in cream and light fawn. Teeth strong, with a perfect, regular and complete scissor bite, i.e. upper teeth closely overlapping lower teeth and set square to the jaws. Padding of lower lip should not be so excessive as to interfere with the bite.

NECK Short, strong, full; set well on shoulders, with loose skin under neck.

FOREQUARTERS Shoulders muscular, well laid and sloping. Forelegs straight, moderate length, good bone; pasterns slightly sloping, strong and flexible.

BODY Chest broad and deep, underline rising slightly under loin; back short, strong; topline dips slightly behind withers then rises over short, broad loin. Excessive skin on body when mature highly undesirable.

HINDQUARTERS Muscular, strong; moderately angulated: hocks well let down.

FEET Moderate size, compact, toes well knuckled. Fore and hind dewclaws may be removed.

TAIL Rounded, narrowing to fine point, base set very high. May be carried high and curved, carried in tight curl, or curved over. Lack of tail highly undesirable.

GAIT/MOVEMENT Free, balanced, vigorous.

COAT Distinctive feature of breed. Short and bristly; harsh to touch. Straight and off-standing on body and generally flatter on limbs. No undercoat. Over 2.5 cm (1 in) long undesirable. Never trimmed.

COLOUR Solid colours – black, red, light or dark shades of fawn and cream. Frequently shaded on tail and back of thighs with lighter colour; patched white or spotted undesirable.

SIZE Height: 46–51 cm (18–20 in) at withers.

FAULTS Any departure from the foregoing points should be considered a fault and the seriousness with which this fault should be regarded should be in exact proportion to its degree.

NOTE Male animals should have two apparently normal testicles fully descended into the scrotum.

SHIH TZU

PEOPLE TEND TO GET CONFUSED between the Apso and the Shih Tzu, but there are a number of very distinct differences. Roots of this breed are in Tibet but it was developed in China, where dogs like these lived in the imperial palaces. China became a republic in 1912 after which examples of the breed found their way to the West, though the first recorded importation to Britain was not until 1931. It was recognised as a breed separate from other Oriental breeds in 1934 and granted a separate register by The Kennel Club in 1940, with challenge certificates on offer from 1949.

The breed standard calls for the maximum height of the Shih Tzu to be just 1.2 centimetres (½ inch) more than that of the Apso.

Temperamentally he is a bouncy character, and very outgoing, a complete extrovert, full of infectious enthusiasm.

The chrysanthemum look to the Shih Tzu's head is most appealing, and this is caused by the hair growing upwards on the bridge of the nose. His long coat requires regular attention, but is not difficult to keep in good order.

A delightful companion, and happy to be part of any family.

GENERAL APPEARANCE Sturdy, abundantly coated dog with distinctly arrogant carriage and chrysanthemum-like face.

CHARACTERISTICS Intelligent, active and alert.

TEMPERAMENT Friendly and independent.

HEAD AND SKULL Head broad, round, wide between eyes. Shock-headed with hair falling well over eyes. Good beard and whiskers, hair growing upwards on the nose giving a distinctly chrysanthemum-like effect. Muzzle of ample width, square, short, not wrinkled; flat and hairy. Nose black, but dark liver in liver or liver-marked dogs, and about 2.5 cm (1 in) from tip to definite stop. Nose level or slightly tip-tilted. Top of nose leather should be on a line with or slightly below lower eye rim. Wide-open nostrils. Down-pointed nose highly undesirable, as are pinched nostrils. Pigmentation of muzzle as unbroken as possible.

EYES Large, dark, round, placed well apart but not prominent. Warm expression. In liver or liver-marked dogs, lighter eye colour permissible. No white of eye showing.

EARS Large, with long leathers, carried drooping. Set slightly below crown of skull, so heavily coated they appear to blend into hair of neck.

MOUTH Wide, slightly undershot or level. Lips level.

NECK Well proportioned, nicely arched. Sufficient length to carry head proudly.

FOREQUARTERS Shoulders well laid back. Legs short and muscular with ample bone, as straight as possible, consistent with broad chest being well let down.

BODY Longer between withers and root of tail than height of withers, well coupled and sturdy, chest broad and deep, shoulders firm, back level.

HINDQUARTERS Legs short and muscular with ample bone. Straight when viewed from the rear. Thighs well rounded and muscular. Legs looking massive on account of wealth of hair.

FEET Rounded, firm and well padded, appearing big on account of wealth of hair.

TAIL Heavily plumed, carried gaily well over back. Set-on high. Height approximately level with that of skull to give a balanced routine.

GAIT/MOVEMENT Arrogant, smooth-flowing, front legs reaching well forward, strong rear action and showing full pad.

COAT Long, dense, not curly, with good undercoat. Slight wave permitted. Strongly recommended that hair on head tied up.

COLOUR All colours permissible, white blaze on forehead and white tip to tail highly desirable in parti-colours.

SIZE Height at withers not more than 26.7 cm (10½ in), type and breed characteristics of the utmost importance and on no account to be sacrificed to size alone. Weight: 4.5-8.1 kg (10-18 lb). Ideal weight: 4.5-7.3 kg (10-16 lb).

FAULTS Any departure from the foregoing points should be considered a fault and the seriousness with which the fault should be regarded should be in exact proportion to its degree.

NOTE Male animals should have two apparently normal testicles fully descended into the scrotum.

TIBETAN SPANIEL

THE TIBETAN BREEDS HAVE ACHIEVED great popularity over the past sixty years or so and this is no surprise. The Tibetan Spaniel was one of the first Tibetan breeds to reach England, coming here in around 1900. It was a breed favoured by Tibetan monks and was brought here by returning medical missionaries. It had established a firm hold by 1920 and really came into its own after the end of the Second World War.

The Tibetan Spaniel has a delightful temperament, for while he obviously likes to stress his superiority of breeding by his somewhat haughty expression, he is only too ready to let his hair down in a mad rush round the garden with his friends.

He comes in a great variety of colours, but his coat never varies in its gleaming, silky texture, which in spite of its length is not hard to keep in good condition.

He likes company and exercise, but he is quite happy to let life take its course, and is a healthy chap needing relatively little food and a minimum of fuss.

GENERAL APPEARANCE Small, active and alert. Well balanced in general outline, slightly longer in body than height at withers.

CHARACTERISTICS Gay and assertive, highly intelligent, aloof with strangers.

TEMPERAMENT Alert, loyal but independent.

HEAD AND SKULL Small in proportion to body, carried proudly. Masculine in dogs but free from coarseness. Skull slightly domed, moderate width and length. Stop slight but defined. Medium length of muzzle, blunt with cushioning, free from wrinkle. Chin showing some depth and width. Nose: black preferred.

EYES Dark brown, oval, bright and expressive, medium size, set fairly well apart but forward-looking. Rims black.

EARS Medium size, pendant, well feathered in adults, set fairly high. Slight lift from the skull desirable but must not fly. Large, heavy, low-set ears untypical.

MOUTH Slightly undershot. Teeth evenly placed and the lower jaw wide between the canine teeth. Full dentition desirable. Teeth and tongue not showing when mouth closed.

NECK Moderately short, strong and well set-on. Covered with a mane or 'shawl' of longer hair, more pronounced in dogs than bitches.

FOREQUARTERS Moderate bone. Forelegs slightly bowed but firm at shoulder. Shoulder well laid.

BODY Slightly longer from withers to root of tail than the height at withers, good spring of rib, level back.

HINDQUARTERS Well made and strong, hocks well let down, straight when viewed from behind. Moderate turn of stifle.

FEET Harefoot. Small and neat with feathering between toes often extending beyond the feet. Round cat-feet undesirable.

TAIL Set high, richly plumed and carried in gay curl over back when moving (Not to be penalised for dropping tail when standing.)

GAIT/MOVEMENT Quick-moving, straight, free, positive.

COAT Top coat silky in texture, smooth on face and front of legs, of moderate length on body, but lying rather flat. Undercoat fine and dense. Ears and back of forelegs nicely feathered, tail and buttocks well furnished with longer hair. Not overcoated, bitches tend to carry less coat and mane than dogs.

COLOUR All colours and mixture of colours permissible.

SIZE Height about 25.4 cm (10 in). Ideal
weight: 4.1 to 6.8 kg (9-15 lb).

FAULTS Any departure from the foregoing
points should be considered a fault and the
seriousness with which the fault should be
regarded should be in exact proportion to its
degree.

NOTE Male animals should have two apparently
normal testicles fully descended into the
scrotum.

TIBETAN TERRIER

THE TALLEST OF THE TIBETAN BREEDS IN the Utility Group, this chap is even more lively than the others. He is built on square lines, being much the same height at the shoulder as he is long in the body. He carries a coat of moderate length which is fine rather than silky.

The breed has gained rapidly in popularity, his energy and enthusiasm balancing his ability as a miniature guard dog along the lines of a small Old English Sheepdog. He needs a fairly firm hand but will reward his owners with loyalty and devotion.

In spite of the name, this breed is not a terrier but a herding dog, doubling as a guard for traders as they journeyed to and from China. He succeeded in his job not so much by size but through the awe in which he was held. This is believed to be the original Holy Dog of Tibet.

GENERAL APPEARANCE Sturdy, medium-sized, long-haired, generally square outline; resolute expression.

CHARACTERISTICS Lively, good-natured. Loyal companion dog with many engaging ways.

TEMPERAMENT Outgoing, alert, intelligent and game; neither fierce nor pugnacious. Sparing of affection to strangers.

HEAD AND SKULL Skull of medium length, neither broad nor coarse, narrowing slightly from ear to eye, neither domed nor absolutely flat between ears. Zygomatic arch curved, but not overdeveloped so as to bulge. Marked stop in front of eyes but not exaggerated. Muzzle strong; well developed lower jaw. Length from eye to tip of nose equal to length from eye to base of skull. Nose black. Head well furnished with long hair, falling forward over eyes. Lower jaw carrying small, but not exaggerated amount of beard.

EYES Large, round, neither prominent nor sunken; set fairly wide apart; dark brown. Eye rims black.

EARS Pendant, carried not too close to head, V-shaped, not too large, heavily feathered.

MOUTH Scissor or reverse scissor bite. Incisors set in slight curve, evenly spaced and set perpendicular to jaw.

FOREQUARTERS Heavily furnished. Shoulders well laid; legs straight and parallel; pasterns slightly sloping.

BODY Well muscled, compact and powerful. Length from point of shoulder to root of tail equal to height at withers. Well ribbed up. Back level over ribs; loin short, slightly arched; croup level.

HINDQUARTERS Heavily furnished. Stifles well bent, hocks low-set.

FEET Large, round, heavily furnished with hair between toes and pads. Standing well down on pads; no arch in feet.

TAIL Medium length, set-on fairly high and carried in a gay curl over back. Very well feathered. Kink near tip often occurring and permissible.

GAIT/MOVEMENT Smooth; good reach; powerful drive. When walking or trotting hindlegs should track neither inside nor outside the front legs.

COAT Double coat. Undercoat fine and woolly. Top coat profuse, fine but not silky nor woolly; long; either straight or waved but not curled.

COLOUR White, golden, cream, grey or smoke, black, parti-colour and tricolours; in fact any colour except chocolate or liver permissible.

SIZE Height at shoulder: dogs: 35.6–40.6 cm (14–16 in); bitches: slightly smaller.

FAULTS Any departure from the foregoing points should be considered a fault and the seriousness with which the fault should be regarded should be in exact proportion to its degree.

NOTE Male animals should have two apparently normal testicles fully descended into the scrotum.

WORKING
GROUP

LEFT: Dick Turpin *by Cecil Aldin (1870–1935). This pastel of an Alsatian probably dates from the late 1920s. It is believed to have been commissioned by an unknown bridegroom as a present for his bride.*

ALASKAN MALAMUTE

(INTERIM)

HAILING FROM THE RUGGED WESTERN area of Alaska, and taking his name from the Malamute settlement of the Eskimos, this dog has had to be hardy to stay alive. He is a really big dog, the male scaling well over a hundredweight and standing up to 71 centimetres (28 inches) at the shoulder. His purpose in life is to pull sledges and he can cope with prodigious loads, though he is not designed to be a racer. Although he is a truly handsome fellow, he does not have the spectacular glamour of his smaller sledding cousins.

The Malamute is a Nordic type dog who moved into the northern Polar regions when people began to occupy the land. The Mahlemut tribes were a hard-working and skilled Inuit (Eskimo) race who loved and cared for their dogs, which were first discovered by settlers as far back as the 1750s. Though breed type was nearly lost by crossing with faster animals for sled racing, some Inuit continued to breed to type. Eventually promotion of the pure-bred Malamute was taken up by the American fancy.

Not only massively built, he is also dignified; this does not mean he lacks a sense of play, but he sometimes doesn't know his own strength. If he takes off after another dog, his handler needs good brakes.

His coat is thick in the coarse outer guard coat and in the woolly undercoat, so he doesn't notice the cold and will curl up and sleep in a blizzard which would send lesser canines running for shelter. Being large, he requires plenty of food for energy. Though he is not particularly fleet of foot, he likes his exercise, and is not a dog for the lazy.

GENERAL APPEARANCE Heavily boned, powerfully built, not too compact and never appearing short on the leg.

CHARACTERISTICS Sled dog capable of surviving in Arctic temperatures and of pulling heavy loads at steady speeds.

TEMPERAMENT Affectionate, friendly, loyal, devoted companion but not a 'one-man' dog, playful on invitation, generally impressive by his dignity after maturity but tends to show aggression to other dogs.

HEAD AND SKULL Head broad, powerful, not coarse in proportion to size of dog. Skull broad between ears, gradually narrowing to eyes, moderately rounded between ears, flattening on top as it approaches eye, rounding off to moderately flat cheeks. Very slight but perceptible stop. Muzzle large in proportion to size of skull, scarcely diminishing in width or depth from stop. Nose black except in red and white dogs when it is brown. Pink streaked 'snow nose' acceptable.

EYES Brown, almond-shaped, moderately-large, set obliquely. Dark eyes preferred, except in red and white dogs where light eyes are permissible. Blue eyes highly undesirable.

EARS Small in proportion to head. Triangular in shape, slightly rounded at tips, set wide apart, at back of skull. Ears forward when erect. When dog is working sometimes folded against skull.

MOUTH Upper and lower jaws broad with large teeth, with a perfect, regular and complete scissor bite, i.e. upper teeth closely overlapping lower teeth and set square to the jaws.

NECK Strong and moderately arched.

FOREQUARTERS Shoulders moderately sloping; forelegs heavily boned and well muscled, straight as far as pasterns which are short, strong and almost vertical viewed from side.

BODY Strong and powerfully built, chest strong and deep; back straight but not level, sloping slightly downwards from shoulder to croup. Loins well muscled, never so short as to interfere with movement. No excess weight.

HINDQUARTERS Hindlegs broad and powerfully muscled through thighs; stifles moderately bent, hock joints broad and strong, moderately bent and well let down. Viewed from behind, hindlegs vertical, standing and moving true, in line with movement of front legs. Legs indicate tremendous propelling power. Dewclaws on hindlegs undesirable.

FEET Large and compact, toes close, well arched, pads thick and tough, toenails short and strong. Protective growth of hair between toes.

TAIL Moderately high-set, following line of spine at start then curving gently upwards. At rest may hang straight down. Well furred and carried over back when dog is working, not tightly curled to rest on back, nor short furred and carried like a fox brush, but giving appearance of a waving plume.

GAIT/MOVEMENT Single tracking at trot is normal but movement not too wide or too close at any gait. Easy, tireless, rhythmic movement, produced by powerful drive from hindquarters.

COAT Thick, coarse guard coat, not long and soft. Dense undercoat, from 2.5-5 cm (1-2 in) in depth, oily and woolly. Coarse guard coat stands out, with thick fur around neck. Guard coat varies in length as does undercoat, but in general coat of medium length along sides of body, increasing somewhat around shoulders and neck, down back and over croup, as well as in breeching and plume.

COLOUR Range is from light grey through intermediate shadings to black, or from gold through shades of red to liver, always with white on underbody, parts of legs, feet and part of mask markings. Markings either caplike or masklike on face. Combination of cap and mask not unusual. White blaze on forehead, white collar, or spot on nape permissible. Heavy mantling of unbroken colour acceptable, broken colour extending over body in spots or uneven splashings undesirable. Only solid colour permissible is all white.

SIZE Height: dogs: 64-71 cm (25-28 in); bitches: 58-66 cm (23-26 in). Weight between 38-56 kg (85-125 lb), size consideration not to outweigh type.

FAULTS Any departure from the foregoing points should be considered a fault and the seriousness with which the fault should be regarded should be in exact proportion to its degree.

NOTE Male animals should have two apparently normal testicles fully descended into the scrotum.

Anatolian Shepherd Dog

(INTERIM)

THIS IS A TALL DOG ALTHOUGH OF mastiff type. The largest males will measure as much as 81 centimetres (32 inches) and weigh in in the true heavyweight range. Prized by the shepherds of his native Turkey for his faithful devotion to his role as a flock-guard, he must present an awesome sight to marauders, whether wolves or men. Despite his purpose in life he can be a remarkably gentle animal in firm hands.

The breed descends directly from the ancient mastiff and flock-guarding dogs of the Middle East and has a strong scenting power. Tough and long lived, he often works until well into old age.

His relatively short, thick coat is not difficult to keep clean, and in spite of his size he is remarkably agile. A breed which requires sensible exercise, he stands up to variations of weather well.

GENERAL APPEARANCE Large, upstanding, tall, powerfully built, with broad, heavy head and short dense coat. Must have size, stamina and speed.

CHARACTERISTICS Active breed used originally as a guard dog for sheep; hard working; capable of enduring extremes of heat and cold.

TEMPERAMENT Steady and bold without aggression, naturally independent, very intelligent. Proud and confident.

HEAD AND SKULL Skull large, broad and flat between ears. Slight furrow between eyes and slight stop. Mature males have broader head than females. Foreface one-third of total head length. Slightly pendulous black lips. Square profile. Nose black.

EYES Rather small in proportion to size of skull, set well apart and deep, showing no haw. Golden to brown in colour. Eye rims black.

EARS Medium-sized, triangular in shape, rounded at tip, carried flat to skull and pendant, higher when alert.

MOUTH Teeth strong, with a perfect, regular and complete scissor bite, i.e. upper teeth closely overlapping lower teeth and set square to the jaws. Lips black.

NECK Slightly arched, powerful, muscular, moderate in length, rather thick. Slight dewlap.

FOREQUARTERS Shoulders well muscled and sloping. Forelegs set well apart, straight and well boned; of good length; strong pasterns, slightly sloping when viewed from side. Elbows close to sides.

BODY Chest deep to point of elbow, ribs well sprung. Body powerful, well muscled, never fat. Level back. Body in proportion to leg length, slightly arched over loins, with good tuck-up.

HINDQUARTERS Powerful, lighter than forequarters; moderate turn of stifle.

FEET Strong feet with well arched toes. Nails short.

TAIL Long, reaching at least to hock. Set-on rather high. When relaxed carried low with slight curl, when alert carried high with end curled over back, especially by males.

GAIT/MOVEMENT Relaxed even gait, with impression of latent power, very supple movement. Noticeable straight line of head, neck and body, giving impression of stalking in some dogs. Great drive when viewed from side.

COAT Short, dense with thick undercoat. Flat, close-lying, neither fluffy nor wavy. Slightly longer and thicker at neck, shoulders and tail; no feathering on ears or legs.

COLOUR All colours acceptable but it is desirable that they should be whole colours, cream to fawn, with black mask and ears.

SIZE Height: dogs: 74-81 cm (29-32 in) at the shoulder; bitches: 71-79 cm (28-31 in). Weight: mature dogs: 50-64 kg (110-141 lb); bitches: 41-59 kg (90.5-130 lb).

FAULTS Any departure from the foregoing points should be considered a fault and the seriousness with which the fault should be regarded should be in exact proportion to its degree.

NOTE Male animals should have two apparently normal testicles fully descended into the scrotum.

AUSTRALIAN CATTLE DOG

(INTERIM)

A MEDIUM-SIZED DOG, GREATLY PRIZED in his native Australia for his working ability, he is used for the control and movement of cattle in all environments. He is also known as the Australian Heeler, a name derived from the manner in which he manoeuvres cattle, crouching low behind them and nipping them on the heels. A dog of great stamina and endurance, he is wary of strangers, and protective of his herd and property. He requires plenty of exercise to keep him in hard muscular condition, is very alert, and has an implicit devotion to duty.

The breed was created from intensive and careful crossbreeding when it was found that imported herding dogs could not control tough cattle on long treks to market. Behind the Australian Cattle Dog are breeds such as the Dingo, the Kelpie, the Dalmatian and the Bull Terrier, but the breed has been purebred since the mid-1890s.

GENERAL APPEARANCE Strong, compact, symmetrical, with substance, power and balance. Hard muscular condition conveys agility, strength and endurance. Grossness or weediness undesirable.

CHARACTERISTICS Ability to control and move cattle in all environments. Loyal, protective. Guardian of stockman, herd and property. Naturally suspicious of strangers, but amenable to handling. Biddable.

TEMPERAMENT Alert, intelligent, watchful, courageous, trustworthy, devoted to his work.

HEAD AND SKULL Strong, in balance with body and general conformation. Skull broad and slightly curved between ears, flattening to slight but definite stop. Cheeks muscular but not coarse or prominent. Strong under-jaw, deep and well developed. Broad foreface, well filled in under eyes, tapers gradually down medium length muzzle which is parallel to skull. Nose always black.

EYES Medium, oval, alert and intelligent, dark brown. Neither prominent nor sunken. Warning suspicious glint is characteristic.

EARS Moderate, small rather than large. Broad at base, muscular, pricked and moderately pointed. Oval or bat-eared undesirable. Set wide apart inclining outwards. Sensitive, pricked when alert. Leather thick in texture and inside ear well furnished with hair.

MOUTH Lips tight and clean. Jaws strong with a perfect, regular and complete scissor bite, i.e. upper teeth closely overlapping lower teeth and set square to the jaws.

NECK Exceptionally strong, muscular, of medium length blending into body. Free from throatiness.

FOREQUARTERS Strong, sloping shoulders well laid back, not too closely set at withers. Strong, round bone, legs straight when viewed from front, pasterns flexible and slightly sloping when viewed from side. Loaded shoulder and heavy front undesirable.

BODY Slightly longer from point of shoulder to buttocks than height at withers, as 10 is to 9. Level topline, strong back and couplings. Well sprung ribs, carried well back, but not barrel ribbed. Chest deep, muscular and moderately broad.

HINDQUARTERS Broad, strong and muscular. Croup rather long and sloping. Well turned stifle, hocks strong and well let down. When viewed from behind, hocks to feet straight and set parallel, neither too close nor too wide apart.

FEET Round, short toes, strong, well arched and held tight, pads hard and deep. Nails short and strong.

TAIL Set-on low, following slope of croup/rump. Reaching to back, hanging in

slight curve at rear. When working or excited, may be raised but never carried over back. Good brush.

GAIT/MOVEMENT True, free, supple, tireless, with powerful thrust of hindquarters. Capable of quick and sudden action. Soundness of paramount importance. Stands four square, but when moving at speed, legs tend to converge. Any weaknesses highly undesirable.

COAT Smooth, double with short dense undercoat. Close top coat, hard, straight and weather-resistant. Under body and behind legs, coat is longer to form mild breeching near thighs. Short on head (including inside of ear), front of legs and feet. Thicker and longer on neck. Average hair length 2.5-4 cm (1-1½ in).

COLOUR
BLUE: Blue, blue-mottled or blue speckled with or without other markings. Permissible markings are black, blue or tan markings on head, evenly distributed for preference. Forelegs tan midway up legs and extending up the front to breast and throat, with tan on jaws. Hindquarters tan on inside of hindlegs, and inside of thighs, showing down front of stifles and broadening out to outside of hindlegs from hock to toes. Tan undercoat permissible on body providing it does not show through blue outer coat. Black markings on body undesirable.
RED SPECKLE: Good even red speckle all over, including undercoat (neither white nor cream), with or without darker red markings on head. Even head markings desirable. Red markings on body permissible but undesirable.

SIZE Height at withers: dogs: 46-51 cm (approx 18-20 in); bitches: 43-48 cm (approx 17-19 in).

FAULTS Any departure from the foregoing points should be considered a fault and the seriousness with which the fault should be regarded should be in exact proportion to its degree.

NOTE Male animals should have two apparently normal testicles fully descended into the scrotum.

AUSTRALIAN SHEPHERD

(INTERIM)

THE AUSTRALIAN SHEPHERD DOG DOES not originate from Australia! He is a product of the USA, his origins going back to the Basque/Spanish sheepdogs. Basque shepherds emigrated to Australia in the latter part of the nineteenth century taking their 'blue' dogs with them. When they then in turn went on to the Americas the dogs travelled as well, hence the Americans' naming of them.

Built on powerful lines, he can turn his very intelligent mind to obedience, agility, and tracking as well as to his basic role as a worker on farm or ranch. He has already made himself a wide circle of friends in the dozen or so years since he first appeared in the United Kingdom.

The rapid fashion in which the early 'settlers' have multiplied has resulted in a considerable divergence in type; perhaps the most important quality in any breed is its basic temperament; doubtless, as the breed settles down, this will stabilise, as will the outward look of what is a very handsome and versatile, new addition to the UK pedigree dog scene.

GENERAL APPEARANCE Well balanced, length slightly greater than height. Medium size, solid and muscular. Various colours. Expression alert, keen and friendly.

CHARACTERISTICS Intelligent, strong herding and guarding instincts. Great stamina, loyal, attentive, animated, lithe, agile; able to change speed and direction instantly.

TEMPERAMENT Even disposition. May show initial reserve, never shy or aggressive.

HEAD AND SKULL In proportion to body. Clean-cut. Dry. Muzzle equal to, or a little shorter than length of skull. Skull of equal length and width with slight dome. Occiput may be apparent. From side, top of muzzle and skull on parallel planes. Moderate, well defined stop. Muzzle tapers slightly toward nose, ending in rounded tip. Nose: In blue merles and blacks – black; in red merles and reds – liver/brown. Merles may have small pink spots.

EYES Brown, blue or amber, or combination including flecks and marbling. Oval shaped, of moderate size, neither protruding nor sunken. Eye rims: blue merles and blacks – black; in red merles and reds – liver/brown.

EARS Triangular; of moderate size and thickness, set high. Breaking forward or to side when attracted.

MOUTH Jaws strong with a perfect, regular and complete scissor bite, i.e. the upper teeth closely overlapping the lower teeth and set square to the jaws. Level bite tolerated.

NECK Moderate length, strong, slightly arched; fitting smoothly into shoulders.

FOREQUARTERS Shoulder blades long and flat, well laid back, set close at withers. Upper arms of comparable length. Legs straight from all sides, with strong oval bone. Medium length, slightly sloping pasterns.

BODY Strong, with firm level topline. Croup moderately sloping. Chest deep, of moderate width, with brisket reaching to elbow. Ribs well sprung and long. Underline shows moderate tuck-up.

HINDQUARTERS Same width as forequarters. Corresponding angulation of pelvis and upper thighs to scapulae and upper arms. Well defined stifles, moderate angle of hock joints. Hocks well let down, perpendicular to ground and parallel when viewed from rear.

FEET Oval. Closely set, well arched toes; thick pads.

TAIL Straight, naturally bobbed, or customarily docked to no more than 10 cm (4 in) length.

GAIT/MOVEMENT Agile, smooth, free and easy, with good forward reach. Fore- and hindlegs move straight and parallel but may converge at speed.

COAT Medium length and texture, straight to wavy, weather resistant with undercoat. Short hair on head, ears, front of forelegs and below hock joints. Back of legs moderately feathered. Moderate mane, more pronounced in dogs than bitches.

COLOUR Blue, merle, black, red merle, all with or without tan points. May have white as follows: white collar no further back than point of withers at skin. White on neck as full or part collar, chest, muzzle, underparts, moderate blaze. Coloured coat surrounding pigmented eye rims.

SIZE Dogs: 51-58 cm (20-23 in).
Bitches: 46-53 cm (18-21 in).

FAULTS Any departure from the foregoing points should be considered a fault and the seriousness with which the fault should be regarded should be in exact proportion to its degree.

NOTE Male animals should have two apparently normal testicles fully descended into the scrotum.

BEARDED COLLIE

THERE IS MENTION OF A BREED resembling the Bearded Collie in Scottish records dating back to around the sixteenth century. He has long been known in Scotland and Northern England where he was bred for herding sheep.

Some five hundred years ago dogs which were also said to be the forerunners of the Polish Lowland Sheepdog were abandoned on the shores of Scotland and these bred with native herding dogs. A look at the Polish Lowland will show similarities. But the Bearded Collie as we know it today owes most of what we have to G Olive Willison who, in the 1940s, came into possession of a Beardie puppy called Jeannie. After searching she found a mate for Jeannie, a dog called Bailey, and her Bothkennar kennels set the mould for today's Bearded Collies.

The 'Beardie', as he is affectionately known, is a hardy dog with a lovable temperament. His handy size and adaptability, combined with workmanlike qualities, have given him a following far outside the farming community. Ideally suited to life in the country, with a double weather-resistant coat and active nature, he is a happy dog, neither timid nor aggressive. Ready to join in any activity, he has an enquiring expression that seems to ask 'Well, what shall we do now?' Gentle, good with children and adults, he makes an ideal member of a fun-loving, growing family.

GENERAL APPEARANCE Lean active dog, longer than it is high in an approximate proportion of 5 to 4, measured from point of chest to point of buttock. Bitches may be slightly longer. Though strongly made, should show plenty of daylight under body and should not look too heavy. Bright enquiring expression is a distinctive feature.

CHARACTERISTICS Alert, lively, self-confident and active.

TEMPERAMENT Steady, intelligent working dog, with no signs of nervousness or aggression.

HEAD AND SKULL Head in proportion to size. Skull broad, flat and square, distance between stop and occiput being equal to width between orifices of ears. Muzzle strong and equal in length to distance between stop and occiput. Whole effect being that of a dog with strength of muzzle and plenty of brain room. Moderate stop. Nose large and square, generally black but normally following coat colour in blues and browns. Nose and lips of solid colour without spots or patches. Pigmentation of lips and eye rims follows nose colour.

EYES Toning with coat colour, set widely apart and large, soft and affectionate, not protruding. Eyebrows arched up and forward but not so long as to obscure eyes.

EARS Of medium size and drooping. When alert, ears lift at base, level with, but not above, top of skull, increasing apparent breadth of skull.

MOUTH Teeth large and white. Jaws strong with a perfect, regular and complete scissor bite preferred, i.e. upper teeth closely overlapping lower teeth and set square to the jaws. Level bite tolerated but undesirable.

NECK Moderate length, muscular and slightly arched.

FOREQUARTERS Shoulders sloping well back. Legs straight and vertical with good bone, covered with shaggy hair all round. Pasterns flexible without weakness.

BODY Length of back comes from length of ribcage and not that of loin. Back level and ribs well sprung but not barrelled. Loin strong and chest deep, giving plenty of heart and lung room.

HINDQUARTERS Well muscled with good second thighs, well bent stifles and low hocks.

Lower leg falls at right angle to ground and, in normal stance, is just behind a line vertically below point of buttocks.

FEET Oval with soles well padded. Toes arched and close together, well covered with hair, including between pads.

TAIL Set low, without kink or twist, and long enough for end of bone to reach at least point of hock. Carried low with an upward swirl at tip whilst standing or walking, may be extended at speed. Never carried over back. Covered with abundant hair.

GAIT/MOVEMENT Supple, smooth and long-reaching, covering ground with minimum of effort.

COAT Double with soft, furry and close undercoat. Outer coat flat, harsh, strong and shaggy, free from woolliness and curl, though slight wave permissible. Length and density of hair sufficient to provide a protective coat and to enhance shape of dog, but not enough to obscure natural lines of body. Coat must not be trimmed in any way. Bridge of nose sparsely covered with hair slightly longer on side just to cover lips. From cheeks, lower lips and under chin, coat increases in length towards chest, forming typical beard.

COLOUR Slate grey, reddish-fawn, black, blue, all shades of grey, brown and sandy with or without white markings. When white occurs it appears on foreface, as a blaze on skull, on tip of tail, on chest, legs and feet and, if round the collar, roots of white hair should not extend behind shoulder. White should not appear above hocks on outside of hindlegs. Slight tan markings are acceptable on eyebrows, inside ear, on cheeks, under root of tail and on legs where white joins main colour.

SIZE Ideal height: dogs: 53-56 cm (21-22 in); bitches: 51-53 cm (20-21 in). Overall quality and proportions should be considered before size but excessive variations from the ideal height should be discouraged.

FAULTS Any departure from the foregoing points should be considered a fault and the seriousness with which the fault should be regarded should be in exact proportion to its degree.

NOTE Male animals should have two apparently normal testicles fully descended into the scrotum.

BEAUCERON

THE BEAUCERON, AS ITS NAME suggests, originates from the French Plains of Beauce. It has been seen in the United Kingdom before, but was recently re-introduced in 1995. The French also refer to the breed by the familiar name of Bas Rouge or Red Stockings.

He is an extremely agile and active dog, used extensively as a livestock herder/guarder. He seems to have a very good memory to add to his working ability, and is tolerant by nature, so he fits into family situations. He doesn't appreciate harsh handling, is gentle with children, which is just as well as the male can reach a height of 70 centimetres (27.5 inches), and is solid to boot.

He takes to dogs he knows, but is not enthusiastic about intruders. He obviously needs plenty of exercise and reacts well to training.

He comes in black and tan markings, or as a harlequin pattern where the base colour is grey with black and rust torn patches.

It is hoped that the Beauceron's standard will be published in 1998. It was not finalised when this book went to press.

BELGIAN SHEPHERD DOG

THIS IS A BREED WHICH COMES IN FOUR varieties. As far as the physical characteristics are concerned the breed standards are identical, with only one area of difference. This relates to the coat in respect of colour, texture and length. In alphabetical order the varieties are the Groenendael, the Laekenois, the Malinois and the Tervueren. The names refer to their geographic areas of origin within Belgium. These Belgian sheepdogs date back to the Middle Ages but began to be separated only in 1891 when Prof Adolphe Reul of the Belgian Veterinary School established the standards for the types.

A restaurant owner is credited with fostering the Groenendael; a brewer who first whelped a litter from a mating of two long-haired black-tipped fawns produced the Tervueren; the Malinois takes its name from Malines; and the Laekenois comes from Boom, near Antwerp, taking its name from the Château de Laeken, a royal residence of Queen Marie Henriette, whose favourite variety was the Laekenois.

It is not appropriate to detail the existing differences as these are covered in the coat and colour clauses, but the Groenendael is fundamentally longhaired and with a black harsh-textured coat; the Laekenois, as yet

BELOW: *The Groenendael*

ABOVE: *The Laekenois*

the rarest variety in the UK, has a pretty, short, wiry type of coat which is reddish-fawn; the Malinois is possessed of a shortish firm-textured coat which may be red, fawn or grey with a black overlay; while the Tervueren, now the most rapidly increasing of the four, has the same range of colouring as the Malinois, but the outer coat is long, straight and abundant.

The varieties are described as both sheep dogs and guards. They are essentially graceful without being too refined. They give the appearance of being purposeful creatures, and their somewhat laconic gait clause 'brisk, free and even', while being very economic in words, does not give the full flavour of a unique mode of progression which is one of efficiency above all, with a high style. It is always a debatable point whether we should take what is in truth a working breed and try to turn it into a family companion/pet, but it has been done in many breeds in the past, especially the recent past, and doubtless it will be done in

respect of the Belgian Shepherd. Provided owners do not lose sight of the fact that these are active animals requiring adequate exercise, both physical and mental, little harm will be done. But, as in many other working breeds, we must never lose sight of their history of service, or we shall find ourselves with dogs whose basic temperaments have been changed for the worse and out of all recognition.

GENERAL APPEARANCE Medium-sized dog, well proportioned, intelligent, attentive, hardy and alert. [Four Varieties: Groenendael, Laekenois, Malinois and Tervueren.]

CHARACTERISTICS With fine proportions and proud carriage of head, conveying an impression of graceful strength. Not only a sheep dog, but a guard dog.

TEMPERAMENT Wary, neither timid, nervous nor aggressive.

HEAD AND SKULL Head finely chiselled, long but not excessively so. Skull and muzzle roughly equal in length, with at most slight bias in favour of muzzle, giving impression of a balanced whole. Skull of medium width in proportion to length of head, forehead flat, centre line not very pronounced; in profile, parallel to imaginary line extending muzzle line. Muzzle of medium length tapering gradually to nose. Nose black, well-flared nostrils. Moderate stop. Arches above eyes not prominent, muzzle finely chiselled under eyes. Cheeks spare, quite flat but well muscled.

EYES Medium size, neither protruding nor sunken, slightly almond-shaped, preferably dark brown; black-rimmed eyelids. Direct, lively and enquiring look.

EARS Distinctly triangular appearance, stiff and erect, set high, moderate length with external ear well rounded at base.

MOUTH Wide, lips thin-textured, very firm, strongly pigmented. Strong white teeth firmly set in well developed jaws. Scissor bite, i.e. upper teeth closely overlapping lower teeth and set square to the jaws. Pincer bite tolerated.

NECK Very supple. Neck slightly elongated, well muscled and without dewlap, broadening slightly towards shoulders. Nape very slightly arched.

FOREQUARTERS Withers distinct, strongly boned throughout with wiry, powerful muscle structure. Shoulder blades long and oblique, firmly attached, flat, forming such angle with humerus as to enable elbows to work easily. Forelegs long, well muscled, parallel. Pasterns strong and short. Carpus clearly defined. Dewclaws permissible.

BODY Body powerful but elegant. In males, length from point of shoulders to point of buttocks approximately equal to height at withers. In females slightly longer permissible. Chest deep and well let down. Ribs moderately well sprung. Upper line of body straight, broad and powerfully muscled. Belly moderately developed neither drooping nor unduly cut up continuing lower line of chest in a graceful curve. Rump very slightly sloping, broad but not excessively so. Skin springy but quite taut over whole body. All external mucous membranes highly pigmented.

HINDQUARTERS Well muscled and powerful. Good but not excessive angulation; hocks well let down. Viewed from behind, legs parallel. Dewclaws to be removed.

FEET Toes arched, very close together; soles thick and springy with large dark claws. Forefeet round. Hindfeet slightly oval.

TAIL Firmly set, strong at base, of medium length. When at rest, hangs down, with tip slightly bent backwards at level of hock; when moving it should lift accentuating curve towards tip, never curled, nor bent to one side. Tip may be carried slightly higher than topline.

GAIT/MOVEMENT Brisk, free and even.

COAT There are three distinct coat types:
GROENENDAEL/TERVUEREN
Outer coat long, straight and abundant. Texture of medium harshness. Not silky or wiry. Undercoat extremely dense. Hair shorter on head, outside of ears and lower part of legs. Opening of ear protected by hair. Hair especially long and abundant, ruff-like around neck, particularly in males. Fringe of long hair down back of forelegs, long and abundant hair evident on hindquarters and tail. Males longer coated than females.

OPPOSITE: *The Tervueren*

ABOVE: *The Malinois*

LAEKENOIS
Harsh, wiry, dry and not curly. Any sprinkling of fluffy fine hair in locks in rough coats is undesirable. Length of coat about 6 cm (2½ in) on all parts of body. Hair around eyes but not to obscure them. Muzzle hair not so long as to make head appear square or heavy. Tail not plumed.

MALINOIS
Hair very short on head, exterior of ears and lower parts of legs. Short on rest of body, thicker on tail and around neck where it resembles a ridge or collar, beginning at base of ear and extending to throat. Hindquarters fringed with longer hair. Tail thick and bushy. Coat thick, close, of good firm texture with woolly undercoat, neither silky nor wiry.

NO VARIATION IN THESE TYPES IS ACCEPTABLE.

COLOUR The acceptable colours relate directly to coat type.

GROENENDAEL
Black or black with limited white as follows: small to moderate patch or strip on chest, between pads of feet and on tips of hind toes. Frosting (white or grey) on muzzle.

LAEKENOIS
Reddish fawn with black shading, principally in muzzle and tail.

TERVUEREN/MALINOIS

All shades of red, fawn, grey with black overlay. Coat characteristically double pigmented, wherein tip of each light-coloured hair is blackened. On mature males this blackening especially pronounced on shoulders, back and rib sections. Black mask on face, not extended above line of eyes and ears mostly black. Tail should have a darker or black tip. Small to moderate white patch or strip permitted on chest, between pads of feet and on tips of hind toes. Frosting (white or grey) on the muzzle. Beyond the age of 18 months a washed out colour or colour too black undesirable.

NO VARIATION ON THESE COLOURS BY COAT TYPE IS ACCEPTABLE.

SIZE Ideal height: dogs: 61-66 cm (24-26 in); bitches: 56-61 cm (22-24 in). Weight, in proportion to size.

FAULTS Any departure from the foregoing points should be considered a fault and the seriousness with which the fault should be regarded should be in exact proportion to its degree.

NOTE Male animals should have two apparently normal testicles fully descended into the scrotum.

BELOW: *The Laekenois*

Bergamasco

THIS HERDER/GUARDER ORIGINATES from the mountains of Northern Italy where his protective streak is employed effectively. He sports a harsh coat which is abundant, to put it mildly. It forms into loose mats which hang from the topline, and grooming is not a simple matter.

Powerfully built but relatively cautious in temperament, he will need intelligent control. He will expect plenty of exercise and will prefer a countryside environment. Not a chap to be taken on lightly.

GENERAL APPEARANCE Medium-sized sheepdog of ancient origin. Powerfully constructed, square in profile, heavily coated.

CHARACTERISTICS Vigilant guard with strong protective instinct. Tight skin. Unusual and distinctive coat.

TEMPERAMENT Intelligent, cautious, patient. Good companion/guard.

HEAD AND SKULL Skull and muzzle of equal length. Tight skin with no wrinkle. Broad skull, slightly convex between high-set ears, but rounded forehead. Width of skull no more than half length of head from occiput to nostril. Top of skull and top of muzzle parallel in profile. Prominent occiput. Definite stop with marked median furrow. Fairly deep truncated muzzle tapers slightly towards nose, but never pointed with rather flat foreface and strong under-jaw. Well pigmented, tight lips just cover front of jaw.

EYES Oval, large, dark chestnut colour preferred, but depends on colour of coat. Soft, serene but attentive expression. Tight fitting black eye rims. Long lashes hold head hair back from eyes.

EARS Set high, top two-thirds semi-drooping. Ear lifts from base when attracted. Triangular shape, wide base tapers into neckline. Slightly rounded tips. Covered with soft, slightly wavy hair forming fringes at tips.

MOUTH Well split lips, with inner corner directly below vertical line from outer corner of eye. Scissor bite, i.e. upper teeth closely overlapping lower teeth and set square to the jaws.

NECK Medium length, strong, well arched, no dewlap. Densely coated. Joins back in gentle slope to high-set withers.

FOREQUARTERS Straight when seen from front and side. Well angulated shoulder with good lay-back, and length and angulation of upper arm. Elbows set under body. Straight forelegs, with strong bone and muscle. Short pasterns.

BODY Depth is half height at withers, which are well defined. Length from point of shoulder to point of buttocks equal to height at withers. Brisket reaches to elbow. Broad back. Well sprung ribs. Straight topline. Sloping croup.

HINDQUARTERS Long, wide, well muscled upper thigh, good turn of stifle, fairly high-set hocks. Straight when viewed from rear.

FEET Oval with well closed and arched toes. Strong well pigmented nails. Hard pads of dark colour. Dewclaws may be removed.

TAIL Strong at root, tapering towards tip. Reaches hock easily, but preferably no longer. Slightly curved towards tip at rest, carried flag-like when animated.

GAIT/MOVEMENT Free, long steps. Extended trot is desirable. Capable of maintaining free gallop.

COAT Abundant and long. Harsh texture on front of body, softer on head and limbs. Short, dense undercoat obscures skin. Tends to form into strands or loose mats from topline of body (not cords). Greasy to the touch.

COLOUR Solid grey, or with patches of all shades of grey through to black. White patches allowed providing no more than one-fifth of coat. Black, Isabella and light fawn allowed.

SIZE Height: dogs: 58–62 cm (23–25 in); bitches: 54–58 cm (21–23 in). Weight: dogs: 32–38 kg (70–84 lb); bitches: 26–32 kg (56–70 lb).

FAULTS Any departure from the foregoing points should be considered a fault and the seriousness with which the fault should be regarded should be in exact proportion to its degree.

NOTE Male animals should have two apparently normal testicles fully descended into the scrotum.

BERNESE MOUNTAIN DOG

ONE OF THE MOST BEAUTIFUL OF SWISS dogs, used by the weavers of Berne as a draught dog, and also employed in herding sheep and cattle. He is still occasionally harnessed to a light cart, which he enjoys pulling, often to the delight of the small children riding inside.

Though the Bernese carries the traditional Swiss colouring of black and tan with white markings. The breed can be traced back to the Roman invasion of what we now call Switzerland some 2,000 years ago. Caesar's troops, which were always on the move, needed dogs to guard their supplies and the mastiff types they brought with them eventually mated with local flock-guarders, from which the Bernese evolved with an ability to withstand the severe weather of the Alps.

The name is taken from the canton of Berne, and the Bernese has also attracted other less flattering names, such as Gelbbacken (Yellow Cheeks) and Vieraugen (Four Eyes) while the association as a draft dog also earned them the name of 'Cheese Factory Dog'.

Of imposing stature, the striking tricolour markings of his soft, silky coat add to his impressive appearance. Never aggressive, he is a gentleman, kind and courteous, well mannered and affectionate. Not a noisy dog, but obedient and easily trained, he makes a perfect companion for children and a devoted family pet.

GENERAL APPEARANCE Strong, sturdy working dog, active, alert, well boned, of striking colour.

CHARACTERISTICS A multi-purpose farm dog capable of draught work. A kind and devoted family dog. Slow to mature.

TEMPERAMENT Self-confident, good-natured, friendly and fearless. Aggressiveness not to be tolerated.

HEAD AND SKULL Strong with flat skull, very slight furrow, well defined stop; strong straight muzzle. Lips slightly developed.

EYES Dark brown, almond-shaped, well fitting eyelids.

EARS Medium-sized; set high, triangular-shaped, lying flat in repose, when alert brought slightly forward and raised at base.

MOUTH Jaws strong, with a perfect, regular and complete scissor bite, i.e. upper teeth closely overlapping lower teeth and set square to the jaws.

NECK Strong, muscular and medium length.

FOREQUARTERS Shoulders long, strong and sloping with upper arm forming a distinct angle, flat lying, well muscled. Forelegs straight from all sides. Pasterns flexing slightly.

BODY Compact rather than long. Height to length 9:10. Broad chest, good depth of brisket reaching at least to elbow. Well ribbed; strong loins. Firm, straight back. Rump smoothly rounded.

HINDQUARTERS Broad, strong and well muscled. Stifles well bent. Hock strong, well let down and turning neither in nor out. Dewclaws to be removed.

FEET Short, round and compact.

TAIL Bushy, reaching just below hock. Raised when alert or moving but never curled or carried over back.

GAIT/MOVEMENT Stride reaching out well in front, following well through behind, balanced stride in all gaits.

COAT Soft, silky with bright natural sheen, long, slightly wavy but should not curl when mature.

COLOUR Jet black, with rich reddish-brown on cheeks, over eyes, on all four legs and on chest. Slight to medium-sized symmetrical white head marking (blaze) and white chest marking (cross) are essential. Preferred but not essential, white paws, white not reaching higher than pastern, white tip to tail. A few white hairs at nape of neck, and white anal patch undesirable but tolerated.

SIZE Height: dogs: 64-70 cm (25-27½ in); bitches: 58-66 cm (23-26 in).

FAULTS Any departure from the foregoing points should be considered a fault and the seriousness with which the fault should be regarded should be in exact proportion to its degree.

NOTE Male animals should have two apparently normal testicles fully descended from the scrotum.

BORDER COLLIE

THIS HIGHLY INTELLIGENT DOG HAS AN inborn instinct to work, and responds readily and eagerly to training. He was originally used for working sheep in the hills and mountains, mainly in the border counties of England, Scotland and Wales, but his prowess as a working sheepdog has now spread country-wide throughout Britain and even farther afield.

It was only in the latter quarter of the twentieth century that the Border collie assumed an important role in the showrings of Britain.

He is graceful, but with sufficient substance to withstand the elements. A silent worker, he responds to any signal, audible or visual. His disposition is kindly as he is loyal and faithful by nature. Capable of thinking for himself, he is often used in mountain rescue work, makes an excellent tracker, and is also used as a sniffer dog.

He needs a lot of exercise, thrives on company, and will participate in any activity. He is dedicated to serving man, but is the type of dog who needs to work to be happy and is not content to sit at home by the hearth all day.

GENERAL APPEARANCE Well proportioned, smooth outline showing quality, gracefulness and perfect balance, combined with sufficient substance to give impression of endurance. Any tendency to coarseness or weediness undesirable.

CHARACTERISTICS Tenacious, hard-working sheep dog, of great tractability.

TEMPERAMENT Keen, alert, responsive and intelligent. Neither nervous nor aggressive.

HEAD AND SKULL Skull fairly broad, occiput not pronounced. Cheeks not full or rounded. Muzzle, tapering to nose, moderately short and strong. Skull and foreface approximately equal in length. Stop very distinct. Nose black, except in brown or chocolate colour when it may be brown. In blues nose should be slate colour. Nostrils well developed.

EYES Set wide apart, oval-shaped, of moderate size, brown in colour except in merles where one or both or part of one or both may be blue. Expression mild, keen, alert and intelligent.

EARS Medium size and texture, set well apart. Carried erect or semi-erect and sensitive in use.

MOUTH Teeth and jaws strong with a perfect, regular and complete scissor bite, i.e. upper teeth closely overlapping lower teeth and set square to the jaws.

NECK Of good length, strong and muscular, slightly arched and broadening to shoulders.

FOREQUARTERS Front legs parallel when viewed from front, pasterns slightly sloping when viewed from side. Bone strong but not heavy. Shoulders well laid back, elbows close to body.

BODY Athletic in appearance, ribs well sprung, chest deep and rather broad, loins deep and muscular, but not tucked-up. Body slightly longer than height at shoulder.

HINDQUARTERS Broad, muscular, in profile sloping gracefully to set-on of tail. Thighs long, deep and muscular with well turned stifles and strong well let down hocks. From hock to ground, hindlegs well boned and parallel when viewed from rear.

FEET Oval, pads deep, strong and sound, toes arched and close together. Nails short and strong.

TAIL Moderately long, the bone reaching at least to hock, set-on low, well furnished and with an upward swirl towards the end, completing graceful contour and balance of dog. Tail may be raised in excitement, never carried over back.

GAIT/MOVEMENT Free, smooth and tireless, with minimum lift of feet, conveying impression of ability to move with great stealth and speed.

COAT Two varieties: a) Moderately long; b) Smooth. In both top coat dense and medium textured, undercoat soft and dense giving good weather resistance. In moderately long-coated variety, abundant coat forms mane, breeching and brush. On face, ears, forelegs (except for feather), hindlegs from hock to ground, hair should be short and smooth.

COLOUR Variety of colours permissible. White should never predominate.

SIZE Ideal height: dogs: 53 cm (21 in); bitches: slightly less.

FAULTS Any departure from the foregoing points should be considered a fault and the seriousness with which the fault should be regarded should be in exact proportion to its degree.

NOTE Male animals should have two apparently normal testicles fully descended into the scrotum.

BOUVIER DES FLANDRES

A RUGGED, POWERFUL DOG, ORIGINALLY used for herding and protecting cattle in Belgium and France, he has found his way into the towns where he can adapt to family life. His impressive head accentuated by eyebrows, beard and moustache gives him a formidable appearance which belies his stable temperament, and amiable disposition. However, he can and will protect home and family. He is good with children, quiet in the house, but ever vigilant. His rough, dry coat is easy to care for and, although large, he requires only a medium amount of exercise, is not a clumsy dog, but is very social and happy to live in country or city, mansion or flat.

Bouvier can be translated as 'oxherd' or 'cattle herder', with each French or Belgian region having its own type. This is the one from Flanders, which gained a wider reputation during the First World War when it was used both as an ambulance dog and a messenger. Many modern pedigrees trace back to a dog saved by a Belgian army vet after the breed all but died out.

GENERAL APPEARANCE Compact body, short coupled, powerfully built, well boned, strongly muscled limbs, giving impression of great power but without clumsiness in general deportment.

CHARACTERISTICS Lively appearance revealing intelligence, energy and audacity. Its harsh beard is very characteristic giving forbidding expression.

TEMPERAMENT Calm and sensible.

HEAD AND SKULL In proportion to build and stature general impression is of massiveness, accentuated by beard and moustache. Head clean-cut. Skull well developed, flat, somewhat longer than wide. Proportions of skull to muzzle are 3:2. Stop shallow, but appears deep due to upstanding eyebrows. Muzzle broad, powerful, well boned, straight in upperline, sloping slightly toward nose which should never become pointed. Circumference measured just in front of eyes approximately equal to length of head. Nose should be very well developed, thus extending the foreface in a slightly convex line towards its tip, rounded at edges, always black. Nostrils wide. Cheeks flat and clean.

EYES Alert in expression. Neither protruding nor sunken. Slightly oval in shape and horizontally placed but not too close together. As dark as possible in relation to coat colour. Light or wild-looking eyes highly undesirable. Eyes always black, lack of pigmentation undesirable. Haw never visible.

EARS Set-on high, very flexible, triangular and in proportion to head.

MOUTH Jaws strong. Teeth strong and white with a perfect, regular and complete scissor bite, i.e. upper teeth closely overlapping lower teeth and set square to the jaws.

NECK Strong, well muscled and thickening slightly towards shoulders. A little shorter than length of head, nape strong and slightly arched. Without dewlap.

FOREQUARTERS Forelegs very strong and absolutely straight. Shoulders relatively long, muscular without heaviness, obliquely placed. Shoulder blade and upper arm of equal length. Elbows well set into body and parallel, turning neither in nor out. Forearms, seen from front or side, straight, parallel to each other, perpendicular to ground. Well muscled, heavy boned. Pasterns strong, fairly short, sloping very slightly.

BODY Short, strong, deep, broad, compact with very little tuck-up. Length from point of shoulder to point of buttock about equal to height at withers. Chest descends to level of elbows and is not cylindrical, although ribs well sprung. Croup extends horizontal line of back,

blends imperceptibly with curve of rump; broad but not excessively so in dogs, broader in bitches. A rising croup, or one which falls away very definitely undesirable.

HINDQUARTERS Moderate angulation, firm and well muscled, with large, powerful thighs. Legs strong and sturdy with hocks well let down and perfectly perpendicular when viewed from rear. No dewclaws.

FEET Short, round and compact. Toes tight and well arched. Nails black and strong. Pads thick and hard.

TAIL Customarily docked to 2-3 vertebrae. Continuing normal line of vertebral column and carried gaily when moving. Dogs born tailless permissible.

GAIT/MOVEMENT Powerful, driving, free and easy; ambling permitted but not desirable.

COAT Abundant, so thick that when separated by hand skin barely visible. Hair coarse to touch, dry and matt. Neither too long nor too short, about 6 cm (2½ in). Unkempt-looking but never woolly nor curly, gradually becoming short as it comes down the legs, always harsh.

Flat coat denoting lack of undercoat highly undesirable. Undercoat dense and close-grained. On head shorter, outside of ears very short. Upper lip well moustached, lower carrying a full harsh beard giving forbidding expression so characteristic of breed. Eyebrows formed of backward-sweeping hairs accentuating shape of eyebrows but never veiling eyes.

COLOUR From fawn to black including brindle. White star on chest permissible. White predominating or chocolate brown highly undesirable. Light washed-out shades undesirable.

SIZE Height: dogs: 62-68 cm (25-27 in); bitches: 59-65 cm (23-25½ in). Weight: dogs: approx 35-40 kg (77-88 lb); bitches: approx 27-35 kg (59-77 lb).

FAULTS Any departure from the foregoing points should be considered a fault and the seriousness with which the fault should be regarded should be in exact proportion to its degree.

NOTE Male animals should have two apparently normal testicles fully descended into the scrotum.

BOXER

DEVOTEES OF THE BOXER NEED TO BE fit to stand up to their charges; a gentle, meek Boxer does not exist; extrovert and energetic are two adjectives which spring to mind as soon as the breed is mentioned, along with loyal and fun-loving. Once converted to the Boxer, owners never give up the breed.

Home for the Boxer is Germany and behind the breed are believed to be dogs such as the Great Dane and the Bulldog. It is thought his name may have come from a corruption of the German word *beisser*, the Boxer being a refined version of *bullenbeisser*, meaning 'bull biter'. The breed has been in its present form since the late 1800s and in Germany and America has its ears cropped (upright) but in Britain this is not so.

A guarding breed of a high order, the Boxer is intelligent and, with patient firmness, tractable, but he needs to be convinced of the rightness of what he is asked to do. On the other hand, he will enter into the spirit of the most riotous of family games.

Hardy and full of stamina, his idea of a country walk is to get as wet and muddy as possible, but the shortness of his coat permits easy cleaning.

A good trencherman, he is rarely finicky or faddy. Truly a delightful breed, he is not quick to pick a fight but ready to prove that his slightly pugnacious face with its upturned chin can be backed to the hilt.

GENERAL APPEARANCE Great nobility, smooth-coated, medium-sized, square build, strong bone and evident, well developed muscles.

CHARACTERISTICS Lively, strong, loyal to owner and family, but distrustful of strangers. Obedient, friendly at play, but with guarding instinct.

TEMPERAMENT Equable, biddable, fearless, self-assured.

HEAD AND SKULL Head imparts its unique individual stamp and is in proportion to body, appearing neither light nor too heavy. Skull lean without exaggerated cheek muscles. Muzzle broad, deep and powerful, never narrow, pointed, short or shallow. Balance of skull and muzzle essential, with muzzle never appearing small, viewed from any angle. Skull cleanly covered, showing no wrinkle, except when alerted. Creases present from root of nose running down sides of muzzle. Dark mask confined to muzzle, distinctly contrasting with colour of head, even when white is present. Lower jaw undershot, curving slightly upward. Upper jaw broad where attached to skull, tapering very slightly to front. Muzzle shape completed by upper lips, thick and well padded, supported by well separated canine teeth of lower jaw. Lower edge of upper lip rests on edge of lower lip, so that chin is clearly perceptible when viewed from front or side. Lower jaw never to obscure front of upper lip, neither should teeth or tongue be visible when mouth closed. Top of skull slightly arched, not rounded, nor too flat and broad. Occiput not too pronounced. Distinct stop, bridge of nose never forced back into forehead, nor should it be downfaced. Length of muzzle measured from tip of nose to inside corner of eye is one-third length of head measured from tip of nose to occiput. Nose broad, black, slightly turned up, wide nostrils with well defined line between. Tip of nose set slightly higher than root of muzzle. Cheeks powerfully developed, never bulging.

EYES Dark brown, forward looking, not too small, protruding or deeply set. Showing lively, intelligent expression. Dark rims with good pigmentation showing no haw.

EARS Moderate size, thin, set wide apart on highest part of skull lying flat and close to cheek in repose, but falling forward with definite crease when alert.

MOUTH Undershot jaw, canines set wide apart with incisors (six) in straight line in lower jaw. In upper jaw set in line curving slightly forward. Bite powerful and sound, with teeth set in normal arrangement.

NECK Round, of ample length, strong, muscular, clean-cut, no dewlap. Distinctly marked nape and elegant arch down to withers.

FOREQUARTERS Shoulders long and sloping, close lying, not excessively covered with muscle. Upper arm long, making right angle to shoulder blade. Forelegs seen from front, straight, parallel, with strong bone. Elbows not too close or standing too far from chest wall. Forearms perpendicular, long and firmly muscled. Pasterns short, clearly defined, but not distended, slightly slanted.

BODY In profile square, length from forechest to rear of upper thigh equal to height at withers. Chest deep, reaching to elbows. Depth of chest half height at withers. Ribs well arched, not barrel-shaped, extending well to rear. Withers clearly defined. Back short, straight, slightly sloping, broad and strongly muscled. Loin short, well tucked up and taut. Lower abdominal line blends into curve to rear.

HINDQUARTERS Very strong with muscles hard and standing out noticeably under skin. Thighs broad and curved. Broad croup slightly sloped, with flat, broad arch. Pelvis long and broad. Upper and lower thigh long. Good hind angulation; when standing, the stifle is directly under the hip protuberance. Seen from side, leg from hock joint to foot not quite vertical. Seen from behind, legs straight, hock joints clean, with powerful rear pads.

FEET Front feet small and cat-like, with well arched toes, and hard pads; hind feet slightly longer.

TAIL Set-on high, customarily docked and carried upward.

GAIT/MOVEMENT Strong, powerful with noble bearing, reaching well forward, and with driving action of hindquarters. In profile, stride free and ground covering.

COAT Short, glossy, smooth and tight to body.

COLOUR Fawn or brindle. White markings acceptable not exceeding one-third of ground colour.
FAWN: Various shades from dark deer red to light fawn.
BRINDLE: Black stripes on previously described fawn shades, running parallel to ribs all over body. Stripes contract distinctly to ground colour, neither too close nor too thinly dispersed. Ground colour clear, not intermingling with stripes.

SIZE Height: dogs: 57-63 cm (22½-25 in); bitches: 53-59 cm (21-23 in). Weight: dogs: approx 30-32 kg (66-70 lb); bitches: approx 25-27 kg (55-60 lb).

FAULTS Any departure from the foregoing points should be considered a fault and the seriousness with which the fault should be regarded should be in exact proportion to its degree.

NOTE Male animals should have two apparently normal testicles fully descended into the scrotum.

BRIARD

ENEATH THE REFINED APPEARANCE OF
the long coat on the show Briard there
is a truly rugged worker. The varied
shades of fawn and the blacks, sometimes
with white hairs scattered through the coat,
make this a striking and handsome dog.
He is extrovert, loving to engage in games
which can turn rough but never nasty;
definitely not a dog for the weak-willed!

Originating from the province of Brie
in France, he has a dual role as a guard
against marauding predators as well as a
sheep-herder. He has also occasionally been
employed by armies as a pack dog among
other general duties.

He is a fairly large dog, so he takes some
feeding, and his very flowing coat with its
moustache, beard and eyebrows requires
regular and thorough grooming if it is not
to become a mess.

Blessed with a fearless temperament, he
makes a good household dog with no hint
of aggression in his make-up, but he does
need exercise.

GENERAL APPEARANCE Rugged appearance;
supple, muscular and well proportioned.

CHARACTERISTICS Very intelligent, gay and
lively.

TEMPERAMENT Fearless, with no trace of
timidity or aggressiveness.

HEAD AND SKULL Skull slightly rounded and slightly longer from occiput to stop than it is wide when measured through points of cheek bones. Head is composed of two equal rectangles, occiput to stop and stop to end of nose, when viewed in profile from above. Muzzle square and very strong; any tendency to snipiness highly undesirable. Stop clearly defined. Nose large and square, always black.

EYES Horizontally placed, well open and rather large, not oblique. Intelligent and gentle in expression. Dark brown, eye rims always black.

EARS Set-on high and covered with long hair. Should not lie too flat against side of head. Fairly short, length of ear being equal to or slightly less than half length of head. When dog alert ears should be lifted slightly and swing very slightly forward.

MOUTH Teeth very strong and white with a perfect, regular and complete scissor bite, i.e. upper teeth closely overlapping lower teeth and set square to the jaws. Lips always black.

NECK Of good length; strong and muscular; arched, giving proud carriage of head and flowing smoothly into well placed shoulders.

FOREQUARTERS Shoulders well angulated and well laid back, forelegs well muscled, strongly boned.

BODY Back firm and level, chest broad, medium spring of rib, well let down, very slight slope at croup, determining set of tail. Very slightly longer in body than height at shoulder.

HINDQUARTERS Well angulated, with hocks set not too low and turning neither in nor out, but leg below hock not quite vertical. Hindlegs, particularly thighs, well muscled. Double dewclaws set low on hindlegs of utmost importance.

FEET Strong, turning neither in nor out, slightly rounded, about midway between cat-foot and harefoot. Nails always black, pads firm and hard, toes close together. Well covered with hair.

TAIL Long, well covered with hair with upward hook at tip. Carried low but always held centrally. Bone of tail reaching at least point of hock.

GAIT/MOVEMENT Effortless, and when dog extends himself covering a great deal of ground. Extremely supple, enabling dog to turn quickly. Strong, firm, very smooth with plenty of drive.

COAT Long, not less than 7 cm (3 in) on body. Slightly wavy and very dry. A fine dense undercoat required all over body. Head carries hair forming a moustache, beard and eyebrows, lightly veiling eyes.

COLOUR All black, or with white hairs scattered through black coat. Fawn in all its shades, darker shades preferred. Fawns may have dark shadings on ears, muzzle, back and tail, but these shadings must blend gradually into rest of coat since any demarcation line denotes a bi-colour which is not permissible. May also be slate grey.

SIZE Height: dogs: 62-68 cm (24-27 in) at withers; bitches: 56-64 cm (23-25½ in) at withers. Slight undersize before 18 months, or slight oversize in maturity permissible.

FAULTS Any departure from the foregoing points should be considered a fault and the seriousness with which the fault should be regarded should be in exact proportion to its degree.

NOTE Male animals should have two apparently normal testicles fully descended into the scrotum.

BULLMASTIFF

A BRITISH BREED EVOLVED FROM THE Old English Mastiff and the Bulldog. Primarily used as a guard dog and, in olden times, to help the gamekeeper in the apprehension of poachers.

Naturally intelligent and observant, he is easily trained but likes to have a reason for doing things. Highly spirited, he makes a happy companion who is totally reliable both physically and mentally. Devoted to his 'family', his bravery and courage are legendary, defending them against intruders. He can quickly assess a situation and this, combined with his acute hearing, makes him an excellent housedog. He is very strong, but amenable to kindly discipline.

GENERAL APPEARANCE Powerful build, symmetrical, showing great strength, but not cumbersome; sound and active.

CHARACTERISTICS Powerful, enduring, active and reliable.

TEMPERAMENT High-spirited, alert and faithful.

HEAD AND SKULL Skull large and square, viewed from every angle, fair wrinkle when interested, but not when in repose. Circumference of skull may equal height of dog measured at top of shoulder; broad and deep with well filled cheeks. Pronounced stop. Muzzle short; distance from tip of nose to stop approximately one-third of length from tip of nose to centre of occiput, broad under eyes and sustaining nearly same width to end of nose; blunt and cut off square, forming right angle with upper line of face, and at same time proportionate with skull. Under-jaw broad to end. Nose broad with widely spreading nostrils; flat, neither pointed nor turned up in profile. Flews not pendulous, never hanging below level of lower jaw.

EYES Dark or hazel, of medium size, set apart the width of muzzle with furrow between. Light or yellow eyes highly undesirable.

EARS V-shaped, folded back, set-on wide and high, level of occiput giving square appearance to skull which is most important. Small and deeper in colour than body. Point of ear level with eye when alert. Rose ears slightly undesirable.

MOUTH Level desired but slightly undershot allowed but not preferred. Canine teeth large and set wide apart, other teeth strong, even and well placed.

NECK Well arched, moderate length, very muscular and almost equal to skull in circumference.

FOREQUARTERS Chest, wide and deep, well let down between forelegs, with deep brisket. Shoulders muscular, sloping and powerful, not overloaded. Forelegs powerful and straight, well boned, set wide apart, presenting a straight front. Pasterns straight and strong.

BODY Back short and straight, giving compact carriage, but not so short as to interfere with activity. Roach and sway backs highly undesirable.

HINDQUARTERS Loins wide and muscular with fair depth of flank. Hindlegs strong and muscular, with well developed second thighs, denoting power and activity, not cumbersome. Hocks moderately bent. Cow-hocks highly undesirable.

FEET Well arched, cat-like, with rounded toes, pads hard. Dark toenails desirable. Splayed feet highly undesirable.

TAIL Set high, strong at root and tapering, reaching to hocks, carried straight or curved, but not hound-fashion. Crank tails highly undesirable.

GAIT/MOVEMENT Movement indicates power and sense of purpose. When moving straight neither front nor hindlegs should cross or plait, right front and left rear leg rising and falling at same time. A firm backline unimpaired by powerful thrust from hindlegs denoting a balanced and harmonious movement.

COAT Short and hard, weather-resistant, lying flat to body. Long silky or woolly coats highly undesirable.

COLOUR Any shade of brindle, fawn or red; colour to be pure and clear. A slight white marking on chest permissible. Other white markings undesirable. Black muzzles essential, toning off towards eye, with dark markings around eyes contributing to expression.

SIZE Height at shoulder: dogs: 63.5–68.5 cm (25–27 in); bitches: 61–66 cm (24–26 in). Weight: dogs: 50–59 kg (110–130 lb); bitches: 41–50 kg (90–110 lb).

FAULTS Any departure from the foregoing points should be considered a fault and the seriousness with which the fault should be regarded should be in exact proportion to its degree.

NOTE Male animals should have two apparently normal testicles fully descended into the scrotum.

ROUGH COLLIE

THE ROUGH COLLIE IS THE SAME AS the Smooth Collie with the exception of coat length. The breed is thought to have evolved from dogs brought originally to Scotland by the Romans as far back as 50 BC which then mated with native types. Purists may point to subtle differences which have appeared as individual breeders selected stock for future breeding, but the fact remains that the two breeds derived very recently from the same stock and, in truth, share lines which can be found in common to this day. The Rough Collie is, of course, the somewhat refined version of the original working collie of the Scottish shepherd, from which it has been selected over at least a hundred years. As a result we now see a glamorous show dog which draws applause because of his aesthetic appearance, in the same way that his working cousin thrills audiences with his skill in the competitive obedience ring.

This is not to suggest that the work of the pedigree breeder has made the Rough Collie the equivalent of the human 'dumb blonde'. Far from it: many of the breed can perform satisfactorily, offered the chance, and it is as well for owners to remember the 'origin of the species' when taking their companions across farmland and hillside; all too easily the quiet pet can prick up his ears at the sight of a grazing flock with disastrous results as the old instincts take charge. The basic message is that for all his beauty, the Collie is a worker and must never be dismissed as 'just a pretty face'.

The coat does not look glamorous as a result of negligence; grooming is hard work, but that work is very rewarding. Surprisingly enough the Rough Collie does not seem to demand vast amounts of exercise, but care must be taken to stop him from putting on too much weight.

The winning Rough Collie needs a working award before he can be crowned Champion rather than Show Champion.

GENERAL APPEARANCE Appears as dog of great beauty, standing with impassive dignity, with no part out of proportion to whole.

CHARACTERISTICS Physical structure on lines of strength and activity, free from cloddiness and with no trace of coarseness. Expression most important. In considering relative values it is obtained by perfect balance and combination of skull and foreface, size, shape, colour and placement of eyes, correct position and carriage of ears.

TEMPERAMENT Friendly disposition with no trace of nervousness or aggressiveness.

HEAD AND SKULL Head properties of great importance, must be considered in proportion to size of dog. Viewed from front or side, head resembles a well-blunted clean wedge, being smooth in outline. Skull flat. Sides taper gradually and smoothly from ears to end of black nose, without prominent cheek bones or pinched muzzle. Viewed in profile, top of skull and top of muzzle lie in two parallel straight lines of equal length divided by a slight, but perceptible stop or break. A mid-point between inside corner of eyes (which is centre of a correctly placed stop) is centre of balance in length of head. End of smooth, well rounded muzzle blunt, never square. Under-jaw strong, clean-cut. Depth of skull from brow to underpart of jaw never excessive (deep through). Nose always black.

EYES Very important feature giving sweet expression. Medium size (never very small) set somewhat obliquely, of almond shape and dark brown colour, except in the case of blue merles when eyes are frequently (one or both, or part of one or both) blue or blue-flecked. Expression full of intelligence, with quick, alert look when listening.

EARS Small, not too close together on top of skull, nor too far apart. In repose carried thrown

back, but on alert brought forward and carried semi-erect, that is, with approximately two-thirds of ear standing erect, top third tipping forward naturally, below horizontal.

MOUTH Teeth of good size. Jaws strong with a perfect, regular and complete scissor bite, i.e. upper teeth closely overlapping lower teeth and set square to the jaws.

NECK Muscular, powerful, of fair length, well arched.

FOREQUARTERS Shoulders sloping and well angulated. Forelegs straight and muscular, neither in nor out at elbows, with moderate amount of round bone.

BODY Slightly long compared with height, back firm with a slight rise over loins; ribs well sprung, chest deep, fairly broad behind shoulders.

HINDQUARTERS Hindlegs muscular at thighs, clean and sinewy below, with well bent stifles. Hocks well let down and powerful.

FEET Oval; soles well padded. Toes arched and close together. Hindfeet slightly less arched.

TAIL Long with bone reaching at least to hock joint. Carried low when quiet but with slight upward swirl at tip. May be carried gaily when excited, but never over back.

GAIT/MOVEMENT Distinctly characteristic in this breed. A sound dog is never out at the elbow, yet moves with front feet comparatively close together. Plaiting, crossing or rolling are highly undesirable. Hindlegs from hock joint to ground when viewed from rear to be parallel but not too close; when viewed from side, action is smooth. Hindlegs powerful with plenty of drive. A reasonably long stride is desirable and should be light and appear effortless.

COAT Fits outline of body, very dense. Outer coat straight and harsh to touch, undercoat soft, furry and very close almost hiding the skin; mane and frill very abundant, mask and face smooth, ears smooth at tips, but carrying more hair towards base, front legs well feathered, hindlegs above hocks profusely feathered, but smooth below hock joint. Hair on tail very profuse.

COLOUR Three recognised colours: Sable and white, Tricolour and Blue Merle.
SABLE: any shade of light gold to rich mahogany or shaded sable. Light straw or cream coloured highly undesirable.
TRICOLOUR: predominantly black with rich tan markings about legs and head. A rusty tinge in top coat highly undesirable.
BLUE MERLE: predominantly clear, silvery blue, splashed and marbled with black. Rich tan markings preferred, but absence should not be penalised. Large black markings, slate colour, or rusty tinge either of top or undercoat are highly undesirable.

All should carry typical white Collie markings to a greater or lesser degree. Following markings are favourable – white collar, full or part, white shirt, legs and feet, white tail tip. A blaze may be carried on muzzle or skull, or both.

SIZE Height: dogs: 56-61 cm (22-24 in) at shoulder; bitches: 51-56 cm (20-22 in).

FAULTS Any departure from the foregoing points should be considered a fault and the seriousness with which the fault should be regarded should be in exact proportion to its degree.

NOTE Male animals should have two apparently normal testicles fully descended into the scrotum.

SMOOTH COLLIE

THE OBVIOUS DIFFERENCE BETWEEN THE breeds is the coat length, which in the case of the Smooth is short and flat with a harsh texture on a dense undercoat. Colour range is the same although one tends to see more blue merles in Smooths than in Roughs. As a result the blue and blue-flecked eye is more characteristically seen in Smooths. Both breeds' standards call for a gay, friendly disposition without a trace of nervousness or aggression.

GENERAL APPEARANCE Appears as gifted with intelligence, alertness and activity. Stands with dignity governed by perfect anatomical formation, with no part out of proportion, giving appearance of working capability.

CHARACTERISTICS Physical structure on lines of strength and activity, free from cloddiness and with no trace of coarseness. Expression, most important. In considering relative values, it is obtained by perfect balance and combination of skull and foreface, size and shape, colour and placement of eye, correct position and carriage of ears.

TEMPERAMENT Gay and friendly, never nervous or aggressive.

HEAD AND SKULL Head properties of great importance, must be considered in proportion to size of dog. Viewed from front or side, head resembles a well-blunted, clean wedge, being smooth in outline. Skull flat. Sides taper gradually and smoothly from ears to end of black nose, without prominent cheek bones or pinched muzzle. Viewed in profile, top of skull and top of muzzle lie in two parallel straight lines of equal length divided by a slight, but perceptible stop or break. A mid-point between inside corner of eyes (which is centre of a correctly-placed stop) is centre of balance in length of head. End of smooth, well rounded muzzle blunt, never square. Under-jaw strong,

clean-cut. Depth of skull from brow to underpart of jaw never excessive (deep through). Nose always black.

EYES Very important feature, giving sweet expression. Medium size (never very small), set somewhat obliquely, of almond shape and dark brown colour, except in case of blue merles when eyes are frequently (one or both, or part of one or both) blue or blue-flecked. Expression full of intelligence, with quick, alert look when listening.

EARS Moderately large, wider at base, and placed not too close together nor too much on side of head. When in repose carried thrown back, but on alert brought forward and carried semi-erect, that is, with approximately two-thirds of ear standing erect, top third tipping forward naturally, below horizontal.

MOUTH Teeth of good size, jaws strong with a perfect, regular and complete scissor bite, i.e. upper teeth closely overlapping lower teeth and set square to the jaws.

NECK Muscular, powerful, of fair length; well arched.

FOREQUARTERS Shoulders sloping and well angulated. Forelegs straight and muscular, neither in nor out at elbows, with a moderate amount of bone. Forearm somewhat fleshy, pasterns showing flexibility without weakness.

BODY Slightly long compared with height, back level and firm with slight rise over loins; ribs well sprung; chest deep and fairly broad behind shoulders.

HINDQUARTERS Hindlegs muscular at thighs, clean and sinewy below, with well bent stifles. Hocks well let down and powerful.

FEET Oval soles well padded. Toes arched and close together. Hindfeet slightly less arched.

TAIL Long with bone reaching at least to hock joint. To be carried low when quiet but with a slight upward swirl at tip. May be carried gaily when excited, but never over back.

GAIT/MOVEMENT Distinctly characteristic of this breed. A sound dog is never out at elbow, yet moves with front feet comparatively close together. Plaiting, crossing or rolling are highly undesirable. Hindlegs, from hock joint to ground, when viewed from rear, parallel. Hindlegs powerful and full of drive. Viewed from side, action is smooth. A reasonably long stride is desirable and should be light and appear quite effortless.

COAT Short, flat top coat of harsh texture, with very dense undercoat. Not trimmed or clipped.

COLOUR Three recognised colours: Sable and white, Tricolour and Blue Merle.
SABLE: any shade from light gold to rich mahogany or shaded sable. Light straw or cream colour is highly undesirable.
TRICOLOUR: predominantly black with rich tan markings about the legs and head. A rusty tinge in top coat is highly undesirable.
BLUE MERLE: predominantly clear, silvery blue, splashed and marbled with black. Rich tan markings preferred but absence should not be penalised. Large black markings, slate colour or rusty tinge top or undercoat are highly undesirable.

All may carry typical white collie markings to a greater or lesser degree. Following markings are favourable: white collar full or part; white front, legs and feet; white tail tip. A blaze may be carried on muzzle or skull, or both. All white or predominantly white is most undesirable.

SIZE Height: dogs: 56-61 cm (22-24 in) at shoulder; bitches: 51-56 cm (20-22 in) at shoulder. Weight: dogs: 20.5-29.5 kg (45-65 lb); bitches: 18-25 kg (40-55 lb).

FAULTS Any departure from the foregoing points should be considered a fault and the seriousness with which the fault should be regarded should be in exact proportion to its degree.

NOTE Male animals should have two apparently normal testicles fully descended into the scrotum.

DOBERMANN

ORIGINALLY FROM GERMANY, THIS elegant, intelligent dog has made his mark in the canine popularity polls throughout the world. Extremely alert, with a clean outline encompassing strength and agility, he is a skilful tracker, and is often used for police work. His gleaming, short, hard coat is easily cared for. Usually black and tan, he can also be brown, blue or fawn with rust-red markings.

He has a very adaptable outlook to life and fits into a family well, playing with and guarding children. He enjoys riding in a car, and will take over the most comfortable chair without even a second thought. He makes an excellent obedience dog, and the breed is numerically strong in the showring.

A German tax collector, Louis Dobermann, is credited with the development of the breed. He needed a dog to protect him and one which would 'encourage' slow payers. It was in the late 1860s that he decided his dog should be a larger version of the Pinscher and he quickly fixed breed type, using the old-style German Shepherd and the Pinscher to obtain a mix of brain, soundness, toughness of character and quick terrier-like reaction. Other breeds such as the Weimaraner, Rottweiler, Greyhound and Manchester Terrier gave refinements in scenting powers, strength, speed and the coat.

GENERAL APPEARANCE Medium size, muscular and elegant, with well set body. Of proud carriage, compact and tough. Capable of great speed.

CHARACTERISTICS Intelligent and firm of character, loyal and obedient.

TEMPERAMENT Bold and alert. Shyness or viciousness very highly undesirable.

HEAD AND SKULL In proportion to body. Long, well filled out under eyes and clean-cut, with good depth of muzzle. Seen from above and side, resembles an elongated blunt wedge. Upper part of head flat and free from wrinkle. Top of skull flat, slight stop; muzzle line extending parallel to topline of skull. Cheeks flat, lips tight. Nose solid black in black dogs, solid dark brown in brown dogs, solid dark grey in blue dogs and light brown in fawn dogs. Head out of balance in proportion to body, dish-faced, snipy or cheeky very highly undesirable.

EYES Almond-shaped, not round, moderately deep-set, not prominent, with lively, alert expression. Iris of uniform colour, ranging from medium to darkest brown in black dogs, the darker shade being more desirable. In browns, blues, or fawns, colour of iris blends with that of markings, but not of lighter hue than markings; light eyes in black dogs highly undesirable.

EARS Small, neat, set high on head. Normally dropped, but may be erect.

MOUTH Well developed, solid and strong with a complete dentition and a perfect, regular and complete scissor bite, i.e. upper teeth closely overlapping lower teeth and set square to the jaws. Evenly placed teeth. Undershot, overshot or badly arranged teeth highly undesirable.

NECK Fairly long and lean, carried with considerable nobility; slightly convex and in proportion to shape of dog. Region of nape very muscular. Dewlap and loose skin undesirable.

FOREQUARTERS Shoulder blade and upper arm meet at an angle of 90 degrees. Shoulder blade and upper arm approximately equal in length. Short upper arm relative to shoulder blade highly undesirable. Legs seen from front and side, perfectly straight and parallel to each other from elbow to pastern; muscled and sinewy, with round bone in proportion to body structure. Standing or gaiting, elbow lies close to brisket.

BODY Square, height measured vertically from ground to highest point at withers equal to length from forechest to rear projection of upper thigh. Forechest well developed. Back short and firm, with strong, straight topline sloping slightly from withers to croup; bitches may be slightly longer to loin. Ribs deep and well sprung, reaching to elbow. Belly fairly well tucked up. Long, weak, or roach backs highly undesirable.

HINDQUARTERS Legs parallel to each other and moderately wide apart. Pelvis falling away from spinal column at an angle of about 30 degrees. Croup well filled out. Hindquarters well developed and muscular; long, well bent stifle; hocks turning neither in nor out. When standing, hock to heel perpendicular to the ground.

FEET Well arched, compact, and cat-like, turning neither in nor out. All dewclaws removed. Long, flat deviating feet and/or weak pasterns highly undesirable.

TAIL Customarily docked at first or second joint; appears to be a continuation of spine without material drop.

GAIT/MOVEMENT Elastic, free, balanced and vigorous, with good reach in forequarters and driving power in hindquarters. When trotting, should have strong rear drive, with apparent rotary motion of hindquarters. Rear and front legs thrown neither in nor out. Back remains strong and firm.

COAT Smooth, short, hard, thick and close-lying. Imperceptible undercoat on neck permissible. Hair forming a ridge on back of neck and/or along spine highly undesirable.

COLOUR Definite black, brown, blue or fawn (Isabella) only, with rust red markings. Markings to be sharply defined, appearing above each eye, on muzzle, throat and forechest, on all legs and feet and below tail. White markings of any kind highly undesirable.

SIZE Ideal height at withers: dogs: 69 cm (27 in); bitches: 65 cm (25½ in). Considerable deviation from this ideal undesirable.

FAULTS Any departure from the foregoing points should be considered a fault and the seriousness with which the fault should be regarded should be in exact proportion to its degree.

NOTE Male animals should have two apparently normal testicles fully descended into the scrotum.

ESKIMO DOG

(INTERIM)

WORKING

272

THE ESKIMO DOG, AS HIS NAME IMPLIES, is the dog traditionally employed by the Eskimo tribes as an all-purpose haulage dog. Similar in general construction to the Alaskan Malamute and the Siberian Husky, he comes mid-way between the two breeds in both height and weight, and obviously has distinct similarities.

The Eskimo Dog originated in Greenland but Canada is listed as the breed's home country because it was there that it was saved and fostered. It is extremely hardy and on one Polar expedition a six-dog team hauled a 317.5-kilogram (700-pound) fully laden sled 1,200 kilometres (750 miles) in 14 days.

The breed was never 'domesticated' by its original keepers and is not a dog geared to fit easily into a pet situation. In their homeland, they were expected to catch any prey which could form part of their rations and they cannot be considered safe with other livestock. As a result, good fences are a must.

The Eskimo Dog's basic nature includes a certain wariness, which means that early socialisation is even more necessary than in other breeds. While he can be surprisingly obliging, traditional methods of training may not work with the Eskimo Dog. Those whose hearts go out to the breed at first sight should be possessed of patience coupled with a sense of humour.

They will also require stamina as these dogs are energetic and exercise will never tire them. They enjoy life to the full, are happy extroverts, and while they are normally quiet, they will indulge *en masse* in an impromptu howl-in. They need company, human or canine. In youth they are irrepressible, in middle age they tend to mellow – a bit.

It has been said of the breed, 'They have the persistence and tenacity of the wild animal; and the domestic dog's admirable devotion to his master.' What more need be said?

GENERAL APPEARANCE Powerful body and heavy coat, striking appearance. Marked contrast in size between dogs and bitches.

CHARACTERISTICS A working sledge dog, primarily assessed for freighting capacity in Arctic conditions, adaptable, distinctly independent, alert and bold. Bitches more amenable.

TEMPERAMENT Sound, dignified, intelligent, good-natured, affectionate.

HEAD AND SKULL Head well proportioned, broad and wedge-shaped with moderate stop. Skull strong and flat; powerful jaws. Nose and lips black or brown. Muzzle medium length, gently tapering to nose.

EYES Dark brown or tawny. Placed slightly obliquely, neither prominent nor too deep-set. Expression alert and fearless.

EARS Short and firm, well set apart. Carried sharply erect and facing forward. Internally protected by fur.

MOUTH Teeth large, strong and uncrowded. Jaws strong with perfect, regular and complete scissor bite, i.e. upper teeth closely overlapping lower teeth and set square to the jaws.

NECK Rather short, heavy and muscular, with loose skin.

FOREQUARTERS Shoulders broad, big-boned and muscular. Forelegs perfectly straight and vertical in stance, powerful and heavy-boned.

BODY Chest deep and broad with well sprung ribs. Body strong and well muscled, with level back, presenting a well balanced and compact appearance. Length of body slightly greater than height at shoulder.

HINDQUARTERS Thighs broad, strong and heavily muscled. Stifles well bent, hocks well let down. Heavy bone. Legs straight when viewed from rear. Dewclaws should be removed.

FEET Rather large and strong, with strong nails. Thick pads with protective growth of fur between toes.

TAIL Large and bushy. Set high, curled loosely over back and falling either side.

GAIT/MOVEMENT Strong drive, limbs moving parallel, back held level.

COAT Thick double coat consisting of an impenetrable undercoat 2.5-5 cm (1-2 in) long, uniform over body, with well protruding outer coat of coarser longer hair, which is quite straight. Outer coat at its longest on neck and withers, breeches and underside of tail. Underbelly also well covered. Hair on head and legs rather short.

COLOUR All known dog colours, or combinations of these colours.

SIZE Height: dogs: 58-68 cm (23-27 in) at shoulder; bitches: 51-61 cm (20-24 in) at

shoulder. Weight: dogs: 34-47.6 kg
(75-105 lb); bitches: 27-41 kg (60-90 lb).

FAULTS Any departure from the foregoing
points should be considered a fault and the
seriousness with which the fault should be

regarded should be in exact proportion to its
degree.

NOTE Male animals should have two apparently
normal testicles fully descended into the
scrotum.

ESTRELA MOUNTAIN DOG

(INTERIM)

THE ESTRELA MOUNTAIN RANGE IS IN the central part of Portugal and the Estrela is the Portuguese relation of the flock-guarding dogs which can be found anywhere from Asia halfway across the world to the shores of the Atlantic. The breed standard isn't joking when it describes this dog as sturdy and well built. He is made on a generous scale and that goes for his nature as well. His devotees say that he is almost too good with children, as he tends to tow his owners towards them at high speed.

He is relatively trainable in the basics of good canine behaviour, but doesn't consider that retrieving is any part of a dog's normal way of life. He is easy to groom and a good trencherman, being unfaddy in his appetite.

Lest he should appear to be altogether too good to be true, he has a loud voice which he delights in using at frequent intervals, not always at the most convenient moments. He is also a prodigious leaper, so runs have to be well made to confine him if that is the way an owner reckons to keep him.

This is a breed which has not yet been seen in the UK in any numbers, but has much to commend it if a large dog is appropriate.

GENERAL APPEARANCE A sturdy, well built dog of mastiff type, conveying an impression of strength and vigour.

CHARACTERISTICS A hardy guard dog, active and of considerable stamina.

TEMPERAMENT Loyal, affectionate to owners, indifferent to others, intelligent and alert, inclined to be stubborn.

HEAD AND SKULL Head long and powerful with broad, slightly rounded skull. Moderate stop mid-way between the end of the nose and the slightly defined occiput. Muzzle tapers moderately, but a narrow head and pointed muzzle are undesirable. Nose black, a pale or partly pigmented nose being undesirable. Nostrils wide. Jaws well developed. Lips black, meeting closely and not pendulous. Roof of mouth intensely pigmented with black.

EYES Neither deep nor prominent, of medium size, oval in shape with calm and intelligent expression, preferably amber or darker. Black-rimmed eyelids closing well, with rather prominent eyebrows.

EARS Small in relation to body, thin, triangular, rounded at the tips, set-on moderately high, carried falling backwards against the side of the head with a small portion of the inner edge showing.

MOUTH Teeth very strong. Jaw strong with perfect, regular and complete scissor bite, i.e. upper teeth closely overlapping lower teeth and set square to the jaws.

NECK Short, thick and well set-on. What may appear to be a dewlap, especially in dogs, should be a thick tuft of hair under the throat. A true dewlap undesirable.

FOREQUARTERS Forelegs straight, well muscled and with strong bone, shoulders moderately sloping, rounded forearms and short pasterns which appear nearly vertical when viewed from the side.

BODY Back slightly higher at withers than at loins and preferably short. Chest deep and well sprung without being barrel chested. Loins short and well muscled. The lower line rising gradually but gently from the sternum to the groin.

HINDQUARTERS Thighs well muscled with moderate angulation. Hocks moderately well let down. Slightly sloping croup. Vertical pastern when viewed either from front or back. Strong bone well angulated.

FEET Well made, neither very round nor excessively long. Thick, well closed toes with abundant hair between pads, which are thick and hard. Claws well protruding but not overgrown, dark and preferably black. Dewclaws customarily removed from hindlegs.

TAIL Long, reaching to the hock, well furnished with hair and feathered, forming a hook at the end resembling a scimitar. When excited the tail passes the horizontal.

GAIT/MOVEMENT Distinctive, free and easy with a driving, purposeful jog trot. Tendency for closeness behind acceptable without any sign of weakness. Dogs should not be penalised for carrying the head level with topline in motion.

COAT Two types:
LONG COAT: The outer coat is thick and moderately harsh, resembling goat hair, lying close over the body, flat or slightly waved, never curly. Undercoat very dense and normally lighter in colour than the outer coat. Short and smooth hair on head, diminishing in length from the base of ears to tip, is thick and abundant round the neck and chest forming a ruff, particularly in the male. Thighs, lower hocks and backs of the forearm abundantly feathered, as is the tail. Front of legs, short smooth hair. A woolly or fluffy coat undesirable.

SHORT COAT: Short, thick, moderately harsh and straight, calling to mind goat's hair, with shorter dense undercoat. Any feathering should be in proportion.

COLOUR Recognised colours are:
FAWN: which varies from burnt yellow through reddish gold to a deep red, with or without guard hairs. The fawn should never be so pale as to be a dirty white.
BRINDLE: any of the previous permitted colours with the addition of streaks or smudges of black or brown varying in intensity.
WOLF GREY: all black and all white, skewbald and piebald unacceptable. Black muzzle or mask is highly desirable. White markings on chest, underside, feet or tail are tolerated but undesirable.

SIZE Height: dogs: 65-72 cm (25½-28½ in); bitches: 62-68 cm (24½-27 in). A tolerance of 4 cm (1½ in) above these limits is allowed.

FAULTS Any departure from the foregoing points should be considered a fault and the seriousness with which the fault should be regarded should be in exact proportion to its degree.

NOTE Male animals should have two apparently normal testicles fully descended into the scrotum.

FINNISH LAPPHUND

(INTERIM)

THE FINNISH LAPPHUND IS A SURVIVOR. HE would have to be in order to cope with life under the harsh climate of Lapland. His original role in Finland was to herd reindeer and he still does so as well as sorting out cattle and sheep.

He lives his life in the family and likes nothing so much as to please his owners in whatever activity his quick brain allows him to become involved. An ideal companion for an outdoor household, he is a typical Spitz and his thick jacket comes in all manner of colours.

He seems to enjoy the company of children and is fortunately not quite as fiercely vocal as some members of the Spitz gang! He needs adequate food because he always appears to be bursting with energy.

GENERAL APPEARANCE A Spitz-type dog of medium size, strongly built, slightly longer than height at withers.

CHARACTERISTICS Tendency to herd.

TEMPERAMENT Intelligent, brave, calm, faithful. Suitable as companion and watchdog.

HEAD AND SKULL Strong featured, comparatively broad, bitch's more refined; forehead slightly rounded; stop clearly defined. Muzzle shorter than skull, straight and slightly tapering when viewed from both above and side. Nose black.

EYES Oval-shaped; dark.

EARS Erect, pointed, medium-sized, set far apart, rather broad at base and very mobile.

MOUTH Jaws strong with perfect, regular and complete scissor bite, i.e. upper teeth closely overlapping lower teeth and set square to the jaws. Lips tight.

NECK Medium long, strong, covered with thick hair.

FOREQUARTERS Legs well boned, strong and straight. Elbows level with lowest edge of brisket. Shoulders well laid back.

BODY Firm. Back strong, straight and broad. Brisket deep and long; moderate tuck-up.

HINDQUARTERS Strong boned. Strong and straight when viewed from behind. Hock of medium size. Dewclaws permitted.

FEET Well arched, oval, covered with thick hair.

TAIL Medium length, covered wih long hair. Carried curved over the back when dog is moving.

GAIT/MOVEMENT Free with parallel movement fore and aft.

COAT Profuse. Outer coat long and coarse. Undercoat soft and thick. Shorter on the head and front parts of legs.

COLOUR All colours are allowed, but the main colour must dominate. Marks differing from the dominant colour are permitted on head, neck, chest, legs and on tip of tail.

SIZE Height: dogs: 46-52 cm (18-20½ in) at withers; bitches: 41-47 cm (16-18½ in) at withers.

FAULTS Any departure from the foregoing points should be considered a fault and the seriousness with which the fault should be regarded should be in exact proportion to its degree.

NOTE Male animals should have two apparently normal testicles fully descended into the scrotum.

GERMAN SHEPHERD DOG (ALSATIAN)

ARGUABLY THE MOST POPULAR BREED worldwide, the Shepherd, as he is known to most people, provokes fiercer loyalties in enthusiasts' hearts than virtually any other breed. The breed as we know it today was founded at the very end of the 1800s and a German cavalry captain, Rittmeister Max von Stephanitz, has been credited as the father of the breed. A group of people led by him promoted the Shepherd for thirty-five years to bring it to a position of respect. As demand for them as herding dogs fell away Rittmeister Stephanitz encouraged their use by police and the military and in the First World War alone 48,000 were enlisted in the German army.

It is difficult to talk about German Shepherds without being drawn into the discussion on type; the style of the dog varies tremendously even if the wording of the standards throughout the world is based on that of the country of origin. The appearance of the animal may vary according to the attitude of the fancier, but one thing will be agreed by all: that a genuine German Shepherd must be possessed of a truly steady temperament, greeting all he meets with a calm firmness. He ranks with any breed in his trainability for a veritable plethora of purposes. From his original work as a shepherd, acting as both herder and flock-guard, he has become by far the most widely used military and police dog for forces all over the globe.

He rates with the best as a guide dog for the blind; he is a tracker of great quality; and his devotees consider him the ultimate as an obedience worker.

In short, temperament is deemed the most important single attribute, but conscientious breeders strive also for physical perfection.

In spite of his thick double coat, he is not a difficult dog to keep groomed provided his owner is vigorous and determined. In truth, determination may well need to be an important facet in an owner's make-up, as a Shepherd needs a firm, consistent hand. He is a highly intelligent creature and, like many highly intelligent creatures, he needs to be kept occupied if he is not to become bored and, in turn, mischievous.

GENERAL APPEARANCE Slightly long in comparison to height; of powerful, well muscled build with weather-resistant coat. Relation between height, length, position and structure of fore and hindquarters (angulation) producing far-reaching, enduring gait. Clear definition of masculinity and femininity essential, and working ability never sacrificed for mere beauty.

CHARACTERISTICS Versatile working dog, balanced and free from exaggeration. Attentive, alert, resilient and tireless with keen scenting ability.

TEMPERAMENT Steady of nerve, loyal, self-assured, courageous and tractable. Never nervous, over-aggressive or shy.

HEAD AND SKULL Proportionate in size to body, never coarse, too fine or long. Clean-cut; fairly broad between ears. Forehead slightly domed; little or no trace of central furrow. Cheeks forming softly rounded curve, never protruding. Skull from ears to bridge of nose tapering gradually and evenly, blending without too pronounced stop into wedge-shaped powerful muzzle. Skull approximately 50 per cent of overall length of head. Width of skull corresponding approximately to length, in males slightly greater, in females slightly less. Muzzle strong, lips firm, clean and closing tightly. Top of muzzle straight, almost parallel to forehead. Short, blunt, weak, pointed, overlong muzzle undesirable.

EYES Medium-sized, almond-shaped, never protruding. Dark brown preferred, lighter shade permissible, provided expression good and general harmony of head not destroyed. Expression lively, intelligent and self-assured.

EARS Medium-sized, firm in texture, broad at base, set high, carried erect, almost parallel, never pulled inwards or tipped, tapering to a point, open at front. Never hanging. Folding back during movement permissible.

MOUTH Jaws strongly developed. With a perfect, regular and complete scissor bite, i.e. upper teeth closely overlapping lower teeth and set square to the jaws. Teeth healthy and strong. Full dentition desirable.

NECK Fairly long, strong, with well developed muscles, free from throatiness. Carried at 45 degree angle to horizontal, raised when excited, lowered at fast trot.

FOREQUARTERS Shoulder blades long, set obliquely (45 degrees) laid flat to body. Upper arm strong, well muscled, joining shoulder blade at approximately 90 degrees. Forelegs straight from pasterns to elbows viewed from any angle, bone oval rather than round. Pasterns firm, supple and slightly angulated. Elbows neither tucked in nor turned out. Length of foreleg exceeding depth of chest.

BODY Length measured from point of breast bone to rear edge of pelvis, exceeding height at withers. Correct ratio 10 to 9 or 8 and a half. Undersized dogs, stunted growth, high-legged dogs, those too heavy or too light in build, over-loaded fronts, too short overall appearance, any feature detracting from reach or endurance of gait, undesirable. Chest deep (45-48 per cent) of height at shoulder, not too broad, brisket long, well developed. Ribs well formed and long; neither barrel-shaped nor too flat; allowing free movement of elbows when gaiting. Relatively short loin. Belly firm, only slightly drawn up. Back between withers and croup, straight, strongly developed, not too long. Overall length achieved by correct angle of well laid shoulders, correct length of croup and hindquarters. Withers long, of good height and well defined, joining back in a smooth line without disrupting flowing topline, slightly sloping from front to back. Weak, soft and roach backs undesirable and should be rejected. Loin broad, strong, well muscled. Croup long, gently curving downwards to tail without disrupting flowing topline. Short, steep or flat croups undesirable.

HINDQUARTERS Overall strong, broad and well muscled, enabling effortless forward propulsion of whole body. Upper thighbone, viewed from side, sloping to slightly longer lower thighbone. Hind angulation sufficient if imaginary line dropped from point of buttocks cuts through lower thigh just in front of hock, continuing down slightly in front of hindfeet. Angulations corresponding approximately with front angulation, without over-angulation, hock strong. Any tendency towards over-angulation of hindquarters reduces firmness and endurance.

FEET Rounded toes well closed and arched. Pads well cushioned and durable. Nails short, strong and dark in colour. Dewclaws removed from hindlegs.

TAIL Bushy-haired, reaches at least to hock – ideal length reaching to middle of metatarsus. At rest tail hangs in slight sabre-like curve; when moving raised and curve increased, ideally never above level of back. Short, rolled, curled, generally carried badly or stumpy from birth, undesirable.

GAIT/MOVEMENT Sequence of step follows diagonal pattern, moving foreleg and opposite hindleg forward simultaneously; hindfoot thrust forward to midpoint of body and having equally long reach with forefeet without any noticeable change in backline.

COAT Outer coat consisting of straight, hard, close-lying hair as dense as possible; thick undercoat. Hair on head, ears, front of legs, paws and toes short; on back, longer and thicker; in some males forming slight ruff. Hair longer on back of legs as far down as pasterns and stifles and forming fairly thick trousers on hindquarters. No hard and fast rule for length of hair; mole-type coats undesirable.

COLOUR Black or black saddle with tan, or gold to light grey markings. All black, all grey with lighter or brown markings referred to as Sables. Nose black. Light markings on chest or very pale colour on inside of legs permissible but undesirable, as are whitish nails, red-tipped tails or wishy-washy faded colours defined as lacking in pigmentation. Blues, livers, albinos, whites (i.e. almost pure white dogs with black noses) and near whites *highly undesirable*. Undercoat, except in all black dogs, usually grey or fawn. Colour in itself is of secondary importance having no effect on character or fitness for work. Final colour of a young dog only ascertained when outer coat has developed.

SIZE Ideal height (from withers and just touching elbows): dogs: 62.5 cm (25 in); bitches: 57.5 cm (23 in). 2.5 cm (1 in) either above or below ideal permissible.

FAULTS Any departure from the foregoing points should be considered a fault and the seriousness with which the fault should be regarded should be in exact proportion to its degree.

NOTE Male animals should have two apparently normal testicles fully descended into the scrotum.

GIANT SCHNAUZER

AT ONE TIME THE THREE VARIETIES OF Schnauzer were in the Utility Group, but because of his size and working ability the Giant was moved to the Working Group. An imposing dog, large and square in outline, he combines strength with agility. His outlook is bold and vigorous.

Farmers around the Munich area used him from the fifteenth century as a droving dog until the coming of the railways when large cattle drives vanished. Interest in the breed was lost in the rural communities and he re-emerged in the towns and cities as a guard or even a mascot in beer halls and butchers' shops. He also became a breed used widely for police and security work in Europe.

Amenable to training, not aggressive unless provoked, he is a good house dog and a lovable pet. His coat is harsh and wiry, and should be trimmed regularly. Prominent eyebrows, a bristly moustache and whiskers give his strong head a keen expression. He is slow to mature, but a good stayer.

GENERAL APPEARANCE Powerfully built, robust, sinewy, appearing almost square. Imposing, with keen expression and alert attitude. Correct conformation of the utmost importance.

CHARACTERISTICS Versatile, strong, hardy, intelligent and vigorous. Adaptable, capable of great speed and endurance and resistant to weather.

TEMPERAMENT Bold, reliable, good-natured and composed.

HEAD AND SKULL Head strong, of good length, narrowing from ears to eyes and then gradually toward end of nose. The overall length (from nose to occiput) is in proportion to the back (from withers to set-on of tail) approximately 1:2. Upper part of head (occiput to base of forehead) moderately broad between ears – with flat creaseless forehead. Well muscled but not over-developed cheeks. Medium stop accentuated by bushy eyebrows. Powerful muzzle ending in a moderately blunt wedge, with bristly stubby moustache and chin whiskers. Ridge of nose straight, running parallel to extension of forehead. Nose black with wide nostrils.

EYES Medium-sized, dark, oval, set forward, with lower lid fitting closely.

EARS Neat, V-shaped, set high and dropping forward to temple.

MOUTH Jaws strong with a perfect, regular and complete scissor bite, i.e. upper teeth closely overlapping lower teeth and set square to the jaws. Lips black, closing tightly but not overlapping.

NECK Moderately long, strong and slightly arched, skin close to throat, neck set cleanly on shoulders.

FOREQUARTERS Shoulders flat, well laid back. Forelegs straight viewed from any angle. Muscles smooth and lithe rather than prominent, bone strong, carried straight to feet. Elbows set close to body and pointing directly backward.

BODY Chest moderately broad and deep, reaching at least to height of elbow rising slightly backward to loins. Breast bone clearly extends to beyond joint of shoulder and upper arm forming the conspicuous forechest. Back strong and straight, slightly higher at shoulder than at hindquarters, with short, well developed loins. Slightly sloping croup. Ribs well sprung. Length of body equal to height at top of withers to ground.

HINDQUARTERS Strongly muscled. Stifles forming a well defined angle. Upper thighs vertical to stifle, from stifle to hock in line with extension of upper neck line, from hock vertical to ground. When viewed from rear, hindlegs parallel.

FEET Pointing directly forward, short, round, compact with closely arched toes. Deep, dark and firm pads. Dark nails.

TAIL Set-on high and carried at an angle slightly above topline, customarily docked to two joints.

GAIT/MOVEMENT Free, balanced and vigorous, with good reach of forequarters and good driving power from hindquarters. Topline remains level in action.

COAT Top coat harsh and wiry, just short enough for smartness on body. Slightly shorter on neck and shoulders, but blending smoothly into body coat. Clean on throat, skull, ears and under tail. Good undercoat. Harsh hair on legs.

COLOUR
(a) Pure black (b) Pepper and salt: shades range from dark iron grey to light grey; hairs banded black/light/black. Dark facial mask essential,

harmonising with corresponding body colour. On both colours white markings on head, chest and legs undesirable. Good pigmentation essential.

SIZE Height: dogs: 65-70 cm (25½-27½ in); bitches: 60-65 cm (23½-25½ in). Variations outside these limits undesirable.

FAULTS Any departure from the foregoing points should be considered a fault and the seriousness with which the fault should be regarded should be in exact proportion to its degree.

NOTE Male animals should have two apparently normal testicles fully descended into the scrotum.

GREAT DANE

IN SPITE OF HIS GREAT SIZE THE DANE makes an excellent house-dog. True, he will stretch out in front of the fire, blocking the warmth from the rest of the family, and will commandeer the most comfortable armchair, or settee. These are his privileges. His kindly disposition, affection for children, devotion to his family, and easy tolerance of other animals more than compensate. He is clean in his habits and his short coat is easy to groom. Dignified and noble, with a look of dash and daring, ready to go anywhere at any time, an excellent guard and watchdog – these are just some of his many attributes.

This handsome, elegant dog comes in a variety of striking colours. Used as a hunting dog in the pursuit of wild boar, the Dane is the national dog of Germany and has been since 1876. While he is also known as the German Mastiff, his mastiff characteristics were altered by a crossing with hounds over the years. The Great Dane was introduced to Britain in 1877.

GENERAL APPEARANCE Very muscular, strongly though elegantly built, with look of dash and daring, of being ready to go anywhere and do anything. Head and neck carried high, tail in line with back, or slightly upwards, but never curled over hindquarters. Elegance of outline and grace of form most essential.

CHARACTERISTICS Alert expression, powerful, majestic action displaying dignity.

TEMPERAMENT Kindly without nervousness, friendly and outgoing.

HEAD AND SKULL Head, taken altogether, gives idea of great length and strength of jaw. Muzzle broad, skull proportionately narrow, so that whole head when viewed from above and in front, has appearance of equal breadth throughout. Length of head in proportion to height of dog. Length from nose to point between eyes about equal or preferably of greater length than from this point to back of occiput. Skull flat, slight indentation running up centre, occipital peak not prominent. Decided rise or brow over the eyes but not abrupt stop between them; face well chiselled, well filled in below eyes with no appearance of being pinched: foreface long, of equal depth throughout. Cheeks showing as little lumpiness as possible, compatible with strength. Underline of head, viewed in profile, runs almost in a straight line from corner of lip to corner of jawbone, allowing for fold of lip, but with no loose skin hanging down. Bridge of nose very wide, with slight ridge where cartilage joins bone (this is a characteristic of breed). Nostrils large, wide and open, giving blunt look to nose. Lips hang squarely in front, forming right angle with upper line of foreface.

EYES Fairly deep-set, not giving the appearance of being round, of medium size and preferably dark. Wall, or odd eyes permissible in harlequins.

EARS Triangular, medium size, set high on skull and folded forward, not pendulous.

MOUTH Teeth level. Jaws strong with a perfect, regular and complete scissor bite, i.e. upper teeth closely overlapping lower teeth and set square to the jaws.

NECK Neck long, well arched, quite clean and free from loose skin, held well up, well set in shoulders, junction of head and neck well defined.

FOREQUARTERS Shoulders muscular, not loaded, well sloped back, with elbows well under body. Forelegs perfectly straight with big flat bone.

BODY Very deep, brisket reaching elbow, ribs well sprung, belly well drawn up. Back and loins strong, latter slightly arched.

HINDQUARTERS Extremely muscular, giving strength and galloping power. Second thigh long and well developed, good turn of stifle, hocks set low, turning neither in nor out.

FEET Cat-like, turning neither in nor out. Toes well arched and close, nails strong and curved. Nails preferably dark in all coat colours, except harlequins, where light are permissible.

TAIL Thick at the root, tapering towards end, reaching to or just below hocks. Carried in straight line level with back, when dog is moving, slightly curved towards end, but never curling or carried over back.

GAIT/MOVEMENT Action lithe, springy and free, covering ground well. Hocks move freely with driving action, head carried high.

COAT Short, dense and sleek-looking, never inclined to roughness.

COLOUR
BRINDLES: must be striped, ground colour from lightest buff to deepest orange, stripes always black, eyes and nails preferably dark, dark shadings on head and ears acceptable.
FAWNS: colour varies from lightest buff to deepest orange, dark shadings on head and ears acceptable, eyes and nails preferably dark.
BLUES: colour varies from light grey to deep slate, the nose and eyes may be blue.
BLACKS: black is black.
In all above colours white is only permissible on chest and feet, but it is not desirable even there. Nose always black, except in blues and harlequins. Eyes and nails perfectly black.
HARLEQUINS: pure white underground with preferably all black patches or all blue patches, having appearance of being torn. Light nails permissible. In harlequins, wall eyes, pink noses, or butterfly noses permissible but not desirable.

SIZE Minimum height of an adult dog over 18 months: 76 cm (30 in); bitches: 71 cm (28 in).

Weight, minimum weight over 18 months: dogs: 54 kg (120 lb); bitches: 46 kg (100 lb).

FAULTS Any departure from the foregoing points should be considered a fault and the seriousness with which the fault should be regarded should be in exact proportion to its degree.

NOTE Male animals should have two apparently normal testicles fully descended into the scrotum.

HOVAWART

THIS IS A BREED OF CONSIDERABLE antiquity, having been known for many centuries as a guard dog, mainly of the farmyard; indeed, this type of dog is recorded as far back as the 1200s. Then there came a blank space in the breed's history, with it re-emerging in the early 1900s through the efforts of a Kurt Konig.

This led to an argument as to whether or not it had been truly resurrected or was a re-invented breed. But it is thought that dogs of the old-type Hovawart had survived in isolated farm and rural areas and it was these which were the basis of today's breed, recognised by the German Kennel Club in 1937. He has only been seen in the UK in the last twenty years or so, and is only now emerging as a truly recognisable breed.

The variation of colour permitted by the breed standard perhaps makes his recognition less than universal, as he bears considerable resemblance at first glance to several other breeds.

An intelligent, trainable breed, with a good nose and an ability to hunt, he makes a good, companionable house-dog, relatively easy to keep tidy coat-wise, not hard to feed, a practical dog, and now stabilising into a recognisable style.

GENERAL APPEARANCE Medium size, strong but not heavy.

CHARACTERISTICS Hardy, works in all weathers, watchful, agile, swift, dignified, self-assured.

TEMPERAMENT Playful, alert, intelligent, devoted to his family, can be wilful and dominant towards other dogs.

HEAD AND SKULL Strong head, skull moderately broad, free from wrinkle. Equal length of skull and muzzle. Moderate stop. Nose never blunt, but pointed.

EYES Dark preferred, toning with pigmentation. Oval, medium-sized, alert and intelligent expression.

EARS Triangular, hanging, set medium to high. May be covered with long or short hair.

MOUTH Tight lips, scissor bite preferred, i.e. upper teeth closely overlapping lower teeth and set square to the jaws, but pincer bite tolerated.

NECK Strong, medium length, no dewlap.

FOREQUARTERS Well laid shoulder, strong and muscular. Forelegs straight when viewed from front. Moderate slope on pastern, flexible and well feathered. Free-moving elbow, not too tight. Dewclaws optional.

BODY Well balanced. Longer from point of breast bone to buttocks, than height at withers. Strong topline, level from withers to croup, which is not too long, and slightly sloping. Foreribs fairly flat, but gradual spring to centre of body. Deep brisket. Loin moderately deep.

HINDQUARTERS Muscular, with width. Well angulated, without exaggeration. From hock joint to foot, of medium length. Strong, flexible hock joint. Legs parallel when viewed from rear.

FEET Oval. Hard pads, well arched, tight. Strong nails.

TAIL Long and bushy, reaching below hock but not to ground. Carried high when moving, loosely curled over croup, but not in a complete circle or falling to either side. When standing, tail hangs straight down.

GAIT/MOVEMENT Free, supple, tireless. Soundness very important, with no stilted action. Head tends to drop at high speed. When trotting, tends to converge.

COAT Long in appearance, but short on face and front legs. Not so long on ribcage and thighs. Fine, light undercoat, straight or lightly waved. Long coat averages 10-22.5 cm (4-9 in) but feathering may be 15-30 cm (6-12 in). Never trimmed, except around feet.

COLOUR
BLACK/GOLD: deep shining coal-black, with no signs of rustiness, with medium gold to gold-brown markings. Markings on head should begin below back of nose and below eye, and reach to beginning of neck and on breast, should be present, but must not extend continously to forelegs. At forelegs the marks should reach (seen from the side) from toes to the carpal joint, and on inner side should reach nearly to vent. Beginning from toes, (from the side) a middle blond or solid brown strip should be visible above hock joint. Underneath beginning of tail, marking should be visible. A small white spot on breast, and a few white hairs at end of tail are permissible.
BLOND: middle blond coat should reach from back of nose to end of tail, and should lighten to belly. A small white spot on breast and a few white hairs at point of tail are permissible.
BLACK: deep shining coal black with no signs of rustiness, a few white spots on breast and a few white hairs at point of tail are permissible. All other pigment to suit colour of dog, i.e. a blond can have brown nose and eye is darker than gold of dog.

SIZE Height: dogs: 63-70 cm (24-27½ in); bitches: 58-65 cm (23-25½ in). Weight: dogs: 30-40 kg (66-68 lb); bitches: 25-35 kg (55-77 lb).

FAULTS Any departure from the foregoing points should be considered a fault and the seriousness with which the fault should be regarded should be in exact proportion to its degree.

NOTE Male animals should have two apparently normal testicles fully descended into the scrotum.

Hungarian Kuvasz

(INTERIM)

THE KUVASZ IS AN INDEPENDENT powerful dog used for the protection of flocks in Hungary by nomadic herdsmen, although he has adapted to become guard for people and property. He does not take kindly to unfair discipline, requiring firm treatment coupled with companionship and attention in order to socialise him to fit modern home conditions.

His medium-length white, wavy coat is relatively easy to groom and is thick enough to withstand extremes of wintry weather. He stands up to 75 centimetres (29 inches) at the withers and can weigh as much as 50 kilograms (110 pounds) or so – he is not bulky, but his weight lies in his muscular frame.

Although he will live as a family member within the home, he should also be provided with an adequately fenced territory to patrol and protect. He is not a breed for the casual owner.

GENERAL APPEARANCE Large, sturdily built, well-balanced dog of power and mobility.

CHARACTERISTICS Bold, courageous and fearless. Protective of owners, good guard.

TEMPERAMENT Devoted, gentle and patient but suspicious of strangers.

HEAD AND SKULL Long, medium width, skull slightly rounded, occiput broad and pronounced. Muzzle tapers slightly from base to nose but not too pointed at tip, ridge of nose straight, slight stop. Prominent eyebrows.

EYES Dark, brown, almond-shaped. Slightly slanted, set well apart. Eye rims black.

EARS Set high on side of skull; V-shaped and rather thick, slightly rounded tips. Inner edge carried close to cheek.

MOUTH Roof of mouth slate grey; lips black.

NECK Medium length, strong and muscular. Slightly arched; no dewlap.

FOREQUARTERS Shoulders well muscled. Scapula and humerus of equal length; forelegs straight; pasterns long and slightly sloping.

BODY Pronounced sternum, ribs well sprung; deep brisket. Withers above the level of back. Back level and firm, good tuck-up.

HINDQUARTERS Upper thigh of good length, stifles well angulated. Metatarsus short, strong and perpendicular to ground.

FEET Tight, well arched. Forefeet round, thick pads. Hindfeet longer than forefeet. Pads black. Nails slate grey or black. Dewclaws removed.

TAIL Low set in line with croup; tip to reach hock; when relaxed carried low, on the alert carried level with loin, tip slightly curved upwards.

GAIT/MOVEMENT Walk slow, dignified; at the trot, light rhythmic; at speed legs converge to a centre line often single stacking. Head carried low at speed.

COAT Slight wavy. Double-coated; top coat medium coarse; undercoat, fine and woolly. Shorter and smooth on head, muzzle, ears, front of fore- and hindlegs, below hocks and on feet. Mane on neck thick and long reaching down to brisket. Feathering on back of fore- and hindlegs 5-7.5 cm (2-3 in). Medium length on body.

Back of thighs and tail profusely coated, hair 10-15 cm (4-6 in) long.

COLOUR Pure white. Skin highly pigmented with patches of slate grey.

SIZE Height: dogs: 71-75 cm (28-29 in); bitches: 66-70 cm (26-27½ in). Weight: dogs: 40-52 kg (88-114 lb); bitches: 30-42 kg (66-92 lb).

FAULTS Any departure from the foregoing points should be considered a fault and the seriousness with which the fault should be regarded should be in exact proportion to its degree.

NOTE Male animals should have two apparently normal testicles fully descended into the scrotum.

HUNGARIAN PULI

THERE CAN BE NO MISTAKING THE PULI, although the casual observer may well be confused as to which way the dog is heading. It must also come as something of a surprise to find a coat which seems to glory in getting itself into the sort of tangle which in another breed would be regarded as having been neglected by its owner. But the Puli, in his native Hungary, is expected to withstand intense cold as he goes about his work as a herder for the flocks, so he needs a thick coat, which will keep out the rain as well.

This is a breed whose origins are obscure. Much of Hungary's culture derives from the Far East and as the Magyars moved westwards and into Hungary they brought with them many things, including dogs. There are those who can see in the Puli a likeness to the Tibetan Terrier, a resemblance to other mid-European breeds and a relationship to the Poodle whose coat will cord similarly, given the opportunity.

He is a highly intelligent and trainable dog and makes an excellent house-dog as he is a great barker at the least sound. His natural disposition is friendly and consequently he is highly companionable. He is, however, not a dog for the idle, as his coat, which starts life fluffy, and only cords as he matures, requires a deal of attention. He also demands a fair share of exercise and is an active chap who does not appreciate a life of sybaritic ease.

GENERAL APPEARANCE Sturdy, muscular, wiry, with fine bone. Whole well covered with long (according to age), profuse corded coat. Long hair overshadows eyes like an umbrella. Viewed from side, trunk and limbs should present square figure.

CHARACTERISTICS Herding, dog, medium-sized, nimble and extremely intelligent.

TEMPERAMENT Lively, wary of strangers, but not displaying nervousness or unprovoked aggression.

HEAD AND SKULL Disregarding hair, head small and fine with slightly domed skull. From front it appears round, from side almost elliptical. Muzzle one-third length of head, with well defined stop, not snipy but bluntly rounded. Arches of eye socket well defined, nose relatively large and black, eye rims and flews black in all colours.

EYES Medium size, dark brown with lively expression.

EARS Set slightly below level of skull, V-shaped, pendant, of medium size, covered with long hair. Length of ears about half length of head. Ears do not appear noticeable, even when alert.

MOUTH Roof uniformly dark or variegated with deep pigmented spots on dark base. Flews tight and black. Tongue bright red. Jaws and teeth strong with perfect scissor bite, i.e. upper teeth closely overlapping lower teeth and set square to the jaws.

NECK Set at an angle of 45 degrees to horizontal, of medium length, tight skinned and muscular. When fully coated, neck appears to merge with body.

FOREQUARTERS Shoulders well laid. Elbows tight. Forelegs straight and muscular, and viewed from any angle, vertical.

BODY Withers slightly higher than level of back, which is of medium length. Loin short and broad, belly slightly tucked-up. Ribs deep, ribcage broadening from behind elbows and well sprung. Rump short and slightly sloping but this is not obvious because of tightly curled tail.

HINDQUARTERS Strong, and well muscled. Pelvis forming an angle of 90 degrees with thighbone. Well bent stifle. Hocks set fairly low. When viewed from the rear, the legs should be parallel, with feet turning neither in nor out. Wide pelvis desirable, especially in bitches.

FEET Short, round, tight. Hindfeet slightly longer than forefeet. Nails strong, black or slate grey. Pads springy, dark grey in colour.

TAIL Medium length, curled tightly over rump-loin area; long hair of tail mixes indistinguishably with similar hair of rump so that tail does not appear separate.

GAIT/MOVEMENT Stride not far-reaching. Gallop short. Typical movement short-stepping, very quick, in harmony with lively disposition. Movement never heavy, lethargic or lumbering.

COAT Correct proportion of top and undercoat creates, naturally, the desired cords. Matting and felting to be avoided, and a combed coat is as undesirable as a neglected one. Coat generally longest on hindquarters, shortest on head and feet. Some dogs will grow a floor-length coat.

COLOUR Acceptable colours black, rusty black, white and various shades of grey and apricot. Black sometimes appears weathered, rusty, or with slight intermingling of white hairs. Grey and apricot in all their shades may have an intermingling of black or white hairs, with or without black mask, ear tips and tail tip. The overall appearance of all variants must be that of a solid colour. A white spot on chest of not more than 5 cm (2 in) is permissible. A few white hairs on feet also permissible. Body skin should be well pigmented and slate grey in colour, especially in blacks and greys.

SIZE Height: dogs: 40-44 cm (16-17½ in); bitches: 37-41 cm (14½-16 in). Weight: dogs: 13-15 kg (28½-33 lb); bitches: 10-13 kg (22-28½ lb).

FAULTS Any departure from the foregoing points should be considered a fault and the seriousness with which the fault should be regarded should be in exact proportion to its degree.

NOTE Male animals should have two apparently normal testicles fully descended into the scrotum.

KOMONDOR

(INTERIM)

THE KOMONDOR HAILS FROM HUNGARY where he is a guarding dog for the herds and flocks on the farms. A dog never to be trifled with, he will take care of anything or any place which he has been taught to regard as his charge and he will do so to the utmost of his ability.

As a result he is totally unsuited to a town life, where he would be miserable as well as a liability; even in the country, he requires a very well defined territory on which he is not going to encounter the casual hiker or even a visiting postman.

Known in Hungary for a thousand years, the Komondor is descended from the Owtcharki taken into Hungary by the nomadic Magyars who moved westwards from the East.

He is not a dog demanding a great deal of food and he has an easy-going attitude to exercise. Those who consider taking him on should study the breed carefully and closely before taking steps to acquire such a dog.

GENERAL APPEARANCE Large, cord-coated muscular dog, of great strength, with plenty of bone and substance. Powerful conformation.

CHARACTERISTICS Excellent guard, wary of strangers, noted for imposing strength and courageous manner.

TEMPERAMENT Faithful and devoted. This strong, sharp guard dog must be treated with respect.

HEAD AND SKULL Head somewhat short in comparison with width. Skull slightly arched viewed from side. Stop moderate; muzzle slightly shorter than length of skull. Broad, rather coarse muzzle, not pointed. Nostrils wide. Nose black, though dark grey or dark brown nose acceptable but undesirable.

EYES Medium-sized, not too deeply set, darker the better; rims dark grey or black, closely fitting.

EARS Medium-sized, hanging U-shaped. Erect or partially erect ears incorrect.

MOUTH Powerful jaws, strong teeth. Scissor bite ideal, i.e. upper teeth closely overlapping lower teeth and set square to the jaws, (pincer bite tolerated but undesirable). Lips tight fitting and black. Ideally gums and roof of mouth black or dark grey.

NECK Strong, medium length, moderately arched, no dewlap.

FOREQUARTERS Straight, well boned, muscular, forelegs vertical, viewed from front and side; well laid tight shoulders.

BODY Broad, deep muscular chest, back level. Rump broad, slightly sloping towards root of tail. Body slightly longer than height at withers. Belly tucked-up.

HINDQUARTERS Strong bone, very muscular. Viewed from rear, legs fairly wide apart, parallel, well angulated. Dewclaws should be removed.

FEET Large, strong and compact, well arched toes. Nails strong, grey or black; toes slightly longer on hindfeet. Pads firm, elastic and dark.

TAIL Continuation of rump line; reaching to hock, slightly curved at tip; when excited, raised in line with body.

GAIT/MOVEMENT Light and easy, moving with very long stride.

COAT Long coarse outer coat, which may be wavy or curly, with softer undercoat. Hair tends to cling together like tassels, giving a corded appearance. Cords of an adult strong and heavy, and felt-like to touch. If neglected, forms into large, matted 'plates'. Coat longest on rump, loins and tail, of medium length on back, shoulders and chest, shorter on cheeks, around eyes, mouth and lower parts of legs. Coat is

fairly slow in cording and may not be fully formed before two years of age. Puppy coat should be soft and fluffy, adult coat usually starts appearing 6–9 months of age. Presented corded.

COLOUR Always white. Ideally skin grey but pink skin acceptable.

SIZE Height: dogs: average 80 cm (31½ in), minimum 65 cm (25 in); bitches: average 70 cm (27½ in), minimum 60 cm (23½ in). No maximum height, but it should be taken into consideration with overall appearance.

Weight: dogs: 50–61 kg (110–135 lb); bitches: 36–50 kg (80–110 lb).

FAULTS Any departure from the foregoing points should be considered a fault and the seriousness with which the fault should be regarded should be in exact proportion to its degree.

NOTE Male animals should have two apparently normal testicles fully descended into the scrotum.

LANCASHIRE HEELER

(INTERIM)

HIS ORIGINS ARE NOT CLEARLY defined; it has been suggested that cattle were herded from Wales by Corgis to slaughter in the Ormskirk area and the 'Welsh heeler' met the Manchester Terrier, with obvious results. Certainly the breed is found in that area and has been bred there for many generations.

The Heeler is an intelligent, eager-to-please fellow, with a love of people; he enjoys being with children because he likes joining in games. He is trainable but does best under a firm, kindly owner; he can be a handful if he is not kept occupied as he is possessed of a prodigious amount of energy in his small frame. If he gets excited he can revert to his calling and take a nip at the rear end of anyone who is handy, but he is not basically a 'biter', being content to warn the intruder by noise accompanied by a furiously wagging tail. He has a hearty appetite to go with his super-abundant energy.

He requires only a damp chamois-leather and a quick brush to restore him to acceptable in-house cleanliness. He is reasonably friendly to other dogs, but has a tendency to want to be the pack-leader. If he lives with other pack-leader candidates, this may cause problems.

He is tough, basically very sound in construction, and doesn't ail a great deal, although it might be hard to tell if he was out of sorts as he doesn't like to admit it.

GENERAL APPEARANCE Small, powerful, sturdily built, alert energetic worker.

CHARACTERISTICS Works cattle but has terrier instincts when rabbiting and ratting.

TEMPERAMENT Courageous, happy, affectionate to owner.

HEAD AND SKULL In proportion to body. Skull flat and wide between ears, tapering towards eyes which are set wide apart. Moderate stop equidistant between nose and occiput. Tapering continues towards nose. Skull and muzzle to be on parallel planes.

EYES Almond-shaped, medium size, dark colour.

EARS Showing alert lift, or erect. Drop ears showing no lift undesirable.

MOUTH Lips firm. Scissor bite – jaws strong with a perfect, regular and complete scissor bite, i.e. upper teeth closely overlapping lower teeth and set square to the jaws. Under or overshot to be discouraged.

NECK Moderate length, well laid into shoulders.

FOREQUARTERS Well laid shoulder, elbows firm against ribs. Amply boned. Pasterns allow feet to turn slightly outwards, but not enough to cause weakness or affect freedom of movement.

BODY Well sprung ribbing, extending well back with close coupling. Firm, level topline, never dipping at withers or falling at croup. Approximately 2.5 cm (1 in) longer than height at withers. (Measured from withers to set-on of tail).

HINDQUARTERS Muscular, with well turned stifles, hocks well let down. From rear should be parallel, when moving or standing. Never bandy or cow-hocked.

FEET Small, firm and well padded.

TAIL Set-on high, left natural. Carried over back in a slight curve when alert, but not forming a complete ring.

GAIT/MOVEMENT Smart and brisk. Natural, free movement.

COAT Fine undercoat is covered throughout by weather-resistant, short, thick, hard, flat top coat. Top coat slightly longer on neck. Undercoat should not show through top coat nor allow any longer hair at the mane to stand off. Long or excessively wavy coat highly undesirable.

COLOUR Black with rich tan marking on muzzle, spots on cheeks and often above eyes, from knees downwards, with desirable thumb-mark above feet, inside hindlegs and under tail. Richness of tan may fade with age. White to be discouraged, except for a very small spot on forechest being permitted, but not desired.

SIZE Ideal height at shoulder: dogs: 30 cm (12 in); bitches: 25 cm (10 in).

FAULTS Any departure from the foregoing points should be considered a fault and the seriousness with which the fault should be regarded should be in exact proportion to its degree.

NOTE Male animals should have two apparently normal testicles fully descended into the scrotum.

MAREMMA SHEEPDOG

STILL USED IN ITALY TO GUARD THE flocks and property of the shepherds, he is named after the plains of Maremma which have been used for centuries as grazing land. His exact origins are unknown, but he is believed to be a descendant of the white working dogs of the Magyars.

A majestic, large dog with a thick white weather-proof coat, agile, with a preference for the outdoors, he is muscular and strongly built. Independent by nature, he is somewhat aloof and not easy to train. Very intelligent, with a highly developed guarding instinct which he automatically exercises to protect his family and home.

His first appearance in Britain was recorded in 1872, but the breed was still relatively rare until 1976 when a concerted effort was made to import and breed good stock.

GENERAL APPEARANCE Majestic, large size, lithe, strongly built, of 'outdoor' appearance. Expression of aloof awareness.

CHARACTERISTICS Intelligent, distinguished, sturdy, courageous but not aggressive.

TEMPERAMENT Lively, any tendency to nervousness or aggression highly undesirable.

HEAD AND SKULL Head conical in shape and appearing large in proportion to size of body. Skull rather wide between ears, narrowing towards foreface. Occipital ridge little emphasised with medium stop. Area under eyes slightly chiselled. Length of muzzle very slightly less than skull. Muzzle converges without snipiness. Jaws powerful and with plenty of substance in foreface. Lips close fitting, not pendulous. Pigmentation of lips and nose black.

EYES Bold, neither large nor small, ball neither sunk nor protruding – aperture almond-shaped, dark eye preferred. Rims black.

EARS Small in relation to size of head, V-shaped, set high on head, covered with short hair. Hanging flat to side of head in repose, moving forward when alert. The extremity of the ear forming a narrow point, never a rounded end.

MOUTH Teeth white, strong, regularly spaced and set in a level jaw. Scissor bite, i.e. upper teeth closely overlapping lower jaw and set square to the jaws.

NECK Strong of medium length, devoid of dewlap.

FOREQUARTERS Shoulders long, sloping, well muscled. Forelegs well boned and muscular without heaviness, straight when viewed from front; elbows close to ribcage, not turning in or out. Viewed from side, pasterns slope very slightly forward.

BODY Strong, muscles well developed, withers slightly above level of back; back broad and straight, rising to slight arch over loins, and falling to broad, strong rump. Length of body, measured from point of shoulder to point of buttocks, slightly longer than height at shoulder. Ribcage full, let down to level of elbow; well sprung ribs, not barrel chested. Sternum long, gradually curving up to the abdomen, which shows a waist without tucking up.

HINDQUARTERS Wide and powerful; thighs strongly muscled, legs straight when viewed from behind, hocks well down, strong, moderate bend of stifle.

FEET Large and almost round. Hindfeet slightly more oval. Pads black.

TAIL Set-on low, reaching below joint of hock, hangs down when dog is quiet, but carried level with back when dog is alert, with tip gently curved. Well covered with thick hair but without forming fringes.

GAIT/MOVEMENT Movement free and active, giving impression of nimble dog, able to move easily over rough ground and turn quickly.

COAT Fits outline of dog and is long, plentiful and rather harsh. Slight waviness, not curliness, permitted. Forms thick collar on neck. Hair short on muzzle, skull, ears, feet and front of limbs, forming slight feathering on rear limbs. Thick, close undercoat, especially in winter. Tail well covered with thick hair.

COLOUR All white. A little shading of ivory or pale fawn is permissible.

SIZE Ideal height: dogs: 65-73 cm (25½-28½ in); bitches: 60-68 cm (23½-26½ in).
Ideal weight: dogs: 35-45 kg (77-99 lb); bitches: 30-40 kg (66-88 lb).

FAULTS Any departure from the foregoing points should be considered a fault and the seriousness with which the fault should be regarded should be in exact proportion to its degree.

NOTE Male animals should have two apparently normal testicles fully descended into the scrotum.

WORKING

297

MASTIFF

THIS BREED, PERHAPS NOT IN EXACTLY the form as we know it today, has been with us for many hundreds of years, and played its part in history since well before the Battle of Agincourt, in the early fifteenth century. Even then the Mastiff was known for his courage and guarding instincts. It is recorded that when the Romans invaded Britain they found a mastiff-type dog already here, and were so impressed that they took some back to fight in the arenas of Rome. When the Normans came to Britain the mastiff type was so common that the French word *dogue* found its way into the English language.

The breed almost became extinct in Britain after the Second World War. Stock was then imported, and since that time the numerical strength and quality of the breed have taken an upsurge. Combining grandeur with good nature, he is an extremely large dog in both height and girth, broad and deep in body, full of substance, with large strong bones.

A very intelligent dog, not excitable, but affectionate towards his owner, he is a dog who requires plenty of human contact and plenty of good food. He is best suited to a home where there are opportunities for exercise.

GENERAL APPEARANCE Head, in general outline, giving a square appearance when viewed from any point. Breadth greatly desired; in ratio to length of whole head and face as 2:3. Body massive, broad, deep, long, powerfully built, on legs wide apart and squarely set. Muscles sharply defined. Size a great desideratum, if combined with quality. Height and substance important if both points are proportionately combined.

CHARACTERISTICS Large, massive, powerful, symmetrical, well knit frame. A combination of grandeur and courage.

TEMPERAMENT Calm, affectionate to owners, but capable of guarding.

HEAD AND SKULL Skull broad between ears, forehead flat, but wrinkled when attention is excited. Brows (superciliary ridges) slightly raised. Muscles of temples and cheeks (temporal and masseter) well developed. Arch across skull of a rounded, flattened curve, with depression up centre of forehead from median line between eyes, to halfway up sagittal suture. Face or muzzle short, broad under eyes, and keeping nearly parallel in width to end of nose; truncated, i.e. blunt and cut off squarely, thus forming a right angle with upper line of face, of great depth from point of nose to under-jaw. Under-jaw broad to end. Nose broad, with widely spreading nostrils when viewed from front, flat (not pointed or turned up) in profile. Lips diverging at obtuse angles with septum, and slightly pendulous so as to show a square profile. Length of muzzle to whole head and face as 1:3. Circumference of muzzle (measured mid-way between eyes and nose) to that of head (measured before the ears) as 3:5.

EYES Small, wide apart, divided by at least space of two eyes. Stop between eyes well marked but not too abrupt. Colour hazel brown, darker the better, showing no haw.

EARS Small, thin to touch, wide apart, set-on at highest points of sides of skull, so as to continue outline across summit, and lying flat and close to cheeks when in repose.

MOUTH Canine teeth healthy; powerful and wide apart; incisors level, or lower projecting beyond upper but never so much as to become visible when mouth is closed.

NECK Slightly arched, moderately long, very muscular, and measuring in circumference about 2.5-5 cm (1-2 in) less than skull before ears.

FOREQUARTERS Shoulder and arm slightly sloping, heavy and muscular. Legs straight, strong and set wide apart; bones being large. Elbows square. Pasterns upright.

BODY Chest wide, deep and well let down between forelegs. Ribs arched and well rounded. False ribs deep and well set back to hips. Girth one-third more than height at shoulder. Back and loins wide and muscular; flat and very wide in bitch, slightly arched in dog. Great depth of flanks.

HINDQUARTERS Broad, wide and muscular, with well developed second thighs, hocks bent, wide apart, and quite squarely set when standing or walking.

FEET Large and round. Toes well arched. Nails black.

TAIL Set-on high, and reaching to hocks, or a little below them, wide at its root and tapering to end, hanging straight in repose, but forming a curve with end pointing upwards, but not over back, when dog is excited.

GAIT/MOVEMENT Powerful, easy extension.

COAT Short and close-lying, but not too fine over shoulders, neck and back.

COLOUR Apricot-fawn, silver-fawn, fawn, or dark fawn-brindle. In any case, muzzle, ears and nose should be black with black around orbits, and extending upwards between them.

FAULTS Any departure from the foregoing points should be considered a fault and the seriousness with which the fault should be regarded should be in exact proportion to its degree.

NOTE Male animals should have two apparently normal testicles fully descended into the scrotum.

NEAPOLITAN MASTIFF

(INTERIM)

WORKING

300

THIS ANCIENT BREED IS A DESCENDANT of the Roman Molossus, and is the native Mastiff of Italy. His appearance is somewhat forbidding especially in his homeland where his ears are closely cropped adding to his ferocious expression and giving the appearance of a very formidable guard dog.

The breed so impressed the painter Piero Scanziani that he started his own kennel and is considered the modern father of the breed.

He is an extremely large, heavy dog with loose skin forming a dewlap around the neck; this combined with his pendulous lips gives his already large head the impression of being even bigger. He is said to be of a very reliable temperament, and will only use his full force to attack when so commanded.

The Neapolitan was bred originally to fight in the arena but over the years has seen service as a war dog, police dog, guard and draught dog, yet it was not until 1946 that the breed was seen at a show in Naples.

GENERAL APPEARANCE Well boned, large, strongly built, vigorous, alert and muscular. Of majestic bearing, with intelligent expression.

CHARACTERISTICS A degree of loose-fitting skin over body and head, with some dewlap, is a feature, not to be excessive.

TEMPERAMENT Devoted and loyal guard of owner and property.

HEAD AND SKULL Head large, broad short skull. Broad across cheeks. Head proportion: skull length 2:3 to muzzle 1:3. Top of skull parallel to topline of muzzle. Well pronounced, definite stop, nose should not protrude beyond vertical line of muzzle. Nose large with well opened nostrils, lips full and heavy. Upper lip resembles inverted V. Muzzle deep, sides flat and vertical, showing flews. Head deep and spherical.

EYES Set forward, well apart, rather rounded. Set fairly deep. Rim pigmentation to tone with nose colour.

EARS Small for size of head, set forward, high and well apart. Triangular, hanging flat towards cheeks, but not reaching beyond line of throat.

MOUTH Teeth white and regular. Strong, well developed jaws, with scissor bite, but level tolerated. Scissor bite, i.e. upper teeth closely overlapping lower teeth and set square to the jaws.

NECK Short, stocky, very muscular, dewlap from lower jaw reaching mid-point of neck.

FOREQUARTERS Shoulder long, slightly sloping with well developed and definite muscle. Elbows not too close to body to allow very free action. Pasterns slightly sloping, legs vertical when viewed from front.

BODY Longer than height at withers. Broad, well muscled chest, ribcage reaching at least to elbow. Ribs long and well sprung. Topline straight, slightly lower than withers, line of belly parallel to topline.

HINDQUARTERS Broad loin, well let into backline, slightly rounded with well developed muscle. Croup broad, muscular, with slight slope. Thighs long, broad, moderate stifle, powerful hocks. Dewclaws (single or double) removed.

FEET Oval; close, arched toes. Pads thick, hard and dark-coloured. Nails curved, strong and dark. Hindfeet slightly smaller than front.

TAIL Thick at root, set-on slightly lower than topline. Tapering towards tip. Customarily docked by one-third length. Never carried up or over back, but may be carried level with topline when moving.

GAIT/MOVEMENT Slow, free, bear-like. Slow trot, long steps covering ground well. Rarely gallops.

COAT Short, dense, even, fine, hard texture, with good sheen. No fringe.

COLOUR Preferred black, blue, all shades of grey, brown varying from fawn to red. Brindling on either of the latter colours. Small star on chest and white on toes permissible. Pigmentation to tone with coat colours.

SIZE Height: 65–75 cm (26–29 in).
Weight: 50–70 kg (110–154 lb). Some tolerance allowed. Bitches somewhat less.

FAULTS Any departure from the foregoing points should be considered a fault and the seriousness with which the fault should be regarded should be in exact proportion to its degree.

NOTE Male animals should have two apparently normal testicles fully descended into the scrotum.

NEWFOUNDLAND

A GENTLE GIANT, THIS LARGE, STRONG, heavily built dog combines great gentleness with a mild, guarding instinct. Robust and eager to please, he makes a very suitable companion for children, joining in their games and keeping a watchful eye on them in the absence of adults.

As a puppy he looks like a cuddly teddy bear, but does grow remarkably quickly into a very large, thick-coated adult. He loves water, and is a powerful swimmer, capable of pulling a rowing boat, or 'rescuing' anyone he feels might be in distress!

Mystery seems to surround the origin of the Newfoundland, and history books tell us that the breed, as we know it today, almost certainly did not originate in North America. Legend has it that the Newfoundland developed from an early Tibetan Mastiff type which accompanied tribes who crossed the Polar region. Examples of the Newfoundland came to Britain on trade ships, the original examples being lighter boned and smaller than today's breed and with a wide variance in colour. The standard for today's Newfoundland was written in the late 1800s and about this time the solid black became all the rage in England, becoming almost the only type known here.

Definitely not for the flat-dweller, he requires a moderate amount of exercise. Colours range from black and brown to Landseer, which is white with black markings. The name was derived from Sir Edwin Landseer who depicted many of these dogs in his famous paintings.

GENERAL APPEARANCE Well balanced, impresses with strength and great activity. Massive bone throughout, but not giving heavy inactive appearance. Noble, majestic and powerful.

CHARACTERISTICS Large draught and water dog, with natural life-saving instinct, and devoted companion.

TEMPERAMENT Exceptionally gentle, docile nature.

HEAD AND SKULL Head broad and massive, occipital bone well developed, no decided stop, muzzle short, clean-cut and rather square, covered with short fine hair.

EYES Small, dark brown, rather deeply set, not showing haw, set rather wide apart.

EARS Small, set well back, square with skull, lying close to head, covered with short hair without fringe.

MOUTH Soft and well covered by lips. Scissor bite preferred, i.e. upper teeth closely overlapping lower teeth and set square to the jaws, but pincer tolerated.

NECK Strong, well set-on to shoulders.

FOREQUARTERS Legs perfectly straight, well muscled, elbows fitting close to sides, well let down.

BODY Well ribbed, back broad with level topline, strong muscular loins. Chest deep, fairly broad.

HINDQUARTERS Very well built and strong. Slackness of loins and cow-hocks most undesirable. Dewclaws should be removed.

FEET Large, webbed, and well shaped. Splayed or turned out feet most undesirable.

TAIL Moderate length, reaching a little below hock. Fair thickness well covered with hair, but not forming a flat. When standing hangs downwards with slight curve at end; when moving, carried slightly up, and when excited, straight out with only a slight curve at end. Tails with a kink or curled over back are most undesirable.

GAIT/MOVEMENT Free, slight rolling gait. When in motion slight toe-ing in at front acceptable.

COAT Double, flat and dense, of coarse texture and oily nature, water-resistant. When brushed wrong way it falls back into place naturally. Forelegs well feathered. Body well covered but chest hair not forming a frill. Hindlegs slightly feathered.

COLOUR Only permitted colours are:
BLACK: dull jet black may be tinged with bronze. Splash of white on chest, toes and tip of tail acceptable.
BROWN: can be chocolate or bronze. In all other respects follow black except for colour. Splash of white on chest, toes and tip of tail acceptable.
LANDSEER: white with black markings only. For preference black head with narrow blaze, evenly marked saddle, black rump extending to tail. Beauty in markings to be taken greatly into consideration. Ticking undesirable.

SIZE Average height at shoulder:
dogs: 71 cm (28 in); bitches: 66 cm (26 in). Average weight: dogs: 64-69 kg (140-150 lb); bitches: 50-54.5 kg (110-120 lb). While size and weight are important it is essential that symmetry is maintained.

FAULTS Any departure from the foregoing points should be considered a fault and the seriousness with which the fault should be regarded should be in exact proportion to its degree.

NOTE Male animals should have two apparently normal testicles fully descended into the scrotum.

NORWEGIAN BUHUND

THE BUHUND IS A TYPICAL SPITZ WITH HIS pointed face and his erect ears. He is both a sharp guard and an efficient herder; he thrives on work, always giving the appearance of being active and bustling.

Hailing from Norway, the Buhund is one of the earliest known Nordic herding dogs but was not recognised officially until the turn of the twentieth century. *Bu* in Norwegian means 'homestead' and Buhund is the 'dog found on the homestead or farm'.

The commonest colour is the basic wheaten, but the wolf-sable and the black are recognised, as is the light red. The youngsters are especially attractive and it is surprising that the breed, which has been known in the UK for many years, has not become more widely appreciated.

The temperament is one of friendly reserve; he does not fawn, but is delighted to be included in the conversation. With his harsh but smooth coat he is extremely easy to keep clean and, being fairly small, he does not eat great quantities.

GENERAL APPEARANCE Lightly built, short compact body, fairly smooth-lying coat, erect pointed ears, curled tail carried over back.

CHARACTERISTICS Well balanced, medium size, free from exaggeration, and capable of arduous work.

TEMPERAMENT Fearless, brave and energetic.

HEAD AND SKULL Head-lean, light, rather broad between ears, wedge-shaped, narrowing towards point of nose. Skull and back of head almost flat; marked but not sharp stop; muzzle medium length, tapering evenly from above and side, straight bridge, lips tightly closed. Nose black.

EYES Not protruding, dark brown, lively with fearless expression.

EARS Placed high, erect, height greater than base; sharply pointed, very mobile.

MOUTH Jaws strong with a perfect, regular and complete scissor bite, i.e. upper teeth closely overlapping lower teeth and set square to the jaws. Complete dentition.

NECK Medium length, lean without loose skin, moderately arched.

FOREQUARTERS Legs lean, straight and strong, elbows tightly placed.

BODY Strong, short, but light, chest deep with good ribs; straight line of back, firm loins, short couplings, slightly drawn up.

HINDQUARTERS Legs strong and only a little angulated, straight when viewed from behind.

FEET Rather small, oval in shape, toes tightly closed.

TAIL Set-on high, short, thick, and hair longer on underside, tightly curled and carried over back.

GAIT/MOVEMENT Without exaggeration, straight coming and going. From side, light, active, with good stride.

COAT Outer coat close, harsh, but smooth; undercoat soft and woolly. On head and front legs, short, close and smooth; longer on chest, neck and shoulders, back of legs and underside of tail.

COLOUR Wheaten, black, red (red not too dark), wolf-sable. Self-coloured but small symmetrical markings, e.g. white on chest and legs, blaze on head and narrow ring on neck, black mask and ears and black tip to tail permissible.

SIZE Ideal height: dogs: 45 cm (17¾ in); bitches somewhat less. Weight in proportion to size.

FAULTS Any departure from the foregoing points should be considered a fault and the seriousness with which the fault should be regarded should be in exact proportion to its degree.

NOTE Male animals should have two apparently normal testicles fully descended into the scrotum.

OLD ENGLISH SHEEPDOG

THOUGH THE OLD ENGLISH SHEEPDOG registry is listed as Britain its actual ancestry is thought to be from the European Shepherd Dogs of the Owtcharka and Bergamasco types bred to sheepdogs of Britain. It is now regarded as a native British breed, often called the Bob-Tail. Strong, compact and profusely coated; his coat is a distinctive feature and is weather-resistant. This is not the dog for those without plenty of time and patience to groom.

Boisterous, lovable puppies soon grow into large, strong adults requiring plenty of exercise. Basically a country dog, intelligent and friendly; he has a particularly resonant bark sufficient to frighten off any intruder, and is protective of his family and friends.

His use as an advertising symbol has probably not been in the breed's interest.

GENERAL APPEARANCE Strong, square-looking dog with great symmetry and overall soundness. Absolutely free from legginess, profusely coated all over. A thick-set, muscular, able-bodied dog with a most intelligent expression. The natural outline should not be artificially changed by scissoring or clipping.

CHARACTERISTICS Of great stamina, exhibiting a gently rising topline, and a pear-shaped body when viewed from above. The gait has a typical roll when ambling or walking. Bark has a distinctive toned quality.

TEMPERAMENT A biddable dog of even disposition. Bold, faithful and trustworthy, with no suggestion of nervousness or unprovoked aggression.

HEAD AND SKULL In proportion to the size of the body. Skull capacious, rather square. Well arched above eyes, stop well defined. Muzzle strong, square and truncated, measuring approximately half of the total head length. Nose large and black. Nostrils wide.

EYES Set well apart. Dark or wall eyes. Two blue eyes acceptable. Light eyes undesirable. Pigmentation on the eye rim is preferred.

EARS Small and carried flat to side of head.

MOUTH Teeth strong, large, and evenly placed. Scissor bite – jaws strong with a perfect, regular and complete scissor bite, i.e. upper teeth closely overlapping lower teeth and set square to the jaws. Pincer tolerated but undesirable.

NECK Fairly long, strong, arched gracefully.

FOREQUARTERS Forelegs perfectly straight, with plenty of bone, holding body well from ground. Elbows fitting close to brisket. Shoulders should be well laid back, being narrower at the point of withers than at the point of shoulder. Loaded shoulders undesirable. Dog standing lower at withers than loin.

BODY Rather short, and compact, with well sprung ribs, and deep capacious brisket.

HINDQUARTERS Loin very sturdy, broad and gently arched, quarters well covered round and muscular, the second thigh is long and well developed, the stifle well turned, and the hocks set low. From the rear the hocks should be quite straight, with the feet turning neither in nor out.

FEET Small, round and tight, toes well arched, pads thick and hard. Dewclaws should be removed.

TAIL Customarily completely docked.

GAIT/MOVEMENT When walking, exhibits a bear-like roll from the rear. When trotting, shows effortless extension and strong driving rear action, with legs moving straight along line of travel. Very elastic at the gallop. At slow speeds, some dogs may tend to pace. When moving, the head carriage may adopt a naturally lower position.

COAT Profuse, of good harsh texture, not straight, but shaggy and free from curl. Undercoat of waterproof pile. Head and skull well covered with hair, ears moderately coated, neck well coated, forelegs well coated all round, hindquarters more heavily coated than rest of body. Quality, texture, and profusion to be considered above mere length.

COLOUR Any shade of grey, grizzle or blue. Body and hindquarters of solid colour with or without white socks. White patches in the solid area to be discouraged. Head, neck, forequarters and under belly to be white with or without markings. Any shade of brown undesirable.

SIZE Height: dogs: 61 cm (24 in) and upwards; bitches: 56 cm (22 in) and upwards. Type and symmetry of greatest importance, and on no account to be sacrificed to size alone.

FAULTS Any departure from the foregoing points should be considered a fault and the seriousness with which the fault should be regarded should be in exact proportion to its degree.

NOTE Male animals should have two apparently normal testicles fully descended into the scrotum.

PINSCHER

A MEDIUM-SIZED, SMOOTH-COATED DOG of German origin. He is the middle-sized member of the family, fitting in between the larger Dobermann, and the smaller Miniature Pinscher. The breed was officially recognised by the German Kennel Club in 1879 with type set around the start of the twentieth century. Pinscher is the German word for terrier but the German farmers' terriers were larger than terriers in England and were too long in the leg to go to ground, though they did make an effective guard of the home.

A stylish dog of sturdy build and elegant lines, his smooth, glossy coat requires minimum attention. He is responsive and obedient, a little distrustful of strangers, and this makes him an excellent watchdog.

GENERAL APPEARANCE Well balanced, smooth coated, medium size with elegant and flowing outlines but strong and well muscled.

CHARACTERISTICS Alert, good-natured, playful. Loyal, watchful and fearless.

TEMPERAMENT High-spirited and self-possessed.

HEAD AND SKULL Seen from above and side resembles a blunt wedge. Strong but not heavy, elongated without pronounced occiput. Overall length in proportion to back (from withers to base of tail) is approximately 1:2. Top of muzzle parallel with extended line of unwrinkled flat forehead; slight but distinct stop. Cheek muscles strong but not prominent. Deep muzzle. Nose full and black; in reds, nose of corresponding shade. Lips tight and dark. Snipiness undesirable.

EYES Dark, of medium size, oval and directed forward. Eye rims tight.

EARS Set high. V-shaped, folded down close to head.

MOUTH Jaws strong with a perfect, regular and complete scissor bite, i.e. upper teeth closely overlapping lower teeth and set square to the jaws.

NECK Elegant and strong. Neither short nor stout. Nape well arched. Skin of throat tight without dewlap.

FOREQUARTERS Well laid shoulder with good but flat muscle. Forelegs straight viewed from all sides, parallel elbows are close to body.

BODY Chest moderately wide with flat ribs. Brisket extends below elbow. Forechest extends beyond point of shoulder. Compact and short-coupled. Length of body approximately equal to height at withers. Back short and slightly sloping. Slightly rounded croup.

HINDQUARTERS Seen from behind parallel, with sufficient width. Upper thigh slanted and strongly muscled. Good length and bend of stifle, hocks turning neither in nor out.

FEET Well arched, compact and cat-like with dark nails. Turning neither in nor out. Tough, hard pads.

TAIL Set and carried high. Customarily docked to three joints.

GAIT/MOVEMENT Free, well balanced and vigorous with good reach in front and strong rotary driving action from rear. Front and hindlegs should not be thrown outwards. Topline should remain strong and firm. Hackney movement undesirable.

COAT Short and dense, smoothly fitting, glossy without bald spots.

COLOUR All solid colours from fawn (Isabella) to stag red in various shades. Black and blue with reddish/tan markings. In bi-coloured dogs sharply marked red/tan markings desirable.

Markings distributed as follows: at cheeks, lips, lower jaw, above eyes, at throat, at forechest as two triangles seperated from each other, at metatarsus, forelegs, feet, inner side of hindlegs and vent region.

SIZE Height at withers: 43-48 cm (17-19 in).

FAULTS Any departure from the foregoing points should be considered a fault and the seriousness with which the fault should be regarded should be in exact proportion to its degree.

NOTE Male animals should have two apparently normal testicles fully descended into the scrotum.

POLISH LOWLAND SHEEPDOG

WORKING

310

I N ITS NATIVE COUNTRY THIS DOG rejoices in the name Polski Owczarek Nizinny, affectionately shortened to 'Pons'. It is said that he originally came to Britain in the sixteenth century when sailors from Gdansk exchanged their dogs for other animals at their Scottish ports of call. However, he is a relative newcomer to the British dog-show scene, where new imports were first exhibited in the mid 1980s.

Originally a herding dog, he is very adaptable and easy to train, making good use of his excellent memory. In appearance he is not unlike the Bearded Collie, but is usually born without a tail. He is exceptionally fond of children, and is a lively playmate. His stable temperament and medium size makes him an ideal family pet. Regular grooming is required to keep his shaggy, thick coat free from becoming matted.

The breed has a long history and derives from the Hungarian Puli and native long-coated herding dogs of Poland. He has been a working dog since at least the 1500s but has gone through periods of decline due to European wars.

GENERAL APPEARANCE Medium size, cobby, strong, muscular, fairly long, thick coat.

CHARACTERISTICS Lively but self-controlled, watchful, bright, clever, perceptive with excellent memory. Easy to train, works as a herding and watchdog.

TEMPERAMENT Alert, equable.

HEAD AND SKULL Medium size, proportionate to body, not too heavy, carried moderately low. Profuse hair on forehead, cheeks and chin make head appear larger than it is. Proportions of occiput to stop and stop to nose approximately equal, but muzzle may be fractionally shorter. Skull moderately broad, slightly domed, furrow from stop to occiput apparent when handled. Well defined stop. Nose blunt, wide opened nostrils, colour dark as possible.

EYES Medium size, lively penetrating gaze, oval-shaped. Colour hazel to brown. Eye rims as dark as possible, closely fitting and showing no haw.

EARS Medium size, heart-shaped, large at base and set moderately high, drooping with fore edge close to cheeks.

MOUTH Jaws strong with a perfect, regular and complete scissor bite, i.e. upper teeth closing overlapping lower teeth and set square to the jaws. Strong and evenly placed teeth. Lips tightly closed and as dark as possible.

NECK Strong, muscular, medium length without dewlap.

FOREQUARTERS Shoulders well placed with good lay-back, muscular. Legs when viewed from front or side, straight with slightly slanting pastern.

BODY Rectangular rather than square when viewed from side. Deep brisket with moderate spring of rib, neither flat nor barrel shaped. Withers distinctly marked; back level, muscular, with broad loin. Belly slightly drawn up. Croup short and slightly sloping. Proportions – height to length as 9:10.

HINDQUARTERS Well angulated, with broad and well muscled thigh. From behind, legs straight, turning neither in nor out. Hocks strong and distinctly angled.

FEET Oval, slightly arched but tightly fitting toes, with hard pads, nails dark. Hind dewclaws should be removed.

TAIL Customarily docked if not born tailless.

GAIT/MOVEMENT Smooth walking or trotting. Inclined to amble.

COAT Whole body covered with long, dense, shaggy thick coat of harsh texture with soft undercoat. Long hair covers eyes. Slight wave permissible. No loose skin anywhere on body.

COLOUR All colours acceptable.

SIZE Height: dogs: 43-52 cm (17-20 in); bitches: 40-46 cm (16-18½ in).

FAULTS Any departure from the foregoing points should be considered a fault and the seriousness with which the fault should be regarded should be in exact proportion to its degree.

NOTE Male animals should have two apparently normal testicles fully descended into the scrotum.

PORTUGUESE WATER DOG

WORKING

312

(INTERIM)

A FAIRLY RECENT NEWCOMER TO THE UK, the Portuguese Water Dog was at one time a hunting dog. Nowadays the fishermen of his native Portugal employ his great love of water in service with their boats. He can be trained to retrieve lost nets and to swim from boats close in to the shore. He is also a keen guard.

He is a friendly dog even if, as his standard says, he is self-willed. He needs firm handling when young to counteract this stubborn streak. His coat is customarily clipped over the hindquarters and on the tail, leaving a profuse plume at the end. Unusually there are two distinct types of recognised coat. One is long and loosely waved while the other is short and harsh with compact curls.

Though the listed home country is Portugal the breed shares a common background with other European water dogs and was taken to Portugal by traders, probably Moors, by way of North Africa.

GENERAL APPEARANCE Robust, well balanced, rectangular in outline, very strongly muscled on shoulders. Hard, penetrating and attentive expression.

CHARACTERISTICS Very intelligent and tremendously energetic 'fisherman's dog' with great swimming and diving traits.

TEMPERAMENT Pleasant disposition, self-willed but very obedient to owner. Brave and tireless.

HEAD AND SKULL Large, well proportioned, skull slightly longer than muzzle, well defined occiput. Muzzle tapers slightly. Forehead has central furrows for two-thirds of length of head, frontal bones prominent. Nose wide, nostrils well open. Black in black, black and white, and white dogs, liver in brown, brown and white, and brown tones.

EYES Medium, round, set well apart. Black or dark brown with dark eye rims.

EARS Heart-shaped, dropped, thin, set well above eye level, held close to head, except at back. Tips not below neck line.

MOUTH Scissor bite, jaws strong with a perfect, regular and complete scissor bite, i.e. upper teeth closely overlapping lower teeth and set square to the jaws, strongly developed canines.

NECK Short, straight, strongly muscled. Carried high, no mane or dewlap.

FOREQUARTERS Straight, strong boned and well muscled. Shoulders muscular and well laid. Pasterns long and upright.

BODY Chest wide and deep, reaching to elbow. Ribs long, well sprung. Withers wide, not prominent. Back short, good tuck-up, croup only slightly inclined.

HINDQUARTERS Straight and very strongly muscled, well angulated, buttocks long and well curved, strong hock, metatarsals long, no dewclaws.

FEET Round, rather flat, toes not too long or too knuckled up. Membrane reaching to tip of toes, covered with hair. Central pads very thick.

TAIL Medium set, thick at base and tapering, length not below hock, carried in a ring, clipped, leaving plume at end.

GAIT/MOVEMENT Walking, lively short steps. A light trot and energetic gallop.

COAT Profuse, covering whole body except under forelegs and thighs. Two distinct types, born without undercoats.
(a) Hair fairly long, loosely waved with slight sheen, hair on head erect, ears well feathered.
(b) Hair short, fairly harsh and dense, compact

curls, lacking lustre, head hair similar to body, hair on ears somewhat wavy.

COLOUR Black, white, various shades of brown, black and white, brown and white. Skin bluish under black, white, and black and white dogs. Entire hindquarters clipped from the last rib, tail clipped two-thirds, one-third left long.

SIZE Height: dogs: 50-57 cm (19½-22½ in): bitches: 43-52 cm (17-20½ in).

Weight: dogs: 19-25 kg (42-55 lb); bitches: 16-22 kg (35 lb – 48 lb).

FAULTS Any departure from the foregoing points should be considered a fault and the seriousness with which the fault should be regarded should be in exact proportion to its degree.

NOTE Male animals should have two apparently normal testicles fully descended into the scrotum.

PYRENEAN MOUNTAIN DOG

IT IS GENERALLY THOUGHT THAT A Pyrenean must be all white, but whilst he is mainly white it is quite permissible for him to have markings of badger (called blaireau), wolf-grey, or pale yellow. His black nose and eye rims make a striking contrast.

He is a substantial, impressive-looking dog, hardy and healthy. Once used as a guard dog, protecting flocks against wolves, he has a very gentle side to his nature and is affectionate and tolerant with children, making him a popular house pet. One of the largest breeds, he does not reach full maturity until he is three or four years old.

His thick, double coat needs grooming thoroughly at least once a week. Not tremendously active; a short walk in town, or a long ramble in the country will suit him equally well.

The breed comes from the Pyrenean mountain range in France where he is known as the Great Pyrenees. They have guarded flocks in France for centuries and dogs of the type pre-date even the Bronze Age (1800-1000 BC) but are said to have been 'discovered' by the French nobility before the Revolution and could be found in the great châteaux. Louis XIV named the breed the Royal Dog of France. As recently as the Second World War Pyreneans carried messages and packs for French troops.

GENERAL APPEARANCE Great size, substance and power; looking immensely strong and well balanced. A certain elegance imparted by attractive coat and correct head.

CHARACTERISTICS A natural guard dog protecting shepherd and sheep.

TEMPERAMENT Quietly confident. Nervousness and unprovoked aggression highly undesirable.

HEAD AND SKULL Strong head without coarseness, not too heavy in relation to size of dog. Top, as seen from front and side, definitely curved to give domed effect. Breadth at widest point about equal to length from occiput to stop. Sides nearly flat and of good depth. No obvious stop, only slight furrow, so that skull and muzzle are joined by gentle slope. Strong muzzle, medium length, slight taper near tip. Nose black. Head seen from above has form of a blunt V, well filled in below eyes.

EYES Almond-shaped, dark amber-brown. Close-fitting eyelids set somewhat obliquely, bordered with black. Drooping lower eyelids undesirable. Intelligent and contemplative expression.

EARS Fairly small, triangular, rounded tips. Root level with eyes. Normally lie flat against head, may be slightly raised when alert.

MOUTH Complete dentition, healthy, strong and even. Scissor bite correct, i.e. upper teeth closely overlapping lower teeth and set square to the jaws but pincer bite tolerated. Two central lower incisors may be set a little deeper than others. Close-fitting lips, upper just covering lower. Roof of mouth and lips black or heavily marked with black.

NECK Fairly short, thick, muscular. Some dewlap permitted.

FOREQUARTERS Powerful shoulders lying close to body. Medium angulation between shoulder blade and upper arm. Forelegs straight, heavily boned, well muscled. Elbows not too close to chest, nor too far off, giving adequate width of stance and free-striding movement. Pasterns flexible without weakness.

BODY Broad chest reaching just below elbows; sides slightly rounded, ribcage extended well to rear. Good length back, broad, muscular, straight, level. Dogs usually have more pronounced waist than bitches, giving greater curve to lower body.

HINDQUARTERS Broad muscular loins, fairly prominent haunches, slightly sloping rump, topline curving smoothly into tail. Very strong heavily muscled thighs tapering gradually to strong hocks. Stifle and hock of medium angulation seen from side. Strongly made double dewclaws on each hindleg; lack of this identifying characteristic totally undesirable. The hindfeet may turn out slightly but legs themselves must be straight.

FEET Short and compact, toes slightly arched, strong nails.

TAIL Thick at root, tapering gradually towards tip, preferably slightly curled; reaching below hocks, thickly coated with fairly long hair forming attractive plume. Carried low in repose, with tip turned slightly to one side. Tail rises as dog becomes interested: curled high above back in a circle when fully alert.

GAIT/MOVEMENT Unhurried, steady and smooth, as if driven by powerful hindquarters, well within its capacity, yet able to produce bursts of speed. Tends to pace at slow speeds.

COAT Profuse undercoat of very fine hairs; outer coat longer, coarser-textured, thick and straight or slightly wavy, never curly or fuzzy. Longer towards tail and forming mane round neck and shoulders. Forelegs fringed. Long, very dense woollier hair on rear of thighs giving pantaloon effect. Bitches tend to be smoother-coated than dogs and have less developed mane.

COLOUR (a) Mainly white with patches of badger, wolf-grey or pale yellow, or (b) White. (a) and (b) are of equal merit. The colour patches may be on the head, ears or base of tail and a few permissible on body. Black patches going right down to the roots highly undesirable. Black nose and eye rims: liver or pink pigmentation highly undesirable.

SIZE Minimum shoulder height: dogs: 70 cm (28 in); bitches: 65 cm (26 in). Most will considerably exceed this, great size is essential provided type and character are retained. Minimum weight: dogs: 50 kg (110 lb); bitches: 40 kg (90 lb); these weights apply only to specimens of minimum height, taller ones should be heavier. Weight always in proportion to height, giving a powerful dog of great strength, but excess weight due to fat undesirable.

FAULTS Any departure from the foregoing points should be considered a fault and the seriousness with which the fault should be regarded should be in exact proportion to its degree.

NOTE Male animals should have two apparently normal testicles fully descended into the scrotum.

PYRENEAN SHEEPDOG

(INTERIM)

THIS IS A TRULY COURAGEOUS working breed. His origins lie in the rural community, and he has been selected to herd large flocks of sheep for as long as his master needs him to do so. He has a particular 'head for heights' when asked to perform in the mountains.

The phrase in the standard which requires him to be 'wary of strangers' is not meant to indicate that he has a doubtful temperament, but that he needs to be properly socialised in his early formative weeks if he is to become an acceptable member of the household.

His coat is densely harsh as befits a breed which prefers to be out in all weathers. He is not difficult to keep tidy, but, in common with all long-coated breeds, grooming should be regular. The breed was first registered with The Kennel Club in 1988 and has increased gradually in numbers since; breeders have been careful to introduce new blood lines over the years.

GENERAL APPEARANCE Energetic, small sheepdog. Medium or long coated with windswept appearance. Alert, lean and racy outline. Mischievous, inquiring.

CHARACTERISTICS Highly intelligent, strong herding instinct. Tremendous energy and stamina for size.

TEMPERAMENT Alert, lively, wary of strangers.

HEAD AND SKULL Head almost triangular when viewed from above, length of skull equal to its widest point, flat on top with central furrow, showing slight occiput, side of skull slightly rounded. Muzzle slightly shorter in length than skull; tapering evenly to nose with no apparent stop; well filled below eyes. Toplines of nose and skull parallel. Nostrils well open. Well pigmented on nose, lips and in roof of mouth.

EYES Expressive, almond, wide open, not bulging or sunken. Dark brown, but one or both may be blue or flecked with blue in merle or slate coloured animals. Eye rims black. Never obscured by head coat.

EARS Fairly short, moderately wide at base, placed on top of head but neither too close nor too wide apart. Bottom part of ear erect and mobile, with top ideally hanging forward or to side when alert, but laid back in repose.

MOUTH Strong teeth, scissor bite, i.e. upper teeth closely overlapping lower teeth and set square to the jaws.

NECK Rather long, muscular, and set well into shoulder.

FOREQUARTERS Forelegs lean, sinewy and straight when seen from front, with single dewclaws. From side, pasterns slope gently and are flexible. Shoulder fairly long and well angulated, with upper arm joining shoulder blade at right angles. Withers prominently visible.

BODY Lean, strong. Ribs slightly rounded and extending well back. Brisket reaching to elbow. Loins strong and slightly arched.

HINDQUARTERS Short, sloping croup; fairly low-set tail. Strong, well muscled thigh, second thigh well developed and long. Well angulated stifle. Hocks lean, low-set and well angulated. Single or double dewclaws on rear.

FEET Lean, rather flat, oval shape. Dark pads and nails, well furred between pads.

TAIL Set low, not too long, reaching to hock joint with upward hook at end. Well covered with hair. Never carried higher than topline. May be docked. Sometimes born with short or stump tail.

GAIT/MOVEMENT Walks with fairly short strides, trots freely with vigour. Smooth gait,

feet never raised very high. Head carried high with slow action, tending to drop with faster action. Good angulations ensure effortless gait. Pacing should not be penalised.

COAT Long or semi-long. Fairly harsh; dense, almost flat or slightly wavy; denser and more woolly on rump and thighs. Hair on muzzle short. Longer on face and cheeks, where it grows away from the nose and eyes.
SEMI-LONG COATS: short hair with fringing on forelegs and short hair below hocks.
LONG COATS: long hair on legs to cover toes.

COLOUR Various shades of fawn, with or without black hairs; there may be a little white on chest and feet. Light to dark grey, often with white on head, chest and legs. Blue merle, slate blue or brindle. Black or black and white.

Unmixed colours preferred. Large areas of white, predominance of white, or black and tan undesirable.

SIZE Height: dogs: 40-48 cm (16-19 in); bitches: 38-46 cm (15-18 in).

FAULTS Any departure from the foregoing points should be considered a fault and the seriousness with which the fault should be regarded should be in exact proportion to its degree.

NOTE Male animals should have two apparently normal testicles fully descended into the scrotum.

ROTTWEILER

THESE DOGS STEM FROM ANIMALS TAKEN to Germany by Roman soldiers as they marched across Europe, and were used to guard livestock. These mastiff-type dogs were discarded as the cattle were eaten or were left to guard outposts and many finished up in Switzerland while others reached southern Germany. They were especially known around the town of Rottweil which for 1,800 years was a centre for livestock trading. The evolving dog became a butcher's dog, drover and draught dog.

The Rottweiler, which first appeared in Britain in 1936 and was shown at Crufts in 1937, is an above average-sized, very agile, black and tan dog. Extremely strong and imposing, he is easily obedience-trained and is, in fact, a dog that enjoys working. He has natural guarding instincts, but is not vicious by nature. His expression is tranquil and kind, but when aroused he will hold his own with any opponent. He is not a dog for the inexperienced and has been much maligned in recent years, when the breed became over-popular, and Rottweilers were often purchased to feed a macho image.

He is a very active dog who needs plenty of exercise and his smooth coat only requires short periods of regular grooming to keep it in the desired shining condition.

GENERAL APPEARANCE Above average size, stalwart dog. Correctly proportioned, compact and powerful form, permitting great strength, manoeuvrability and endurance.

CHARACTERISTICS Appearance displays boldness and courage. Self-assured and fearless. Calm gaze should indicate good humour.

TEMPERAMENT Good-natured, not nervous, aggressive or vicious; courageous, biddable, with natural guarding instincts.

HEAD AND SKULL Head medium length, skull broad between ears. Forehead moderately arched as seen from side. Occipital bone well developed but not conspicuous. Cheeks well boned and muscled but not prominent. Skin on head not loose, although it may form a moderate wrinkle when attentive. Muzzle fairly deep with topline level, and length of muzzle in relation to distance from well defined stop to occiput to be as 2 to 3. Nose well developed with proportionately large nostrils, always black.

EYES Medium size, almond-shaped, dark brown in colour, light eye undesirable, eyelids close fitting.

EARS Pendant, small in proportion rather than large, set high and wide apart, lying flat and close to cheek.

MOUTH Teeth strong, complete dentition with scissor bite, i.e. upper teeth closely overlapping lower teeth and set square to the jaws. Flews black and firm, falling gradually away towards corners of mouth, which do not protrude excessively.

NECK Of fair length, strong, round and very muscular. Slightly arched, free from throatiness.

FOREQUARTERS Shoulders well laid back, long and sloping, elbows well let down, but not

loose. Legs straight, muscular, with plenty of bone and substance. Pasterns sloping slightly forward.

BODY Chest roomy, broad and deep with well sprung ribs. Depth of brisket will not be more, and not much less than 50 per cent of shoulder height. Back straight, strong and not too long, ratio of shoulder height to length of body should be as 9 is to 10, loins short, strong and deep, flanks not tucked-up. Croup of proportionate length, and broad, very slightly sloping.

HINDQUARTERS Upper thighs not too short, broad and strongly muscled. Lower thigh well muscled at top, strong and sinewy below. Stifles fairly well bent. Hocks well angulated without exaggeration, metatarsals not completely vertical. Strength and soundness of hock highly desirable.

FEET Strong, round and compact with toes well arched. Hindfeet somewhat longer than front. Pads very hard, toenails short, dark and strong. Rear dewclaws removed.

TAIL Normally carried horizontally, but slightly above horizontal when dog is alert. Customarily docked at first joint, it is strong and not set too low.

GAIT/MOVEMENT Conveys an impression of supple strength, endurance and purpose. While back remains firm and stable there is a powerful hindthrust and good stride. First and foremost, movement should be harmonious, positive and unrestricted.

COAT Consists of top coat and undercoat. Top coat is of medium length, coarse and flat. Undercoat, essential on the neck and thighs, should not show through top coat. Hair may also be a little longer on the back of the forelegs and breechings. Long or excessively wavy coat highly undesirable.

COLOUR Black with clearly defined markings as follows: a spot over each eye, on cheeks, as a strip around each side of muzzle, but not on bridge of nose, on throat, two clear triangles on either side of the breast bone, on forelegs from carpus downward to toes, on inside of rear legs from hock to toes, but not completely eliminating black from back of legs, under tail. Colour of markings from rich tan to mahogany and should not exceed 10 per cent of body colour. White marking is highly undesirable. Black pencil markings on toes are desirable. Undercoat is grey, fawn or black.

SIZE Height at shoulder: dogs: between 63-69 cm (25-27 in); bitches: between 58-63.5 cm (23-25 in). Height should always be considered in relation to general appearance.

FAULTS Any departure from the foregoing points should be considered a fault and the seriousness with which the fault should be regarded should be in exact proportion to its degree.

NOTE Male animals should have two apparently normal testicles fully descended into the scrotum.

St. Bernard

THE MODERN ST. BERNARD RANKS amongst the most massive of all dogs; he seems to have grown heavier over the years from the days when he was known in the world as the mountain-rescue dog of Switzerland famed by the cartoonist's pencil for his brandy barrel. He was certainly leggier than the dog we see today, even if the breed standard says the 'taller the better, provided symmetry is maintained'. The standard also asks that the temperament, among other desirable qualities, should be benevolent, and that is something which is evident to all in his expression. Just as well, because the concept of a belligerent St. Bernard is not something many of us would wish to imagine.

Many of the larger breeds are surprisingly capable of curling up into a smallish ball and making their presence less obvious. Not so the St. Bernard; he takes up a lot of space in any position and those who have ideas about keeping one in a small flat or cottage with no outside accommodation for the dog should 'borrow' an adult for a test run. Perhaps they should use their tape-measure to check how much living space they will be granted once the new purchase has moved in and grown to full adult size.

There is a fair acreage of dog to be groomed; there are a good few kilograms of dog to be fuelled; there is a deal of dog to be dried on one's return from the slush of an autumn stroll across the fields. And if he needs lifting into a car *en route* to the local veterinary surgery, a low-loader might be a sensible purchase. A delightful breed if you can cope with the size and, dare it be said, the slobber, which often necessitates a bib if the pride of your eye is to arrive at the show in pristine condition.

The story of the dogs of the Hospice of St. Bernard goes back to the saint who built the hospice and whose aim was to help those travelling through the St. Gothard Pass. The monks at first used a mix of mastiff dogs but gradually established a proper breeding programme and produced dogs with the general name of Alpine Mastiffs. At first they were shorthaired and of modest size but outcrossing, made necessary by disease and losses from bad winters, brought in blood from thicker-coated and larger breeds. So evolved today's St. Bernard.

GENERAL APPEARANCE Well proportioned and of great substance.

CHARACTERISTICS Distinctly marked, large-sized, mountain-rescue dog.

TEMPERAMENT Steady, kindly, intelligent, courageous, trustworthy and benevolent.

HEAD AND SKULL Large, massive, circumference of skull being rather more than double its length. Muzzle short, full in front of eye and square at nose end. Cheeks flat, great depth from eye to lower jaw. Lips deep but not too pendulous. From nose to stop perfectly straight and broad. Stop somewhat abrupt and well defined. Skull broad, slightly rounded at top, with fairly prominent brow. Nose large and black with well developed nostrils.

EYES Of medium size, neither deep-set nor prominent, eyelids should be reasonably tight, without any excessive haw. Dark in colour and not staring. There should be no excessive loose wrinkle on brow which would detract from a healthy eye.

EARS Medium size, lying close to cheeks, not heavily feathered.

MOUTH Jaws strong with a perfect, regular and complete scissor bite, i.e. upper teeth closely overlapping lower teeth and set square to the jaws.

NECK Long, thick, muscular, slightly arched, dewlap well developed.

FOREQUARTERS Shoulders broad and sloping, well up at withers. Legs straight, strong in bone, of good length.

BODY Back broad, straight, ribs well rounded. Loin wide, very muscular. Chest wide and deep, but never projecting below elbows.

HINDQUARTERS Legs heavy in bone, hocks well bent, thighs very muscular.

FEET Large, compact with well arched toes. Dewclaws removed.

TAIL Set-on rather high, long, carried low when in repose, when excited or in motion should not curl over back.

GAIT/MOVEMENT Easy extension, unhurried or smooth, capable of covering difficult terrain.

COAT
ROUGHS: dense and flat, rather fuller round

neck, thighs and tail well feathered. SMOOTHS: close and hound-like, slight feathering on thighs and tail.

COLOUR Orange, mahogany-brindle, red-brindle, white with patches on body of any of the above named colours. Markings as follows: white muzzle, white blaze on face, white collar, white chest, white forelegs, feet and end of tail, black shadings on face and ears.

SIZE Taller the better, provided symmetry is maintained.

FAULTS Any departure from the foregoing points should be considered a fault and the seriousness with which the fault should be regarded should be in exact proportion to its degree.

NOTE Male animals should have two apparently normal testicles fully descended into the scrotum.

SAMOYED

RULY THE CANINE EQUIVALENT OF the Laughing Cavalier, he beams on all and sundry with a smile from ear to ear. A bad-tempered Samoyed is something that the devotees would shudder to contemplate, and fortunately he is a real rarity.

The Samoyed of today developed from dogs used for sledding by two nomadic tribes of north-central Siberia, the Samoyedes and the Nentsy. It was fur traders who first brought the breed to Britain and the European explorers described both black dogs and white dogs. Black and white dogs were used on the first Polar exploration but now the sparkling white, stand-off coat, with occasional tones of cream and biscuit quite acceptable, is the hallmark of an instantly recognisable dog.

His Arctic ancestry as a working dog has decreed that he should have flat feet and a deal of hair between the toes and under the soles, acting like canine snow-shoes and preventing snow balling up in between the toes as happens in many other breeds whose feet are 'well knuckled-up'.

The thick luxuriant coat takes a lot of physical effort to keep at its best, but that effort is well worth the considerable time which has to be expended.

He is not a big eater for such a solid dog; he is relatively obedient in what might be described as a fairly casual fashion, but then a true Sam looks on the world as something to be enjoyed to the full and too much going by the book can get one down! Incidentally, he does tend to be vocal.

GENERAL APPEARANCE Most striking. Medium and well balanced. Strong, active and graceful, free from coarseness but capable of great endurance.

CHARACTERISTICS Intelligent, alert, full of action. 'Smiling expression'.

TEMPERAMENT Displays affection to all mankind. Unprovoked nervousness or aggression highly undesirable.

HEAD AND SKULL Head powerful, wedge-shaped, with broad, flat skull, muzzle medium length, tapering foreface not too sharply defined. Lips black. Hair short and smooth before ears. Nose black for preference, but may be brown or flesh-coloured.

EYES Almond-shaped, set slanted, medium to dark brown, set well apart with alert, intelligent expression. Eye rims unbroken black. Light or black eyes undesirable.

EARS Thick, not too long, slightly rounded at tips, set well apart and well covered inside with hair. Fully erect in adults.

MOUTH Jaws strong with a perfect, regular and complete scissor bite, i.e. upper teeth closely overlapping lower teeth and set square to the jaws.

NECK Strong, not too short, and proudly arched.

FOREQUARTERS Shoulders well laid, legs straight and muscular with good bone and not too short.

BODY Back medium in length, broad and very muscular with exceptionally strong loin. Chest deep but not too broad, well sprung deep ribs, giving plenty of heart and lung room.

HINDQUARTERS Very muscular, stifles well angulated. Viewed from rear, legs straight and parallel, with well let down hocks. Cow-hocks or straight stifles highly undesirable.

FEET Long, flattish, slightly spread and well feathered. Soles well cushioned with hair. Round cat-feet highly undesirable.

TAIL Long, profusely coated, carried over the back and to side when alert, sometimes dropped when at rest.

GAIT/MOVEMENT Moves freely with strong, agile drive, showing power and elegance.

COAT Body should be well covered with thick, close, soft and short undercoat, with harsh but not wiry hair growing through it, forming weather-resistant outer coat, which should stand straight away from body and be free from curl.

COLOUR Pure white, white and biscuit, cream, outer coat silver tipped.

SIZE Height: dogs: 51-56 cm (20-22 in) at shoulder; bitches: 46-51 cm (18-20 in) at shoulder. Weight in proportion to size.

FAULTS Any departure from the foregoing points should be considered a fault and the seriousness with which the fault should be regarded should be in exact proportion to its degree.

NOTE Male animals should have two apparently normal testicles fully descended into the scrotum.

SHETLAND SHEEPDOG

THE SHETLAND ISLANDS IN THE north-east of Scotland lay claim to a number of animals small in size. The Shetland Sheepdog is one, an active, intelligent and glamorous dog who always wants to be 'on the go', and is virtually tireless. Affectionate with his owner, he is a little reserved with strangers. A sturdy, cheerful little dog, whose soft undercoat and harsh outer coat make him well able to withstand the winter elements. He is alert, makes a good house pet and is easy to train.

It was a Shetlander called Loggie who standardised the breed for the showring and it was first entered at Crufts in 1906 where it was shown as a miniature Collie.

GENERAL APPEARANCE Small, long-haired working dog of great beauty, free from cloddiness and coarseness. Outline symmetrical so that no part appears out of proportion to whole. Abundant coat, mane and frill, shapeliness of head and sweetness of expression combine to present the ideal.

CHARACTERISTICS Alert, gentle, intelligent, strong and active.

TEMPERAMENT Affectionate and responsive to his owner, reserved towards strangers, never nervous.

HEAD AND SKULL Head refined; when viewed from top or side a long, blunt wedge, tapering from ear to nose. Width of skull in proportion to length of skull and muzzle. Whole to be considered in connection with size of dog. Skull flat, moderately wide between ears, with no prominence of occipital bone. Cheeks flat, merging smoothly into well rounded muzzle. Skull and muzzle of equal length, dividing point inner corner of eye. Topline of skull parallel to topline of muzzle, with slight but definite stop. Nose, lips and eye rims black. The characteristic expression is obtained by the perfect balance and combination of skull and foreface, shape, colour and placement of eyes, correct position and carriage of ears.

EYES Medium size, obliquely set, almond shape. Dark brown except in the case of merles, where one or both may be blue or blue flecked.

EARS Small, moderately wide at base, placed fairly close together on top of skull. In repose, thrown back; when alert brought forward and carried semi-erect with tips falling forward.

MOUTH Jaws level, clean, strong with well-developed under-jaw. Lips tight. Teeth sound with a perfect, regular and complete scissor bite, i.e. upper teeth closely overlapping lower teeth and set square to the jaws. A full complement of 42 properly placed teeth highly desired.

NECK Muscular, well arched, of sufficient length to carry head proudly.

FOREQUARTERS Shoulders very well laid back. At withers, separated only by vertebrae, but blades sloping outwards to accommodate desired spring of ribs. Shoulder joint well angled. Upper arm and shoulder blade approximately equal in length. Elbow equidistant from ground and withers. Forelegs straight when viewed from front, muscular and clean with strong bone. Pasterns strong and flexible.

BODY Slightly longer from point of shoulder to bottom of croup than height at withers. Chest deep, reaching to point of elbow. Ribs well sprung, tapering at lower half to allow free play of forelegs and shoulders. Back level, with graceful sweep over loins, croup slopes gradually to rear.

HINDQUARTERS Thigh broad and muscular, thigh bones set into pelvis at right angles. Stifle joint has distinct angle, hock joint clean-cut, angular, well let down with strong bone. Hocks straight when viewed from behind.

FEET Oval, soles well padded, toes arched and close together.

TAIL Set low; tapering bone reaches to at least hock; with abundant hair and slight upward sweep. May be slightly raised when moving but never over level of back. Never kinked.

GAIT/MOVEMENT Lithe, smooth and graceful with drive from hindquarters, covering the maximum amount of ground with the minimum of effort. Pacing, plaiting, rolling, or stiff, stilted, up and down movement highly undesirable.

COAT Double; outer coat of long hair, harsh-textured and straight. Undercoat soft, short and close. Mane and frill very abundant, forelegs well feathered. Hindlegs above hocks profusely covered with hair, below hocks fairly smooth. Face smooth. Smooth-coated specimens highly undesirable.

COLOUR
SABLE: clear or shaded, any colour from pale gold to deep mahogany, in its shade, rich in tone. Wolf-sable and grey undesirable.
TRICOLOUR: intense black on body, rich tan markings preferred.

BLUE MERLE: clear silvery blue, splashed and marbled with black. Rich tan marking preferred but absence not penalised. Heavy black markings, slate or rusty tinge in either top or undercoat highly undesirable; general effect must be blue.
BLACK AND WHITE, AND BLACK AND TAN: also recognised colours. White markings may appear (except on black and tan) in blaze, collar and chest, frill, legs and tip of tail. All or some white markings are preferred (except on black and tan) but absence of these markings not to be penalised. Patches of white on body highly undesirable.

SIZE Ideal height at withers:
dogs: 37 cm (14½ in); bitches: 35.5 cm (14 in). More than 2.5 cm (1 in) above or below these heights highly undesirable.

FAULTS Any departure from the foregoing points should be considered a fault and the seriousness with which the fault should be regarded should be in exact proportion to its degree.

NOTE Male animals should have two apparently normal testicles fully descended into the scrotum.

SIBERIAN HUSKY

THE LIGHTEST BUILT AND FASTEST OF the sled-dog breeds, this dog is strictly for the active. He was bred to pull sleighs and, truth to tell, he has few other thoughts in his head. Put him on a lead and he will usually stretch your arm for you; put two or more on a couple of leads and they will dislocate your shoulder; let him off the lead and you may be lucky to see him as he gallops over the horizon!

Temperament wise, he is a delight, although his greeting may be so effusive that he will wind you if he catches you in the midriff. He seems to love the human race and never forgets a friend.

Though the breed takes its name from Siberia, the country of registration is America. It can also be known as the Arctic Husky and this stems from a tribe based on the Arctic and Pacific oceans known as the Chukchi who had great need of a long distance sled-hauling dog. Chukchi translates into 'husky'.

When the breed standard talks of all colours and markings, including white, being allowed, it is quite serious; and the comment about striking patterns not seen in other breeds being found on the head is not an exaggeration. And as for the eyes, just read the phrase in the standard for yourself!

He eats well; he's easy to groom; he can be vocal and every now and then a group of Sibes will form a choir of doubtful harmony and howl in chorus as they lie cheerfully tethered out in the worst of weathers. That is another breed characteristic – complete indifference to cold and snow. Just push your snout farther under your tail and it will go away!

And by the way, he can jump anything from the standstill or dig his way under any fence!

GENERAL APPEARANCE Medium-sized working sled-dog, quick and light on feet. Free and graceful in action, with well furred body, erect ears and brush tail. Proportions reflect a basic balance of power, speed and endurance, never appearing so heavy or coarse as to suggest a freighting animal, nor so light and fragile as to suggest a sprint-racing animal. Males are masculine but never coarse, bitches feminine but without weakness of structure. Muscle firm and well developed, no excess weight.

CHARACTERISTICS Medium size, moderate bone, well balanced proportions, ease and freedom of movement, and good disposition.

TEMPERAMENT Friendly and gentle, alert and outgoing. Does not display traits of the guard dog, not suspicious with strangers or aggressive with dogs but some measure of reserve expected in mature dog. Intelligent, tractable and eager disposition. An agreeable companion and willing worker.

HEAD AND SKULL Medium size in proportion to the body, presents a finely chiselled fox-like appearance. Slightly rounded on top, tapering gradually from widest point to eyes. Muzzle medium length and width, neither snipy nor coarse, tapering gradually to rounded nose. Tip of nose to stop equidistant from stop to occiput. Stop clearly defined but not excessive. Line of the nose straight from the stop to tip. Nose black in grey, tan or black dogs; liver in copper dogs; and may be flesh-coloured in pure white. In winter, pink-streaked 'snow nose' is acceptable.

EYES Almond-shaped, moderately spaced and set obliquely. Any shade of blue or brown, one of each colour, or parti-colours equally acceptable. Expression keen, but friendly, interested, even mischievous.

EARS Medium size, relatively close together, triangular in shape, the height slightly greater than width at base. Set high on head, strongly erect, the inner edges being quite close together at the base, when the dog is at attention carried practically parallel. Slightly arched at the back. Thick, well furred outside and inside, tips slightly rounded.

MOUTH Lips well pigmented, close fitting. Jaws strong, with a perfect, regular and complete scissor bite, i.e. upper teeth closely overlapping lower teeth and set square to the jaws.

NECK Medium length and thickness, arched and carried proudly erect when standing. When moving at a trot, extended so that the head is carried slightly forward.

FOREQUARTERS Shoulder blade well laid back, upper arm angles slightly backward from point of shoulder to elbow, never perpendicular to the ground. Muscle holding shoulder to ribcage firm and well-developed. Straight or loose shoulders highly undesirable. Viewed from the front, forelegs moderately spaced, parallel and straight with elbows close to the body, turning neither in nor out. Viewed from the side,

Longer on brisket, thighs and tail. Forming a ruff round neck. Undercoat dense and finely curled.

COLOUR Bear-brown, black, brown, a combination of black and brown, solid colours preferred. White mark on chest, white feet and white tip of tail acceptable. More white markings objectionable.

SIZE Height: dogs: 45-51 cm (18-20 in), ideal height 48 cm (19 in); bitches: 40-46 cm (16-18½ in), ideal 43 cm (17 in).

FAULTS Any departure from the foregoing points should be considered a fault and the seriousness with which the fault should be regarded should be in exact proportion to its degree.

NOTE Male animals should have two apparently normal testicles fully descended into the scrotum.

SWEDISH VALLHUND

THIS IMPORT TO BRITAIN MAY LOOK like an unusually coloured Welsh Corgi but he is nothing of the sort. Although he is fairly long in the back he stands up on strong, thick-set legs, and gives the impression of concentrated power in a fairly small frame. The harsh, close-fitting coat is easy to keep clean and wholesome. He is very active, a good guard from the point of view of giving warning of an approaching stranger, but he has a friendly, cheerful disposition, and will take all the exercise you want to give him.

The Vallhund is also called the Swedish Cattle Dog, identifying both his purpose and country of origin. The breed nearly died out in the 1930s but, mainly through the efforts of a Count Bjorn von Rosen, was saved and was recognised by the Swedish Kennel Club in 1948 and granted recognition in Britain in 1984.

GENERAL APPEARANCE Small, powerful, sturdily built working dog, with fairly long body. (Ratio of height at withers to length of body 2:3).

CHARACTERISTICS Appearance and expression denote a watchful, alert, energetic dog.

TEMPERAMENT Friendly, active, eager to please.

HEAD AND SKULL Rather long and a clean-cut, blunt wedge with almost flat skull and well defined stop. Viewed from above, shows an even wedge shape from skull to tip of nose. Muzzle, viewed from side, looks rather square, slightly shorter than skull. Lower jaw strong. Although a dark mask is acceptable, a well defined mask is highly desirable with lighter hair around eyes, on muzzle and under the throat, giving a distinct contrast to the upper mask. Tightly closed lips. Nose black.

EYES Medium size, oval, very dark brown.

EARS Medium size, pointed, pricked, leather hard from base to tip, but fine, smooth-haired and mobile.

MOUTH Scissor bite – jaws strong with a perfect, regular and complete scissor bite, i.e. upper teeth closely overlapping lower teeth and set square to the jaws.

NECK Long, strongly muscled with good reach.

FOREQUARTERS Shoulder blades long and well laid. Upper arm slightly shorter than shoulder blade and set at a distinct angle. Upper arm lies close to ribs, but is still very mobile. Forearm, when viewed from front, slightly bent, just enough to give free action to chest's lower part; straight when viewed from side. Legs well boned.

BODY Back level, well muscled, with short, strong loin. Chest long with good depth. Well sprung ribs. Viewed from front, chest oval, from side elliptical. Reaching two-fifths of length of forearm. When viewed from side the lowest point of chest is immediately behind back part of foreleg. Sternum visible but not excessively pointed. Croup broad and slightly sloping. Belly slightly tucked-up. Harness markings should be clearly defined.

HINDQUARTERS Well angulated, well bent stifles and low hocks, thighs strongly muscled. Legs well boned.

FEET Medium, short, oval, pointing straight forward with strong pads. Well knuckled up.

TAIL If present, length not exceeding 10 cm (4 in) when adult. Carried horizontally or slightly downwards, may be raised at attention but never higher than level of back. Puppies born with tails may be docked.

GAIT/MOVEMENT Free and active, elbows fitting closely to sides, forelegs moving well forward without too much lift, in unison with powerful, thrusting hind action.

COAT Medium length, harsh, close and tight topcoat, undercoat abundant, soft, woolly.

COLOUR Steel grey, greyish brown, greyish yellow, reddish yellow, reddish brown with darker guard hairs on back, neck and sides of body. Lighter hair same shade of colour as mentioned above is desirable on muzzle, throat, chest, belly, buttocks, feet and hocks. Instead of these lighter shades, white markings are acceptable, but never in excess of one-third of total colour.

SIZE Height at withers: dogs: 33-35 cm (13-13¾ in); bitches: 31-33 cm (12-13 in). The relation between height at withers and length of body should be 2:3. Weight: 11.4-15.9 kg (25-35 lb).

FAULTS Any departure from the foregoing points should be considered a fault and the seriousness with which the fault should be regarded should be in exact proportion to its degree.

NOTE Male animals should have two apparently normal testicles fully descended into the scrotum.

TIBETAN MASTIFF

(INTERIM)

THIS STRONG, WELL BUILT DOG IS found in the foothills of the Himalayas and the borders of Tibet. He is primarily a guard dog, used to protect the flocks from preying wildlife and the home from intruders.

Though the actual origins of the breed are lost in time it is known that Tibetan villagers originally had two types of mastiff: a guard for livestock and another to guard their territory. The modern Tibetan Mastiff has been known outside its native country now for well over 100 years and there has been a British standard for the breed since the 1930s.

A powerful dog, without the massive frame of the Mastiff, he is well coated, with a bushy tail. Usually black, or black and tan, he can also be found in gold, and shades of grey. In his native environment he is very distrustful of strangers, and can be quite ferocious. However, dogs bred in Europe and America do not generally display these tendencies.

GENERAL APPEARANCE Powerful, heavy, well built, with good bone. Impressive; of solemn but kindly appearance.

CHARACTERISTICS A companion, watch and guard dog, slow to mature, only reaching its best at 2-3 years in females and at least 4 years in males.

TEMPERAMENT Aloof and protective.

HEAD AND SKULL Fairly broad, heavy and strong. Skull massive, with strongly defined

occiput and stop. Proportions from occiput to stop and stop to end of nose equal, but nose may be a little shorter. Muzzle fairly broad, well filled and square, viewed from all sides. Broad nose, well pigmented, well opened nostrils. Lips well developed with moderate flews. Some wrinkling, in maturity, on head, extends from above eyes, down to corner of mouth.

EYES Very expressive, medium size, any shade of brown. Set well apart, oval and slightly slanting.

EARS Medium size, triangular, pendant, carried low, dropping forward and hanging close to head. Raised when alert. Ear leathers covered with soft, short hair.

MOUTH Scissor bite – jaws strong, with perfect, regular and complete scissor bite, i.e. upper teeth closely overlapping lower teeth and set square to the jaws. Level acceptable. Essential that dentition fits tightly, to maintain square form of muzzle.

NECK Strong, well muscled, arched. Not too much dewlap. Shrouded by thick upstanding mane.

FOREQUARTERS Well laid shoulders, muscular, strongly boned. Straight legs with strong, slightly sloping pasterns, and well covered all over with strong hair.

BODY Strong, with straight back, muscular, almost imperceptible croup. Chest rather deep of moderate breadth, with reasonable spring of rib, to give heart-shaped ribcage. Brisket reaching to below elbows. Body slightly longer than height at withers.

HINDQUARTERS Powerful, muscular, with good angulation from well bent stifle and strong low-set hocks. Hindlegs, seen from behind, parallel. Removal of dewclaws (single or double) optional.

FEET Fairly large, strong, compact. Cat-feet having good feathering between toes.

TAIL Medium to long, but not reaching below hock joint. Set high on line with top of back. Curled over back to one side. Well feathered.

GAIT/MOVEMENT Powerful, free, always light and elastic. At speed will tend to single-track. When walking appears slow and very deliberate.

COAT Males carry noticeably more than females. Quality of greater importance than quantity. Mainly fairly long, thick, with heavy undercoat in cold weather which becomes rather sparse in warmer months. Hair fine but hard, straight and stand-off. Never silky, curly or wavy. Heavy undercoat, when present, rather woolly. Neck and shoulders heavily coated, giving mane-like appearance. Tail bushy, densely coated, hindlegs well feathered on upper rear parts.

COLOUR Rich black, black and tan, brown, various shades of gold, grey and blue; grey and blue and tan. Tan ranges from a very rich shade, through to a lighter colour. White star on breast permissible. Minimal white markings on feet acceptable. Tan markings appear above eyes, on chest, lower part of legs and underside of tail. Tan markings on muzzle; spectacle markings around eyes.

SIZE Height; dogs: 66 cm (26 in) minimum; bitches: 61 cm (24 in).

FAULTS Any departure from the foregoing points should be considered a fault and the seriousness with which the fault should be regarded should be in exact proportion to its degree.

NOTE Male animals should have two apparently normal testicles fully descended into the scrotum.

WELSH CORGI (CARDIGAN)

T O THE UNINITIATED THE CARDIGAN looks to be a Pembroke with a tail! Admittedly the two varieties came from a common root-stock and were not divided officially until the mid-1930s, but time has led to some variations which are now more obvious even if not all specifically mentioned in the standards. The Cardigan allows for more colours of coat, in fact it permits any colour so long as white does not predominate.

The ears are a trifle larger and set slightly wider in the Cardigan, and the feet should be round rather than oval. The tail, for such a relatively low-set dog, is long, appears heavy and is carried low, nearly reaching the ground when at rest.

In terms of temperament the Cardigan gives the impression of being a more restful character than his cousin, but he is perfectly capable of coming alive whenever he is asked to. He is known as a true companion and worker, capable of fitting into all kinds of life-styles with the minimum of fuss. It is surprising that such a delightful breed has never achieved the popularity that it deserves.

The Cardigan is thought to be the older of the two varieties of Welsh Corgi with a history going back to around 1200. It has also been called the Yard Dog because its length from tip of nose to end of outstretched tail is the measurement for a Welsh yard.

GENERAL APPEARANCE Sturdy, tough, mobile, capable of endurance. Long in proportion to height, terminating in fox-like brush, set in line with body.

CHARACTERISTICS Alert, active and intelligent.

TEMPERAMENT Alert, intelligent, steady, not shy or aggressive.

HEAD AND SKULL Head foxy in shape and appearance, skull wide and flat between ears tapering towards eyes above which it is slightly domed. Moderate stop. Length of foreface in proportion to head 3 to 5, muzzle tapering moderately towards nose which projects slightly and in no sense blunt. Under-jaw clean-cut. Strong but without prominence. Nose black.

EYES Medium size, clear, giving kindly, alert but watchful expression. Rather widely set with corners clearly defined. Preferably dark, to blend with coat, rims dark. One or both eyes pale blue, blue or blue flecked, permissible only in blue merles.

EARS Erect, proportionately rather large to size of dog. Tips slightly rounded, moderately wide at base and set about 8 cm (3½ in) apart. Carried so that tips are slightly wide of straight line drawn from tip of nose through centre of eyes, and set well back so that they can be laid flat along neck.

MOUTH Teeth strong, with scissor bite, i.e. upper teeth closely overlapping lower teeth and set square to the jaws.

NECK Muscular, well developed, in proportion to dog's build, fitting into well sloping shoulders.

FOREQUARTERS Shoulders well laid, angulated at approximately 90 degrees to upper arm; muscular, elbows close to sides. Strong bone carried down to feet. Legs short but body well clear of the ground, forearms slightly bowed to mould round the chest. Feet turned slightly outwards.

BODY Chest moderately broad with prominent breast bone. Body fairly long and strong, with deep brisket, well sprung ribs. Clearly defined waist. Topline level.

HINDQUARTERS Strong, well angulated and aligned with muscular thighs and second thighs, strong bone carried down to feet, legs short; when standing, hocks vertical, viewed from side and rear.

FEET Round, tight, rather large and well padded. All dewclaws to be removed.

TAIL Like a fox's brush, set in line with the body and moderately long (to touch or nearly touch ground). Carried low when standing but may be lifted a little above body when moving; not curled over back.

GAIT/MOVEMENT Free and active, elbows fitting close to sides, neither loose nor tied. Forelegs reaching well forward without too much lift, in unison with thrusting action of hindlegs.

COAT Short or medium of hard texture. Weather-proof, with good undercoat. Preferably straight.

COLOUR Any colour, with or without white markings, but white should not predominate.

SIZE Height: ideal 30 cm (12 in) at shoulder. Weight in proportion to size with overall balance the prime consideration.

FAULTS Any departure from the foregoing points should be considered a fault and the seriousness with which the fault should be regarded should be in exact proportion to its degree.

NOTE Male animals should have two apparently normal testicles fully descended into the scrotum.

WELSH CORGI (PEMBROKE)

I T IS FAIR TO SAY THAT LIFE COULD never be dull with a Pembroke. His prick ears and his lovely sharp face give him an appearance of being interested in everything that is happening. The breed has had its periods when one or two characters gave it a bad name by nipping people as well as the heels of cattle, but the clause in the standard which describes him as outgoing and friendly is a very good description of a dog which is born busy and stays busy through all its, thankfully, long life.

Possessed of a bark which belies his small stature, his lungs are obviously built to give him the stamina he needs to do a day's work as a farm dog. In addition he is nimble enough to duck away from the retaliatory kick of the cow if his herding instincts cause him to lose patience with his charges.

The coat is truly dense in its undercoat and it would be difficult to imagine a Pembroke feeling the cold, even if he is very happy to share the 'mod cons' of his owners if he is living the life of a companion dog. Grooming is therefore not a hard task, although his propensity to plough his way through the muck and the mire of a long country walk may mean that he does not always come home in a state suitable for immediate contact with the best Wilton.

Being small in size he does not need a great deal of food, but that does not mean that he won't eat more than he needs, so it is no bad idea to make sure that he belongs to a canine Weight Watchers.

A thoroughly practical breed which can live with all sorts of households and add a lot to the fun.

GENERAL APPEARANCE Low-set, strong, sturdily built, alert and active, giving impression of substance and stamina in small space.

CHARACTERISTICS Bold in outlook, workmanlike.

TEMPERAMENT Outgoing and friendly, never nervous or aggressive.

HEAD AND SKULL Head foxy in shape and appearance, with alert, intelligent expression, skull fairly wide and flat between ears, moderate amount of stop. Length of foreface to be in proportion to skull 3:5. Muzzle slightly tapering. Nose black.

EYES Well set, round, medium size, brown, blending with colour of coat.

EARS Pricked, medium-sized, slightly rounded. Line drawn from tip of nose through eye should, if extended, pass through, or close to tip of ear.

MOUTH Jaws strong with perfect, regular and complete scissor bite, i.e. upper teeth closely overlapping lower teeth and set square to the jaws.

NECK Fairly long.

FOREQUARTERS Lower legs short and as straight as possible, upper arm moulded round chest. Ample bone, carried right down to feet. Elbows fitting closely to sides, neither loose nor tied. Shoulders well laid, and angulated at 90 degrees to the upper arm.

BODY Medium length, well sprung ribs, not short-coupled, slightly tapering, when viewed from above. Level topline. Chest broad and deep, well let down between forelegs.

HINDQUARTERS Strong and flexible, well angulated stifle. Legs short. Ample bone carried right down to feet. Hocks straight when viewed from behind.

FEET Oval, toes strong, well arched, and tight, two centre toes slightly in advance of two outer, pads strong and well arched. Nails short.

TAIL Short, preferably natural.

GAIT/MOVEMENT Free and active, neither loose nor tied. Forelegs move well forward, without too much lift, in unison with thrusting action of hindlegs.

COAT Medium length, straight with dense undercoat, never soft, wavy or wiry.

COLOUR Self-colours in Red, Sable, Fawn, Black and Tan, with or without white markings on legs, brisket and neck. Some white on head and foreface permissible.

SIZE Height: approx 25.5-30.5 cm (10-12 in) at shoulder. Weight: dogs: 10-12 kg (22-26 lb); bitches: 10-11 kg (20-24 lb).

FAULTS Any departure from the foregoing points should be considered a fault and the seriousness with which the fault should be regarded should be in exact proportion to its degree.

NOTE Male animals should have two apparently normal testicles fully descended into the scrotum.

BELOW: Three Pomeranians with an Apple *(1904).*
This painting by Maud Earl (1864–1943) depicts three
Champion dogs: Champion Dainty Boy, Champion
Gateace Bibury Belle and Champion Dainty Belle.

TOY GROUP

AFFENPINSCHER

THIS QUAINT LITTLE DOG HAS A captivating monkey-like expression, and is one of the oldest Toy dogs in Europe, dating back to about the seventeenth century. Known as the Black Devil, he originated in Germany. Some think he is descended from wire-coated terrier types of the Nordic dogs of which he is a miniature, while others see in the Affenpinscher something of the pug-like dogs from Asia which are found in Europe. Full of mischief, he is a lively little character, very affectionate, and his comical antics make him a most amusing companion.

He has a rough, harsh-textured coat which requires very little care and no trimming. Dark, sparkling eyes, set off by a halo of hair which stands away from his face, give him his unique expression. He adapts to city or country living, and is an ideal size for house or flat.

GENERAL APPEARANCE Rough-coated, sturdy in build with a mischievous monkey-like expression. Although small, not delicate in any way.

CHARACTERISTICS Lively and self-confident, carrying itself with a comic seriousness.

TEMPERAMENT Loyal and loving companion; watchful of strangers and fearless toward aggressors.

HEAD AND SKULL Fairly small in proportion to body; domed forehead, broad brow and marked stop which is not indented. Muzzle blunt and short but not flattened sufficiently to cause difficulty in breathing or wrinkling of skin. Chin prominent with good turn up. Distance between dark eyes and black nose forming an equal sided triangle.

EYES Round, very dark and sparkling. Medium in size and not protruding.

EARS Small, set high, either drop or erect.

MOUTH Slightly undershot with lower incisors gripping scissor-like in front of uppers. Teeth or tongue not showing when mouth closed.

NECK Short and straight. Skin of throat tight and unwrinkled.

FOREQUARTERS Front legs straight, elbows neither in nor out, carried close to sides.

BODY Back short and straight. Height at withers about equal to length of back. Well sprung ribs with chest not too deep, combined with only a slight tuck-up at loin giving a sturdy appearance.

HINDQUARTERS Hindlegs well set under body without excessive angulation.

FEET Small, round and compact turning neither in nor out. Pads and nails dark.

TAIL Set high and carried high, left a natural length to curve gently over back when moving.

GAIT/MOVEMENT A lively, strutting movement. Lifting feet high when in motion, with no hint of hackneyed action or plaiting.

COAT Correct coat needs no trimming, rough and harsh in texture, short and dense on some parts of body and shaggy on others. In particular, longer on shoulders, neck and

head where loose shaggy hair stands away from skull framing eyes, nose and chin giving desired monkey-like appearance.

COLOUR Black preferable, but grey shading permissible.

SIZE Height: 24-28 cm (9½-11 in). Weight: 3-4 kg (6½-9 lb).

FAULTS Any departure from the foregoing points should be considered a fault and the seriousness with which the fault should be regarded should be in exact proportion to its degree.

NOTE Male animals should have two apparently normal testicles fully descended into the scrotum.

AUSTRALIAN SILKY TERRIER

(INTERIM)

As his name implies this dog originated in Australia and, at one time, was known as the 'Sydney Silky'. A certain MacArthur Little was an early prominent breeder and when he moved to Sydney with his kennel of dogs the name Sydney Silky was born. Although he is in the Toy group he is far from being a quiet little lap dog. His background comes from a mixture of Australian and Yorkshire Terriers, and he retains many of the qualities of these breeds. He is friendly but independent, smart and curious, energetic, affectionate, and has lots of stamina. Primarily he was bred to be a household pet, and he fills this role admirably.

His glossy, silky coat, which is five or six inches long, is easy to look after and a few minutes' daily brushing, with a quick comb and parting down the back, gives him a well groomed appearance.

GENERAL APPEARANCE Compact, moderately low-set, medium length with refined structure; sufficient substance to suggest ability to hunt and kill domestic rodents. Straight silky hair parted from nape of neck to root of tail, presenting a well-groomed appearance.

CHARACTERISTICS Terrier-like, keen, alert, active.

TEMPERAMENT Very friendly, quick and responsive.

HEAD AND SKULL Moderate length, slightly shorter in length from tip of nose to between eyes than from there to top rear of occiput. Moderately broad between ears; skull flat, without fullness between eyes. Nose black.

EYES Small, round, dark as possible, not prominent, keen intelligent expression.

EARS Small V-shaped, with fine leathers, high on skull and pricked; entirely free from long hair.

MOUTH Jaws strong, with a perfect, regular and complete scissor bite, i.e. upper teeth closely overlapping lower teeth and set square to the jaws. Teeth even and not cramped, lips tight and clean.

NECK Medium length, refined, slightly arched. Well covering with long silky hair.

FOREQUARTERS Shoulders fine, well laid back, well angulated upper arms fitting snugly to ribs; elbows turn neither in nor out; forelegs straight with refined round bone, set well under body with no weakness in pasterns.

BODY Slightly longer than height. Level topline; well sprung ribs extending back to strong loins. Chest of moderate depth and breadth.

HINDQUARTERS Thighs well developed. Stifles well turned; when viewed from behind, the hocks well let down and parallel.

FEET Small, well padded and cat-like. Closely knit toes with black or very dark toenails.

TAIL Customarily docked, carried erect; not over-gay; free from feathering.

GAIT/MOVEMENT Free, straight forward without slackness at shoulders or elbows. No turning sideways of feet or pasterns. Hindquarters have strong propelling power with ample flexibility at stifles and hocks. Viewed from behind, movement neither too close nor too wide.

COAT Straight, fine and glossy; silky texture; length of coat 13-15 cm (5-6 in) from behind ears to set-on of tail desirable. Legs, from knees and hocks to feet, free of long hair. Fine silky 'top-knot', not falling over eyes. Long fall of hair on foreface and cheeks undesirable.

COLOUR Blue and tan, grey-blue and tan, the richer these colours the better. Blue on tail very dark. Distribution of blue and tan as follows: Silver-blue or fawn to top-knot, tan around base of ears, muzzle and on side of cheeks; blue from base of skull to tip of tail, running down forelegs to near knees and down thighs to hocks; tan line showing down stifles, and tan from knees and hocks to toes and around vent. Blue colour must be established by 18 months of age.

SIZE Most desirable weight about 4 kg (8-10 lb). Height approximately 23 cm (9 in) at withers, bitches may be slightly less.

FAULTS Any departure from the foregoing points should be considered a fault and the seriousness with which the fault should be regarded should be in exact proportion to its degree.

NOTE Male animals should have two apparently normal testicles fully descended into the scrotum.

BICHON FRISE

HIS ORIGIN IS SAID TO BE IN THE Mediterranean area. The breed is known also as the 'Tenerife Dog' because history has it that fourteenth century sailors found him on that island, fell for his charms and took him back to France. He was recognised by the French Kennel Club in 1934 though his recognition in Britain did not occur until after both America and Canada entered him on their registers in the 1970s. There are several members of the Bichon family and portraits painted centuries ago depict small white dogs so similar in type they must surely have been his ancestors.

A happy little dog who thrives on being the centre of attention, he is a complete extrovert, full of confidence and intelligence. He loves companionship and has a deep regard for his family, of which he soon becomes an integral part, and he shows his appreciation of all home comforts. Potential owners must remember that he does require a considerable amount of grooming to maintain his glamorous image.

GENERAL APPEARANCE Well balanced dog of smart appearance, closely coated with handsome plume carried over the back. Natural white coat curling loosely. Head carriage proud and high.

CHARACTERISTICS Gay, happy, lively little dog.

TEMPERAMENT Friendly and outgoing.

HEAD AND SKULL Ratio of muzzle length to skull length 3:5. On a head of the correct width and length, lines drawn between the outer corners of the eyes and nose will create a near equilateral triangle. Whole head in balance with body. Muzzle not thick, heavy or snipy. Cheeks flat, not very strongly muscled. Stop moderate but definite, hollow between eyebrows just visible. Skull slightly rounded, not coarse, with hair accentuating rounded appearance. Nose large, round, black, soft and shiny.

EYES Dark, round with black eye rims, surrounded by dark haloes, consisting of well pigmented skin. Forward-looking, fairly large but not almond-shaped, neither obliquely set nor protruding. Showing no white when looking forward. Alert, full of expression.

EARS Hanging close to head, well covered with flowing hair longer than leathers, set-on slightly higher than eye level and rather forward on skull. Carried forward when dog alert, forward edge touching skull. Leather reaching approximately half-way along muzzle.

MOUTH Jaws strong, with a perfect, regular and complete scissor bite, i.e. upper teeth closely overlapping lower teeth and set square to the jaws. Full dentition desirable. Lips fine, fairly tight and completely black.

NECK Arched neck fairly long, about one-third the length of body. Carried high and proudly. Round and slim near head, gradually broadening to fit smoothly into shoulders.

FOREQUARTERS Shoulders oblique, not prominent, equal in length to upper arm. Upper arm fits close to body. Legs straight, perpendicular, when seen from front; not too finely boned. Pasterns short and straight viewed from front, very slightly sloping viewed from side.

BODY Forechest well developed, deep brisket. Ribs well sprung, floating ribs not terminating abruptly. Loin broad, well muscled, slightly arched and well tucked-up. Pelvis broad, croup slightly rounded. Length from withers to tailset should equal height from withers to ground.

HINDQUARTERS Thighs broad and well rounded. Stifles well bent; hocks well angulated and metatarsals perpendicular.

FEET Tight, rounded and well knuckled up. Pads black. Nails preferably black.

TAIL Normally carried raised and curved gracefully over the back but not tightly curled. Never docked. Carried in line with backbone, only hair touching back; tail itself not in contact. Set-on level with topline, neither too high nor too low. Corkscrew tail undesirable.

GAIT/MOVEMENT Balanced and effortless with an easy reach and drive maintaining a steady and level topline. Legs moving straight along line of travel, with hind pads showing.

COAT Fine, silky with soft corkscrew curls. Neither flat nor corded, and measuring 7-10 cm (3-4 in) in length. The dog may be presented untrimmed or have muzzle and feet slightly tidied up.

COLOUR White, but cream or apricot markings acceptable up to 18 months. Under white coat, dark pigment desirable. Black, blue or beige markings often found on skin.

SIZE Ideal height 23-38 cm (9-11 in) at withers.

FAULTS Any departure from the foregoing points should be considered a fault and the seriousness with which the fault should be regarded should be in exact proportion to its degree.

NOTE Male animals should have two apparently normal testicles fully descended into the scrotum.

BOLOGNESE

(INTERIM)

THE BOLOGNESE (PRONOUNCED Bol-o-neeese) is an ancient, charming and intelligent breed of small dog hailing from the centre of Northern Italy. It is after the style of other Bichon types, but has a distinctive non-shedding coat which forms into flocks. Regular grooming is necessary but this does not include trimming as a means of keeping it neat and tidy. An attractive apricot shading appears occasionally on the ears, but otherwise the colour is white.

Temperamentally the Bolognese delights in family activities and expects to be included in the long walks as well as indoor or garden games. Historically the breed seems to have been regarded as a most acceptable gift in fashionable circles. Today, he is equally acceptable in cottage or castle.

GENERAL APPEARANCE Small white toy dog with square, compact outline and distinctive coat.

CHARACTERISTICS Intelligent, companionable.

TEMPERAMENT Reserved.

HEAD AND SKULL Wide flat skull. Nose to stop slightly shorter than from stop to occiput. Accentuated stop. Nose large, black.

EYES Large, round, dark with well pigmented rims.

EARS Set-on high, long, pendulous, carried away from head giving a broad appearance to head.

MOUTH Jaws level, with perfect, regular scissor bite, i.e. upper teeth closely overlapping lower teeth and set square to the jaws.

NECK Clean, medium length.

FOREQUARTERS Shoulders well laid, legs straight with slightly sloping pasterns. Elbows close to body.

BODY Well sprung ribs, brisket reaching to elbows making half overall height at withers. Level back, loins slightly arched. Point of shoulder to point of buttock equals height at withers.

HINDQUARTERS Well muscled, moderate turn of stifle, hocks well let down.

FEET Oval, black nails and pads. Dewclaws customarily removed.

TAIL Set-on at level of croup carried curved over back. Well feathered.

GAIT/MOVEMENT Normal and smart. Legs moving parallel. Ambling highly undesirable.

COAT Long, flocked without curl covering entire head and body. Shown in natural state.

COLOUR Pure white without markings, not even simple shadings. Lips, eyelids, nose and nails black.

SIZE Dogs: 27-30.5 cm (10½-12 in). Bitches: 22.5-28 cm (10-11 in).

FAULTS Any departure from the foregoing points should be considered a fault and the seriousness with which the fault should be regarded should be in exact proportion to its degree.

NOTE Male animals should have two apparently normal testicles fully descended into the scrotum.

CAVALIER KING CHARLES SPANIEL

HIS LARGE, DARK EYES AND MELTING expression are a true indication of his sweetness of character. Sturdy and hardy, in a range of four such lovely colours it is difficult to know which to choose.

A happy dog whose pleasures are simple – he will enjoy a long country walk, meandering round the shops or sitting beside you in front of the fire. Good with children, he is a devoted companion, absolutely non-aggressive and easy to care for. His silky coat requires little attention and his ever-wagging tail shows how easy he is to please.

His origins are a little hazy; he goes back several centuries though not securing Kennel Club status until 1944, having been revived as a breed separate from the King Charles Spaniel. By the 1970s the breed was in the top twenty of British registrations and continues to attract large show entries. The Cavalier King Charles Spaniel is larger than his relative, the King Charles, and less snub nosed.

GENERAL APPEARANCE Active, graceful and well balanced, with gentle expression.

CHARACTERISTICS Sporting, affectionate, absolutely fearless.

TEMPERAMENT Gay, friendly, non-aggressive; no tendency to nervousness.

HEAD AND SKULL Skull almost flat between ears. Stop shallow. Length from base of stop to tip of nose about 3.8 cm (1½ in). Nostrils black and well developed without flesh marks, muzzle well tapered. Lips well developed but not pendulous. Face well filled below eyes. Any tendency to snipiness undesirable.

EYES Large, dark, round but not prominent; spaced well apart.

EARS Long, set high, with plenty of feather.

MOUTH Jaws strong, with a perfect, regular and complete overlapping lower teeth and set square to the jaws.

NECK Moderate length, slightly arched.

FOREQUARTERS Chest moderate, shoulders well laid back; straight legs moderately boned.

BODY Short-coupled with good spring of rib. Level back.

HINDQUARTERS Legs with moderate bone; well turned stifle – no tendency to cow-hocks or sickle-hocks.

FEET Compact, cushioned and well feathered.

TAIL Length of tail in balance with body, well set-on, carried happily but never much above the level of the back. Docking optional. If docked, no more than one-third to be removed.

GAIT/MOVEMENT Free-moving and elegant in action, plenty of drive from behind. Forelegs and hindlegs move parallel when viewed from in front and behind.

COAT Long, silky, free from curl. Slight wave permissible. Plenty of feathering. Totally free from trimming.

COLOUR Recognised colours are:

BLACK AND TAN: raven black with tan markings above the eyes, on cheeks, inside ears, on chest and legs and underside of tail. Tan should be bright. White marks undesirable.

RUBY: whole coloured rich red. White markings undesirable.

BLENHEIM: rich chestnut markings well broken up, on pearly white ground. Markings evenly divided on head, leaving room between ears for much valued lozenge mark or spot (a unique characteristic of the breed).

TRICOLOUR: black and white well spaced, broken up, with tan markings over eyes, cheeks, inside ears, inside legs, and on underside of tail. Any other colour or combination of colours highly undesirable.

SIZE Weight: 5.4–8 kg (12–18 lb). A small, well balanced dog well within these weights desirable.

FAULTS Any departure from the foregoing points should be considered a fault and the seriousness with which the fault should be regarded should be in exact proportion to its degree.

NOTE Male animals should have two apparently normal testicles fully descended into the scrotum.

CHIHUAHUA

ALTHOUGH THE BREED'S ORIGINS ARE debatable, and probably South American, he may have been originally from China, taking his name from the Mexican state of Chihuahua where first he came to prominence in around 1895. Not long after this he reached El Paso in Texas and it was American dog lovers who refined the breed, seeing it to a high Toy position. The Chihuahua is the smallest breed of dog in the world. Aptly described as cheeky and with a saucy expression, there is no doubt he thinks he is a big dog – and at heart he is. His size makes him easy to take anywhere. He is highly intelligent, easily trained and makes a delightful companion. Elderly people find him an ideal pet, happy to be a much-loved lap dog and also a good house-dog announcing the approach of strangers. However, he is not a suitable pet for small children.

There are two varieties of Chihuahua – the Smooth Coat and the Long Coat.

Both the Smooth and the Long Coats have their special attractions, are equally easy to keep clean and well groomed.

GENERAL APPEARANCE Small, dainty, compact.

CHARACTERISTICS Alert little dog; swift-moving with brisk, forceful action and saucy expression.

TEMPERAMENT Gay, friendly, non-aggressive; no tendency to nervousness.

HEAD AND SKULL Well rounded 'apple dome' skull, cheeks and jaws lean, muzzle moderately short, slightly pointed. Definite stop.

EYES Large, round, but not protruding; set well apart; centre of eye is on a plane with lowest point of ear and base of stop; dark or ruby. Light eyes in light colours permissible.

EARS Large, flaring, set-on at an angle of approximately 45 degrees; giving breadth between ears. Tipped or broken down highly undesirable.

MOUTH Jaws strong, with a perfect, regular and complete scissor bite, i.e. upper teeth closely overlapping lower teeth and set square to the jaws.

NECK Slightly arched, medium length.

FOREQUARTERS Shoulders well laid; lean, sloping into slightly broadening support above straight forelegs, set well under chest giving freedom of movement without looseness.

BODY Level back. Body, from point of shoulder to rear point of croup, slightly longer than height at withers. Well sprung ribs, deep brisket.

HINDQUARTERS Muscular; hocks well let down, with good turn of stifle, well apart, turning neither in nor out.

FEET Small and dainty, turning neither in nor out; toes divided but not spread, pads cushioned, fine, strong, flexible pasterns. Neither hare- nor cat-like, nails moderately short.

TAIL Medium length, set high, carried up and over back (sickle tail). When moving never tucked under or curled below the topline. Furry, flattish in appearance, broadening slightly in centre and tapering to point.

GAIT/MOVEMENT Brisk, forceful action, neither high-stepping nor hackney; good reach without slackness in forequarters, good drive in hindquarters. Viewed from front and behind legs should move neither too close nor too wide, with no turning in or out of feet or pasterns. Topline should remain firm and level when moving.

COAT
LONG COAT: soft texture (never coarse or harsh to touch) either flat or slightly wavy. Never tight and curly. Feathering on ears, feet and legs, pants on hindquarters, large ruff on neck desirable. Tail long and full as a plume.
SMOOTH COAT: smooth, of soft texture, close and glossy, with undercoat and ruff permissible.

COLOUR Any colour or mixture of colours.

SIZE Weight: up to 2.7 kg (6 lb), with 1–1.8 kg (2–4 lb) preferred. If two dogs are equally good in type the more diminutive preferred.

FAULTS Any departure from the foregoing points should be considered a fault and the seriousness with which the fault should be regarded should be in exact proportion to its degree.

NOTE Male animals should have two apparently normal testicles fully descended into the scrotum.

CHINESE CRESTED DOG

THESE UNIQUE LITTLE DOGS COME IN two varieties – the Hairless and the Powder Puff. The 'Hairless' have a crest of hair on their head extending part way down their neck, 'socks' covering their toes, and a plume on their tail. The rest of their body is, as their name implies, hairless, and moisturisers are frequently used to keep the skin fine and supple. The 'Powder Puff' variety is covered entirely with a veil of long soft hair. Both varieties come in a mixture of colours, and can be plain or spotted. This is most definitely a breed for the connoisseur.

While it is difficult to pinpoint their origin, it is said and that they were owned by families of the Han Dynasty of China. The Chinese Cresteds were developed at this time as guardians of the treasure houses and, in a larger, heavier form, as hunting dogs. They were seen at shows in America from 1885 to 1926 but then were rarely ever seen for some fifty years. They are a fastidious breed, keeping themselves scrupulously clean, and have no 'doggy' odour. Affectionate and intelligent, with a strong constitution, they make unique and delightful companions and are good watch dogs.

GENERAL APPEARANCE A small, active and graceful dog; medium- to fine-boned, smooth hairless body, with hair on feet, head and tail only; or covered with a soft veil of hair.

CHARACTERISTICS Two distinct types of this breed; Deer type, racy and fine-boned, and Cobby type, heavier in body and bone.

TEMPERAMENT Happy, never vicious.

HEAD AND SKULL Slightly rounded and elongated skull. Cheeks cleanly chiselled, lean and flat, tapering into muzzle. Stop slightly pronounced but not extreme. Head smooth, without excess wrinkles. Distance from base of skull to stop equal to distance from stop to tip of nose. Muzzle tapering slightly but never pointed, lean without flews. Nose a prominent feature, narrow in keeping with muzzle. Any colour nose acceptable. Head presenting graceful appearance, with alert expression. Lips tight and thin. An ideal crest begins at the stop and tapers off down neck. Long and flowing crest preferred, but sparse acceptable.

EYES So dark as to appear black. Little or no white showing. Medium size, almond in shape. Set wide apart.

EARS Set low: highest point of base of ear level with outside corner of eye. Large and erect, with or without fringe, except in Powder Puffs where drop ears are permissible.

MOUTH Jaws strong, with perfect, regular scissor bite, i.e. upper teeth closely overlapping lower teeth and set square to the jaws.

NECK Lean, free from throatiness, long and sloping gracefully into strong shoulders. When moving, carried high and slightly arched.

FOREQUARTERS Shoulders clean, narrow and well laid back. Legs long and slender, set well under body. Elbows held close to body. Pasterns fine, strong, nearly vertical. Toes turned neither in nor out.

BODY Medium to long. Supple. Chest rather broad and deep, not barrel-ribbed. Breast bone not prominent. Brisket extending to elbows; moderate tuck-up.

HINDQUARTERS Rump well rounded and muscular, loins taut, stifles firm and long, sweeping smoothly into the well let down hocks. Angulation of the rear limbs must be such as to produce a level back. Hindlegs set wide apart.

FEET Extreme harefoot, narrow and very long with unique elongation of small bones between

joints, especially in forefeet, which almost appear to possess an extra joint. Nails any colour, moderately long. Socks ideally confined to toes, but not extending above top of pastern. Feet turning neither in nor out.

TAIL Set high, carried up or out when in motion. Long and tapering, fairly straight, not curled or twisted to either side, falling naturally when at rest. Plume long and flowing, confined to lower two-thirds of tail. Sparse plume acceptable.

GAIT/MOVEMENT Long, flowing and elegant with good reach and plenty of drive.

COAT No large patches of hair anywhere on body. Skin fine-grained, smooth, warm to the touch. In Powder Puffs coat consists of an undercoat with soft veil of long hair, veil coat a feature.

COLOUR Any colour or combination of colours.

SIZE Ideal height in dogs: 28–33 cm (11–13 in) at withers; bitches: 23–30 cm (9–12 in) at withers. Weight varies considerably, but should not be over 5.5 kg (12 lb).

FAULTS Any departure from the foregoing points should be considered a fault and the seriousness with which the fault should be regarded should be in exact proportion to its degree.

NOTE Male animal should have two apparently normal testicles fully descended from the scrotum.

BELOW: *The Powder Puff*

ENGLISH TOY TERRIER (BLACK AND TAN)

BEFORE 1960 THIS BREED WAS KNOWN AS the Miniature Black and Tan Terrier, but devotees felt that this name was one which any terrier type in black and tan could utilise, so the name was changed to English Toy Terrier. Black and Tan terrier types can trace their history back at least to the early sixteenth century. Small Black and Tans were kept in the Regency and Georgian periods and were used variously to help flush foxes and in the rat-fighting pits. But it was as a town dog that the breed really became popular and the late 1800s saw a selective breeding programme.

This oldest of Britain's native toy breeds is not aggressive. The smooth, glossy coat requires minimal care. He makes a charming, intelligent companion.

GENERAL APPEARANCE Well balanced, elegant and compact, sleek and cleanly built.

CHARACTERISTICS Toy with terrier characteristics.

TEMPERAMENT Alert, remembering that historically he could acquit himself satisfactorily in the rat pit. Never unduly nervous.

HEAD AND SKULL Head long, narrow, flat skull, wedge-shaped without emphasis of cheek muscles, well filled up under eyes. Top and bottom jaws held tightly together within compressed lips. Slight stop. Foreface tapers gently to provide wedge-shaped impression, in profile similar to that seen when viewed from front. Although an illusion of being overshot can result, any suggestion of snipy appearance is undesirable. Nose black.

EYES Dark to black, without light shading from iris. Small, almond-shaped, obliquely set and sparkling.

EARS Candle-flame shape, slightly pointed tips, placed high upon back of skull and proportionately close together. A guide to size can be obtained by bending ear forward – it should not reach eye. From nine months of age ear carriage must be erect. Entire inside of ear should face front. Leather of ear thin.

MOUTH Jaws strong, with a perfect, regular and complete scissor bite, i.e. upper teeth closely overlapping lower teeth and set square to the jaws. Teeth level and strong.

NECK Long, graceful, slightly arched. Shoulders well laid back. Line of neck flowing into shoulders, and sloping off elegantly. Throatiness undesirable.

FOREQUARTERS Legs falling straight from shoulders with elbows close to chest providing a straight front. Fine bone eminently desirable.

BODY Body compact, head and legs proportionate thus producing correct balance. Back very slightly curving from behind shoulder to loin, falling again to root of tail. Chest narrow and deep with ribs well sprung. Loins well cut up. Buttocks gently rounded.

HINDQUARTERS Well rounded loin leading to a good turn of stifle; hocks well let down; turning neither in nor out; a 'tucked under' appearance undesirable.

FEET Dainty, compact; split up between toes; well arched, with jet black nails, two middle toes of front feet rather longer than others, hind feet cat-like. Harefeet undesirable.

TAIL Thick at root, tapering to point. Set low and not reaching below hock. 'Gay' tail undesirable if displayed to excess.

GAIT/MOVEMENT Ideal fore-movement akin to the 'extended trot'; hackney action not desirable; equally a 'shuffling gait' undesirable. Hind action smooth with ease and precision combined with drive, there should be flowing quality to indicate true soundness.

COAT Thick, close and glossy. A density of short hair required.

COLOUR Black and Tan. The black ebony, the tan likened to a new chestnut deeply rich. Colours not running or blending into each other, but meeting abruptly, forming clear and well defined lines of colour division. Forelegs tanned to knees in front. The tan then continuing inside and at back of forelegs to point just below elbows, the thin black line up each toe (pencilling) and a clearly defined black mark (thumbmark) on centre of each pastern, and under chin. Hindlegs well tanned in front and inside with black bar dividing tan at centre of lower thigh. Heavy tan on outside of hindquarters (breeching) undesirable. Muzzle well tanned. Nose black, the black continuing along top of muzzle, curving below eyes to base of throat. A tan spot above each eye and a small tan spot on each cheek. Under-jaw and throat tanned, lip line back. Hair inside ears tan (tan behind ears undesirable). Each side of chest has some tan. Vent and under root of tail, tan. White hairs forming a patch anywhere totally undesirable.

SIZE Ideal weight: 2.7-3.6 kg (6-8 lb). Ideal height: 25-30 cm (10-12 in) at the shoulder.

FAULTS Any departure from the foregoing points should be considered a fault and the seriousness with which the fault should be regarded should be in exact proportion to its degree.

NOTE Male animals should have two apparently normal testicles fully descended into the scrotum.

GRIFFON BRUXELLOIS

P ERT, WITH A MONKEY FACE, THIS
enchanting toy dog, whose origins are in
Belgium, is a constant source of
amusement and delight to those fortunate
enough to be owned by him. There are two
varieties – rough and smooth, the latter
known as Petit Brabançon. The breed has
been called the Belgian Street Urchin and
a variety of this little dog appeared in a
painting by the Flemish artist Jan van Eyck
as long ago as 1434. The breed was already
standard in type by the 1600s. The main
ingredient behind the Griffon Bruxellois is
the Affenpinscher and at one time he earned
his keep as a stable dog where horses for
hansom cabs were kept. The Griffon arrived
in Britain in the late 1800s.

His terrier-like qualities make him happy
to indulge in plenty of exercise. He is
fearless, not yappy but a good house-dog,
and a devoted companion who suits either
town or country.

The rough-coated variety do require
stripping once or twice a year, but regular
grooming with a hound glove will keep the
smooth-coated dogs in shining condition.

GENERAL APPEARANCE A cobby, well-
balanced, square little dog, giving appearance of
measuring the same from withers to tail root as
from withers to ground.

CHARACTERISTICS Smart little dog with
disposition of a terrier. Two varieties, rough
coated, Griffon Bruxellois and the smooth
coated, Petit Brabançon. Both with pert,
monkey-like expression, heavy for size.

TEMPERAMENT Lively and alert.

HEAD AND SKULL Head large in
comparison to body, rounded but in no
way domed, wide between the ears. Hair
on skull, in roughs rather coarse. Nose
always black, as short as possible with large
open nostrils, high-set sloping back to skull
with deep stop between nose and skull.
Wide muzzle, neat lips, with good turn-up.
Chin prominent, in roughs furnished
with beard.

EYES Black-rimmed, very dark, large, round,
clear and alert.

EARS Semi-erect, high-set, the smaller the
better.

MOUTH Slightly undershot with even teeth, not
showing teeth or tongue.

NECK Medium length, slightly arched, springing
from well laid back shoulders.

FOREQUARTERS Chest rather wide and deep,
legs straight of medium length and bone.

BODY Short back, level from withers to tail
root, neither roaching nor dipping; deep; well-
sprung ribs, short, strong loin.

HINDQUARTERS Well muscled thighs of good
length, hocks low to ground, turning neither in
nor out, stifles well bent.

FEET Small, thick, cat-like with black toenails.

TAIL Customarily docked short, carried high, emerging at right angles from level topline.

GAIT/MOVEMENT Free with good drive from rear. Moving true coming and going. High-stepping movement undesirable.

COAT
ROUGHS: harsh, wiry, free from curl, preferably with undercoat.
SMOOTHS: short and tight.

COLOUR Clear red, black or black and rich tan without white markings. In clear red, a darker shade on mask and ears undesirable. Ideally each hair should be an even red from tip to root. Frosting on muzzles of mature smooths should not be penalised.

SIZE From 2.2–4.9 kg (5–11 lb); most desirable 2.7–4.5 kg (6–10 lb).

FAULTS Any departure from the foregoing points should be considered a fault and the seriousness with which the fault should be regarded should be in exact proportion to its degree.

NOTE Male animals should have two apparently normal testicles fully descended into the scrotum.

HAVANESE

KNOWN AT HOME AS THE BICHON Habanero, the Havanese ranks as the national dog of Cuba. The breed reached Cuba as a result of either Spanish colonists or Italian traders and ended up as the playthings of the wealthy. When the communist regime took control of Cuba, many major breeders/owners fled to the USA taking their dogs with them.

The Havanese is a lively toy dog, not in any way delicate, but well able to stand up for himself in boisterous play. At one time known as the Havana Silk Dog, his coat should be long and soft; it should not be scissored into shape. All manner of colours are allowed, from white through cream to black, blue, silver and chocolate.

Affectionate and intelligent, the breed enjoys being the centre of the family circle but does not expect to rule the roost.

GENERAL APPEARANCE Small, sturdy, slightly longer in body than height at withers. Profusely coated, tail carried in plume over back.

CHARACTERISTICS Lively, affectionate and intelligent.

TEMPERAMENT Friendly, outgoing.

HEAD AND SKULL Nose to stop and stop to occiput to be equal in length, skull broad, slightly rounded, moderate stop. Muzzle not snipy or blunt, cheeks flat. Nose and lips solid black, although for brown shades the pigment may be brown.

EYES Dark, large, almond-shaped, gentle expression, eye rims black. In brown shades eyes can be a slightly lighter colour, eye rims brown.

EARS Moderately pointed and dropped, set-on just above eye level, slightly raised, neither fly away nor framing the cheeks.

MOUTH Jaws strong with perfect regular scissor bite, i.e. upper teeth closely overlapping the lower teeth and set square to the jaws.

NECK Medium length.

FOREQUARTERS Legs straight, medium bone. Shoulders well laid.

BODY Equal in height from withers to elbow as from elbow to ground. Slightly longer from point of shoulder to point of buttock than height at withers, level topline, slight rise over loin, well sprung ribs, with good tuck-up.

HINDQUARTERS Medium boned, moderate angulation.

FEET Small, tight, harefoot.

TAIL Set high, carried over the back; profusely feathered with long silky hair.

GAIT/MOVEMENT Free with a springy step, legs moving parallel to the line of travel.

COAT Soft, silky, wavy or slightly curled, full coated with an undercoat.

COLOUR Any colour or combination of colours permissible.

SIZE Ideal height: 23–28 cm (9–11 in).

FAULTS Any departure from the foregoing points should be considered a fault and the seriousness with which the fault should be regarded should be in exact proportion to its degree.

NOTE Male animals should have two apparently normal testicles fully descended into the scrotum.

ITALIAN GREYHOUND

A GRACEFUL, RACY LITTLE DOG WHICH claims a background dating back to the days of Pompeii, he found his way to Britain in the seventeenth century. Evidence that small hounds of this type existed can be found in the ancient tombs of Egypt but it was in the Italy of the Romans that the Italian Greyhound was bred to perfection. It is probable that this was the first breed ever to be developed as a pet and a lap dog.

Cheerful, brave and courageous, with exquisitely delicate lines, he has a gentle and loving nature. He is comfort-loving, and will happily wrap himself in a blanket.

Daily grooming is easily carried out with a velvet pad, or a piece of silk. Coat colours come in a particularly attractive range from all shades of gold and blue to parti-colour and pied.

Ideal as a pet for town, he is still a dog that likes plenty of exercise, and can run with the best over fields. He has a Dresden-like quality, but is by no means delicate.

GENERAL APPEARANCE A greyhound in miniature, more slender in all proportions.

CHARACTERISTICS Elegant, graceful and quick-moving.

TEMPERAMENT Intelligent, affectionate and vivacious; may appear aloof.

HEAD AND SKULL Skull long, flat and narrow, slight stop. Muzzle fine and long. Nose dark in colour.

EYES Rather large, bright; full of expression.

EARS Rose-shaped, placed well back, soft and fine, not pricked.

MOUTH Jaws strong, with a perfect, regular and complete scissor bite, i.e. upper teeth closely overlapping lower teeth and set square to the jaws. Teeth even.

NECK Long, gracefully arched.

FOREQUARTERS Shoulders long and sloping. Legs straight; well set under shoulders; fine, strong bone and pasterns.

BODY Chest deep and narrow. Good length of rib and brisket. Back slightly arched over loin.

HINDQUARTERS Long, well muscled thigh: hind legs, parallel when viewed from behind; well bent stifle, hocks well let down.

FEET Hare feet.

TAIL Low-set, long, fine, carried low.

GAIT/MOVEMENT High-stepping and free action. Front and hindlegs to move forward in a straight line with propulsion from behind.

COAT Skin fine and supple. Hair, short, fine and glossy.

COLOUR Black, blue, cream, fawn, red, white, or any of these colours broken with white. White dogs may be broken with one of these colours. Black or blue with tan markings, or brindle not acceptable.

SIZE Weight from 2.7-4.5 kg (6-10 lb).

FAULTS Any departure from the foregoing points should be considered a fault and the seriousness with which the fault should be regarded should be in exact proportion to its degree.

NOTE Male animals should have two apparently normal testicles fully descended into the scrotum.

JAPANESE CHIN

THE JAPANESE CHIN IS AN ORIENTAL aristocrat in bearing and demeanour. History tells us that he originated in China and made his way to Japan as a gift from the Empress of one country to the Empress of the other.

In some parts of the world the breed is known as the Japanese Spaniel. The word 'chin' means cat-like and he does use his paws in the manner of a cat to wash his face. This is a dainty, little dog, but is in no way delicate. He is bright and intelligent, very stylish and extrovert, with a perpetual look of astonishment that is a breed characteristic. Charming and beautiful, he tends to leave tell-tale signs on the furniture as his profuse black and white, or red and white coat does shed and needs regular weekly care. He does not make a suitable pet for small children, who may not be able to resist picking him up and could accidentally drop him.

GENERAL APPEARANCE Elegant and aristocratic, smart, compact, with profuse coat.

CHARACTERISTICS Intelligent, happy, lively little dog who has look of astonishment, peculiar to this breed.

TEMPERAMENT Gay, happy, gentle and good-natured.

HEAD AND SKULL Large in proportion to size of dog, broad skull, rounded in front, and between ears, but never domed. Nostrils large, black, except in red and whites where the colour can be appropriate to markings. Muzzle very short, wide, well cushioned, i.e. upper lips rounded on each side of nostrils, jaws level.

EYES Large, dark, set far apart. Most desirable that white shows in the inner corners, giving characteristic look of astonishment (wrongly called squint), which should on no account be lost.

EARS Small, set wide apart, high on head, carried slightly forward, V-shaped, well feathered.

MOUTH Bite preferably level or slightly undershot; wry mouth or tongue showing highly undesirable.

NECK Moderate length, carried proudly.

FOREQUARTERS Legs straight, fine bone, giving slender appearance, well feathered down to the feet.

BODY Square and compactly built, wide in chest, 'cobby'. Length of body equal to height at withers.

HINDQUARTERS Straight, viewed from behind, good turn of stifle, profusely feathered from the back of thighs.

FEET Slender, harefooted, feathered at tips, pointing neither in nor out.

TAIL Set high on level back, profusely feathered, closely curved or plumed over back.

GAIT/MOVEMENT Stylish, straight in movement, lifting the feet high when in motion, no plaiting, and showing no weakness in hind movement.

COAT Profuse, long, soft, straight, of silky texture. Absolutely free from curl or wave, not too flat, having a tendency to stand out especially at frill of neck.

COLOUR Black and white or red and white. Never tricolour. Red includes all shades of sable, lemon or orange. The brighter and clearer the red the better. Colour evenly distributed on cheeks and ears and as patches on body. White should be clear, not flecked.

SIZE Daintier the better, providing type, quality and soundness are not sacrificed. Ideal weight: 1.8-3.2 kg (4-7 lb).

FAULTS Any departure from the foregoing points should be considered a fault and the seriousness with which the fault should be regarded should be in exact proportion to its degree.

NOTE Male animals should have two apparently normal testicles fully descended into the scrotum.

KING CHARLES SPANIEL

AN OBVIOUS RELATIVE OF THE CAVALIER King Charles Spaniel, this dog is known in some countries as the English Toy Spaniel, and derives his name from a dog which was a great favourite of King Charles II. Toy spaniels have long been treasured as pets both in England and on the Continent and were bred to a smaller and smaller size from setter dogs which established the type for spaniels. Basically these were little gun dogs, but pampered by wealthy owners, admired for their companionship and crossed with toy dogs from the East, giving rise to their facial appearance.

He is compact, with a very distinctive domed skull, and has a wide, deep, turned-up muzzle. His large, dark eyes give him a soft, appealing expression. His long, silky coat is easily cared for, and he is clean and quiet in his habits. A true aristocrat, he is elegant and cheerful, and makes a very affectionate, devoted companion.

GENERAL APPEARANCE Refined, compact and cobby.

CHARACTERISTICS Happy, intelligent, toy spaniel, with distinctive domed head.

TEMPERAMENT Reserved, gentle and affectionate.

HEAD AND SKULL Skull large in comparison to size, well domed, full over eyes. Nose black with large, wide-open nostrils, very short and turned up to meet skull. Stop between skull and nose well defined. Muzzle square, wide and deep, well turned up, lower jaw wide, lips exactly meeting, giving nice finish. Cheeks not falling away under eyes, but well cushioned.

EYES Very large and dark, set wide apart, eyelids block square to face line, pleasing expression.

EARS Set-on low, hanging quite flat to cheeks, very long and well feathered.

MOUTH Bite should be slightly undershot. Protruding tongue highly undesirable.

NECK Of medium length; arched giving proud carriage of head.

FOREQUARTERS Legs short, straight. Shoulders well laid back, elbows close to ribcage, turning neither in nor out.

BODY Chest wide and deep, back short and level.

HINDQUARTERS Sufficient muscle to give positive driving movement, stifles well bent, hocks well let down and defined. Straight when viewed from behind, turning neither in nor out.

FEET Compact, well padded and feathered, toes well knuckled, round cat-shaped foot, well cushioned, pasterns firm. Occasionally central pads and nails fused together.

TAIL Well feathered, not carried over or above level of back. Docking optional.

GAIT/MOVEMENT Free, active and elegant, driving from behind. Sound movement highly undesirable.

COAT Long, silky and straight, slight wave allowed, never curly. Legs, ears and tail profusely feathered.

COLOUR
BLACK AND TAN: rich glossy black, with bright mahogany-tan markings on muzzle, legs, chest, linings of ears, under tail and spots over eyes. White patch on chest undesirable.
TRICOLOUR: ground pearly white, with well distributed black patches, brilliant tan markings on cheeks, linings of ears, under tail and spots over eyes. Wide white blaze between eyes and up forehead.

BLENHEIM: ground pearly white, with well distributed chestnut-red patches. Wide, clear blaze with the 'spot' in centre of skull, should be a clear chestnut red mark about the size of a penny.

RUBY: whole coloured, rich chestnut red. White patch on chest highly undesirable.

SIZE Weight: 3.6–6.3 kg (8–14 lb).

FAULTS Any departure from the foregoing points should be considered a fault and the seriousness with which the fault should be regarded should be in exact proportion to its degree.

NOTE Male animals should have two apparently normal testicles fully descended into the scrotum.

LOWCHEN
(LITTLE LION DOG)

HIS ORIGINS ARE OBSCURE, PROBABLY European, and it is suggested that he has affinities with the Bichon. He is known as the 'Little Lion Dog', because of the manner in which he is trimmed, with his full mane resembling a lion. To the uninitiated he may look like a Poodle, but there are very distinct differences – first and foremost the head, which is short and wide with large eyes. He also has a fine, long, silky coat.

He is most attractive and his coat comes in a variety of colours. A friendly, happy little dog, very active and playful, he is very affectionate, good with children, and makes an excellent house pet.

The Lowchen's home country is listed as France though the breed has been established in Spain and Germany as well as France since the 1500s. As recently as 1960 the Lowchen was described as being the rarest breed in the world, following years of decline and loss of favour, but it has increased in numbers, being registered in Britain for the first time in 1971 and gaining championship status here just five years later.

GENERAL APPEARANCE Coat clipped in traditional lion clip, tail also clipped, topped with plume, giving appearance of a little lion. Strongly built, active, well balanced and alert.

CHARACTERISTICS Gay, happy, lively little dog.

TEMPERAMENT Intelligent, affectionate, showing no sign of aggression.

HEAD AND SKULL Short, fairly broad. Skull flat between the ears, head carried proud and high. Well defined stop; short, strong muzzle.

EYES Round, dark, large and intelligent. Unbroken pigmentation of eye rims, pigment to be in accordance with coat colour.

EARS Ears pendant, of moderate length with long fringing.

MOUTH Jaws strong, with perfect, regular and complete scissor bite, i.e. upper teeth closely overlapping lower teeth and set square to the jaws.

NECK Good length, proudly arched.

FOREQUARTERS Forelegs straight and fine. Shoulders well laid.

BODY Short, strong and well proportioned. Level topline. Ribs well sprung. Strong loin with moderate tuck-up.

HINDQUARTERS Hindlegs well muscled, with good turn of stifle; straight when viewed from rear.

FEET Small, round.

TAIL Medium length, clipped with tuft of hair to resemble a plume. Carried gaily on move.

GAIT/MOVEMENT Free, parallel movement fore and aft, no hackneyed action.

COAT Fairly long, wavy, never curly. Single coat of soft texture.

COLOUR Any colour or combination of colours permissible.

SIZE Height at withers: 25-33 cm (10-13 in).

FAULTS Any departure from the foregoing points should be considered a fault and the seriousness with which the fault should be regarded should be in exact proportion to its degree.

NOTE Male animals should have two apparently normal testicles fully descended into the scrotum.

MALTESE

IN VIEW OF HIS ISLAND ORIGIN, THE Maltese is likely to have been a pure breed for many years. Small dogs of the type have been known around the Mediterranean for centuries and, as with many breeds, were traded by the Phoenicians as they sailed from country to country. There is evidence that the breed was in Malta in Roman times and the dogs were bred as pets, both as lap dogs and 'sleeve' dogs, carried in the coat sleeve.

One of the sweetest of the Toy breeds, the Maltese needs a lot of attention to keep his long, soft, silky coat in immaculate - condition. Much of his beauty comes from the stark contrast of his dark eyes with their black rims, and black nose against his pure white coat. To achieve the correct expression the head must be equally balanced from stop to occiput, and stop to tip of nose.

His temperament is merry and friendly, and he is very bright and intelligent. A lively little dog, full of fun, who belies his chocolate-box appearance.

GENERAL APPEARANCE Smart, white-coated dog, with proud head carriage.

CHARACTERISTICS Lively, intelligent, alert.

TEMPERAMENT Sweet-tempered.

HEAD AND SKULL From stop to centre of skull (centre between forepart of ears) and stop to tip of nose, equally balanced. Stop well defined. Nose black. Muzzle broad, well filled under eye. Not snipy.

EYES Oval, not bulging, dark brown, black eye rims, with dark haloes.

EARS Long, well feathered, hanging close to head; hair to mingle with coat at shoulders.

MOUTH Jaws strong, with perfect, regular and complete scissor bite, i.e. upper teeth closely overlapping lower teeth and set square to the jaws. Teeth even.

NECK Medium length.

FOREQUARTERS Legs short and straight. Shoulders well sloped.

BODY Well balanced, essentially short and cobby. Good spring of rib, back level from withers to tail.

HINDQUARTERS Legs short, well angulated.

FEET Round, pads black.

TAIL Feathered, carried well arched over back.

GAIT/MOVEMENT Free and free-flowing, without weaving.

COAT Good length, not impeding action, straight, of silky texture, never woolly. Never crimped and without woolly undercoat.

COLOUR Pure white, but slight lemon markings permissible.

SIZE Height not exceeding 25.5 cm (10 in) from ground to withers.

FAULTS Any departure from the foregoing points should be considered a fault and the seriousness with which the fault should be regarded should be in exact proportion to its degree.

NOTE Male animals should have two apparently normal testicles fully descended into the scrotum.

MINIATURE PINSCHER

THE BREED IS SMART AND CLEAN IN outline, sturdy and compact in body and features a unique hackney gait. He is lively and high-spirited with quick reactions, and has a keen sense of hearing which makes him a good little guard dog.

He originated in Germany and really started to make his mark in Britain after the Second World War. Stylish, friendly and free from vice, he has a lustrous short coat, and is an ideal size for even a small home. 'Pinscher' in German means terrier and the miniature was developed from the larger smooth-coated variety. Having now been bred for some hundred years, he appeared in the form we know around 1915.

GENERAL APPEARANCE Well balanced, sturdy, compact, elegant, short-coupled, smooth-coated Toy dog. Naturally well groomed, proud, vigorous and alert.

CHARACTERISTICS Precise hackney gait, fearless animation, complete self-possession and spirited presence.

TEMPERAMENT Fearless and alert.

HEAD AND SKULL More elongated than short and round. Narrow, without conspicuous cheek formation. In proportion to body. Skull flat when viewed from front. Muzzle rather strong and proportionate to skull. Nostrils well formed. Nose black with the exception of chocolate and blue in which it may be self-coloured.

EYES Fitting well into face. Neither too full nor round, nor too small or slanting. Black or nearly black.

EARS Set-on high, as small as possible, erect or dropped.

MOUTH Jaws strong, with a perfect, regular and complete scissor bite, i.e. upper teeth closely overlapping lower teeth and set square to the jaws.

NECK Strong yet graceful, slightly arched. Well fitted into shoulders. Free from throatiness.

FOREQUARTERS Forechest well developed and full, moderately broad; shoulders clean, sloping with moderate angulation. Legs straight, medium bone, elbows close to body.

BODY Square, back line straight, sloping towards rear. Belly moderately tucked-up. Ribs well sprung, deep rather than barrelled. Viewed from top slightly wedge-shaped.

HINDQUARTERS Parallel and wide enough apart to fit in with a properly built body. Hindquarters well developed, muscular with good sweep of stifle, and hocks turning neither in nor out. Legs straight, medium bone.

FEET Cat-like; nails dark.

TAIL Continuation of topline carried a little high and customarily docked short.

GAIT/MOVEMENT Co-ordinated to permit a true hackneyed action.

COAT Smooth, hard and short. Straight and lustrous. Closely adhering to and uniformly covering body. Hair forming ridge on any part of head, body or legs highly undesirable.

COLOUR Black, blue, chocolate with sharply defined tan markings on cheeks, lips, lower jaw,

throat, twin spots above eyes and chest, lower half of forelegs, inside of hindlegs and vent region, lower portion of hocks and feet.
All above colours have black pencilling on toes without thumbmarks except chocolates which have brown pencilling. Solid red of various shades. Slight white on chest permissible but undesirable.

SIZE Height from 25.5-30 cm (10-12 in) at withers.

FAULTS Any departure from the foregoing points should be considered a fault and the seriousness with which the fault should be regarded should be in exact proportion to its degree.

NOTE Male animals should have two apparently normal testicles fully descended into the scrotum.

PAPILLON

THIS BREED HAS TWO COUNTRIES LISTED as its home, France and Belgium, in both of which it is known as the Continental Toy Spaniel, Papillon, or, in a drop-eared version, Phalene. The erect-eared version takes its name from the French word for butterfly while the drop-eared is named after the moth.

The Papillon was developing on the Continent at the same time as the King Charles was developing in Britain, both deriving from the toy spaniels of the day.

The Papillon, an exquisite little toy dog, is a lively breed requiring much human companionship. He is happy, easy to teach and train and has proved himself extremely clever in obedience. The breed can be said to be proud and extrovert.

His long silky coat can be kept immaculate by daily brushing with a soft brush, and occasional combing.

He has a long life-span, makes a fascinating and interesting companion, but is not the pet for small children.

GENERAL APPEARANCE Dainty, well balanced little dog. An alert bearing and intelligent expression.

CHARACTERISTICS The name 'Papillon' is derived from the shape and position of the ears. When erect they are carried obliquely like the spread wings of a butterfly, hence the name. When the ears are completely dropped this type is known as the 'Phalene' (Moth). Head markings should be symmetrical, about a narrow white, clearly defined blaze which is desirable but not essential to represent the body of a butterfly.

TEMPERAMENT Lively, intelligent, friendly, with no aggression; always alert.

HEAD AND SKULL Skull slightly rounded between ears, muzzle finely pointed and abruptly finer than the skull, accentuating well defined stop. Length from tip of nose to stop approximately one-third of length of head. Nose black.

EYES Medium size, rounded, never bulging, dark with dark rims, placed rather low in skull.

EARS Very large, mobile with rounded tips, heavily fringed; set towards back of head far enough apart to show slightly rounded shape of skull. Leathers firm but fine. When erect each ear should form an angle of approximately 45 degrees to head.

MOUTH Jaws strong, with perfect regular, and complete scissor bite, i.e. upper teeth closely overlapping lower teeth and set square to the jaws. Lips thin, tight and dark in colour.

NECK Medium length.

FOREQUARTERS Shoulders well developed and sloping. Chest rather deep. Forelegs straight, slender and fine boned. Elbows close to chest.

BODY Fairly long with level topline; well sprung ribs, loin strong, of good length, slightly arched belly.

HINDQUARTERS Well developed, well turned stifle. Legs when viewed from behind parallel. Dewclaws on hindlegs removed.

FEET Fine, fairly long, hare-like. Tufts of hair between toes extending far beyond them.

TAIL Long, well fringed, set-on high, arched over back with fringes falling to side to form plume.

GAIT/MOVEMENT Light, free-flowing, positive and free from any restriction. Viewed from in front or behind, legs and feet moving parallel to each other, with feet turning neither in nor out. Viewed from side, dog covering ground well with no hint of hackneyed action.

COAT Abundant, flowing but without undercoat; long, fine and silky, falling flat on back and sides; profuse frill on chest; short and close on skull, muzzle and front parts of legs. Rear of forelegs to pasterns, tail and thighs covered with long hair.

COLOUR White with patches, which may be any colour except liver. Tricolours, black and white with tan spots over eyes, tan inside ears, on cheeks, and under root of tail.

SIZE Height: 20-28 cm (8-11 in). Dog will appear slightly longer than high when properly furnished with ruff and hind fringes.

FAULTS Any departure from the foregoing points should be considered a fault and the seriousness with which the fault should be regarded should be in exact proportion to its degree.

NOTE Male animals should have two apparently normal testicles fully descended into the scrotum.

PEKINGESE

THE PEKINGESE IS OFTEN THOUGHT OF as a lap dog for elderly ladies, but nothing could be further from the truth. He is an aristocrat, whose ancestry can be traced back to the Tang Dynasty. Similar dogs have been known in China since the eighth century but by the early 1800s had become the favourites of the Imperial court with no commoner being allowed to own one. However, following the British sacking of Peking in 1860 four were found and brought back to England. Subsequently others were obtained by more normal means. The Pekingese was accepted in America in 1909 and in Britain the following year.

He has a sense of humour, but also lots of dignity which he assumes when the mood so takes him. Mischievous and playful, loving and sensitive, he is reputed to have the heart of a lion, and upholds this reputation by guarding his toys and other possessions. He is courageous and, though not naturally aggressive, will stand up for himself if forced to do so.

Although he likes exercise he prefers to take it at his own pace, and is not the long country walk type! Strong and heavy for his size, he is, however, easy to tuck under an arm and take anywhere.

GENERAL APPEARANCE Small, well balanced, thick-set dog of dignity and quality.

CHARACTERISTICS Leonine in appearance with alert and intelligent expression.

TEMPERAMENT Fearless, loyal, aloof but not timid or aggressive.

HEAD AND SKULL Head large, proportionately wider than deep. Skull broad, wide and flat between ears; not domed; wide between eyes. Nose short and broad, nostrils large, open and black; muzzle wide, well wrinkled with firm under-jaw. Profile flat with nose well set between eyes. Pronounced stop. Black pigment essential on nose, lips and eye rims.

EYES Large, clear, round, dark and lustrous.

EARS Heart-shaped, set level with the skull and carried close to the head, with long profuse feathering. Leathers not to come below line of muzzle.

MOUTH Level lips, must not show teeth or tongue. Firm under-jaw essential.

NECK Very short and thick.

FOREQUARTERS Short, thick, heavily boned forelegs; bones of forelegs slightly bowed, firm at shoulder. Soundness essential.

BODY Short, broad chest and good spring of ribs, well slung between forelegs with distinct waist, level back.

HINDQUARTERS Hindlegs lighter than forelegs but firm and well shaped. Close behind but not cow-hocked. Soundness essential.

FEET Large and flat, not round. Standing well up on feet, not on pasterns. Front feet slightly turned out.

TAIL Set high, carried tightly, slightly curved over back to either side. Long feathering.

GAIT/MOVEMENT Slow dignified rolling gait in front. Typical movement not to be confused with a roll caused by slackness of shoulders. Close action behind. Absolute soundness essential.

COAT Long, straight with profuse mane extending beyond shoulders forming a cape round neck; top coat coarse with thick undercoat. Profuse feathering on ears, back of legs, tail and toes.

COLOUR All colours and markings are permissible and of equal merit, except albino or liver. Parti-colours evenly broken.

SIZE Ideal weight not exceeding 5 kg (11 lb) for dogs and 5.5 kg (12 lb) for bitches. Dogs should look small but be surprisingly heavy when picked up; heavy bone and a sturdy well-built body are essential of the breed.

FAULTS Any departure from the foregoing points should be considered a fault and the seriousness with which the fault should be regarded should be in exact proportion to its degree.

NOTE Male animals should have two apparently normal testicles fully descended into the scrotum.

POMERANIAN

THOUGH BRITAIN IS LISTED AS THE country of development of the Pomeranian, he is a Spitz-type dog descended from the much larger sled-hauling dogs of the Arctic and finding himself in the showring by way of Germany. The Pomeranian was bred from the German Spitz before becoming known in Britain in 1870 and entering the kennels of Queen Victoria in 1890, a move which popularised the breed. The Pomeranian Club was formed in 1891.

A dainty little extrovert, and the smallest of the Spitz-type of dogs, he is light-hearted, active and gay. His foxy head and abundant stand-off coat, covering his short barrelled body, give him the appearance of a ball of fluff. Although his undercoat is soft, his outer coat texture is far from fluffy, and requires regular attention to keep it clean and attractive.

He is lively and vivacious, sweet-tempered and affectionate.

GENERAL APPEARANCE Compact, short-coupled dog, well knit in frame. Exhibiting great intelligence in expression; activity and buoyancy in deportment.

CHARACTERISTICS Sound, vivacious and dainty.

TEMPERAMENT Extrovert, lively and intelligent.

HEAD AND SKULL Head and nose foxy in outline, skull slightly flat, large in proportion to muzzle which finishes finely and free from lippiness. Nose black in white, orange and shaded sable dogs; brown in chocolate-tipped sable dogs, but in other colours may be self-coloured, never parti-coloured or flesh.

EYES Medium size, slightly oval, not full, or set too wide apart; bright, dark and showing great intelligence. In white, orange, shaded sable and cream dogs, rims black.

EARS Small, not set too wide apart, nor too low down, but carried perfectly erect.

MOUTH Jaws strong, with a perfect, regular and complete scissor bite, i.e. upper teeth closely overlapping lower teeth and set square to the jaws.

NECK Rather short and well set into shoulders.

FOREQUARTERS Shoulders clean and well laid back. Fine-boned legs, perfectly straight, of medium length in due proportion to size of dog.

BODY Back short, body compact, well ribbed up, barrel well rounded. Chest fairly deep, not too wide but in proportion to size of dog.

HINDQUARTERS Fine-boned, legs neither cow-hocked nor wide behind; medium angulation.

FEET Small, compact and cat-like.

TAIL Characteristic of breed, high-set, turned over back and carried flat and straight, profusely covered with long, harsh, spreading hair.

GAIT/MOVEMENT Free moving, brisk and buoyant.

COAT Two coats, an undercoat and an outer coat. Former soft, fluffy; the latter long, perfectly straight, harsh in texture and covering whole of body; very abundant round neck and fore part of shoulders and chest; forming frill, extending over shoulders. Forequarters well feathered, thighs and hindlegs well feathered to hocks.

COLOUR All permissible, but free from black or white shadings. Whole colours are: white, black, brown, light or dark, blue as pale as possible. Orange which should be self-coloured and bright as possible. Beaver. Cream dogs have black noses and black eye rims. Whites must be quite free from lemon or any other colour. A few white hairs, in any of the self-coloured dogs permissible but undesirable. Dogs (other than white) with white or tan markings highly undesirable and not considered whole coloured specimens. In parti-coloured dogs, colours evenly distributed on body in patches; a dog with white or tan feet or chest not a parti-coloured dog. Shaded sables should be shaded throughout with three or more colours, the hair to be as uniformly shaded as possible, and with no patches of self-colour. In mixed classes, where whole coloured and parti-coloured Pomeranians compete together, the preference should, if in all other points they are equal, be given to the whole coloured specimens.

SIZE Ideal weight: dogs: 1.8-2 kg (4-4½ lb); bitches: 2-2.5 kg (4½-5½ lb).

FAULTS Any departure from the foregoing points should be considered a fault and the seriousness with which the fault should be regarded should be in exact proportion to its degree.

NOTE Male animals should have two apparently normal testicles fully descended into the scrotum.

PUG

A CERTAIN AMOUNT OF SPECULATION has taken place regarding the origin of this breed, which would seem to have come from the Orient. His home country is listed as China, where snub-nosed dogs have always been in favour. He found his way to Europe with traders of the Dutch East India Company and as far back as the 1500s was being admired in the Netherlands. In fact, the Pug became the symbol for the royal patriots just as the Keeshond became the symbol for the patriot commoners. The Pug arrived in England when William III came to the throne. Until 1877 the breed was seen here only in fawn but in that year a black pair was introduced from the Orient and The Kennel Club now allows four colourings. He was very popular with royalty and the aristocracy. These days he has a following in all walks of life.

A dignified dog, very intelligent, good-natured and sociable, he is robust and self-reliant, with great character and personality. An adaptable companion for both young and old, and one who integrates himself very closely with family life. He can talk with his eyes, has his mischievous moments, and usually lives to a ripe old age.

GENERAL APPEARANCE Decidedly square and cobby, it is 'multum in parvo' shown in compactness of form, well knit proportions and hardness of muscle.

CHARACTERISTICS Great charm, dignity and intelligence.

TEMPERAMENT Even-tempered, happy and lively disposition.

HEAD AND SKULL Head large, round, not apple-headed, with no indentation of skull. Muzzle short, blunt, square, not upfaced. Wrinkles clearly defined.

EYES Dark, very large, globular in shape, soft and solicitous in expression, very lustrous, and when excited, full of fire.

EARS Thin, small, soft like black velvet. Two kinds – 'Rose ear' – small drop-ear which folds over and back to reveal the burr. 'Button-ear' – ear flap folding forward, tip lying close to skull to cover opening. Preference given to latter.

MOUTH Slightly undershot. Wry mouth, teeth or tongue showing all highly undesirable. Wide lower jaw with incisors almost in a straight line.

NECK Slightly arched to resemble a crest, strong, thick with enough length to carry head proudly.

FOREQUARTERS Legs very strong, straight, of moderate length, and well under body. Shoulders well sloped.

BODY Short and cobby, wide in chest and well ribbed. Topline level neither roached nor dipping.

HINDQUARTERS Legs very strong, of moderate length, with good turn of stifle, well under body, straight and parallel when viewed from rear.

FEET Neither so long as the foot of the hare, nor so round as that of the cat; well split up toes; the nails black.

TAIL (Twist) High-set, curled as tightly as possible over hip. Double curl highly desirable.

GAIT/MOVEMENT Viewed from in front should rise and fall with legs well under shoulder, feet keeping directly to front, not turning in or out. From behind action just as true. Using forelegs strongly putting them well forward with hindlegs moving freely and using stifles well. A slight roll of hindquarters typifies gait.

COAT Fine, smooth, soft, short and glossy, neither harsh nor woolly.

COLOUR Silver, apricot, fawn or black. Each clearly defined, to make contrast complete between colour, trace (black line extending from occiput to twist) and mask. Markings clearly defined. Muzzle or mask, ears, moles on cheeks, thumbmark or diamond on forehead and trace as black as possible.

SIZE Ideal weight: 6.3-8.1 kg (14-18 lb).

FAULTS Any departure from the foregoing points should be considered a fault and the seriousness with which the fault should be regarded should be in exact proportion to its degree.

NOTE Male animals should have two apparently normal testicles fully descended into the scrotum.

YORKSHIRE TERRIER

A S A SHOW DOG IN ALL THE GLORY OF his full coat he draws the eye like a magnet. When he is kept purely as a pet, his coat is unlikely to achieve such magnificence, as the time required for proper care is rarely available. In either walk of life he is well aware of his importance, and displays this in his carriage and bearing.

The Yorkshire Terrier comes from the same locale as the Airedale and was first seen around the 1850s. The old Black and Tan Terrier is behind the Yorkshire, together with other breeds such as the Maltese and the Skye Terrier. The current name was accepted in 1870.

His terrier-like qualities include the hunting instinct, be it for a toy in the house or a rodent in the garden. He enjoys all sorts of games, and appreciates a good walk. He is a hardy character, and although often very pampered, this is not of his choosing.

GENERAL APPEARANCE Long-coated, coat hanging quite straight and evenly down each side, a parting extending from nose to end of tail. Very compact and neat, carriage very upright conveying an important air. General outline conveying impression of vigorous and well proportioned body.

CHARACTERISTICS Alert, intelligent toy terrier.

TEMPERAMENT Spirited with even disposition.

HEAD AND SKULL Rather small and flat, not too prominent or round in skull, nor too long in muzzle; black nose.

EYES Medium, dark, sparkling, with sharp intelligent expression and placed to look directly forward. Not prominent. Edge of eyelids dark.

EARS Small, V-shaped, carried erect, not too far apart, covered with short hair, colour very deep, rich tan.

MOUTH Perfect, regular and complete scissor bite, i.e. upper teeth closely overlapping lower teeth and set square to the jaws. Teeth well placed with even jaws.

NECK Good reach.

FOREQUARTERS Well laid shoulders, legs straight, well covered with hair of rich golden tan a few shades lighter at ends than at roots, not extending higher on forelegs than elbow.

BODY Compact with moderate spring of rib, good loin. Level back.

HINDQUARTERS Legs quite straight when viewed from behind, moderate turn of stifle. Well covered with hair of rich golden tan a few shades lighter at ends than at roots, not extending higher on hindlegs than stifles.

FEET Round; nails black.

TAIL Customarily docked to medium length with plenty of hair, darker blue in colour than rest of body, especially at the end of tail. Carried a little higher than level of back.

GAIT/MOVEMENT Free with drive; straight action front and behind, retaining level topline.

COAT Hair on body moderately long, perfectly straight (not wavy), glossy; fine silky texture, not woolly. Fall on head long, rich golden tan, deeper in colour at sides of head, about ear roots and on muzzle where it should be very long. Tan on head not to extend on to neck, nor must any sooty or dark hair intermingle with any of tan.

COLOUR Dark steel blue (not silver blue), extending from occiput to root of tail, never mingled with fawn, bronze or dark hairs. Hair on chest rich, bright tan. All tan hair darker at the roots than in middle, shading to still lighter at tips.

SIZE Weight: up to 3.1 kg (7 lb).

FAULTS Any departure from the foregoing points should be considered a fault and the seriousness with which the fault should be regarded should be in exact proportion to its degree.

NOTE Male animals should have two apparently normal testicles fully descended into the scrotum.

GLOSSARY OF CANINE TERMS

ABDOMEN The body cavity between the chest and pelvis.

ACTION Movement. The way a dog walks, trots or runs.

AFFIX The registered Kennel name of breeder/owner.

ALBINO Lacking in pigmentation, usually with pink eyes.

ALMOND EYES The eye, set in surrounding tissue of almond shape.

ALOOF Stand-offish – not over-friendly.

AMBLE A relaxed, easy gait in which the legs on either side move in unison or in some breeds almost, but not quite, as a pair. Often seen as the transition movement between the walk and the faster gaits.

ANGULATION The angles formed at a joint by the meeting of the bones.

ANUS Outlet at end of rectum.

APPLE HEAD Very domed, rounded skull.

APRON Longer hair below the neck on the chest. Frill.

AWARDS Placings decided by a judge.

BABBLER The hound that speaks when not on correct trail.

BACK Region between withers and root of tail but in some standards may refer to region between withers and loin.

BADGER PIED See Pied.

BALANCE A consistent whole; symmetrical, typically proportioned as a whole or as regards its separate parts; i.e. balance of head, balance of body, or balance of head and body.

BANDY LEGS Bowed legs.

BARREL Rounded rib section.

BAT EAR An erect ear, rather broad at the base, rounded in outline at the top, and with opening directly to the front.

BAY The prolonged sound of the hunting hound.

BEARD Thick, long hair on muzzle and under-jaw.

BEAVER Mixture of white, grey, brown, black hairs.

BEEFY Overweight, over-muscled.

BELLY Underpart of abdomen.

BELTON A colour designation. An intermingling of coloured and white hairs as blue belton, lemon, orange or liver belton.

BENCHING Preformed units for housing dogs at shows.

BENCHED SHOW A show where benching is provided.

BEST IN SHOW The over-all winner at a dog show.

BEST OF BREED The best dog or bitch in a breed.

BITCH A female.

BITCHY A feminine-looking male dog.

BITE The relative position of the upper and lower teeth when the mouth is closed. See level bite, scissor bite, undershot, overshot and shark mouth.

BLAIREAU Badger coloured or mixture of brown/black/grey and white hairs.

BLANKET Solid colour of coat on back and upper part of sides, between neck and tail.

BLAZE A white stripe running up the centre of the face.

BLENHEIM A term used to define colour or markings in the King Charles Spaniel and the Cavalier King Charles Spaniel.

BLOOM The sheen of a coat in prime condition.

BLOWN When the coat is moulting or casting.

BLUE MERLE Blue and grey mixed with black. Marbled.

BOBTAIL A naturally tail-less dog or a dog with a tail docked very short. Pseudonym for the Old English Sheepdog.

BODIED UP Mature, well developed.

BOLD IN EYE Giving a foreign expression.

BOLT To drive an animal out of its earth or burrow.

BOLTING EYE Protruding eye.

BONE The relative girth of a dog's leg bones.

BOSSY Overdevelopment of the shoulder muscles.

BOWED Curved outward. See Crook/crooked.

BRACE Two dogs of a kind. A couple or pair.

BRACELETS Rings of hair left on the legs of some breeds in show trim.

BREAST BONE Bone forming floor of chest. Also Sternum/Keel.

BREECHING Hair outside thighs and on back of buttocks.

BREED Pure-bred dogs more or less uniform in size and structure, as produced and maintained by man.

BREED STANDARD Description of the ideal specimen in each breed.

BREED STANDARD (INTERIM) As above for a breed not granted Championship Status.

BREEDER A person who breeds dogs. Under Kennel Club rules the breeder of a dog is the owner (or, if the dam was leased, the lessee) of the dam of the puppy when the litter was whelped.

BREEDING PARTICULARS Sire, dam, date of birth, sex, colour, etc.

BRICK-SHAPED Rectangular.

BRINDLE A fine even mixture of black hairs with hairs of a lighter colour, usually gold, brown or grey, usually in stripes.

BRISKET The forepart of the body below the chest between forelegs.

BROKEN COLOUR Self-colour broken by white or another colour.

BROKEN DOWN EARS Deformed or mis-shapen ears.

BRONZE Copper-coloured.

BROOD BITCH A female used for breeding.

BRUSH A bushy tail; a tail heavy with hair.

BULL NECK Short, thick heavy neck.

BURR The inside of the ear; i.e. the irregular formation visible within the cup.

BUTTERFLY NOSE A parti-coloured nose; i.e. dark, spotted with flesh colour.

BUTTOCKS The rear of upper thigh.

BUTTON EAR The ear flap folding forward, the tip lying

close to the skull so as to cover the opening, and pointing toward the eye.

BYE At field trials, an odd dog remaining after the dogs entered in a stake have been paired in braces by drawing.

CANINES The two upper and two lower long sharp-pointed teeth next to the incisors. Fangs.

CANTER A gait with three beats to each stride, two legs moving separately and two as a diagonal pair. Slower than the gallop and not as tiring.

CARPALS Bones of the wrist.

CAST Attempt by hounds to recover the line when they have lost the original scent.

CASTRATE To remove the testicles of the male dog.

CAT-FOOT Short, round, compact foot like that of a cat.

CERTIFIED Attested by the affixing of an official stamp, the accuracy of a measure.

CHAMPION A dog having acquired the title of Champion as defined in Kennel Club Regulations.

CHARACTER Combination of type, appearance, disposition and behaviour.

CHEEK Fleshy part of the head below eyes and above mouth.

CHEEKY Cheeks prominently rounded; thick, protruding.

CHEST The forepart of the body or trunk that is enclosed by the ribs.

CHINA EYE A clear blue eye.

CHIPPENDALE FRONT Forelegs out at elbows, pasterns close, and feet turned out.

CHISELLED Clean-cut, showing bone structure of foreface.

CHOPS Jowls or pendulous flesh of the lips and jaw.

CHORTLE Chuckle from the throat, can be high or low pitched.

CLODDY Low, thick-set, comparatively heavy.

CLOSE-COUPLED Short in coupling.

COARSE Lacking refinement.

COBBY Short-bodied, compact.

COLLAR A marking around the neck, usually white.

COMPACT Closely put together – not rangy.

CONDITION Health as shown by the body, coat, general appearance and deportment. Denoting overall fitness.

CONFORMATION The form and structure, and arrangement of the parts.

CONJUNCTIVA Thin membrane lining the inner surface of eyelids and reflected over eyeball; often confused with haw or third eyelid.

CORDED COAT Narrow or broad twists of hair like thick string or rope formed by the intertwining of top coat and undercoat. Cords should always be distinctly separate from each other.

CORKSCREW TAIL Twisted tail, not straight.

CORKY Active, lively, alert.

COUPLE Two hounds.

COUPLING The part of the body between the ribs and pelvis; the loin.

COURSING The practice of chasing the hare, often in competition, by sight hounds.

COVERING GROUND Amount of ground covered by a dog when moving or standing.

COW-HOCKED When the hocks turn inwards towards each other.

CRABBING Dog moves with body at an angle to the line of travel.

CRANK TAIL A tail carried down and resembling a crank in shape.

CREST The upper, arched portion of the neck. Also hair starting at stop on head and tapering off down neck, may be full or sparse.

CRIMPED Waved.

CROOK OR CROOKED Not straight. Bent or curved.

CROPPING The cutting or trimming of the ear leather for the purpose of inducing the ears to stand erect. Not allowed by The Kennel Club.

CROSSBRED A dog whose sire and dam are representatives of two different breeds.

CROSSING OVER Unsound gaiting action which starts with twisting elbows and ends with crisscrossing and toeing out. Also called 'knitting' and 'weaving'.

CROUP (RUMP) The part of the back from the front of the pelvis to the root of the tail.

CROWN The highest part of the head. Circular formations of hair at front of ridge as on the Rhodesian Ridgeback.

CRY The baying or 'music' of the hounds.

CRYPTORCHID An adult male whose testicles are abnormally retained in the abdominal cavity. Bilateral cryptorchidism involves both sides; that is, neither testicle has descended into the scrotum. Unilateral cryptorchidism involves one side only; that is, one testicle is retained or hidden and one descended.

CULOTTE The longer hair on the back of the thighs.

CUSHION Fullness or thickness of the upper lips.

CUT-UP See Tuck-up.

DAM The female parent.

DAPPLED Mottled marking of different colours, no one predominating.

DAYLIGHT The light showing underneath body.

DEADGRASS Straw or bracken colour.

DENTITION The number and arrangement of teeth.

DEWCLAW Fifth digit, on the inside of the legs.

DEWLAP Loose, pendulous skin under the throat.

DISH-FACED When the nasal bone is so formed that the nose is higher at the tip than at the stop; or, a slight concavity of the line from the stop to the nose tip.

DISQUALIFY To deprive of an award.

DISTEMPER TEETH Teeth discoloured or pitted as a result of serious illness during eruption of teeth.

DOCK To shorten the tail by cutting.

DOG A male dog; also used collectively to designate both male and female.

DOGGY A masculine-looking bitch.

DOG SHOW A competitive exhibition for dogs at which the dogs are judged in accordance with an established standard of perfection for each breed.

DOMED Evenly rounded in skull; convex instead of flat.

DONATION Bestowal of a gift.

DOUBLE COAT An outer coat resistant to weather, together with an undercoat of softer hair for warmth and waterproofing.

DOWNFACE The muzzle inclining downwards in an unbroken outward arc from the top of the skull to the tip of the nose.

DOWN ON PASTERN Weak or faulty pastern (metacarpus) set at a pronounced angle from the vertical.

DRAWING Selection by lot of dogs to compete.

DRIVE A powerful thrusting of the hindquarters denoting sound locomotion.

DROP EAR The ends of the ear folded or drooping forward, as contrasted with erect or prick ears.

DRY NECK The skin taut; neither loose nor wrinkled.

DUDLEY Liver, brown or putty-coloured.

ECTROPION A condition in which the eyelids are turned outwards.

ELBOW The joint between the upper arm and the forearm.

ELBOWS, OUT AT Turning out or off from body; not held close.

ELONGATED SKULL Long, slender, tapering skull.

ENTROPION A condition in which the eyelids are turning inwards.

EQUILATERAL All sides equal.

EVEN BITE Meeting of front teeth at edges with no overlap of upper or lower teeth.

EWE NECK Concave curavature of the top neckline.

EXHIBITOR Owner of dog entered at a show.

EXPRESSION The general appearance of all features of the head as viewed from the front.

EYEBROWS See Supercillary arches.

EYE-TEETH The upper canines.

FAKING Changing the appearance of a dog by artificial means with the object to deceive.

FALL Long hair surrounding head as in the Yorkshire Terrier.

FALLAWAY Slope of the croup.

FALLOW Light reddish or yellowish brown.

FANCIER A person especially interested and usually active in some phase of the sport.

FANGS See Canines.

FAWN A light brown.

FEATHERING Longer fringe of hair on ears, legs, tail or body.

FEMUR Thigh bone, from hip to stifle point.

FETCH The retrieve of game by the dog; also the command to do so.

FIELD TRIAL CHAMPION A dog having acquired the title of Field Trial Champion as defined in Kennel Club Regulations.

FILBERT EAR Rounded off triangular shape – as a filbert nut.

FINE SHOULDER Well set. In no way heavy or loaded.

FLAG A feathered tail.

FLANGE Projecting edge of rib.

FLANK The side of the body between last rib and hip.

FLARING EARS Gradually spreading outwards from base.

FLAT BONE The leg bone with girth which is elliptical rather than round.

FLAT CATCHER Very flashy dog which by showmanship disguises his bad points.

FLAT SIDED Ribs insufficiently rounded as they approach the sternum or breast bone.

FLECKED Coat lightly ticked with another colour, but not spotted or roan. Also refers to flaw in normal eye colour.

FLEWS Upper lips pendulous, particularly at their inner corners.

FLOATING RIB The last, or 13th, rib, which is unattached to other ribs.

FLOCKED A coat of 'cotton-wool' texture.

FLUFFIES Describes dogs of a medium-coated breed whose coats are too long with exaggerated feathering on ears, chest, legs and feet, underparts and hindquarters.

FLUSH To drive birds from cover, to force them to take flight. To spring or start.

FLYING EARS Any characteristically drop ears or semi-prick ears that stand or 'fly'.

FLYING TROT A fast trotting gait in which all four feet are off the ground for a brief moment during each stride. Because of the long reach, the oncoming hindfeet step beyond the imprint left by the front. Also called Suspended trot.

FORCEFUL ACTION Strong, driving movement.

FOREARM The bone of the forelegs between elbow and wrist.

FORECHEST The front part of the chest.

FOREFACE The front part of the head, before the eyes. Muzzle.

FOREHAND Front part of dog, including head, neck, shoulders, upper arm, legs and feet.

FOREIGN EXPRESSION Expression not typical of the breed.

FORELEG The front leg from elbow to foot.

FOREQUARTERS Front part of dog excluding head and neck.

FOSTER MOTHER A bitch or other animal, used to nurse whelps not her own.

FOXY Sharp expression; pointed foreface and upright ears.

FRILL See Apron.

FRINGES See Feathering.

FROGFACE Extending nose accompanied by a receding jaw, often overshot.

FRONT The forepart of the body as viewed head on, i.e. forelegs, chest, brisket, and shoulder line.

FRONTAL BONE The skull bone over the eyes.

FROSTINGS White hairs intermingling with base colour round muzzle.

FURNISHED Profusely coated.

FURNISHINGS Long hair on head, legs, breechings and tail of certain breeds.

FURROW A slight indentation or median line from stop to occiput.

FUTURITY STAKE A class at dog shows or field trials for young dogs which have been nominated for competition at or before birth.

GAIT The pattern of footsteps at various rates of speed, each pattern distinguished by a particular rhythm and footfall.

GALLOP Fastest of the dog gaits, has a four beat rhythm and often an extra period of suspension during which the body is propelled through the air with all four feet off the ground.

GAME Hunted wild birds or animals.

GASKIN Second or lower thigh.

GAY TAIL The tail carried very high or over dog's back. A term sometimes used when a tail is carried higher than the carriage approved in the breed standard.

GAZEHOUND See Sighthound.

GENEALOGY Recorded family descent.

GENERAL COMMITTEE Governing body of The Kennel Club.

GESTATION The elapsed time between conception and birth; in dogs, usually about 63 days.

GIVING TONGUE Barking or baying of hounds.

GLOBULAR Round, slightly prominent, not bulging.

GLOSSY Shining.

GOGGLED Protruding eye.

GONE TO GROUND Hunting term when the quarry has taken cover from the hounds.

GOOSE RUMP Too steep or sloping a croup.

GRIZZLE A mixture of colours including bluish-grey, red, and black.

GROOM To brush, comb or trim.

GROUPS The breeds as grouped according to Kennel Club classification.

GUARD HAIRS The longer smoother, stiffer hairs which grow through the undercoat and normally conceal it.

GUIDE DOGS Dogs trained to guide the blind.

GUN DOG A dog trained to work to find live game and/or retrieve game that has been shot or wounded.

GUNS Those who do the shooting.

GUN-SHY When the dog fears the sight or sound of a gun.

HACKLES Hair on neck and back raised involuntarily in fright or anger.

HACKNEY ACTION The high lifting of the front feet.

HALOES Dark pigmentation round or over eyes.

HAM Muscular development of hindleg above stifle.

HANDLER A person who handles a dog in the showring or at a field trial. See also Professional handler.

HARD EXPRESSION Hard, staring expression.

HARD-MOUTHED A dog that bites or marks with its teeth the game it retrieves.

HARLEQUIN Patched or pied coloration, usually black on white, or blue on white. A term used of Great Danes.

HAREFOOT An elongated foot like that of a hare.

HARNESS Markings around the shoulders and chest on certain breeds. Also equipment used to control and restrain.

HARSH COAT Stiff, wiry coat.

HAUNCH Buttock or rump.

HAW The third eyelid or membrane in the inside corner of the eye.

HAZEL Light brown eye colour.

HEARING DOGS Dogs trained to aid the deaf.

HEAT Seasonal period of the female. Oestrus. Season.

HEEL See Hock Rear part of the paw. Command to a dog to walk beside handler.

HEIGHT Vertical measurement from the withers to the ground; referred to usually as shoulder height. See Withers.

HERRING GUTTED See Slab-sided.

HINDLEG Leg from pelvis to foot.

HINDQUARTERS Rear part of dog from loin.

HIP DYSPLASIA Abnormal formation of hip joint.

HOCK The tarsus or collection of bones of the hindleg forming the joint between the second thigh and the metatarsus.

HOCKS WELL LET DOWN Hock joints close to the ground.

HONOURABLE SCARS Scars from injuries suffered as result of work.

HOUND A dog originally used for hunting by scent or sight.

HOUND-MARKED A coloration composed of white, black and tan. The ground colour, usually white, may be marked with tan and/or black patches on the head, back, legs and tail. The extent and the exact location of such markings, however, differ in breeds and individuals.

INBREEDING The mating of closely related dogs, i.e. father to daughter, mother to son, or brother to sister.
INCISORS The upper and lower front teeth between the canines.
INTERBREEDING The breeding together of dogs of different varieties of a breed.
IRIS Flat, circular, coloured membrane within the eye. The inner boundary forms pupil which adjusts to control amount of light entering eye.
ISABELLA Fawn colour.

JAWS The bones forming the framework of the mouth.
JEWEL EYE See Ruby eye.
JOWLS Flesh of lips and jaws.
JUDGE An arbiter in any competition involving dogs.

KEEL See Breast bone/Sternum.
KEEN Penetrating expression.
KINK TAIL Malformation of the tail.
KNEE JOINT Stifle joint.
KNITTING See Crossing over.
KNUCKLING OVER Faulty structure of carpus (wrist) joint allowing it to double forward under the weight of the standing dog.

LANDSEER Black and white colouring, term used in Newfoundlands.
LAY-BACK (a) The angle of the shoulder blade, when viewed from the side; (b) Receding nose of the Bulldog.
LEASH Three or more Hounds.
LEATHER The flap of the ear.
LEGGY Too long in the leg for correct balance.
LEONINE Looking like a lion.
LEVEL BACK The line of the back horizontal to ground.
LEVEL BITE When the front teeth (incisors) of the upper and lower jaws meet exactly edge to edge. Pincer bite.
LINE BREEDING The mating of related dogs within a line or family or to a common ancestor.
LINING OF EAR Inside of ear flap.
LINTY Soft coat texture in certain breeds.
LION CLIP Traditionally body clipped from last rib, leaving mane on forequarters. Clipping on legs, back, face and tail according to breed.
LION COLOUR Tawny.
LIPPY Pendulous lip or lips that do not fit tightly.
LITTER The puppy or puppies of one whelping.
LIVER A colour, also known as brown or chocolate.
LOADED SHOULDERS When the shoulder blades are pushed out from the body by overdevelopment of the muscles.
LOIN Region of the body on either side of vertebral column between the last ribs and the hindquarters.
LONG COUPLED Having a long loin.

LOW-SET When tail is set-on below level of topline; or ears set below line of correct placement for the breed.
LOWER THIGH See Second thigh.
LOZENGE MARK Term used for marking on skull of King Charles Spaniel and Cavalier King Charles Spaniel, sometimes known as 'Blenheim spot'.
LUMBERING A heavy gait.

MAIDEN Bitch which has not produced puppies.
MANDIBLE Lower jaw bone.
MANDIBULAR Relating to lower jaw.
MANE Long and profuse hair on top and sides of the neck.
MANTLE Dark-shaded portion of the coat on shoulders, back, and sides.
MASK Dark shading on the foreface.
MATING Sexual coupling of dog and bitch.
MATRON Brood bitch.
MAXILLA Upper jaw bone.
MAXILLARY Relating to upper jaw.
MEDIAN LINE A line in the centre, e.g. furrow, withers, etc.
MERLE A coloration, usually blue-grey with flecks of black.
MERLE EYE Flecked eye, brown and blue, with black iris.
METATARSALS Bones between hock joint and foot.
MILK TEETH First teeth.
MISMARKED Incorrectly marked dog.
MOLAR TEETH There are two molar teeth on each side of the upper jaw and three on each side of the lower jaw (see also Premolars).
MOLERA A small opening on top part of the skull due to the failure of bones to unite.
MONORCHID A dog with only one testicle in the scrotum.
MOULT Casting of the coat.
MOUTH The upper part and lower jaw bones containing the teeth. Also used to describe the bite, e.g. 'a bad mouth' or 'a good mouth'. Sometimes used in retrieving parlance to describe the ability of a dog when carrying game, e.g. 'soft' mouth or 'hard' mouth.
MOVING CLOSE When the hindlimbs move close to each other.
MOVING STRAIGHT Fore- and hindlegs moving parallel.
MULTUM IN PARVO 'Much in little'.
MUSIC The baying of the hounds.
MUTE To run mute, to be silent on the trail.
MUZZLE The head in front of the eyes, nasal bone, nostrils, and jaws; foreface.

N.A.F. Name applied for registration with The Kennel Club.

NECK That part between skull and front of shoulder blade.

NECK WELL SET-ON Good neckline, merging gradually with strong withers, forming a pleasing transition into topline.

NOSE Organ of smell; also, the ability to detect by means of scent.

NOSTRIL Nasal opening admitting air and scent.

OBLIQUE SHOULDERS Shoulders well laid back.

OCCIPUT Upper, back point of skull.

OCCIPITAL PROTUBERANCE A prominently raised occiput characteristic of some breeds.

OESTRUS The period during which a bitch will accept mating. Heat. Season.

OFFICERS Persons elected to office within a Society.

OPEN COAT Sparse, lacking in density.

OTTER TAIL Thick at the root, tapering to blunt end with short thick hair growing round tail, not extending below hock.

OUT AT SHOULDER With shoulder blades loosely attached to the body, leaving the shoulders jutting out in relief and increasing the breadth of the front.

OUT AT WALK To lease or lend a puppy to someone for rearing.

OUTCROSSING The mating of unrelated individuals of the same breed.

OUT OF COAT See Moult.

OVAL CHEST Chest deeper than wide.

OVERREACHING Fault in the trot caused by more angulation and drive from behind than in front, so that the rear feet are forced to step to one side of the forefeet to avoid interference or clipping.

OVERSHOT The front teeth (incisors) of the upper jaw overlap and do not touch the front teeth of the lower jaw when the mouth is closed.

PACE A gait in which the left foreleg and left hindleg advance in unison, then the right foreleg and the right hindleg.

PACK Several hounds kept together in one kennel. 'Mixed pack' composed of dogs and bitches.

PADDLING The front feet thrown out sideways in a loose, uncontrolled manner.

PADS Tough, thickened skin on underside of feet. Soles.

PARTI-COLOUR Variegated in patches of two colours.

PASTERN The region of the foreleg between the carpus or wrist and the digits.

PATELLA A bond, equivalent to the human knee-cap, in front of stifle joint.

PEAK See Occiput.

PEDIGREE The written record of a dog's ancestry.

PELVIS A framework of bones formed by the pelvic arch.

PENCILLED Lay of coat on Dandie Dinmont Terrier.

PENCILLING Black lines on the toes.

PEPPER AND SALT Mixture of light and dark hair.

PIED Unequally proportioned patches of white and another colour. Hare – more tan than black and white giving a coat resembling the colour of a hare. Lemon – mainly lemon or cream hairs mixed with white or black. Badger – unequally proportioned patches of black and white, or tan and white, mixed together.

PIGEON-CHEST A chest with a short protruding breast bone.

PIGEON-TOED Forefeet pointing in; pinning.

PIG-EYE Very small hard eye, as in a pig.

PIG JAW See Overshot.

PIGMENTATION Natural colouring of skin and other tissues.

PILE Dense undercoat of soft hair.

PIN BONES Upper bony protuberance of pelvis.

PINCER BITE See Level bite.

PINTO Dark markings on white background. Markings on head and major part of body.

PIN-TOES See Pigeon-toed.

PLAITING Manner of walking or trotting, in which the legs cross.

PLUME A long fringe of hair hanging from tail.

POINT The static stance of a hound or gundog taken to indicate the presence and position of game.

POINT OF SHOULDER Joint where upper arm meets scapula.

POINTS Colour on face, ears, legs and tail – usually white, black or tan.

POKE To carry the neck stretched forward in an abnormally low, ungainly position, usually when moving.

POMPOM A rounded tuft of hair left on the end of the tail when the coat is clipped.

POUNDING Gaiting fault resultant of dog's stride being shorter in front than in the rear; forefeet strike the ground hard before the rear stride is expended.

PRE-MOLAR TEETH Teeth between canine and molar teeth.

PRICK EAR Carried erect and usually pointed at the tip.

PRINTED AWARDS Documentation confirming a decision.

PRIZE Reward for merit in competition.

PROFILE Side view of head.

PROFESSIONAL HANDLER A person who shows or works dogs for a fee.

PROUD Held high.

PUMP HANDLE Long tail, carried low with upward curve at end.

PUNISHING JAW Of such strength as to hold its prey.

PUT DOWN To prepare a dog for the showring; also used to denote a dog unplaced in competition.

PUPPY A dog under 12 months of age.

PURE-BRED A dog whose sire and dam belong to the same breed, and are themselves of unmixed decent.

QUALITY Refinement, elegance.
QUEEN ANNE FRONT See Chippendale front.

RACY Giving an impression of speed, without loss of substance.
RANGE To cover a wide area of ground.
RANGY Dog of long slender build.
RAT TAIL Thick at the root, tapering to a point, partially or completely devoid of hair.
REACHY With long neck.
REFEREE Person appointed to adjudicate in the event of two Judges failing to reach a joint decision.
REFINED Elegant.
REGISTER To record with The Kennel Club a dog's breeding antecedents.
RETRIEVE Act of bringing back any article or game to the handler.
RIBBED UP Ribs carried well back.
RIDGE Streak of hair growing in reverse direction to main coat.
RINGER A substituted dog closely resembling another.
RING TAIL Carried up and around almost in a circle.
RIOT Term used when a hound goes off to hunt anything other than the original quarry.
ROACH BACK A convex curvature of the back toward the loin.
ROAN A fine mixture of coloured hairs alternating with white hairs; blue roan, orange roan, lemon roan, liver roan, etc.
ROCKING HORSE Both front and rear legs extended out from body as in old-fashioned rocking horse.
ROLLING GAIT Rolling, ambling action when moving.
ROMAN FINISH Slightly sharper downward inclination at end of a downface.
ROMAN NOSE A nose whose bridge is comparatively high forming a slightly convex line from forehead to tip of nose.
ROSE EAR A small drop ear which folds over and back thus revealing the burr.
RUBY EYE Whole eye tinged with red.
RUDDER The tail.
RUFF Thick, longer hair growth around the neck.
RUMP See Croup.
RUNT Weak, undersized puppy in litter.

SABLE Coat colour pattern. Black-tipped hairs overlaid on a background of gold, silver, grey, fawn or tan basic coat.
SABRE TAIL Carried in an upward curve.
SADDLE Variation in colour or coat quality over the back, in the shape of a saddle.
SCAPULA Shoulder blade.

SCENT The odour left by an animal on the trail (ground scent), or wafted through the air (air-borne scent).
SCENTHOUND A hound which hunts by ground scent as distinct from the Sighthound/Gazehound which hunts by sight.
SCIMITAR TAIL See Sabre tail.
SCISSOR BITE Jaws strong, with a perfect, regular and complete scissor bite, i.e. the upper teeth closely overlapping the lower teeth and set square to the jaws.
SCREW TAIL A naturally short tail twisted in more or less spiral formation.
SEASON See Oestrus.
SECOND THIGH That part of the hindquarter from the stifle to the hock. Lower thigh.
SEDGE Red Gold.
SELF-COLOUR One colour or whole colour except for lighter shadings.
SEPTUM The line extending vertically between the nostrils.
SERVICE The act of mating when a bitch is served by a stud dog.
SET-ON Placement of tail on body and position of ears on skull.
SET UP Posed so as to make the most of the dog's appearance for the showring. Stacking.
SHARK MOUTH Jaws are level but teeth are not set at right angles to jaw and protrude.
SHAWL See Mane.
SHED (a) To moult; (b) Coat. To lie in a parting.
SHELLY A weakly formed, shallow, narrow body, lacking substance.
SHORT-COUPLED With very short coupling.
SHOULDER HEIGHT Height of dog's body as measured from withers to ground.
SHOW Exhibition of dogs at which judging takes place.
SHOW CHAMPION The title given to dogs which qualify in accordance with Kennel Club Regulations.
SHOW EXECUTIVE Officers and Committee of a Society.
SHOW MANAGEMENT Persons responsible for the management of a Show.
SICKLE-HOCKED Inability to extend the hock joint on the backward drive of the hindleg.
SICKLE TAIL Carried out and up in a semicircle.
SIGHTHOUND A hound which runs or coarses game by sight rather than scent.
SINGLE TRACKING All footprints falling on a single line of travel.
SIRE The male parent.
SKULL Bony regions of head. Usually meant as section of head from stop to occiput.
SKULLY Thick and coarse through skull.
SLAB-SIDED Flat ribs with too little spring from spinal column. Herring gutted.

SLOPING SHOULDER The shoulder blade set obliquely or 'laid back'.

SMOOTH COAT Short hair, close lying.

SNATCHING HOCKS A gaiting fault indicated by a quick outward snatching of the hock as it passes the supporting leg and twists the rear pastern far in beneath the body. The action causes noticeable rocking in hindquarters.

SNIPY A pointed, weak muzzle.

SNOW NOSE Loss of pigment resulting in pink streak on nose in winter.

SOCIETY Any Club, Society or Association.

SOCKS Hair on the feet to pasterns.

SOFT MOUTH Gentle grip on a retrieve.

SOOTY Black hairs intermingling with tan.

SOUNDNESS The normal state of mental and physical well being. A term particularly applied to movement.

SPAY The surgical removal of the uterus and ovaries.

SPEAK To bark.

SPECTACLES Light shadings or dark markings over or around the eyes or from eyes to ears.

SPLASHED Irregularly patched, colour on white or white on colour.

SPLAYFOOT A flat foot with toes spreading. Open foot, open-toed.

SPONSOR Person or body offering support.

SPRING See Flush.

SPRING OF RIBS Degree of curvature of ribcage.

SQUIRREL TAIL Carried up and curving forward.

STACKING See Set up.

STALLION Dominant stud force.

STANCE Manner of standing.

STANDARD A description of the ideal dog of each recognised breed, by which dogs are judged at shows.

STAND-OFF COAT A coat that stands off from the body.

STARING COAT The hair dry, harsh and open. Out of condition.

STATION Comparative height from ground, as high-stationed, low-stationed.

STEEL BLUE Dark grey/blue, not silvery.

STERN Tail of a sporting dog or hound.

STERNUM See Breast bone/Keel.

STEWARD Person appointed to manage arrangements in the ring.

STIFLE The joint of the hindleg between the thigh and the second thigh. The dog's knee.

STILTED Stiff jerking gait caused by non-flexing of joints.

STOP The step up from muzzle to skull; indentation between the eyes where the nasal bone and skull meet.

STRAIGHT-HOCKED Lacking appreciable angulation at the hock joints.

STRAIGHT IN PASTERN Little or no bend between pastern and foot.

STRAIGHT SHOULDERS Term used to denote insufficient lay-back of shoulder.

STRAIGHT STIFLE Stifle joint in which femur and tibia meet at angle of approximately 180 degrees. Straight behind.

STUD BOOK A record of the breeding particulars of winning dogs.

STUD DOG A male dog used for breeding purposes.

SUBSTANCE Solidity, with correct muscularity and condition.

SUPERCILIARY RIDGES Projection of the frontal bones over the eye; the brow.

SUSPENDED TROT See Flying trot.

SUSPENSION Ban for specified period.

SWAYBACK Concave curvature of the back line between the withers and the hip bones.

SYMMETRY Overall balance.

T.A.F. Transfer of ownership applied for with The Kennel Club.

TAIL SET The position of the tail on the croup.

TEAM Three or more dogs.

TEMPERAMENT Mixture of natural qualities and traits which produce character.

TERRIER A dog originally used for hunting vermin.

TERRIER FRONT Narrow straight front.

TEXTURE Quality or nature of coat.

THICK-SET Broad and solidly built.

THIGH The hindquarter from hip to stifle.

THROAT Part of neck immediately below lower jaw.

THROATINESS An excess of loose skin in the throat area.

THUMBMARKS Black spots on the region of the pastern.

TIBIA Bone between stifle and hock joint (shin bone).

TICKED Small areas of black, flecks or coloured hairs on a white ground.

TIED AT THE ELBOWS Elbows set too close under body, thus restricting movement.

TIMBER Bone, especially of the legs.

TIPPED EARS Ears carried erect with just the tips breaking and falling forward.

TOP-KNOT Longer hair on top of head.

TOPLINE The dog's outline from just behind the withers to the tail set.

TOY DOG Small companion or lap dog.

TRACE A black line extending from occiput to twist on a Pug.

TRAIL To hunt by following ground scent.

TRANSFER Change of ownership.

TRICOLOUR Three-colour; black, white and tan.

TRIM To groom the coat by plucking or clipping.

TROT A rhythmic two-beat diagonal gait in which the feet at diagonally opposite ends of the body strike the ground together; i.e. right hind with left front and left hind with right front.

TUCK-UP Concave underline of body curving upwards from end of rib to waist.

TUFT OF HAIR Bunch or collection of hairs growing together.

TULIP EAR Wide ears carried with a slight forward curve.

TURN-UP An upturned foreface, or under-jaw.

TWIST Term used for tail of a Pug.

TYPE The characteristic qualities distinguishing a breed.

UNDERCOAT Dense, soft, short coat concealed by longer top-coat.

UNDERSHOT The front teeth (incisors) of the lower jaw projecting beyond the front teeth of the upper jaw when the mouth is closed.

UNILATERAL CRYPTORCHID See Cryptorchid.

UP-FACED Short nose, muzzle turned up.

UPPER ARM The humerus or bone of the foreleg, between the shoulder blade and the elbow.

UPRIGHT SHOULDER Without sufficient angulation of shoulder blades.

UTILITY DOGS Miscellaneous breeds of dog mainly of a non-sporting origin.

VARMINTY A keen very bright or piercing expression.

VEILED COAT Fine, wispy long hair.

VENT The anal opening.

VERTEBRAL COLUMN Spine.

VETERINARIAN An individual entitled to practise veterinary surgery in the United Kingdom as result of registration by Royal College of Veterinary Surgeons.

VETERINARY PRACTITIONER Individual on Royal College of Veterinary Surgeons' supplementary register.

VETERINARY SURGEON Individual on Royal College of Veterinary Surgeons' general register.

VICE-LIKE BITE Strongly gripping and well fitting.

WALK Gaiting pattern in which three legs are in support of the body at all times, each foot lifting from the ground one at a time in regular sequence.

WALL EYE Wholly or partly, coloured light blue eyes.

WEAVING See Crossing over.

WEDGINESS Lacking chiselling.

WEEDY Light bone structure, lacking substance.

WELL LAID Optimum shoulder angulation.

WELL SPRUNG RIBS Ribs springing out from spinal column giving correct shape.

WHEATEN Pale yellow or fawn colour.

WHEEL BACK The back line arched markedly over the loin. Excessively roached.

WHELPING Act of giving birth to puppies.

WHELPS Unweaned puppies.

WHIP TAIL Carried out stiffly straight, and tapering.

WHISKER Longer hairs on muzzle sides and under-jaw.

WHITELIES Dogs with untypical predominance of white body colour.

WIND To catch the scent of game.

WIREHAIRED A coat of harsh, crisp, wiry texture.

WITHERS The highest point of the body, immediately behind the neck.

WORKING DOG A dog originally used for work such as herding and guarding.

WRINKLE Loose, folding skin.

WRY MOUTH Lower jaw does not line up with upper jaw.

ZYGOMATIC ARCH Arch of bone forming lower border of eye socket extending to base of ear.

SOURCES

Thanks are due to the following photographers for supplying copyright material:
D. BULL 229; PRUDENCE CUMING ASSOCIATES LIMITED 12-13, 32, 70-71, 120, 126,
130-131, 182-183, 191, 230-231, 342-343; DAVID DALTON 14, 38, 43, 61, 65, 73, 86,
94, 95, 98, 99, 104, 105, 106, 107, 109, 115, 118, 128, 141, 143, 145, 152, 154, 177,
179, 193, 203, 208, 209, 214, 218, 233, 238, 266, 273, 276, 277, 278, 301, 323, 339,
344, 358, 363, 365, 367, 375, 380, 386; DAVE FREEMAN 18, 39, 314, 319; JOHN
HARTLEY 75, 108, 113, 114, 154, 158, 162, 168, 175, 189, 195, 202, 220, 269, 271,
274, 286, 335; MARC HENRIE 33, 37, 315, 378; HUISMAN AND ZONDEROP 40;
CAROL ANN JOHNSON 199; SARAH JOHNSON 110; DIANE PEARCE 15, 19, 47, 49, 58,
81, 127, 144, 148, 171, 172, 178, 187, 219, 244, 245, 247, 257, 261, 285, 294, 297,
299, 306, 309, 310, 320, 333, 349, 357, 368, 377, 381, 385; RUSSELL FINE ART 242;
SALLY ANNE THOMPSON 16, 21, 22, 25, 26, 28, 29, 30, 31, 34, 44, 50, 53, 55, 57, 63,
66, 69, 74, 77, 82, 85, 89, 90, 96, 101, 103, 111, 117, 121, 122, 125, 133, 134, 137,
139, 142, 147, 151, 157, 161, 163, 165, 167, 169, 181, 185, 192, 196, 201, 206, 211,
212, 215, 216, 223, 224, 227, 228, 234, 237, 242, 248, 249, 251, 252, 255, 259, 264,
280, 283, 289, 290, 293, 300, 303, 305, 313, 318, 325, 327, 329, 332, 338, 340, 345,
346, 353, 354, 360, 361, 362, 366, 369, 371, 373, 374, 382, 387; ALAN WALKER 351,
364; R. T. WILLBIE 79, 93, 153, 190, 205, 241, 321.

THE KENNEL CLUB
AND ITS SERVICES

The objective of The Kennel Club is to promote in every way, the general improvement of dogs. Founded in 1873, The Kennel Club achieves its aims through the classification and registration of dogs and associated societies, the licensing of over 5,000 shows, trials and competitions annually, and the promotion of responsible dog ownership.

The Kennel Club frames and enforces Rules and Regulations, publishes breed standards, a Gazette, operates The Kennel Club Junior Organisation and Good Citizen Dog Scheme and, through its Charitable Trust, funds research projects and encourages veterinary development. Europe's definitive canine library is situated at The Kennel Club headquarters in Mayfair.

Crufts, the world's greatest dog show, is organised by The Kennel Club at the NEC, Birmingham every year and Discover Dogs is staged at Earls Court, London, to promote Choice, Care and Training.

General Enquiries	**0171-629 5828**
Registrations	**0171-493 2001** There are 188 breeds currently eligible for registration with The Kennel Club. Some 250,000 pure-bred dogs are registered each year, as well as crossbreeds under the Working Trials and Obedience Register. The Kennel Club operates a free puppy pack service for customers to help in the purchasing process and to provide useful information for new owners.
Healthcare Schemes	**0171-493 2001** The Kennel Club, the British Veterinary Association and the International Sheepdog Society currently operate health schemes for hip dysplasia and inherited eye diseases. There are approximately 20,000 dogs per year tested and the results of all Kennel Club registered dogs are published in the Breed Records Supplement.
Publications	**0171-493 6651 ext 280** The Kennel Club creates a wide variety of publications to help the dog enthusiast including; breeds standards, a Year Book, a Guide for Secretaries of Registered and Affiliated Societies, a Guide for Judges, show guides, a Directory of Affixes, a Directory of Championship Show Judges and The Kennel Gazette monthly magazine.
Shows, Trials and Awards	**0171-493 6651 ext 216** This Kennel Club department is responsible for overseeing the administration of all aspects of canine events providing a wealth of information for the committed show enthusiast.
Kennel Club Junior Organisation	**0171-493 6651 ext 230** This organisation encourages young people between the ages of 8 and 18 to take an interest in the care and training of dogs. Membership provides an introduction to the world of dogs through numerous canine events.
Good Citizen Dog Scheme	**0171-518 1001** The largest dog training scheme in the UK available for all dogs and owners. It is administered by over 800 organisations throughout the country including dog clubs, local councils, agricultural colleges, adult education centres and British Armed Force bases.
Identification Scheme – Petlog	**0171-629 6707** Petlog, the UK's National Pet Register, was launched by The Kennel Club in conjunction with the RSPCA and the Scottish SPCA in 1995 to help reunite stray and abandoned animals with their owners. Microchipping is The Kennel Club's preferred method of identification, but the register encompasses all forms including tags and tattoos.
Healthcare Plan	**(01372) 743472** Recognising the importance of quality veterinary care, The Kennel Club offers all owners of registered dogs an exclusive Healthcare Plan.
Charitable Trust	**0171-518 1037** Registered Charity Number 30208 Donations can be made through The Kennel Club Charity Card.
Library	**0171-518 1009**
Crufts	**0171-493 7838**
Discover Dogs	**0171-493 7838**
Press Office	**0171-518 1008**
Fax	**0171-518 1058**
Internet	**http://www.the-kennel-club.org.uk** **http://www.discover-dogs.org.uk** **http://www.crufts.org.uk**

INDEX